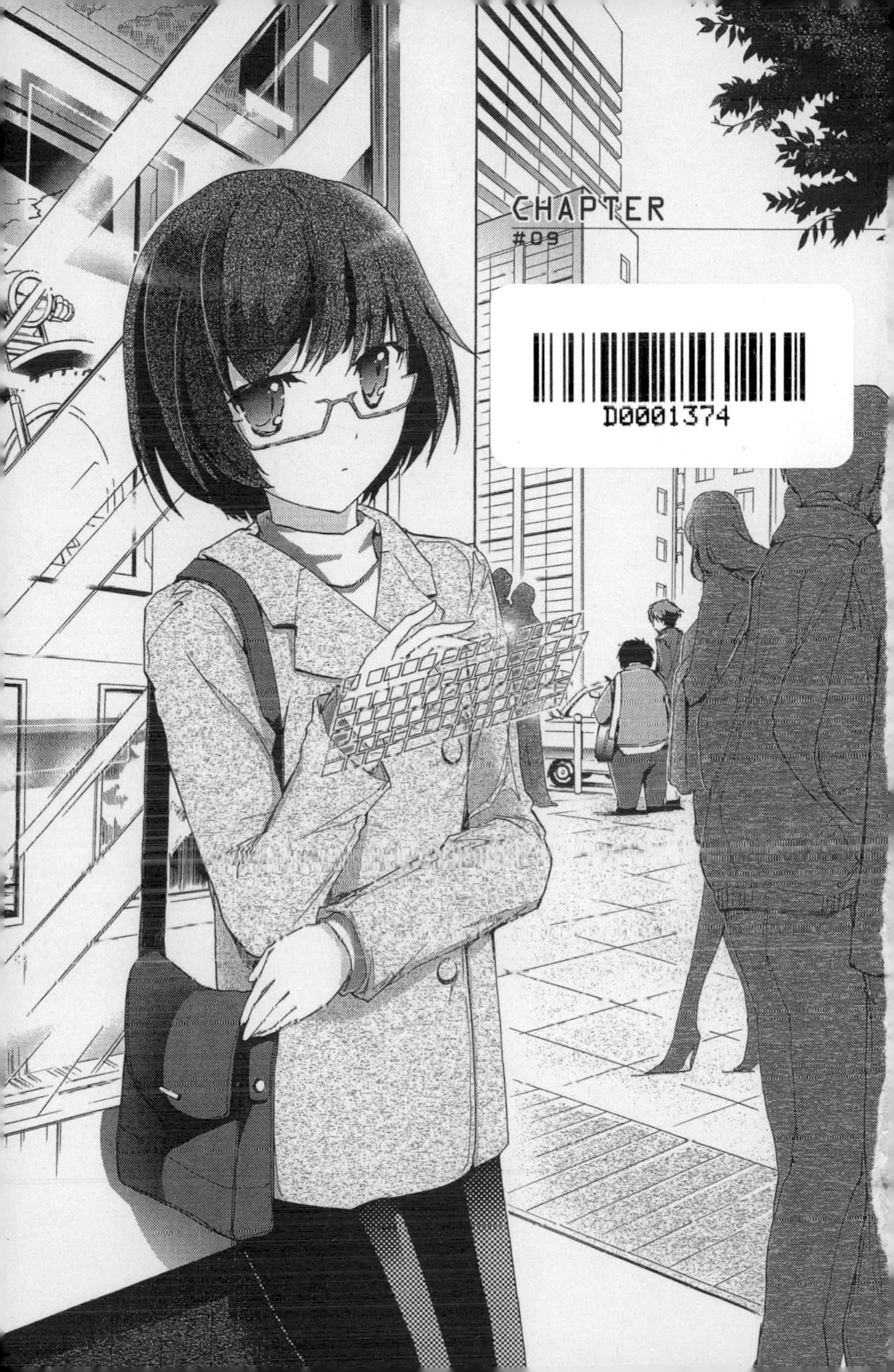
CHAPTER
#09

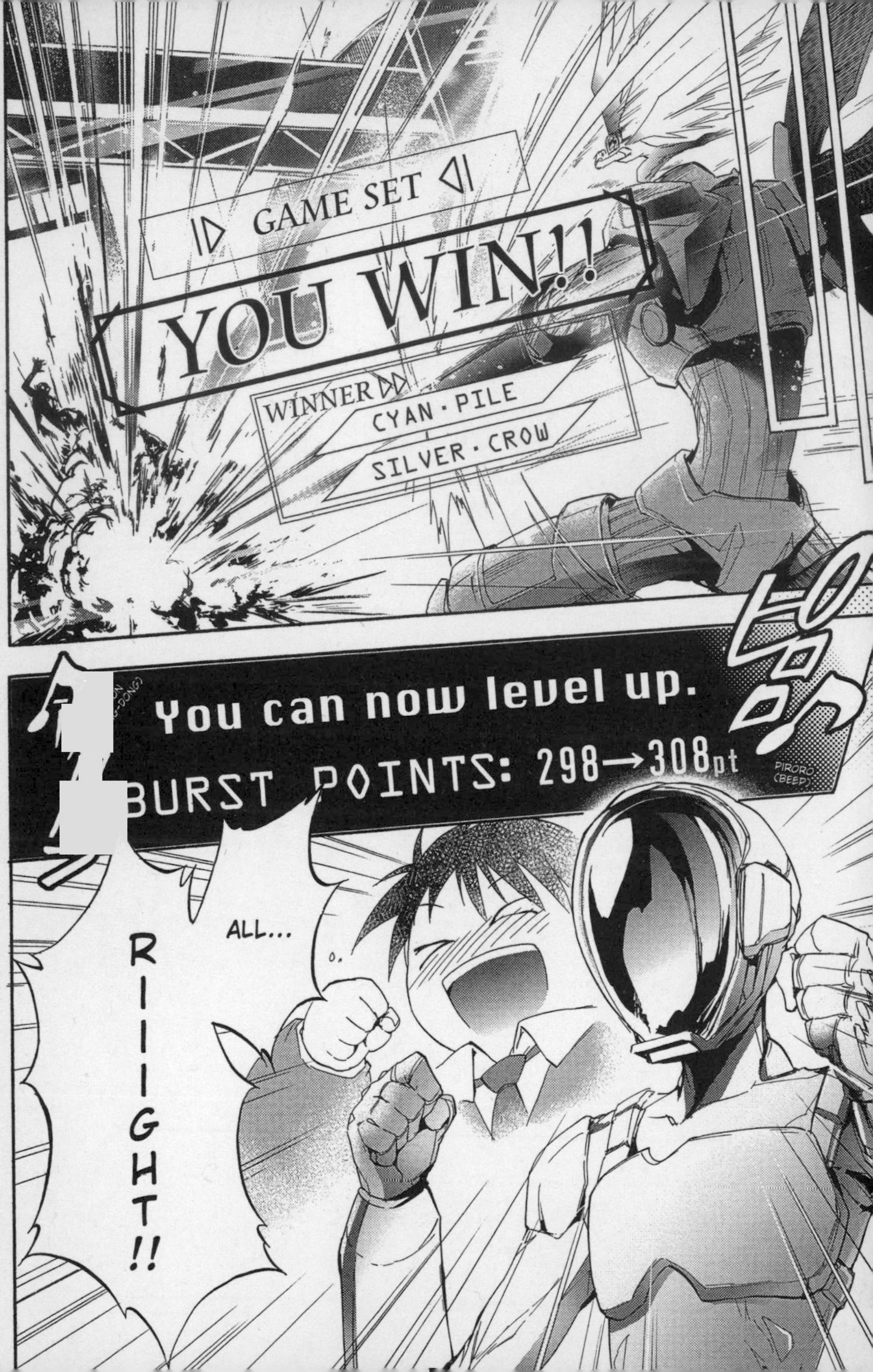
GAME SET
YOU WIN!!
WINNER
CYAN・PILE
SILVER・CROW
PIRORO (BEEP)
You can now level up.
BURST POINTS: 298→308pt
ALL...
O.
RIIIGHT!!

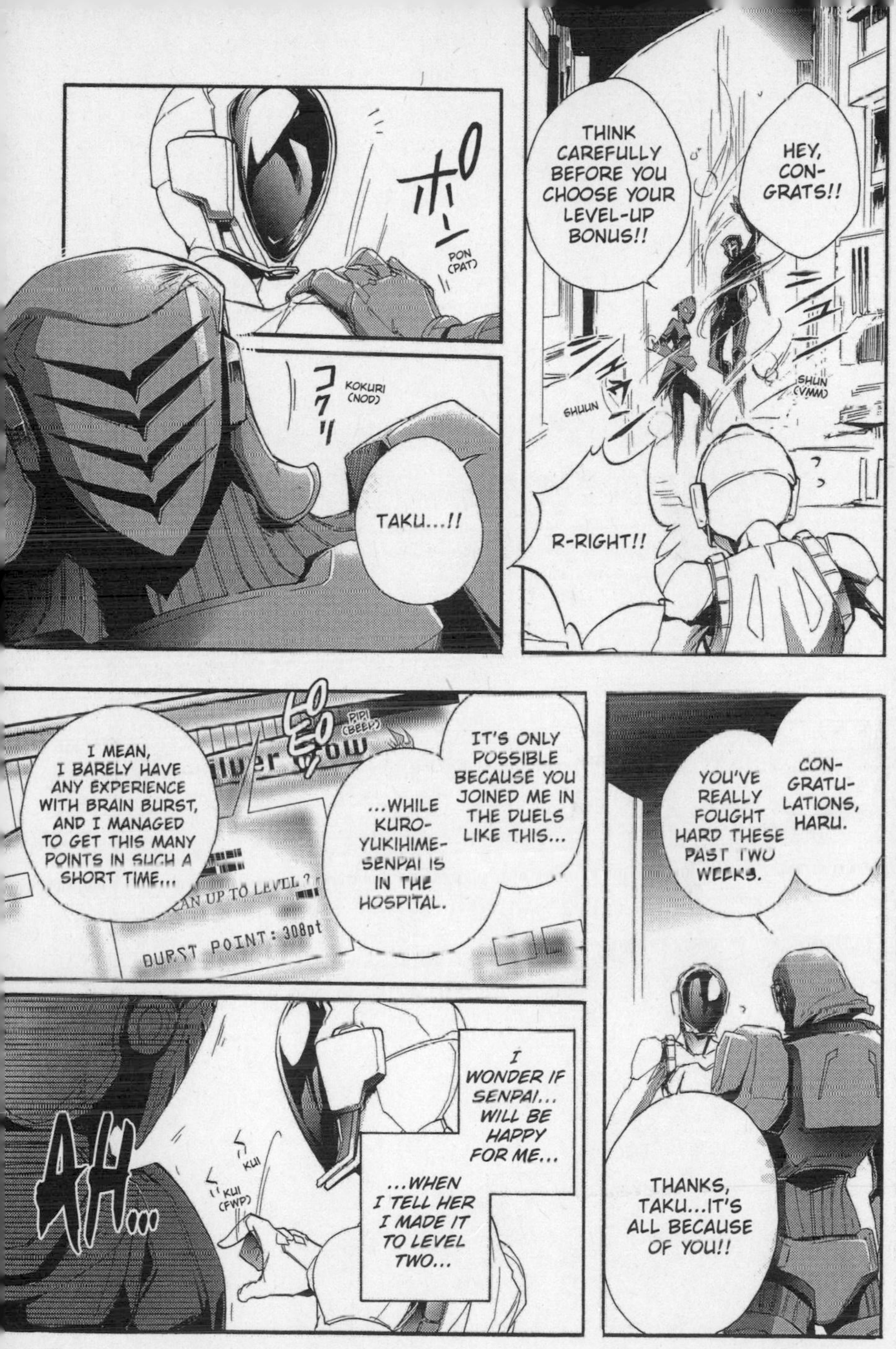
HEY, CON-GRATS!!
THINK CAREFULLY BEFORE YOU CHOOSE YOUR LEVEL-UP BONUS!!
SHUN (VMM)
SHUUN
R-RIGHT!!
PON (PAT)
KOKURI (NOD)
TAKU...!!
CON-GRATU-LATIONS, HARU.
YOU'VE REALLY FOUGHT HARD THESE PAST TWO WEEKS.
THANKS, TAKU...IT'S ALL BECAUSE OF YOU!!
IT'S ONLY POSSIBLE BECAUSE YOU JOINED ME IN THE DUELS LIKE THIS...
...WHILE KURO-YUKIHIME-SENPAI IS IN THE HOSPITAL.
PIPI (BEEP)
I MEAN, I BARELY HAVE ANY EXPERIENCE WITH BRAIN BURST, AND I MANAGED TO GET THIS MANY POINTS IN SUCH A SHORT TIME...
CAN UP TO LEVEL 2
BURST POINT: 308pt
I WONDER IF SENPAI... WILL BE HAPPY FOR ME...
...WHEN I TELL HER I MADE IT TO LEVEL TWO...
KUI
KUI (FWP)
AH...

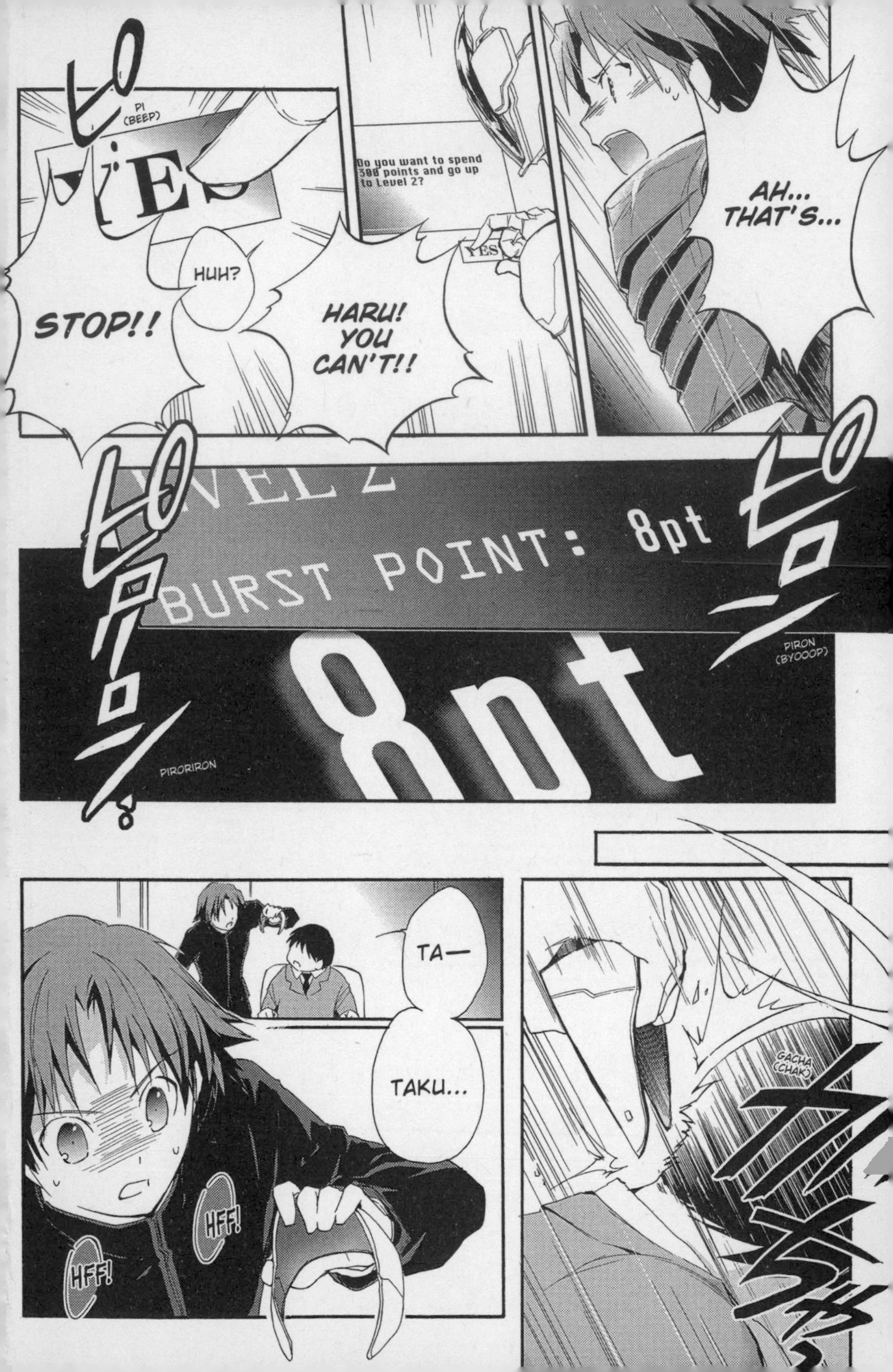
AH... THAT'S...
Do you want to spend 300 points and go up to Level 2?
YES
HARU! YOU CAN'T!!
PI (BEEP)
HUH?
STOP!!
BURST POINT: 8pt
PIRON (BYOOOP)
PIRORIRON
GACHA (CHAK)
TA—
TAKU...
HFF!
HFF!

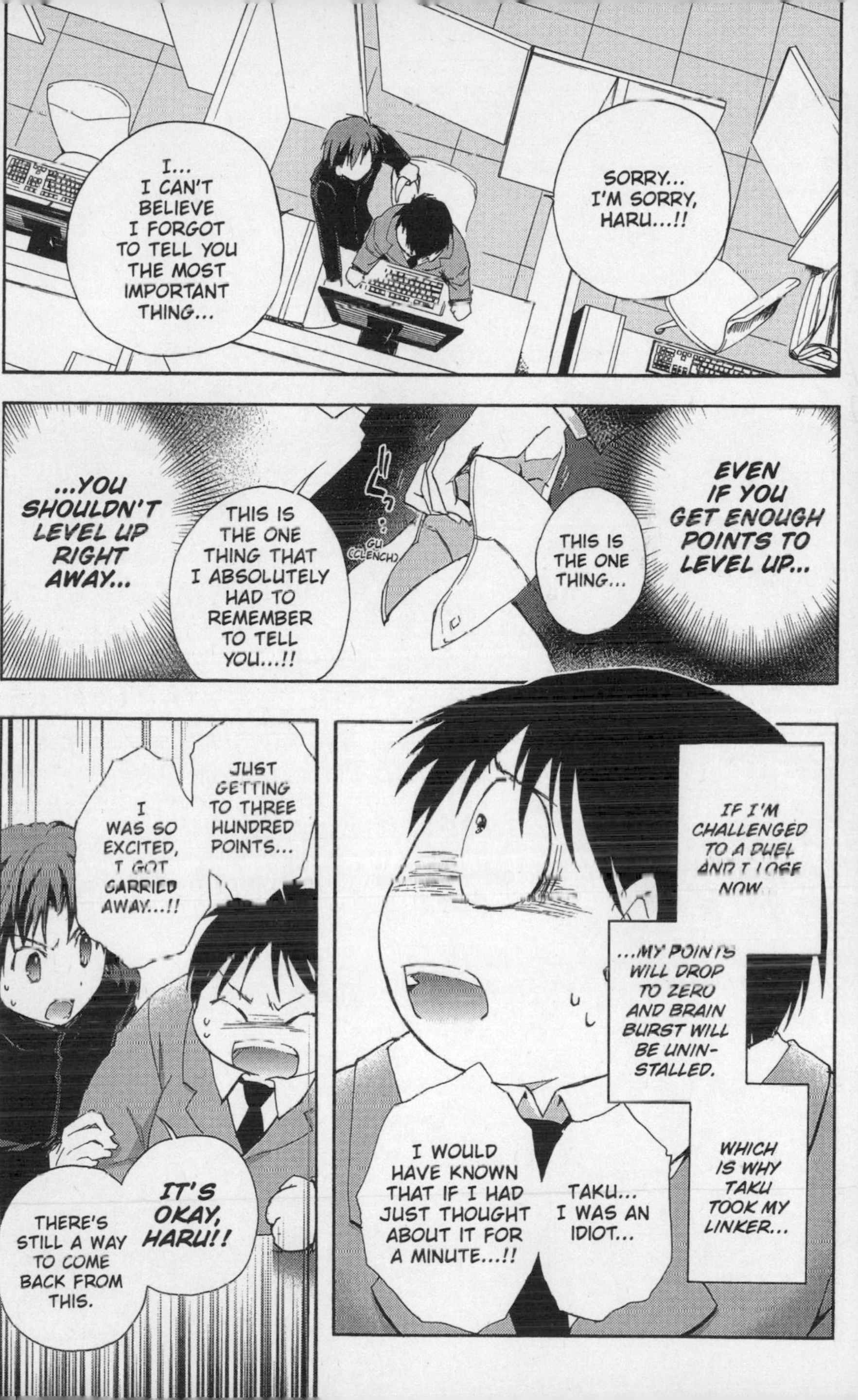
SORRY... I'M SORRY, HARU...!!
I... I CAN'T BELIEVE I FORGOT TO TELL YOU THE MOST IMPORTANT THING...
EVEN IF YOU GET ENOUGH POINTS TO LEVEL UP...
THIS IS THE ONE THING...
GU (CLENCH)
THIS IS THE ONE THING THAT I ABSOLUTELY HAD TO REMEMBER TO TELL YOU...!!
...YOU SHOULDN'T LEVEL UP RIGHT AWAY...
IF I'M CHALLENGED TO A DUEL AND I LOSE NOW...
...MY POINTS WILL DROP TO ZERO AND BRAIN BURST WILL BE UNIN-STALLED.
WHICH IS WHY TAKU TOOK MY LINKER...
TAKU... I WAS AN IDIOT...
I WOULD HAVE KNOWN THAT IF I HAD JUST THOUGHT ABOUT IT FOR A MINUTE...!!
JUST GETTING TO THREE HUNDRED POINTS...
I WAS SO EXCITED, I GOT CARRIED AWAY...!!
IT'S OKAY, HARU!!
THERE'S STILL A WAY TO COME BACK FROM THIS.

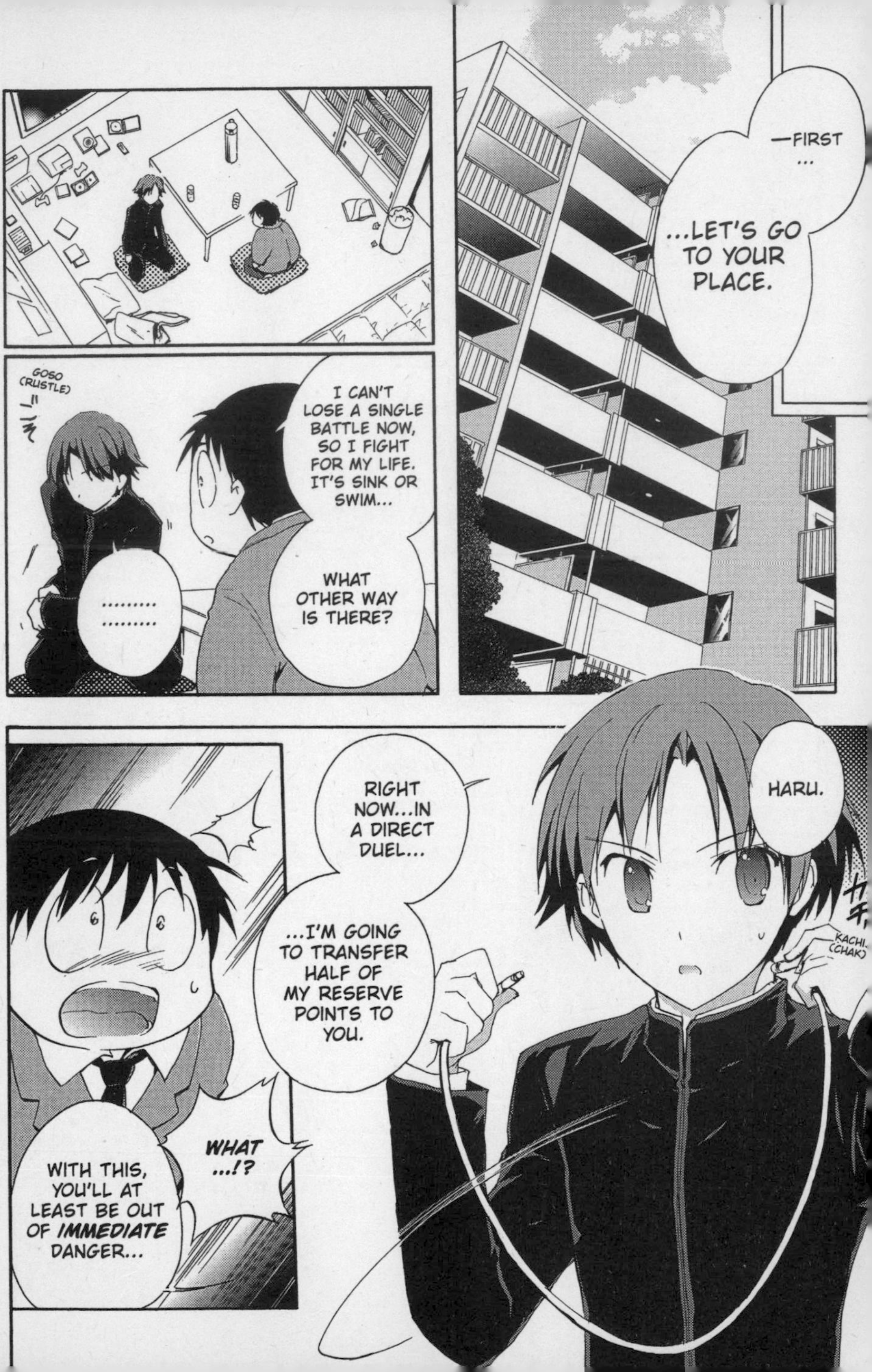
—FIRST
...
...LET'S GO TO YOUR PLACE.
I CAN'T LOSE A SINGLE BATTLE NOW, SO I FIGHT FOR MY LIFE. IT'S SINK OR SWIM...
WHAT OTHER WAY IS THERE?
GOSO (RUSTLE)
....
....
HARU.
KACHI (CHAK)
RIGHT NOW...IN A DIRECT DUEL...
...I'M GOING TO TRANSFER HALF OF MY RESERVE POINTS TO YOU.
WHAT ...!?
WITH THIS, YOU'LL AT LEAST BE OUT OF ***IMMEDIATE*** DANGER...

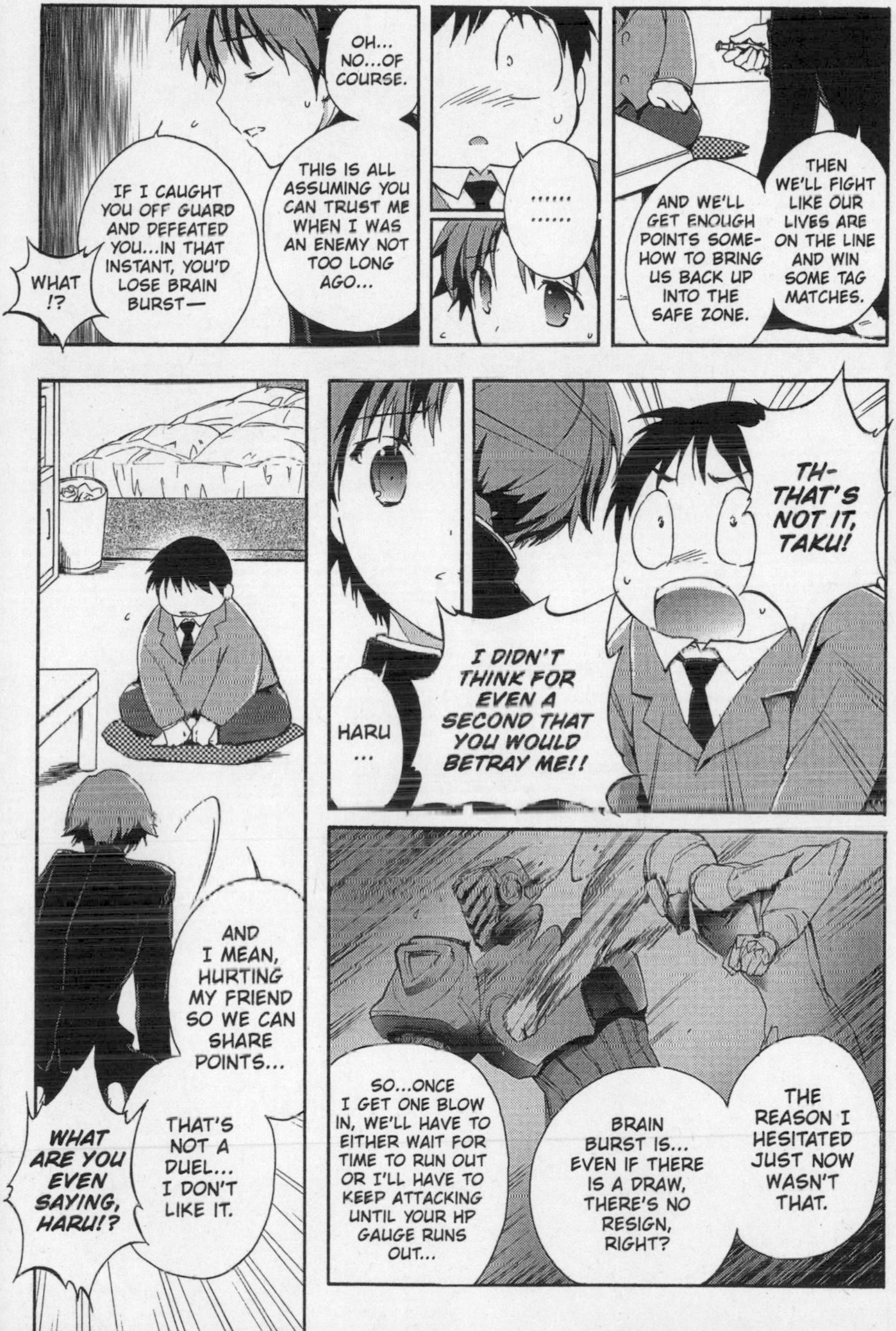
THEN WE'LL FIGHT LIKE OUR LIVES ARE ON THE LINE AND WIN SOME TAG MATCHES.
AND WE'LL GET ENOUGH POINTS SOME-HOW TO BRING US BACK UP INTO THE SAFE ZONE.
......
......
OH... NO...OF COURSE.
THIS IS ALL ASSUMING YOU CAN TRUST ME WHEN I WAS AN ENEMY NOT TOO LONG AGO...
IF I CAUGHT YOU OFF GUARD AND DEFEATED YOU...IN THAT INSTANT, YOU'D LOSE BRAIN BURST—
WHAT!?
TH-THAT'S NOT IT, TAKU!
I DIDN'T THINK FOR EVEN A SECOND THAT YOU WOULD BETRAY ME!!
HARU...
THE REASON I HESITATED JUST NOW WASN'T THAT.
BRAIN BURST IS... EVEN IF THERE IS A DRAW, THERE'S NO RESIGN, RIGHT?
SO...ONCE I GET ONE BLOW IN, WE'LL HAVE TO EITHER WAIT FOR TIME TO RUN OUT OR I'LL HAVE TO KEEP ATTACKING UNTIL YOUR HP GAUGE RUNS OUT...
AND I MEAN, HURTING MY FRIEND SO WE CAN SHARE POINTS...
THAT'S NOT A DUEL... I DON'T LIKE IT.
WHAT ARE YOU EVEN SAYING, HARU!?

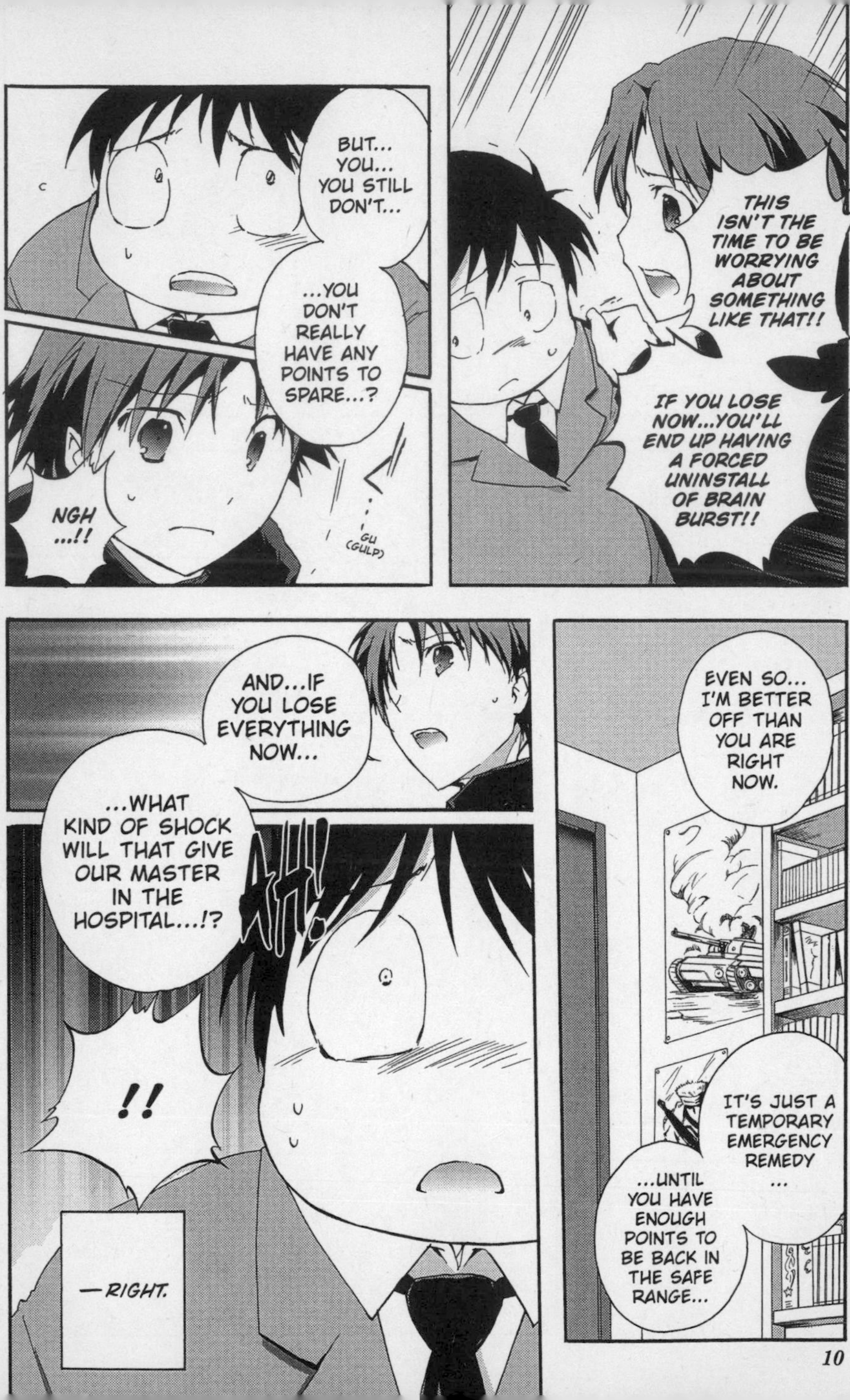
THIS ISN'T THE TIME TO BE WORRYING ABOUT SOMETHING LIKE THAT!!
IF YOU LOSE NOW...YOU'LL END UP HAVING A FORCED UNINSTALL OF BRAIN BURST!!
BUT... YOU... YOU STILL DON'T...
...YOU DON'T REALLY HAVE ANY POINTS TO SPARE...?
NGH ...!!
GU (GULP)
EVEN SO... I'M BETTER OFF THAN YOU ARE RIGHT NOW.
IT'S JUST A TEMPORARY EMERGENCY REMEDY...
...UNTIL YOU HAVE ENOUGH POINTS TO BE BACK IN THE SAFE RANGE...
AND...IF YOU LOSE EVERYTHING NOW...
...WHAT KIND OF SHOCK WILL THAT GIVE OUR MASTER IN THE HOSPITAL...!?
AH!
!!
—RIGHT.

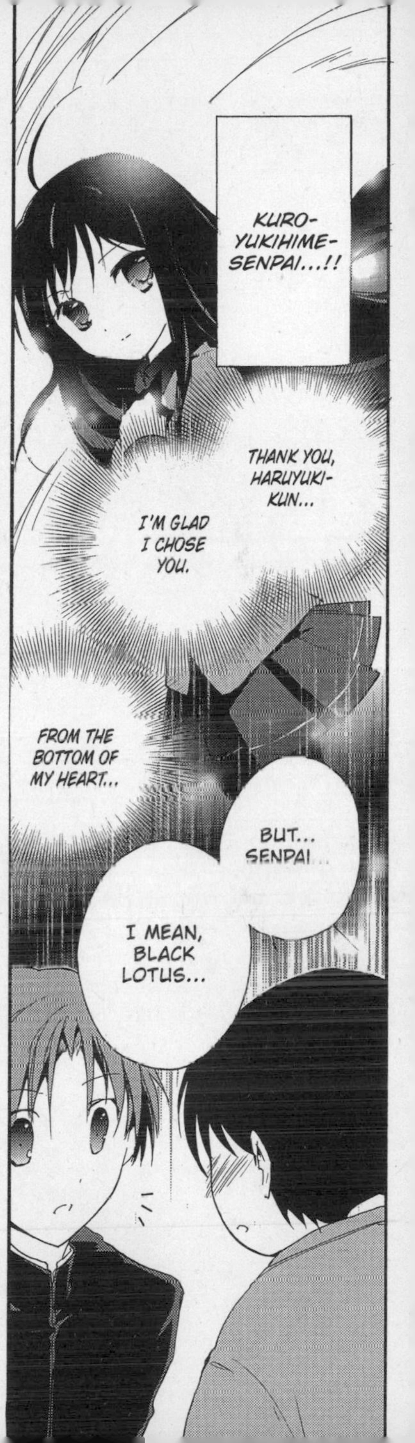
KURO-YUKIHIME-SENPAI...!!
THANK YOU, HARUYUKI-KUN...
I'M GLAD I CHOSE YOU.
FROM THE BOTTOM OF MY HEART...
BUT... SENPAI...
I MEAN, BLACK LOTUS...

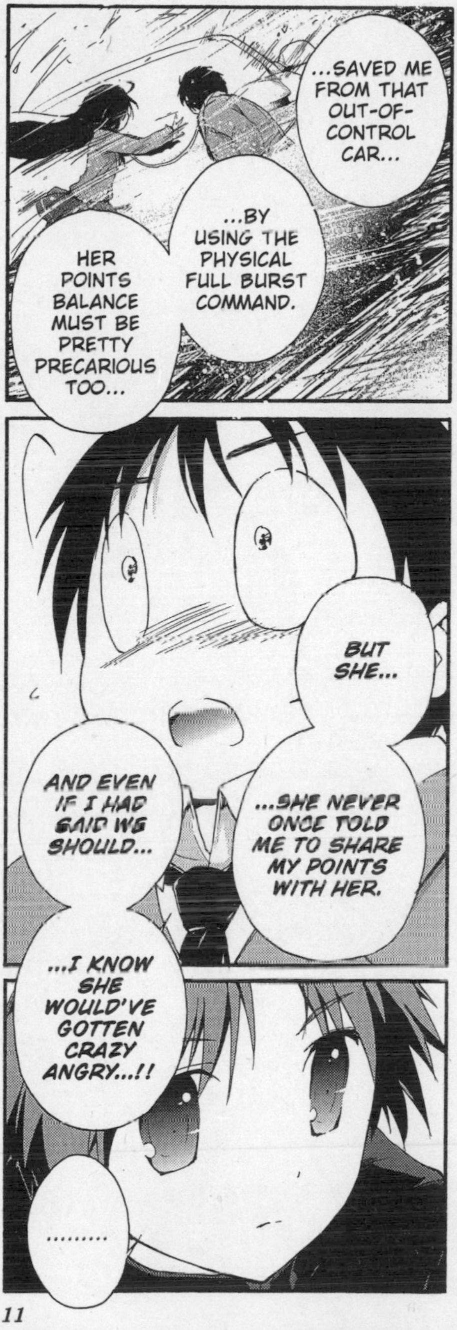
...SAVED ME FROM THAT OUT-OF-CONTROL CAR...
...BY USING THE PHYSICAL FULL BURST COMMAND.
HER POINTS BALANCE MUST BE PRETTY PRECARIOUS TOO...
BUT SHE...
...SHE NEVER ONCE TOLD ME TO SHARE MY POINTS WITH HER.
AND EVEN IF I HAD SAID WE SHOULD...
...I KNOW SHE WOULD'VE GOTTEN CRAZY ANGRY...!!
....

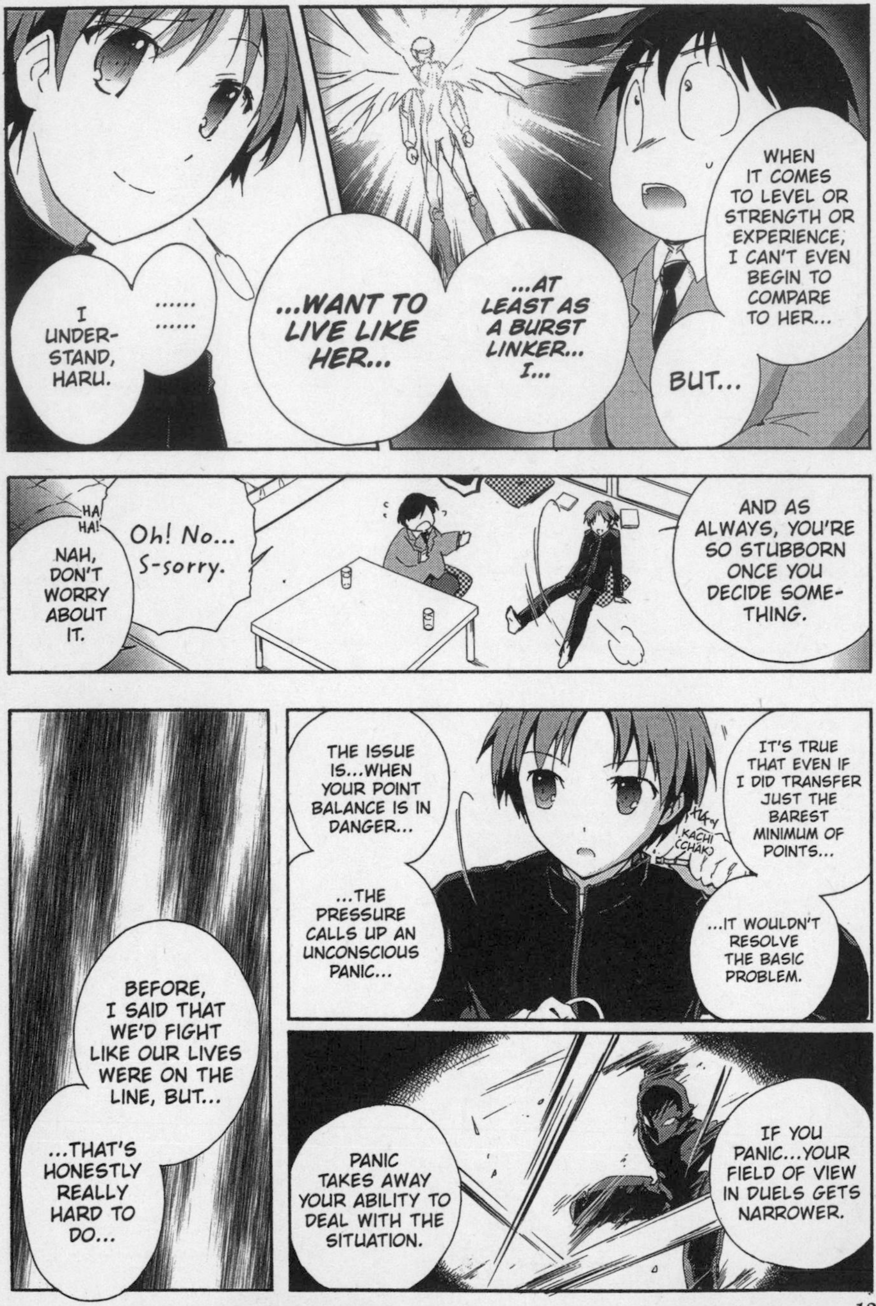
WHEN IT COMES TO LEVEL OR STRENGTH OR EXPERIENCE, I CAN'T EVEN BEGIN TO COMPARE TO HER...
BUT...
...AT LEAST AS A BURST LINKER... I...
...WANT TO LIVE LIKE HER...
....
I UNDER-STAND, HARU.
AND AS ALWAYS, YOU'RE SO STUBBORN ONCE YOU DECIDE SOME-THING.
Oh! No... S-sorry.
HA HA!
NAH, DON'T WORRY ABOUT IT.
IT'S TRUE THAT EVEN IF I DID TRANSFER JUST THE BAREST MINIMUM OF POINTS...
KACHI (CHAK)
...IT WOULDN'T RESOLVE THE BASIC PROBLEM.
THE ISSUE IS...WHEN YOUR POINT BALANCE IS IN DANGER...
...THE PRESSURE CALLS UP AN UNCONSCIOUS PANIC...
IF YOU PANIC...YOUR FIELD OF VIEW IN DUELS GETS NARROWER.
PANIC TAKES AWAY YOUR ABILITY TO DEAL WITH THE SITUATION.
BEFORE, I SAID THAT WE'D FIGHT LIKE OUR LIVES WERE ON THE LINE, BUT...
...THAT'S HONESTLY REALLY HARD TO DO...

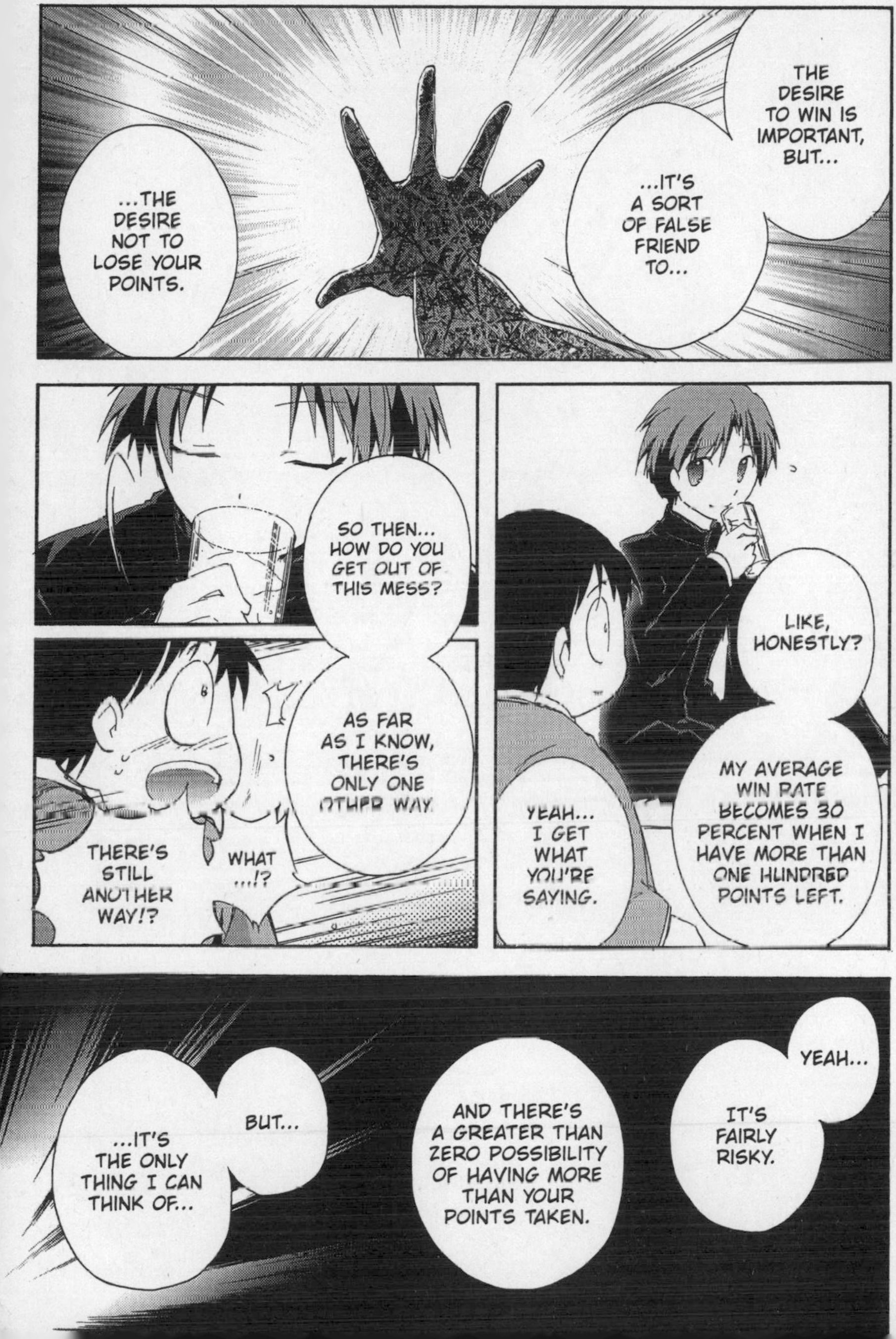
THE DESIRE TO WIN IS IMPORTANT, BUT...
...IT'S A SORT OF FALSE FRIEND TO...
...THE DESIRE NOT TO LOSE YOUR POINTS.
LIKE, HONESTLY?
MY AVERAGE WIN RATE BECOMES 30 PERCENT WHEN I HAVE MORE THAN ONE HUNDRED POINTS LEFT.
YEAH... I GET WHAT YOU'RE SAYING.
SO THEN... HOW DO YOU GET OUT OF THIS MESS?
AS FAR AS I KNOW, THERE'S ONLY ONE OTHER WAY.
WHAT ...!?
THERE'S STILL ANOTHER WAY!?
YEAH...
IT'S FAIRLY RISKY.
AND THERE'S A GREATER THAN ZERO POSSIBILITY OF HAVING MORE THAN YOUR POINTS TAKEN.
BUT...
...IT'S THE ONLY THING I CAN THINK OF...

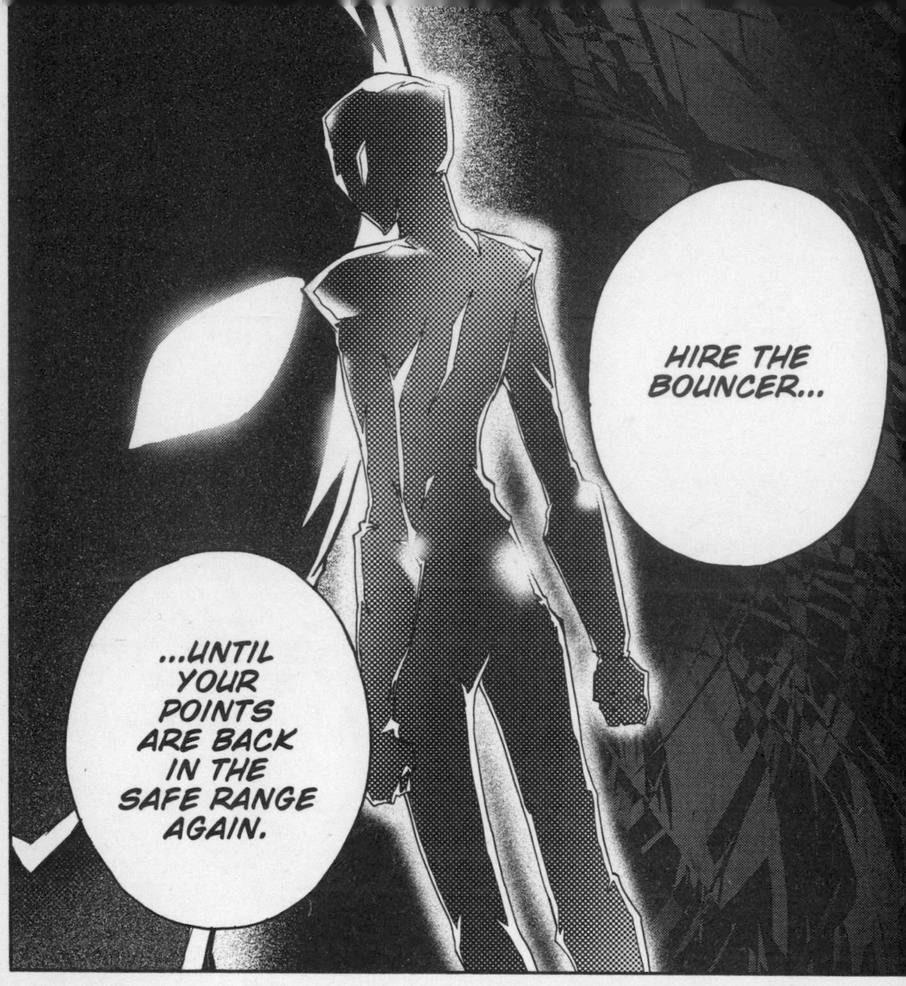
HIRE THE BOUNCER...
...UNTIL YOUR POINTS ARE BACK IN THE SAFE RANGE AGAIN.

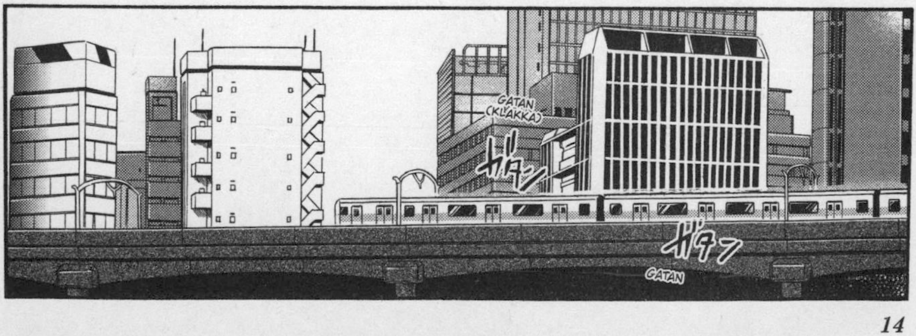
GATAN (KLAKKA)
GATAN

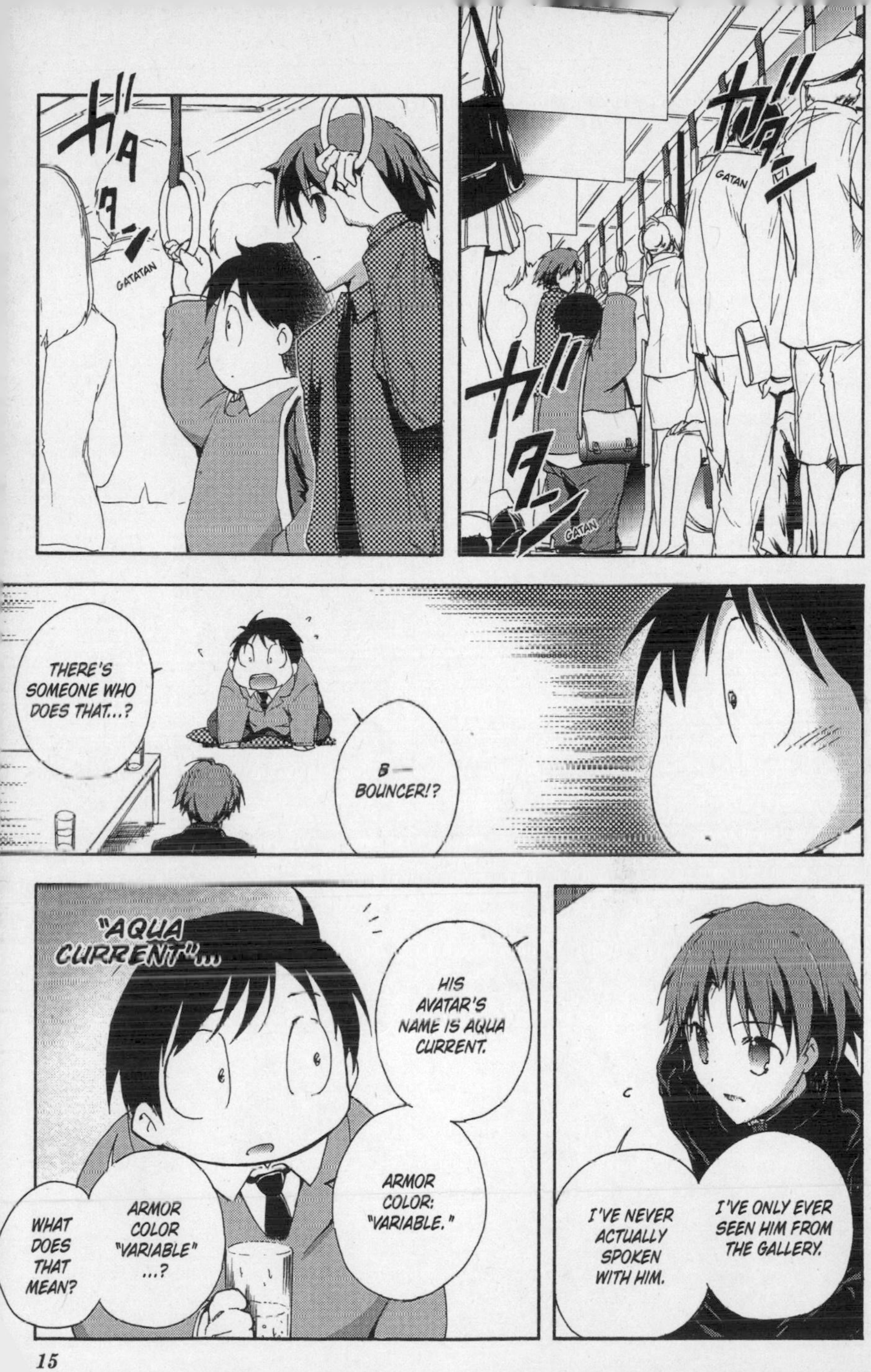
GATAN
GATAN
GATATAN
B— BOUNCER!?
THERE'S SOMEONE WHO DOES THAT...?
I'VE ONLY EVER SEEN HIM FROM THE GALLERY.
I'VE NEVER ACTUALLY SPOKEN WITH HIM.
HIS AVATAR'S NAME IS AQUA CURRENT.
"AQUA CURRENT"...
ARMOR COLOR: "VARIABLE."
ARMOR COLOR "VARIABLE" ...?
WHAT DOES THAT MEAN?

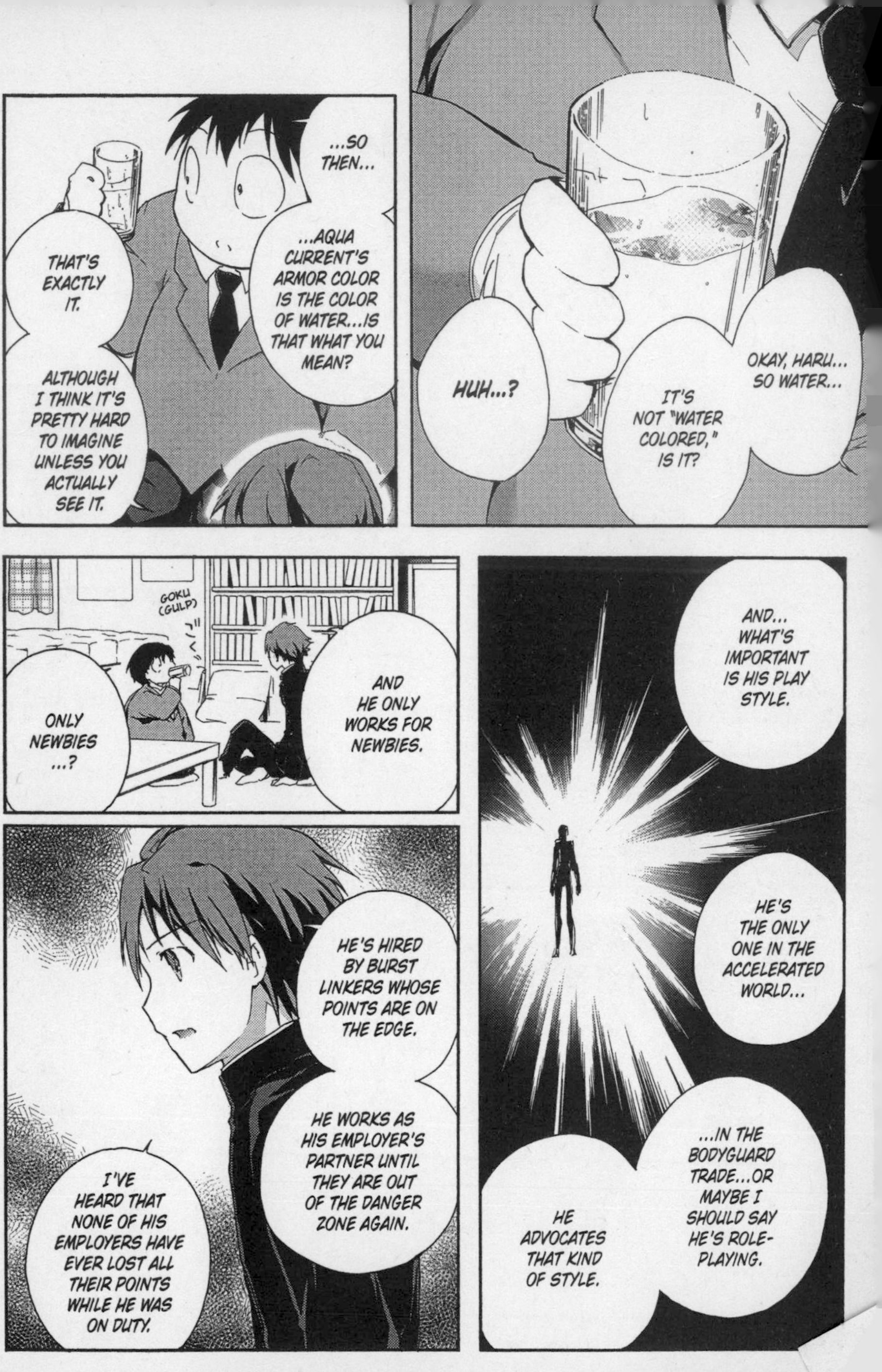
OKAY, HARU... SO WATER...
IT'S NOT "WATER COLORED," IS IT?
HUH...?
...SO THEN...
...AQUA CURRENT'S ARMOR COLOR IS THE COLOR OF WATER...IS THAT WHAT YOU MEAN?
THAT'S EXACTLY IT.
ALTHOUGH I THINK IT'S PRETTY HARD TO IMAGINE UNLESS YOU ACTUALLY SEE IT.
GOKU (GULP)
AND HE ONLY WORKS FOR NEWBIES.
ONLY NEWBIES ...?
HE'S HIRED BY BURST LINKERS WHOSE POINTS ARE ON THE EDGE.
HE WORKS AS HIS EMPLOYER'S PARTNER UNTIL THEY ARE OUT OF THE DANGER ZONE AGAIN.
I'VE HEARD THAT NONE OF HIS EMPLOYERS HAVE EVER LOST ALL THEIR POINTS WHILE HE WAS ON DUTY.
AND... WHAT'S IMPORTANT IS HIS PLAY STYLE.
HE'S THE ONLY ONE IN THE ACCELERATED WORLD...
...IN THE BODYGUARD TRADE...OR MAYBE I SHOULD SAY HE'S ROLE-PLAYING.
HE ADVOCATES THAT KIND OF STYLE.

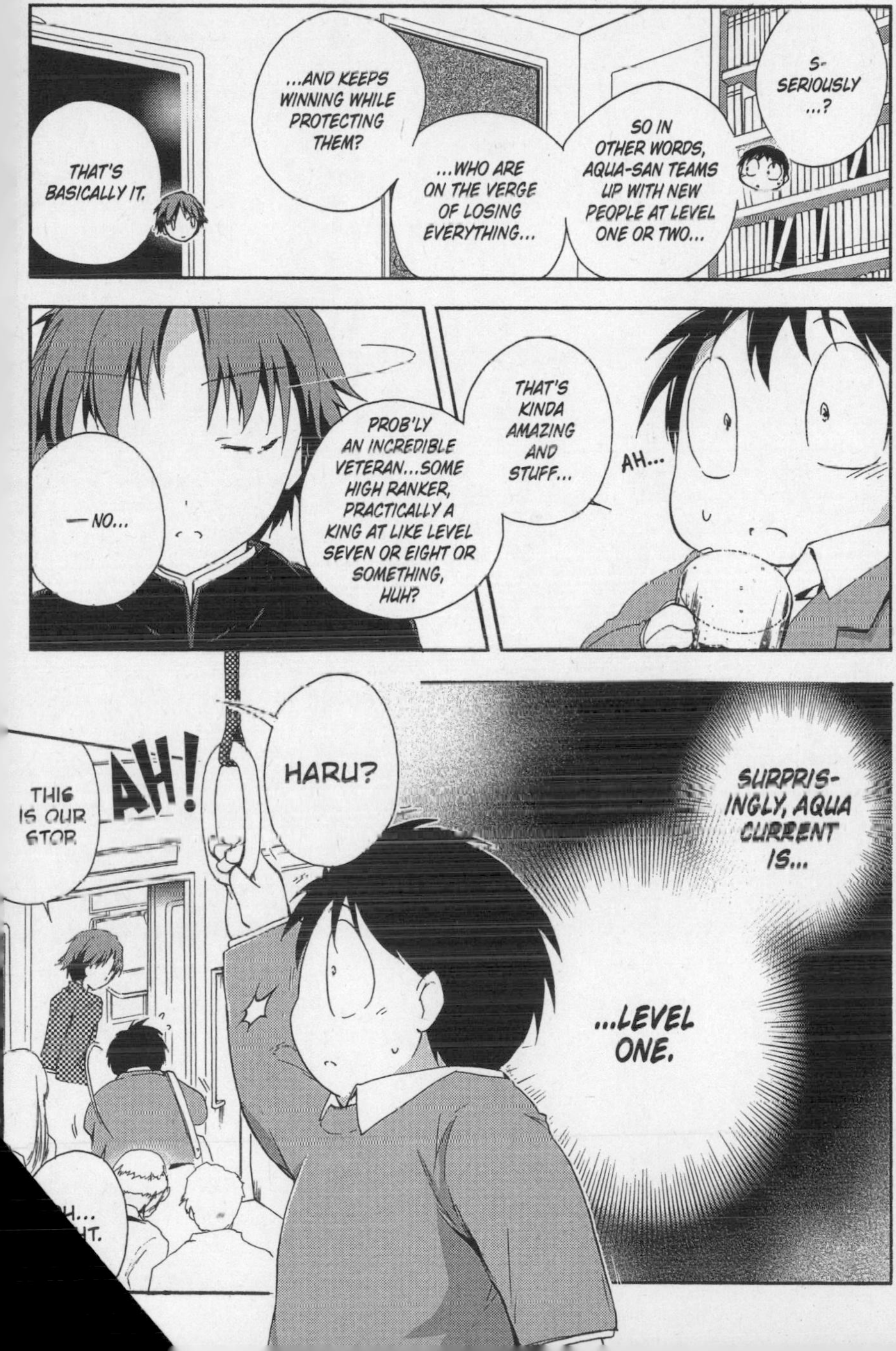
S-SERIOUSLY ...?
SO IN OTHER WORDS, AQUA-SAN TEAMS UP WITH NEW PEOPLE AT LEVEL ONE OR TWO...
...WHO ARE ON THE VERGE OF LOSING EVERYTHING...
...AND KEEPS WINNING WHILE PROTECTING THEM?
THAT'S BASICALLY IT.
AH...
THAT'S KINDA AMAZING AND STUFF...
PROB'LY AN INCREDIBLE VETERAN...SOME HIGH RANKER, PRACTICALLY A KING AT LIKE LEVEL SEVEN OR EIGHT OR SOMETHING, HUH?
—NO...
SURPRIS-INGLY, AQUA CURRENT IS...
...LEVEL ONE.
HARU?
AH!
THIS IS OUR STOP

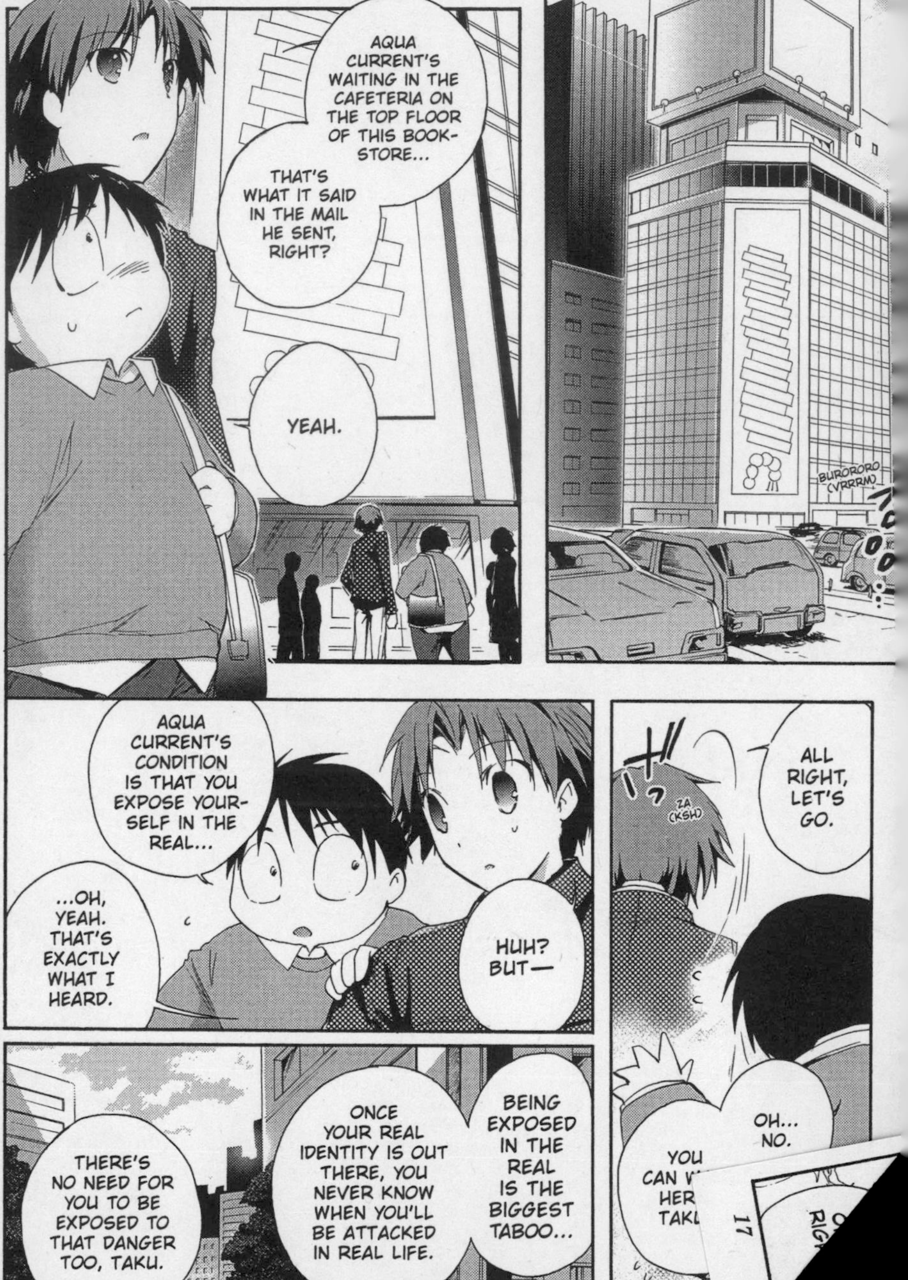
BURORORO (VRRRM)
AQUA CURRENT'S WAITING IN THE CAFETERIA ON THE TOP FLOOR OF THIS BOOK-STORE...
THAT'S WHAT IT SAID IN THE MAIL HE SENT, RIGHT?
YEAH.
ALL RIGHT, LET'S GO.
ZA (KSH)
AQUA CURRENT'S CONDITION IS THAT YOU EXPOSE YOUR-SELF IN THE REAL...
HUH? BUT—
...OH, YEAH. THAT'S EXACTLY WHAT I HEARD.
OH... NO.
YOU
BEING EXPOSED IN THE REAL IS THE BIGGEST TABOO...
ONCE YOUR REAL IDENTITY IS OUT THERE, YOU NEVER KNOW WHEN YOU'LL BE ATTACKED IN REAL LIFE.
THERE'S NO NEED FOR YOU TO BE EXPOSED TO THAT DANGER TOO, TAKU.

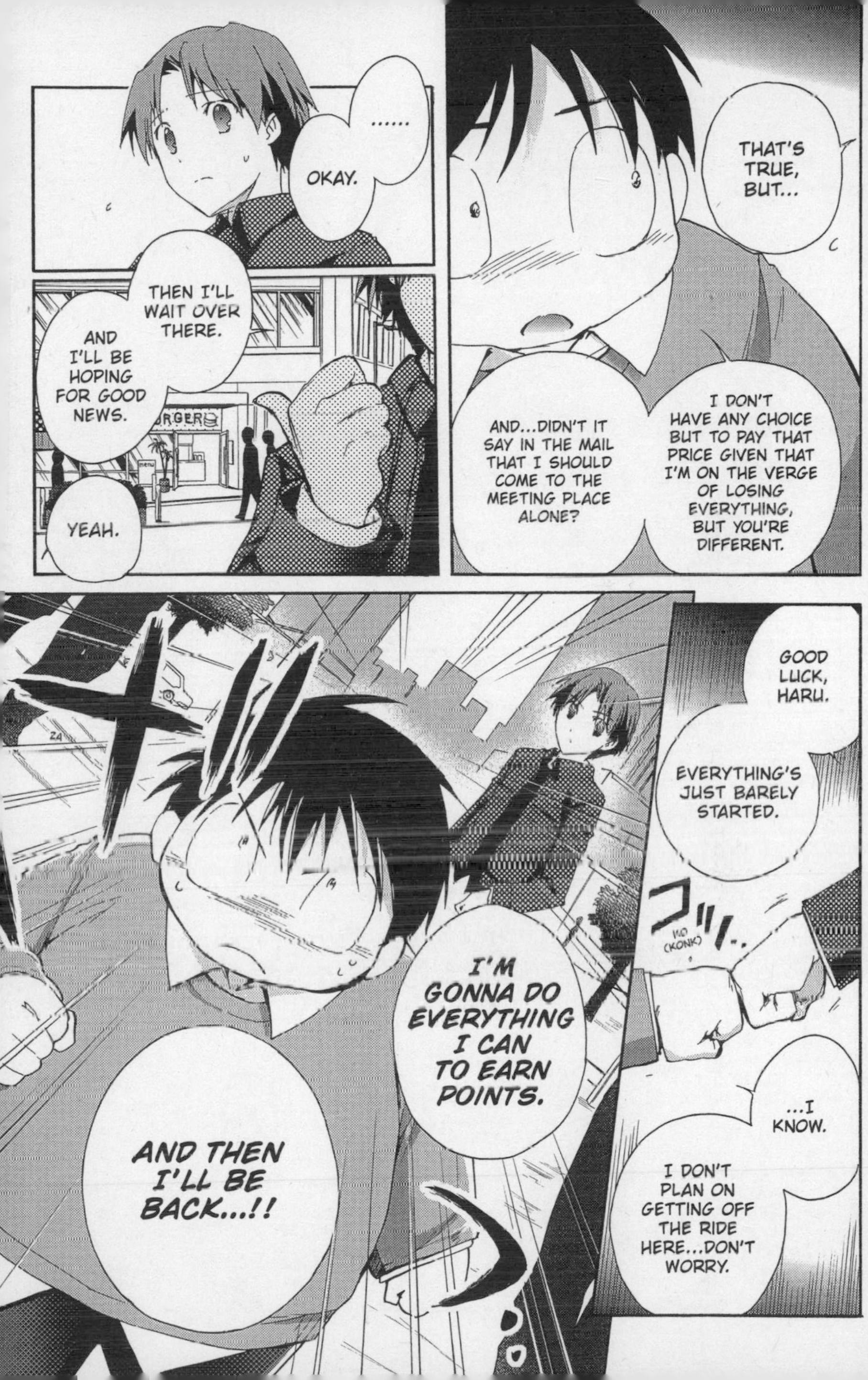
THAT'S TRUE, BUT...
I DON'T HAVE ANY CHOICE BUT TO PAY THAT PRICE GIVEN THAT I'M ON THE VERGE OF LOSING EVERYTHING, BUT YOU'RE DIFFERENT.
AND...DIDN'T IT SAY IN THE MAIL THAT I SHOULD COME TO THE MEETING PLACE ALONE?
......
OKAY.
THEN I'LL WAIT OVER THERE.
AND I'LL BE HOPING FOR GOOD NEWS.
YEAH.
GOOD LUCK, HARU.
EVERYTHING'S JUST BARELY STARTED.
(KONK)
...I KNOW.
I DON'T PLAN ON GETTING OFF THE RIDE HERE...DON'T WORRY.
I'M GONNA DO EVERYTHING I CAN TO EARN POINTS.
AND THEN I'LL BE BACK...!!

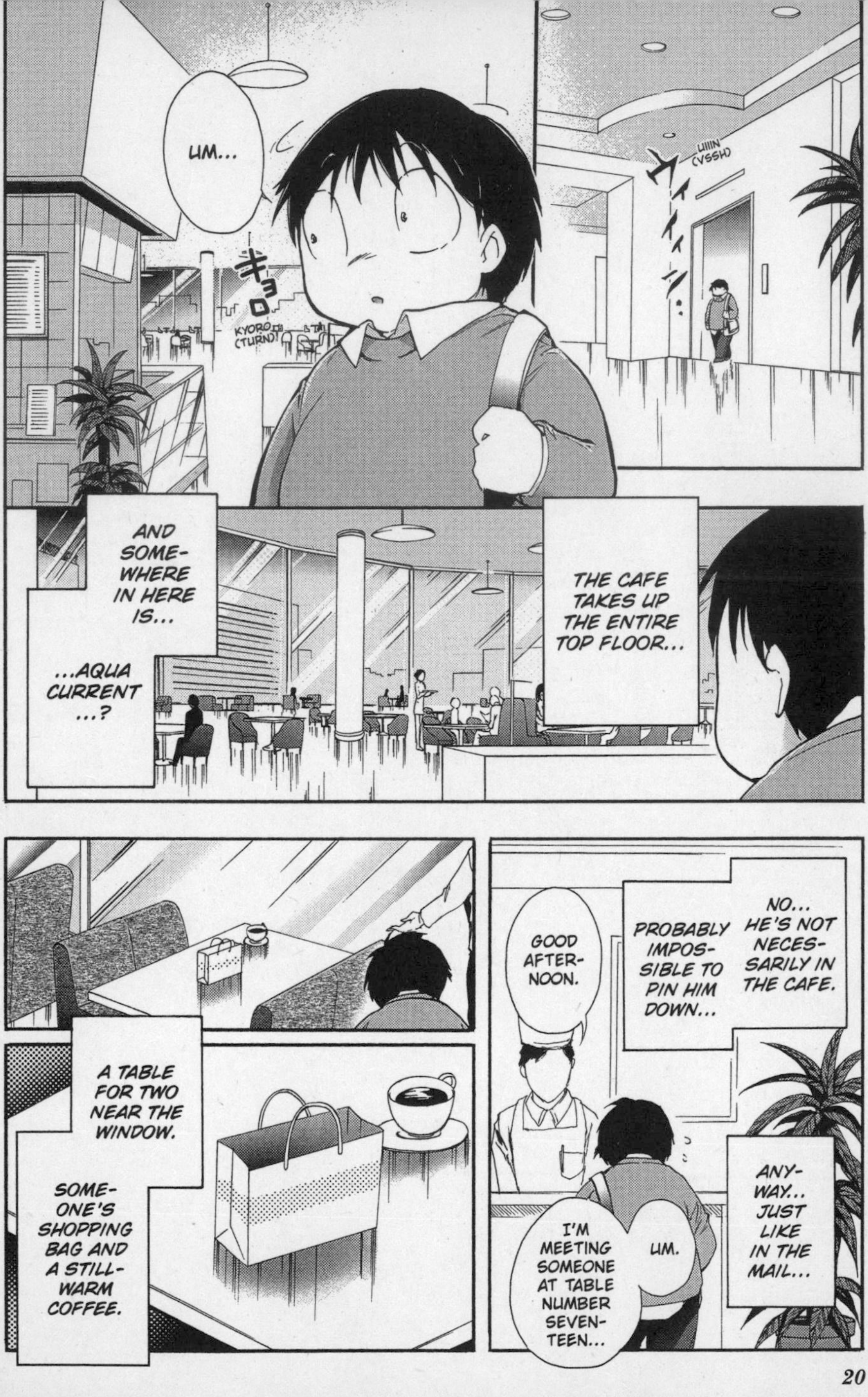
UIIIN (VSSH)
UM...
KYORO (TURN)
THE CAFE TAKES UP THE ENTIRE TOP FLOOR...
AND SOMEWHERE IN HERE IS...
...AQUA CURRENT ...?
NO... HE'S NOT NECESSARILY IN THE CAFE.
PROBABLY IMPOSSIBLE TO PIN HIM DOWN...
GOOD AFTERNOON.
ANYWAY... JUST LIKE IN THE MAIL...
UM.
I'M MEETING SOMEONE AT TABLE NUMBER SEVENTEEN...
A TABLE FOR TWO NEAR THE WINDOW.
SOMEONE'S SHOPPING BAG AND A STILL-WARM COFFEE.

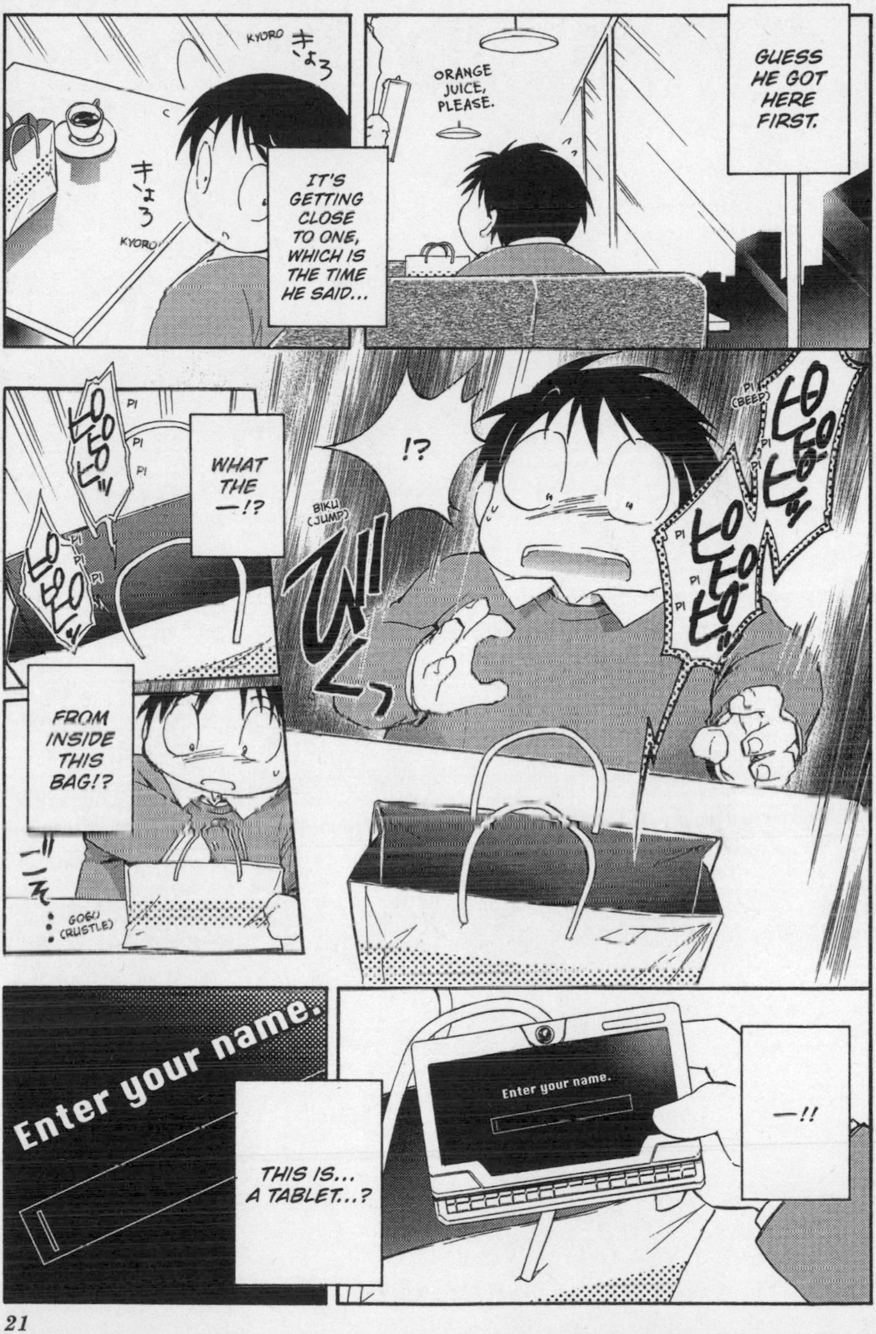
GUESS HE GOT HERE FIRST.
ORANGE JUICE, PLEASE.
KYORO
IT'S GETTING CLOSE TO ONE, WHICH IS THE TIME HE SAID...
KYORO
PI (BEEP)
PI
PI
!?
BIKU (JUMP)
PI
PI
PI
WHAT THE—!?
PI
PI
PI
PI
PI
PI
FROM INSIDE THIS BAG!?
GOSO (RUSTLE)
—!!
Enter your name.
THIS IS... A TABLET...?
Enter your name.

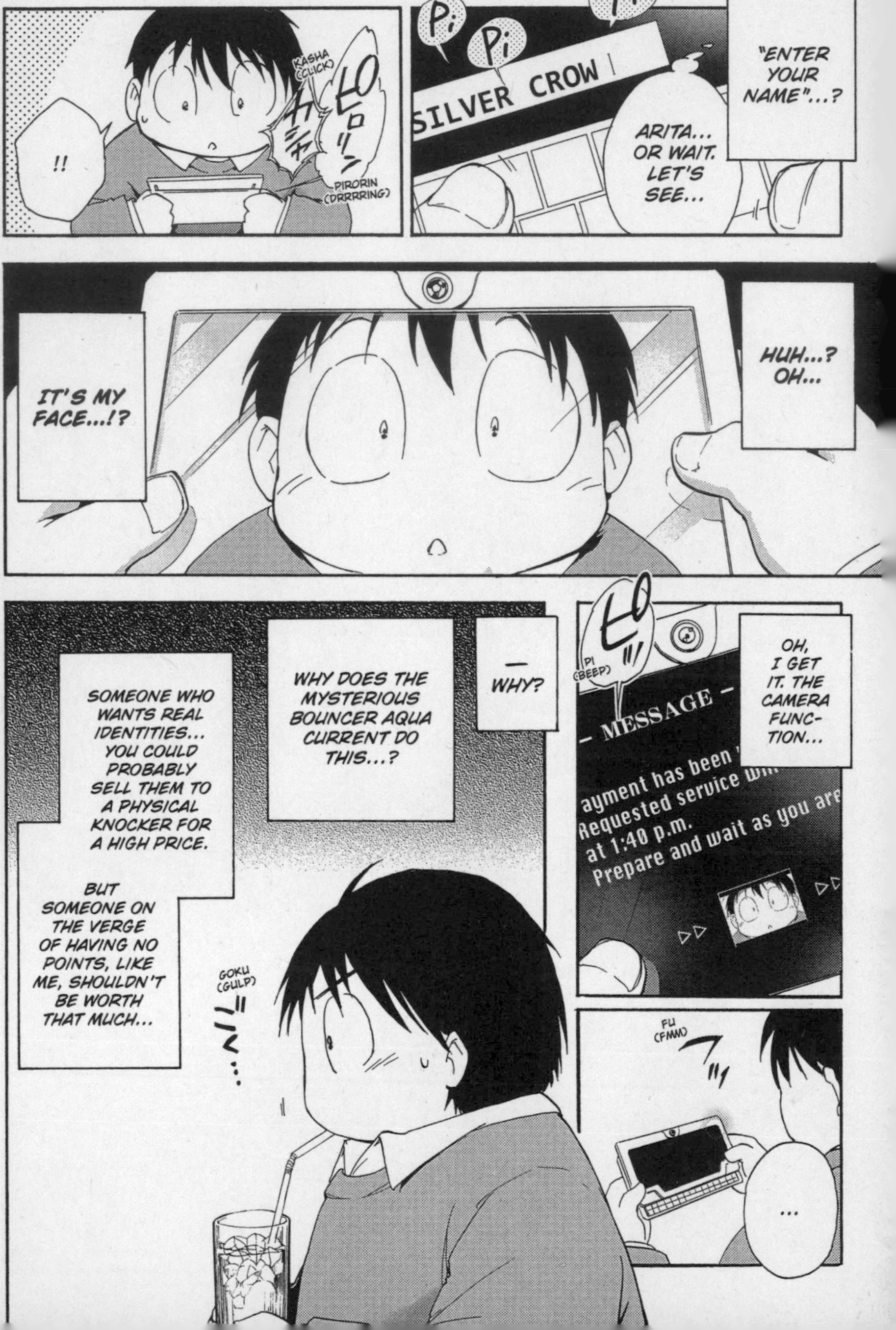
"ENTER YOUR NAME"...?
ARITA... OR WAIT. LET'S SEE...
Pi
Pi
Pi
SILVER CROW
KASHA (CLICK)
PIRORIN (DRRRRING)
!!
HUH...? OH...
IT'S MY FACE...!?
OH, I GET IT. THE CAMERA FUNCTION...
PI (BEEP)
— MESSAGE —
ayment has been
Requested service
at 1:40 p.m.
Prepare and wait as you are
FU (FMM)
...
— WHY?
WHY DOES THE MYSTERIOUS BOUNCER AQUA CURRENT DO THIS...?
SOMEONE WHO WANTS REAL IDENTITIES... YOU COULD PROBABLY SELL THEM TO A PHYSICAL KNOCKER FOR A HIGH PRICE.
BUT SOMEONE ON THE VERGE OF HAVING NO POINTS, LIKE ME, SHOULDN'T BE WORTH THAT MUCH...
GOKU (GULP)

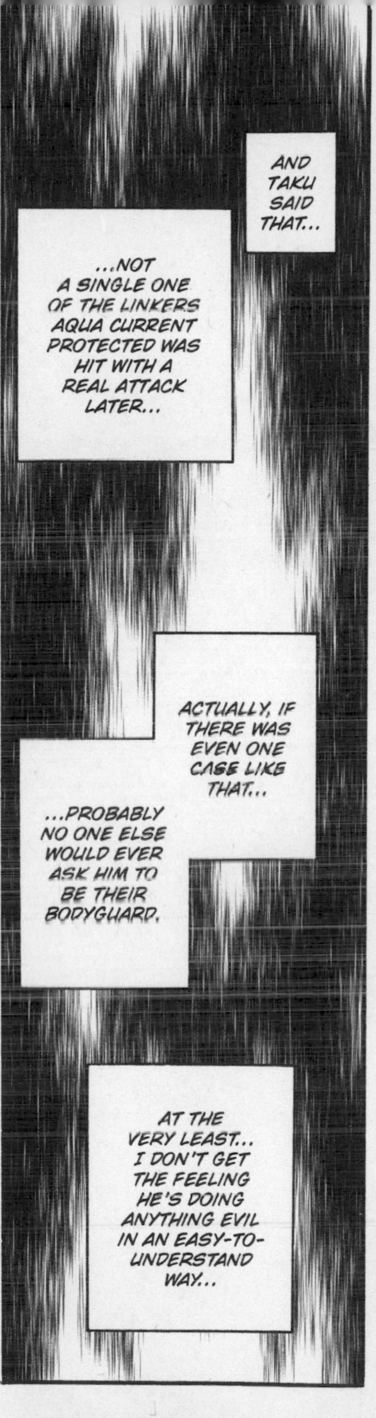
AND TAKU SAID THAT...
...NOT A SINGLE ONE OF THE LINKERS AQUA CURRENT PROTECTED WAS HIT WITH A REAL ATTACK LATER...
ACTUALLY, IF THERE WAS EVEN ONE CASE LIKE THAT...
...PROBABLY NO ONE ELSE WOULD EVER ASK HIM TO BE THEIR BODYGUARD.
AT THE VERY LEAST... I DON'T GET THE FEELING HE'S DOING ANYTHING EVIL IN AN EASY-TO-UNDERSTAND WAY...

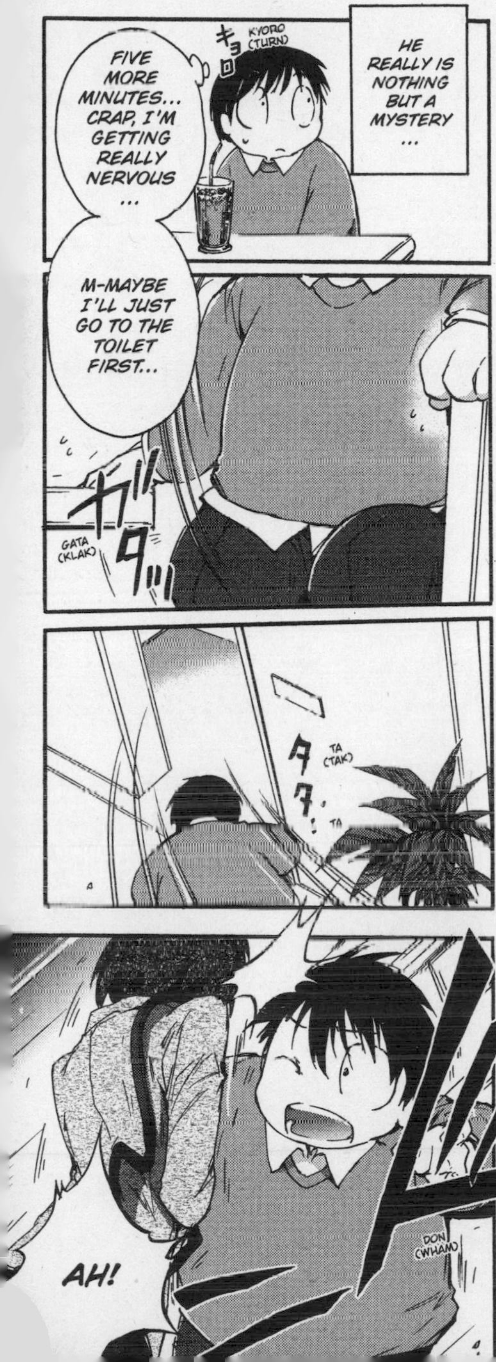
HE REALLY IS NOTHING BUT A MYSTERY...
KYORO (TURN)
FIVE MORE MINUTES... CRAP, I'M GETTING REALLY NERVOUS...
M-MAYBE I'LL JUST GO TO THE TOILET FIRST...
GATA (KLAK)
TA (TAK)
TA
DON (WHAM)
AH!

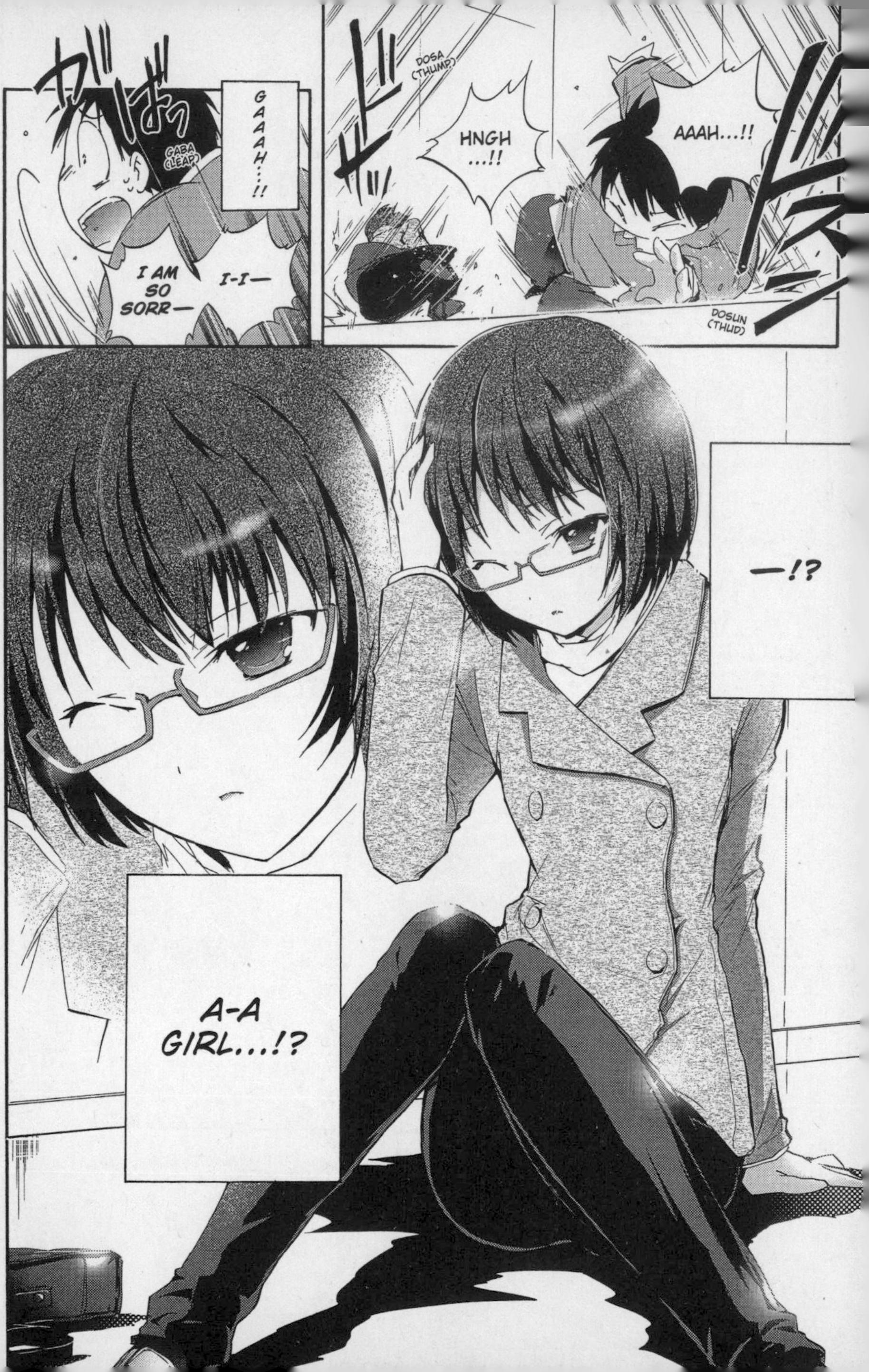
AAAH...!!
HNGH ...!!
DOSA (THUMP)
DOSUN (THUD)
GAAAAH...!!
GABA (LEAP)
I-I—
I AM SO SORR—
—!?
A-A GIRL...!?

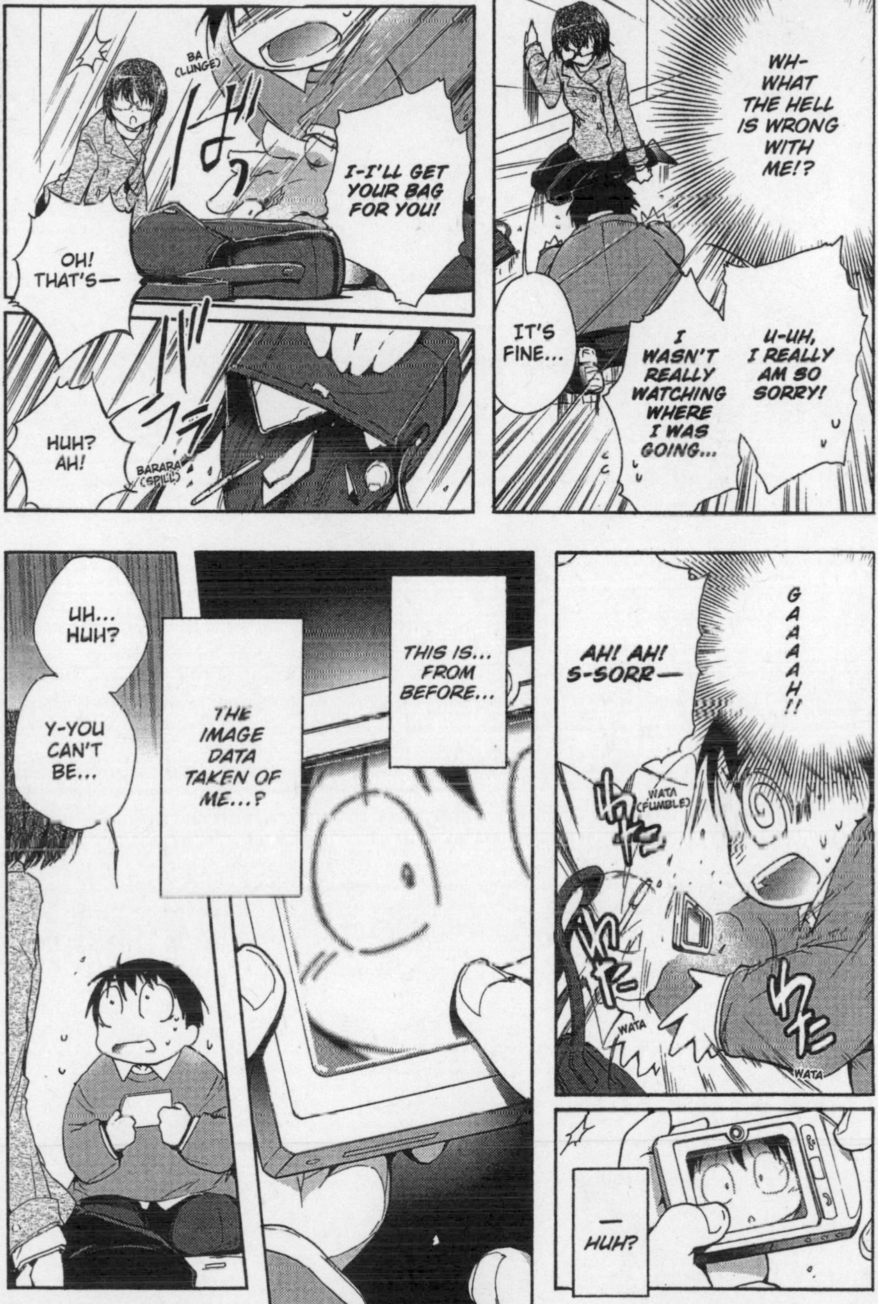
WH-WHAT THE HELL IS WRONG WITH ME!?
U-UH, I REALLY AM SO SORRY!
I WASN'T REALLY WATCHING WHERE I WAS GOING...
IT'S FINE...
BA (LUNGE)
I-I'LL GET YOUR BAG FOR YOU!
OH! THAT'S—
BARARA (SPILL)
HUH? AH!
GAAAAAH!!
AH! AH! S-SORR—
WATA (FUMBLE)
WATA
WATA
—HUH?
THIS IS... FROM BEFORE...
THE IMAGE DATA TAKEN OF ME...?
UH... HUH?
Y-YOU CAN'T BE...

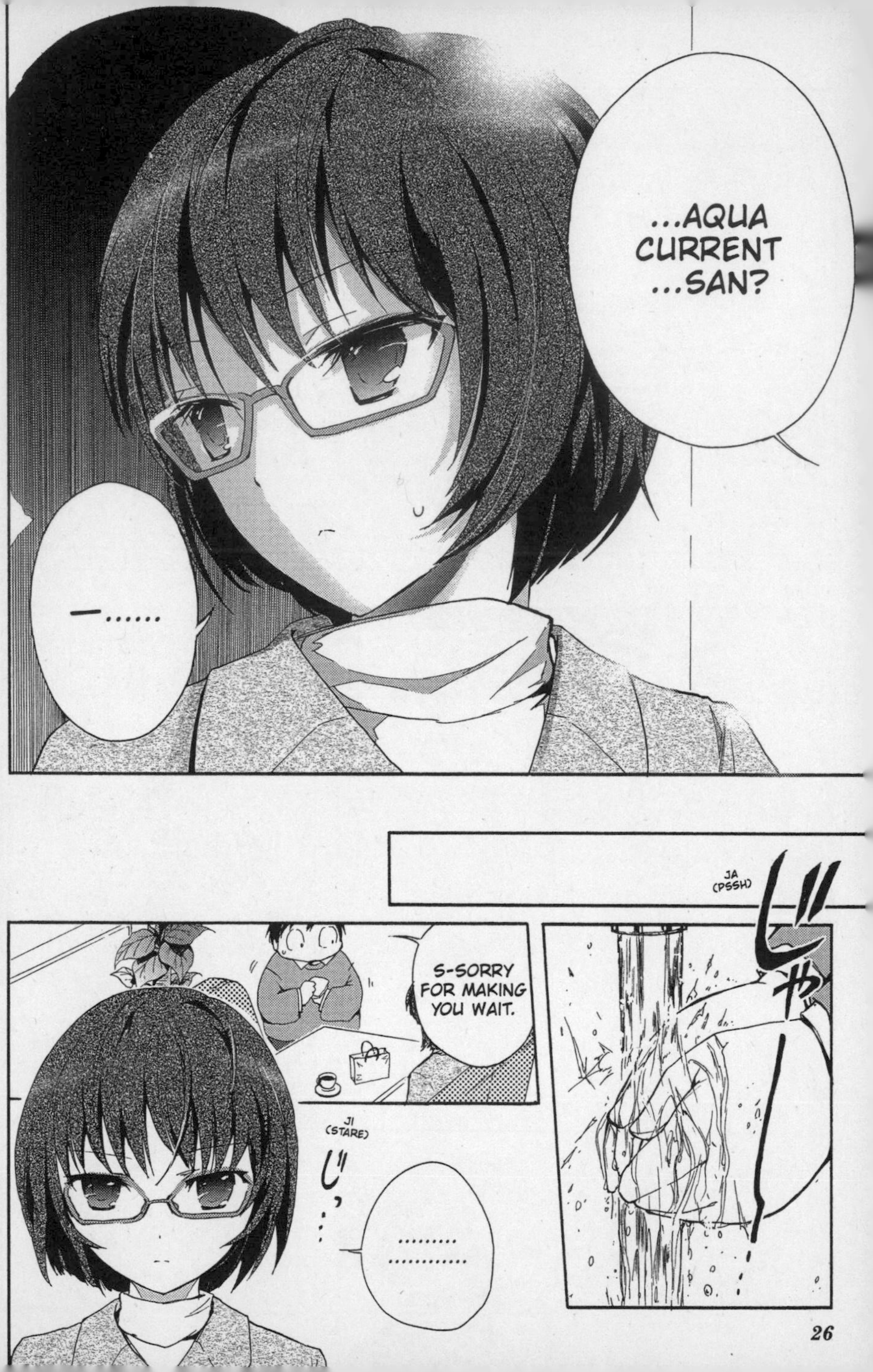
...AQUA CURRENT ...SAN?
—......
JA (PSSH)
S-SORRY FOR MAKING YOU WAIT.
JI (STARE)
....
....

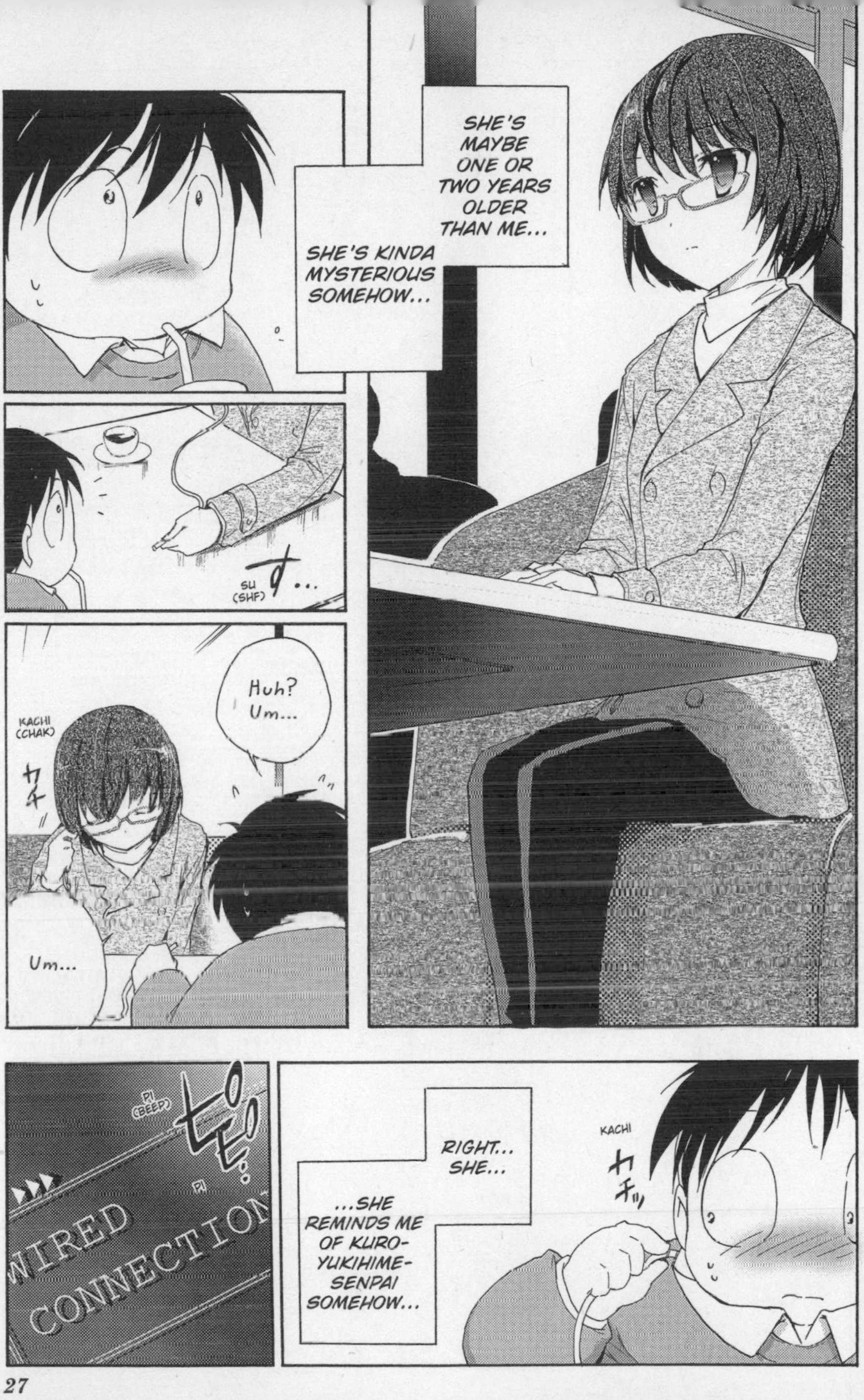

SHE'S MAYBE ONE OR TWO YEARS OLDER THAN ME...
SHE'S KINDA MYSTERIOUS SOMEHOW...
SU (SHF)
Huh? Um...
KACHI (CHAK)
Um...
RIGHT... SHE...
...SHE REMINDS ME OF KURO-YUKIHIME-SENPAI SOMEHOW...
KACHI
PI (BEEP)
PI
WIRED CONNECTION

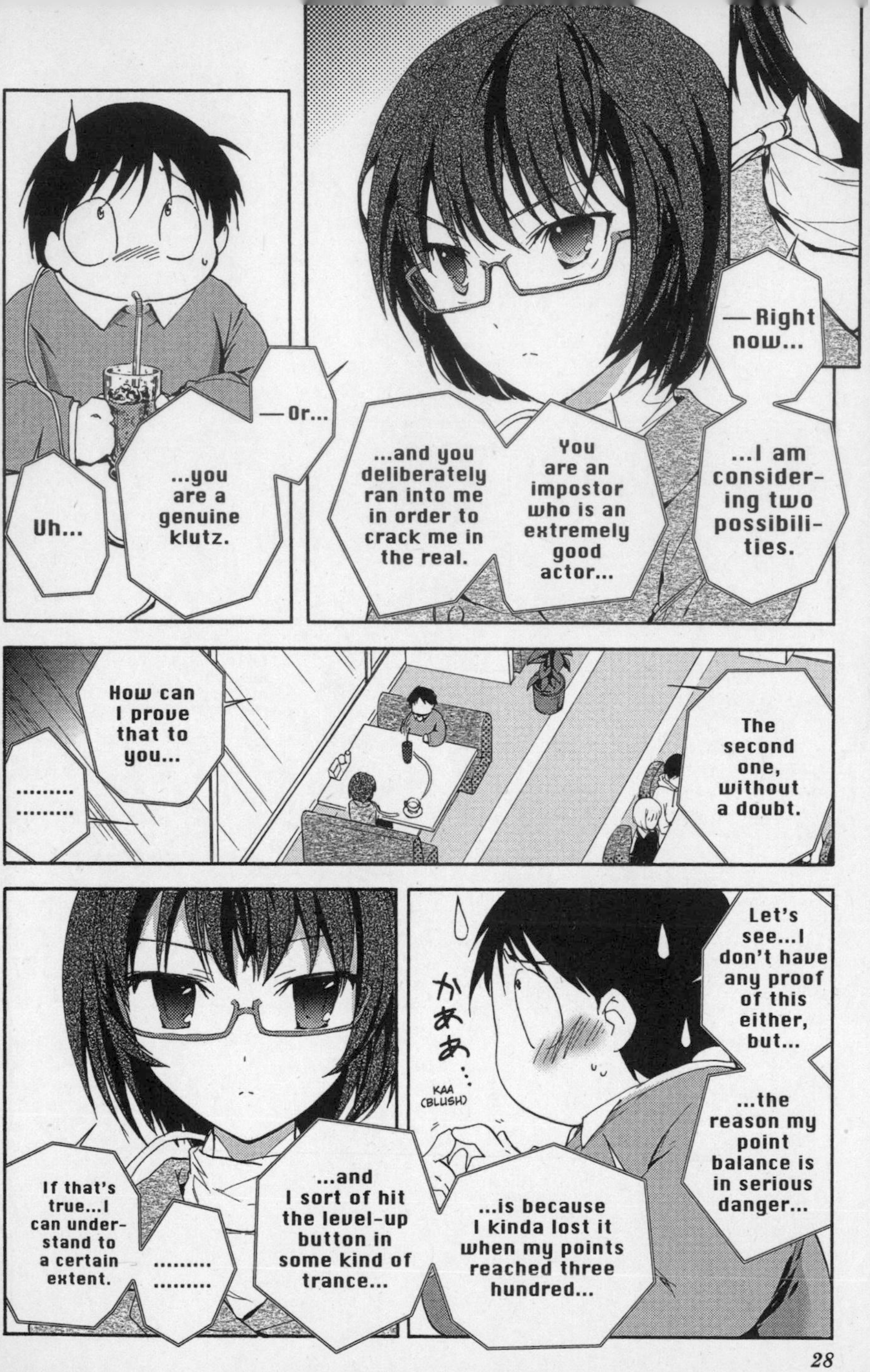
—Right now...
...I am considering two possibilities.
You are an impostor who is an extremely good actor...
...and you deliberately ran into me in order to crack me in the real.
—Or...
...you are a genuine klutz.
Uh...
The second one, without a doubt.
How can I prove that to you...
....
Let's see...I don't have any proof of this either, but...
...the reason my point balance is in serious danger...
...is because I kinda lost it when my points reached three hundred...
かあぁ…
KAA (BLUSH)
...and I sort of hit the level-up button in some kind of trance...
If that's true...I can understand to a certain extent.
....

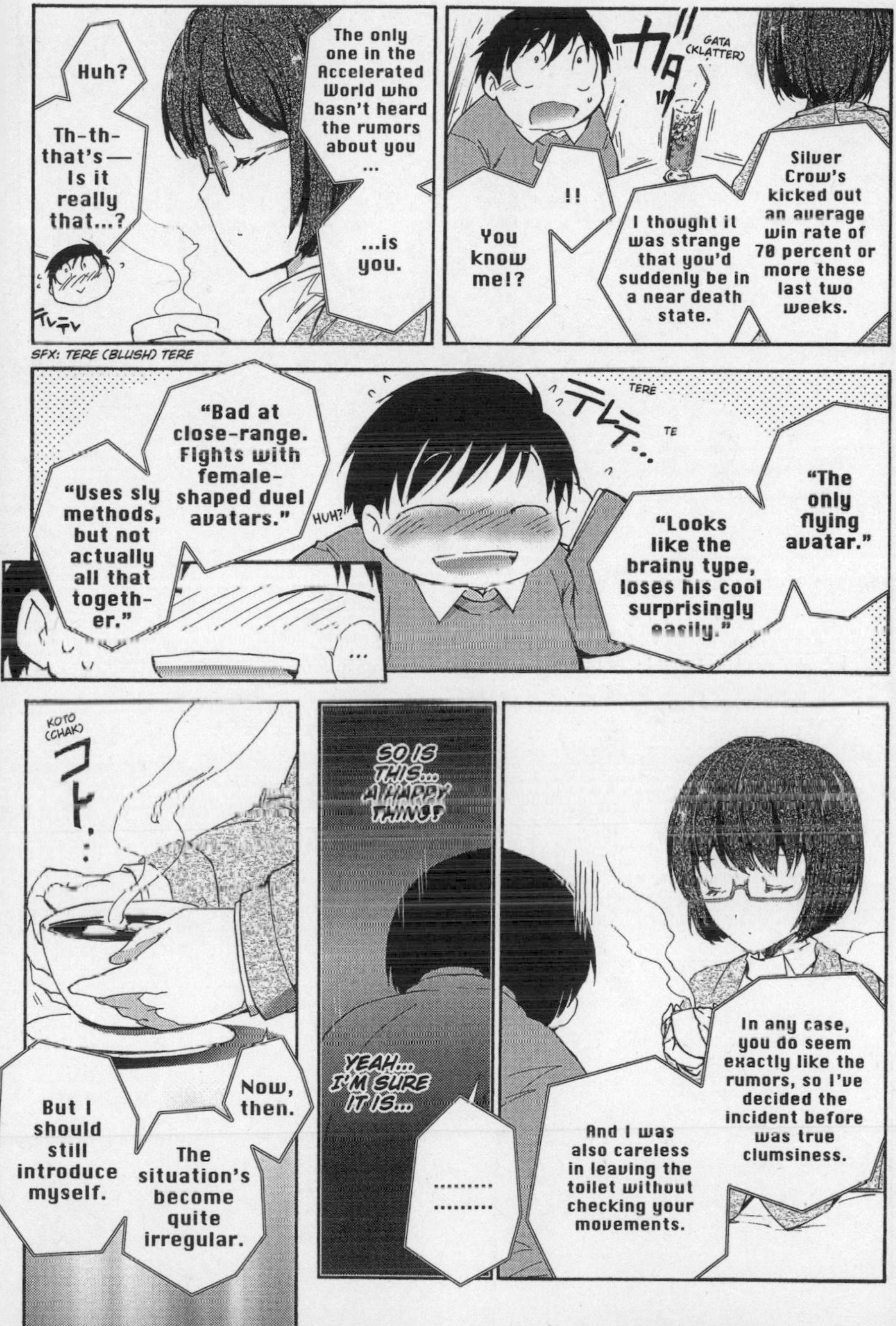
GATA (KLATTER)
Silver Crow's kicked out an average win rate of 70 percent or more these last two weeks.
I thought it was strange that you'd suddenly be in a near death state.
!!
You know me!?
The only one in the Accelerated World who hasn't heard the rumors about you ...
...is you.
Huh?
Th-th-that's— Is it really that...?
SFX: TERE (BLUSH) TERE
TERE
TE
"The only flying avatar."
"Looks like the brainy type, loses his cool surprisingly easily."
HUH?
"Bad at close-range. Fights with female-shaped duel avatars."
"Uses sly methods, but not actually all that togeth-er."
...
In any case, you do seem exactly like the rumors, so I've decided the incident before was true clumsiness.
And I was also careless in leaving the toilet without checking your movements.
SO IS THIS... A HAPPY THING?
YEAH... I'M SURE IT IS...
....
....
KOTO (CHAK)
Now, then.
The situation's become quite irregular.
But I should still introduce myself.

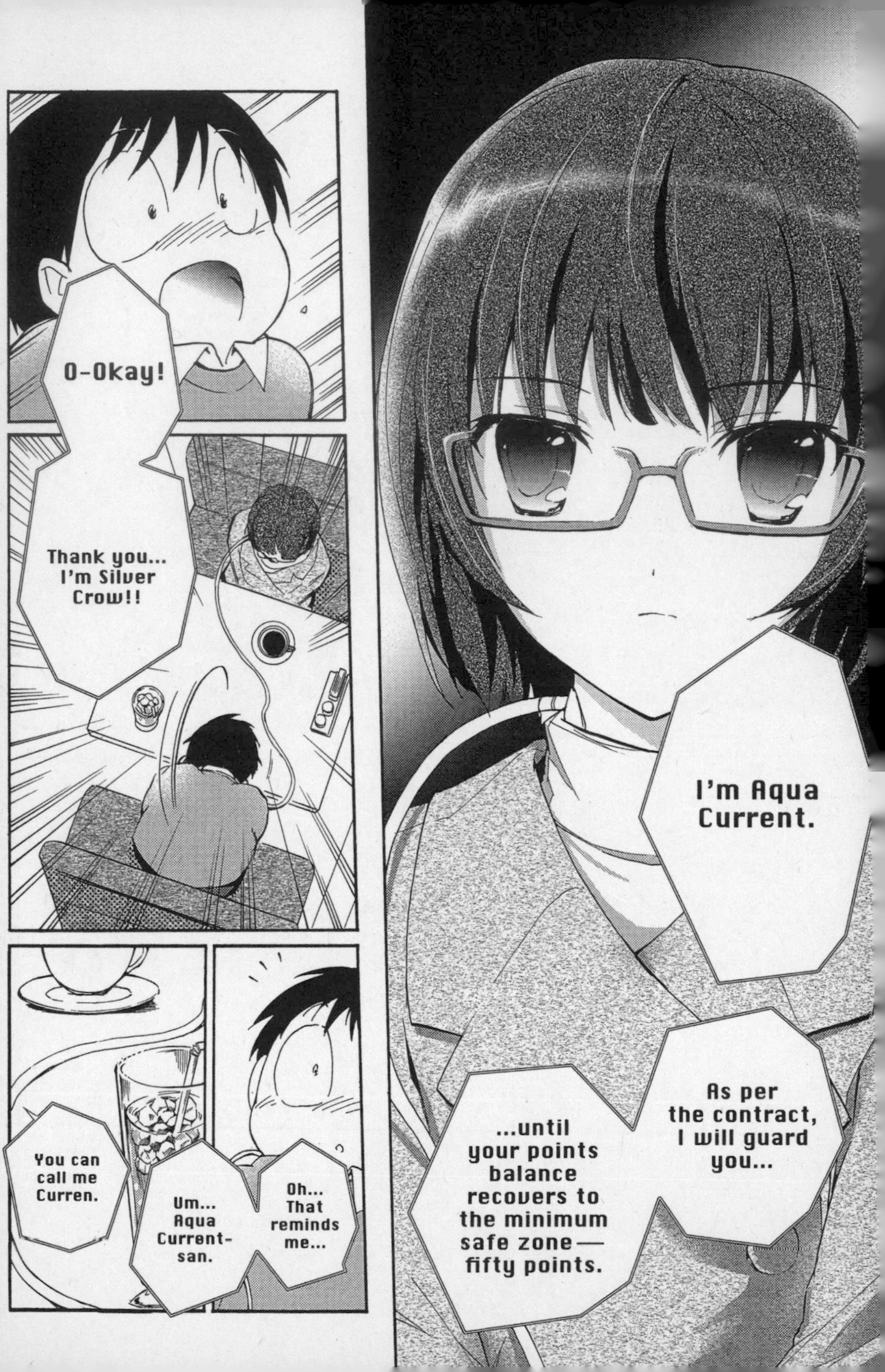
I'm Aqua Current.
As per the contract, I will guard you...
...until your points balance recovers to the minimum safe zone—fifty points.
O-Okay!
Thank you... I'm Silver Crow!!
Oh... That reminds me...
Um... Aqua Current-san.
You can call me Curren.

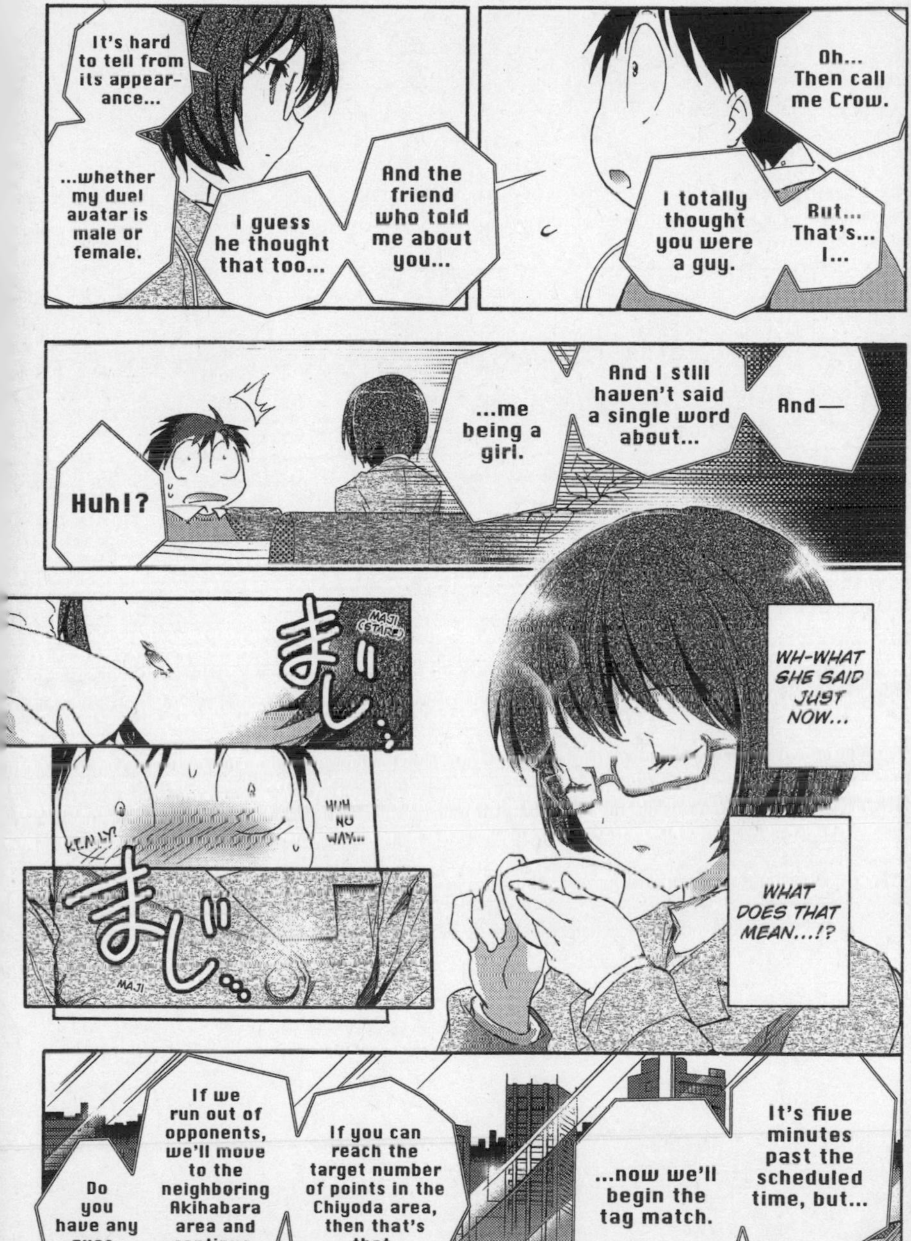
Oh... Then call me Crow.
I totally thought you were a guy.
But... That's... I...
It's hard to tell from its appearance...
...whether my duel avatar is male or female.
And the friend who told me about you...
I guess he thought that too...
And—
And I still haven't said a single word about...
...me being a girl.
Huh!?
WH-WHAT SHE SAID JUST NOW...
WHAT DOES THAT MEAN...!?
まじ…
MAJI (STARE)
HUH NO WAY...
まじ…
MAJI
It's five minutes past the scheduled time, but...
...now we'll begin the tag match.
If you can reach the target number of points in the Chiyoda area, then that's that.
If we run out of opponents, we'll move to the neighboring Akihabara area and continue.
Do you have any questions?

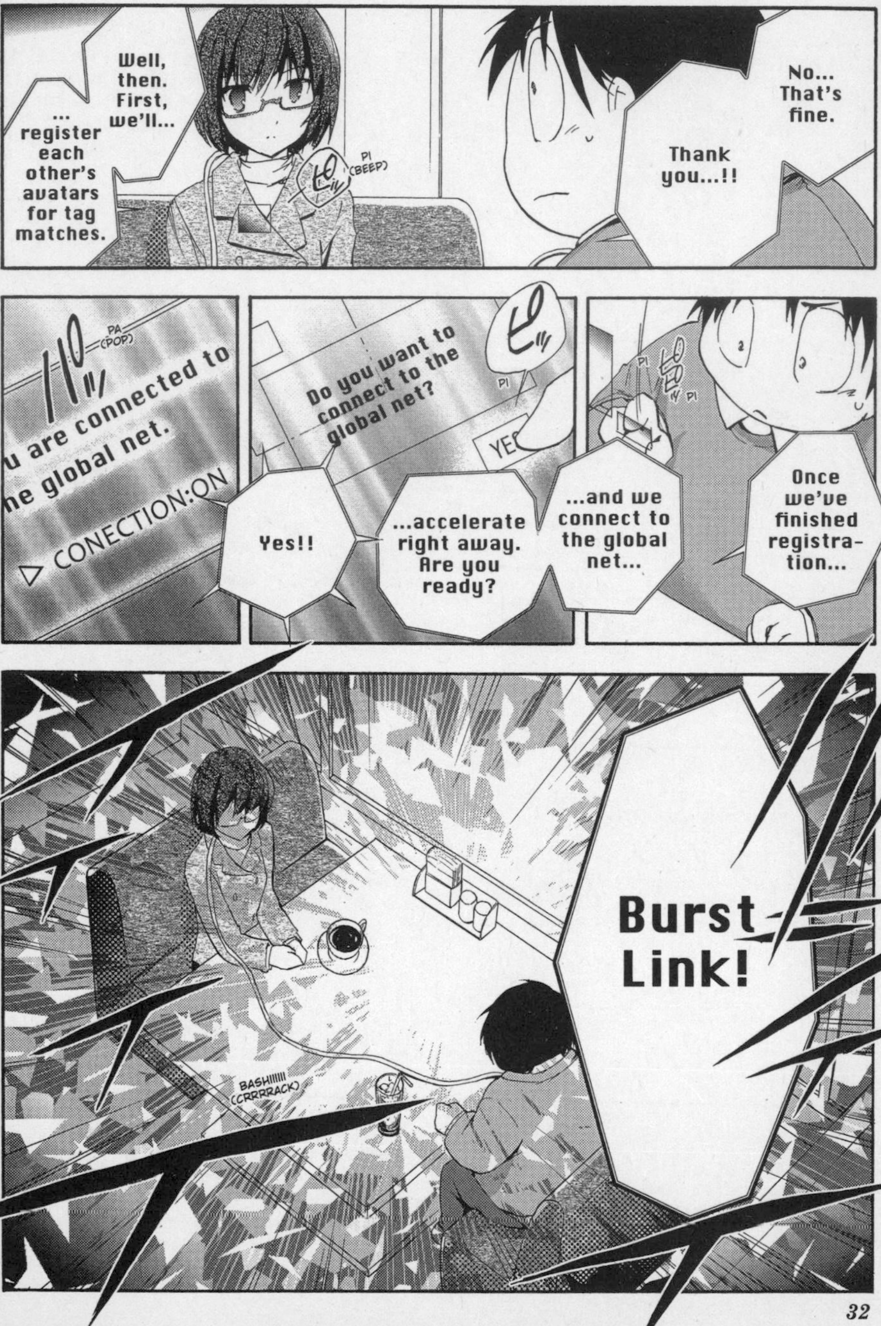
No... That's fine.
Thank you...!!
Well, then. First, we'll...
... register each other's avatars for tag matches.
PI (BEEP)
Once we've finished registra-tion...
PI PI
...and we connect to the global net...
...accelerate right away. Are you ready?
PI
Do you want to connect to the global net?
Yes!!
PA (POP)
u are connected to
he global net.
▽ CONECTION:ON
Burst Link!
BASHIIIIII (CRRRRACK)

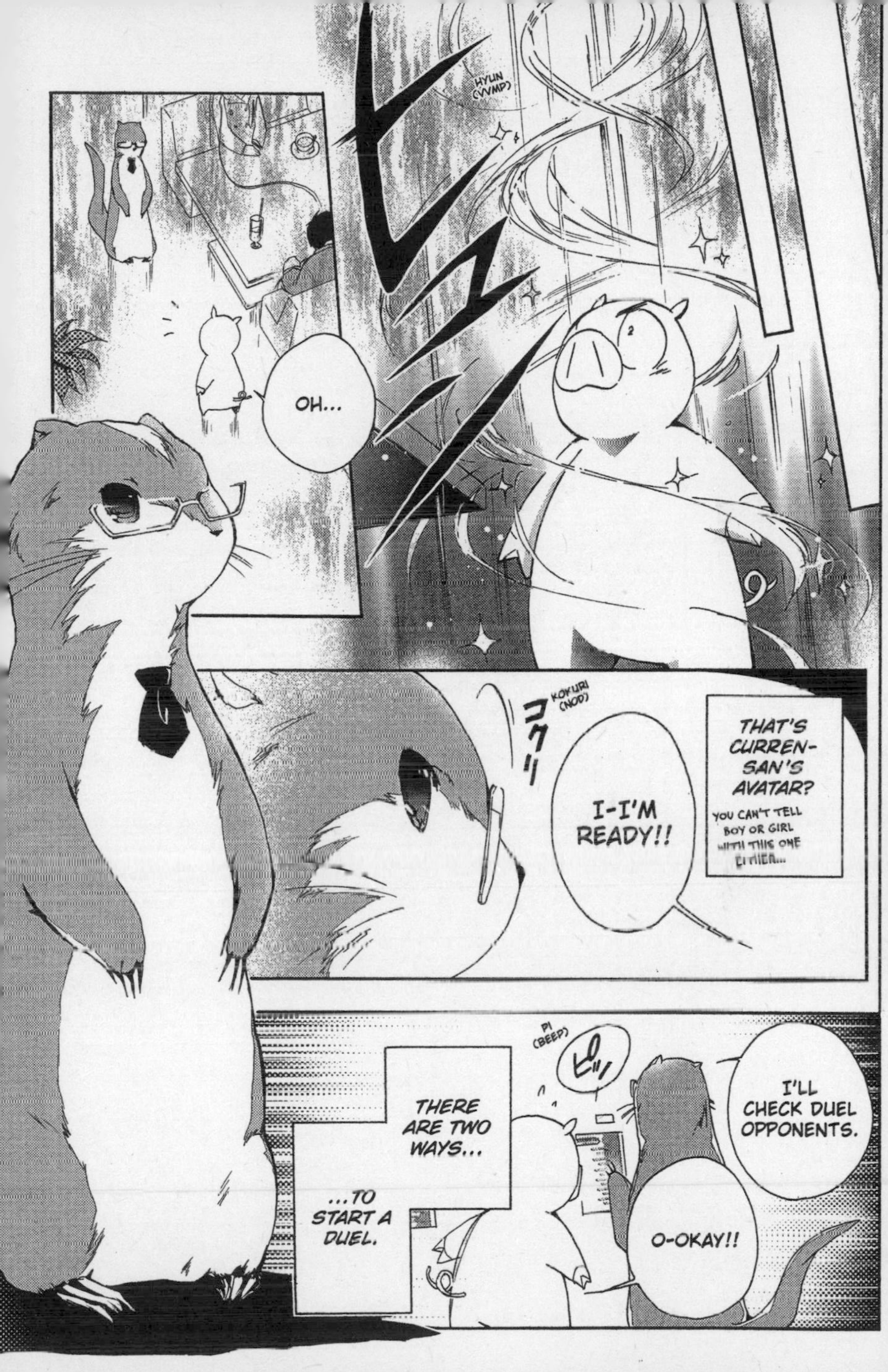
HYUN (VVMP)
OH...
THAT'S CURREN-SAN'S AVATAR?
YOU CAN'T TELL BOY OR GIRL WITH THIS ONE EITHER...
KOKURI (NOD)
I-I'M READY!!
I'LL CHECK DUEL OPPONENTS.
PI (BEEP)
O-OKAY!!
THERE ARE TWO WAYS...
...TO START A DUEL.

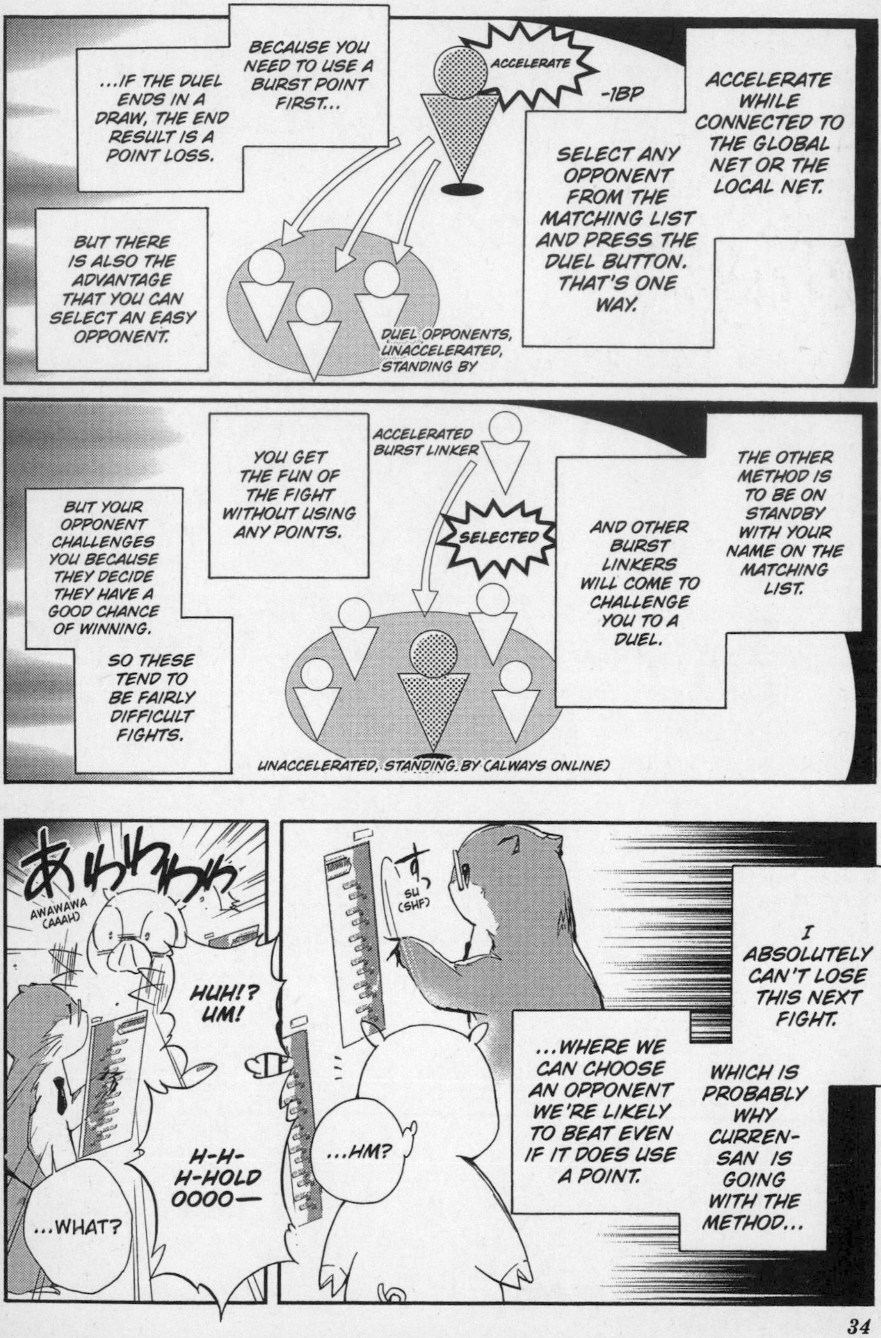
ACCELERATE WHILE CONNECTED TO THE GLOBAL NET OR THE LOCAL NET.
SELECT ANY OPPONENT FROM THE MATCHING LIST AND PRESS THE DUEL BUTTON. THAT'S ONE WAY.
-1BP
ACCELERATE
BECAUSE YOU NEED TO USE A BURST POINT FIRST...
...IF THE DUEL ENDS IN A DRAW, THE END RESULT IS A POINT LOSS.
DUEL OPPONENTS, UNACCELERATED, STANDING BY
BUT THERE IS ALSO THE ADVANTAGE THAT YOU CAN SELECT AN EASY OPPONENT.
THE OTHER METHOD IS TO BE ON STANDBY WITH YOUR NAME ON THE MATCHING LIST.
AND OTHER BURST LINKERS WILL COME TO CHALLENGE YOU TO A DUEL.
ACCELERATED BURST LINKER
SELECTED
YOU GET THE FUN OF THE FIGHT WITHOUT USING ANY POINTS.
BUT YOUR OPPONENT CHALLENGES YOU BECAUSE THEY DECIDE THEY HAVE A GOOD CHANCE OF WINNING.
SO THESE TEND TO BE FAIRLY DIFFICULT FIGHTS.
UNACCELERATED, STANDING BY (ALWAYS ONLINE)
I ABSOLUTELY CAN'T LOSE THIS NEXT FIGHT.
WHICH IS PROBABLY WHY CURREN-SAN IS GOING WITH THE METHOD...
...WHERE WE CAN CHOOSE AN OPPONENT WE'RE LIKELY TO BEAT EVEN IF IT DOES USE A POINT.
すっ
SU (SHF)
...HM?
あわわわ
AWAWAWA (AAAH)
HUH!? UM!
H-H-H-HOLD OOOO—
...WHAT?

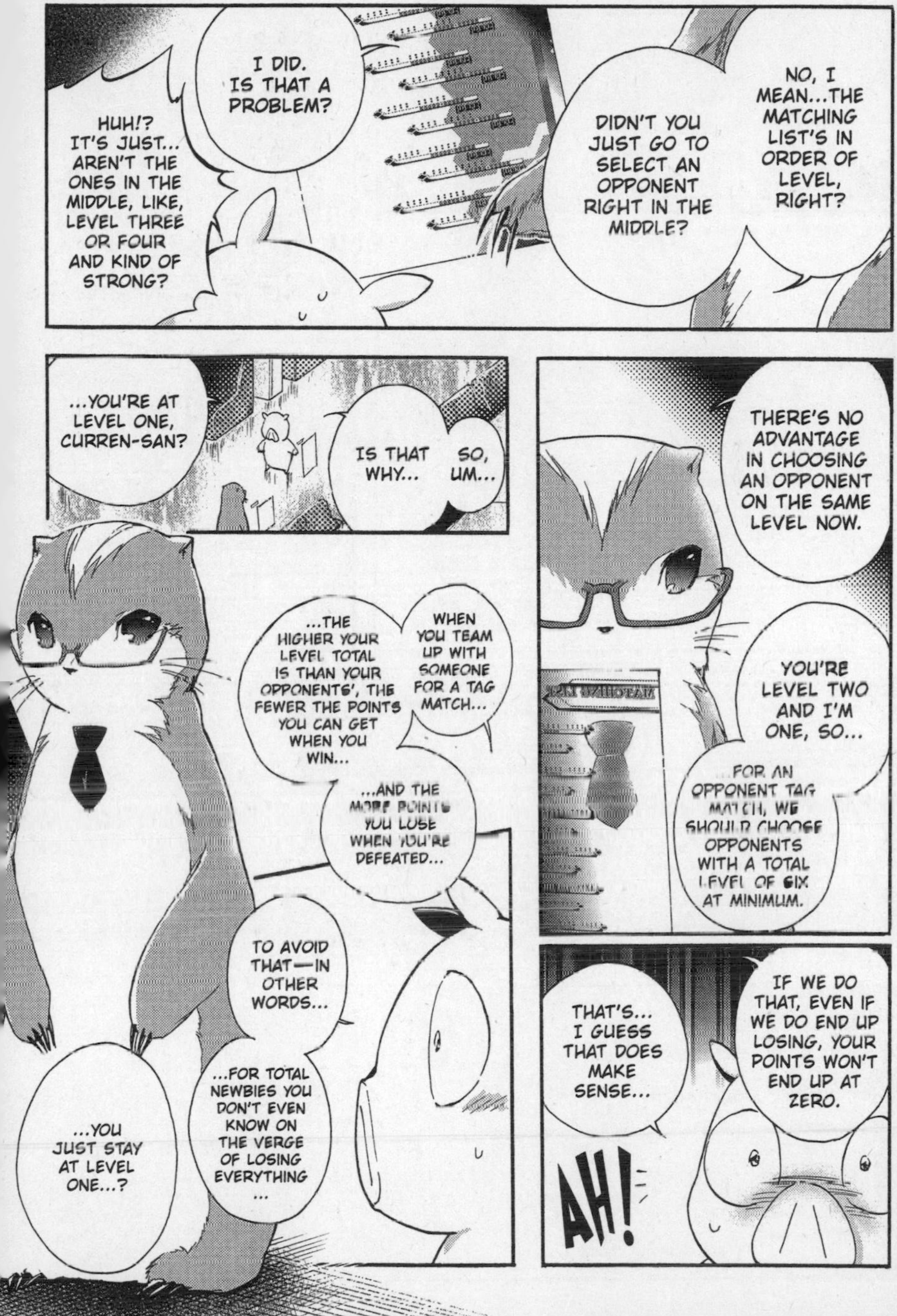
NO, I MEAN...THE MATCHING LIST'S IN ORDER OF LEVEL, RIGHT?
DIDN'T YOU JUST GO TO SELECT AN OPPONENT RIGHT IN THE MIDDLE?
I DID. IS THAT A PROBLEM?
HUH!? IT'S JUST... AREN'T THE ONES IN THE MIDDLE, LIKE, LEVEL THREE OR FOUR AND KIND OF STRONG?
THERE'S NO ADVANTAGE IN CHOOSING AN OPPONENT ON THE SAME LEVEL NOW.
YOU'RE LEVEL TWO AND I'M ONE, SO...
...FOR AN OPPONENT TAG MATCH, WE SHOULD CHOOSE OPPONENTS WITH A TOTAL LEVEL OF SIX AT MINIMUM.
SO, UM...
IS THAT WHY...
...YOU'RE AT LEVEL ONE, CURREN-SAN?
WHEN YOU TEAM UP WITH SOMEONE FOR A TAG MATCH...
...THE HIGHER YOUR LEVEL TOTAL IS THAN YOUR OPPONENTS', THE FEWER THE POINTS YOU CAN GET WHEN YOU WIN...
...AND THE MORE POINTS YOU LOSE WHEN YOU'RE DEFEATED...
TO AVOID THAT—IN OTHER WORDS...
...FOR TOTAL NEWBIES YOU DON'T EVEN KNOW ON THE VERGE OF LOSING EVERYTHING...
...YOU JUST STAY AT LEVEL ONE...?
IF WE DO THAT, EVEN IF WE DO END UP LOSING, YOUR POINTS WON'T END UP AT ZERO.
THAT'S... I GUESS THAT DOES MAKE SENSE...
AH!

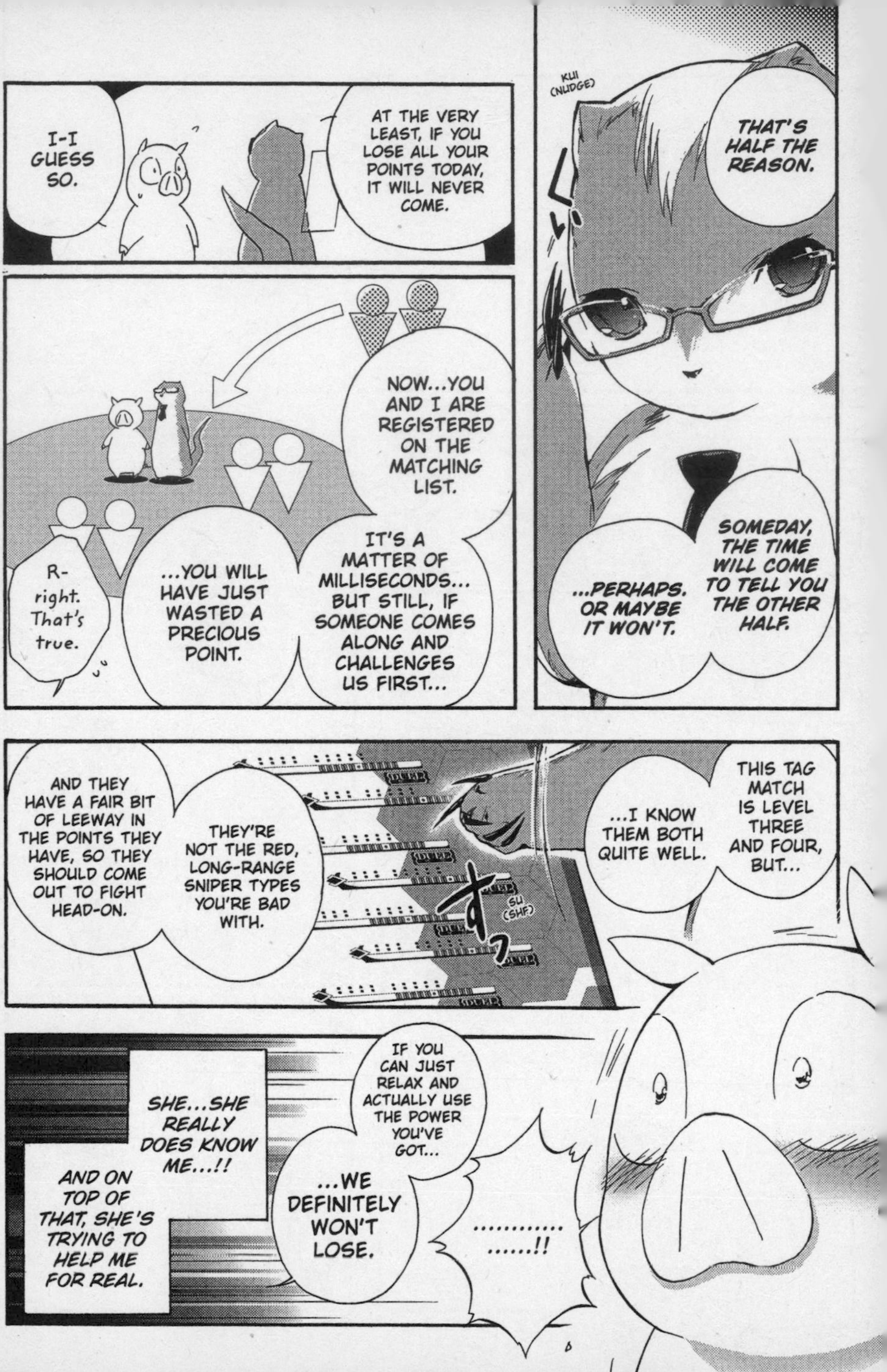
KUI (NUDGE)
THAT'S HALF THE REASON.
SOMEDAY, THE TIME WILL COME TO TELL YOU THE OTHER HALF.
...PERHAPS. OR MAYBE IT WON'T.
AT THE VERY LEAST, IF YOU LOSE ALL YOUR POINTS TODAY, IT WILL NEVER COME.
I-I GUESS SO.
NOW...YOU AND I ARE REGISTERED ON THE MATCHING LIST.
IT'S A MATTER OF MILLISECONDS... BUT STILL, IF SOMEONE COMES ALONG AND CHALLENGES US FIRST...
...YOU WILL HAVE JUST WASTED A PRECIOUS POINT.
R-right. That's true.
THIS TAG MATCH IS LEVEL THREE AND FOUR, BUT...
...I KNOW THEM BOTH QUITE WELL.
SU (SHF)
THEY'RE NOT THE RED, LONG-RANGE SNIPER TYPES YOU'RE BAD WITH.
AND THEY HAVE A FAIR BIT OF LEEWAY IN THE POINTS THEY HAVE, SO THEY SHOULD COME OUT TO FIGHT HEAD-ON.
IF YOU CAN JUST RELAX AND ACTUALLY USE THE POWER YOU'VE GOT...
...WE DEFINITELY WON'T LOSE.
....!!
SHE...SHE REALLY DOES KNOW ME...!!
AND ON TOP OF THAT, SHE'S TRYING TO HELP ME FOR REAL.

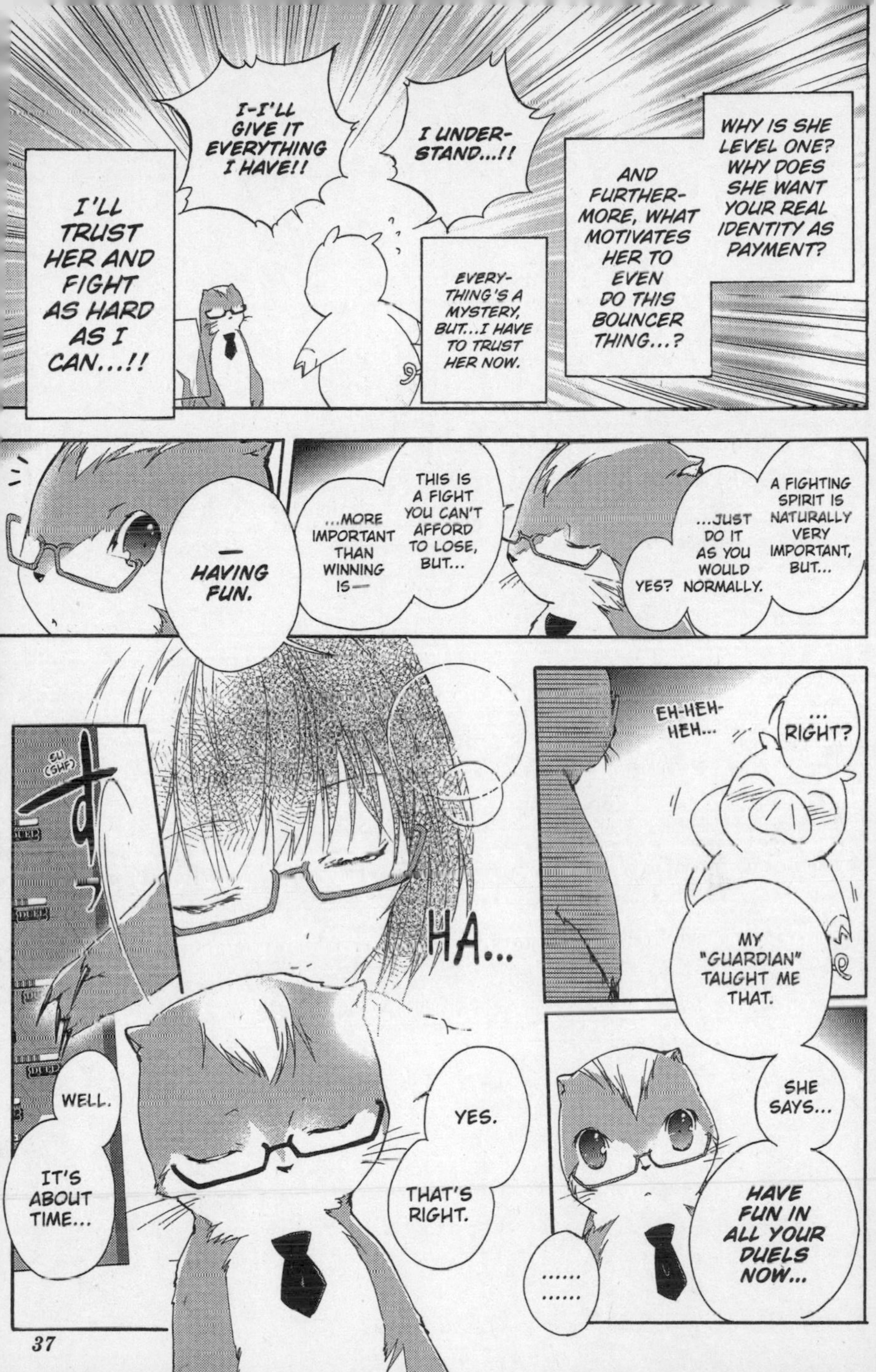
WHY IS SHE LEVEL ONE? WHY DOES SHE WANT YOUR REAL IDENTITY AS PAYMENT?
AND FURTHERMORE, WHAT MOTIVATES HER TO EVEN DO THIS BOUNCER THING...?
EVERYTHING'S A MYSTERY, BUT...I HAVE TO TRUST HER NOW.
I UNDERSTAND...!!
I-I'LL GIVE IT EVERYTHING I HAVE!!
I'LL TRUST HER AND FIGHT AS HARD AS I CAN...!!
A FIGHTING SPIRIT IS NATURALLY VERY IMPORTANT, BUT...
...JUST DO IT AS YOU WOULD NORMALLY.
YES?
THIS IS A FIGHT YOU CAN'T AFFORD TO LOSE, BUT...
...MORE IMPORTANT THAN WINNING IS—
—HAVING FUN.
EH-HEH-HEH...
...RIGHT?
MY "GUARDIAN" TAUGHT ME THAT.
SHE SAYS...
HAVE FUN IN ALL YOUR DUELS NOW...
....
SU (SHF)
HA...
YES.
THAT'S RIGHT.
WELL.
IT'S ABOUT TIME...

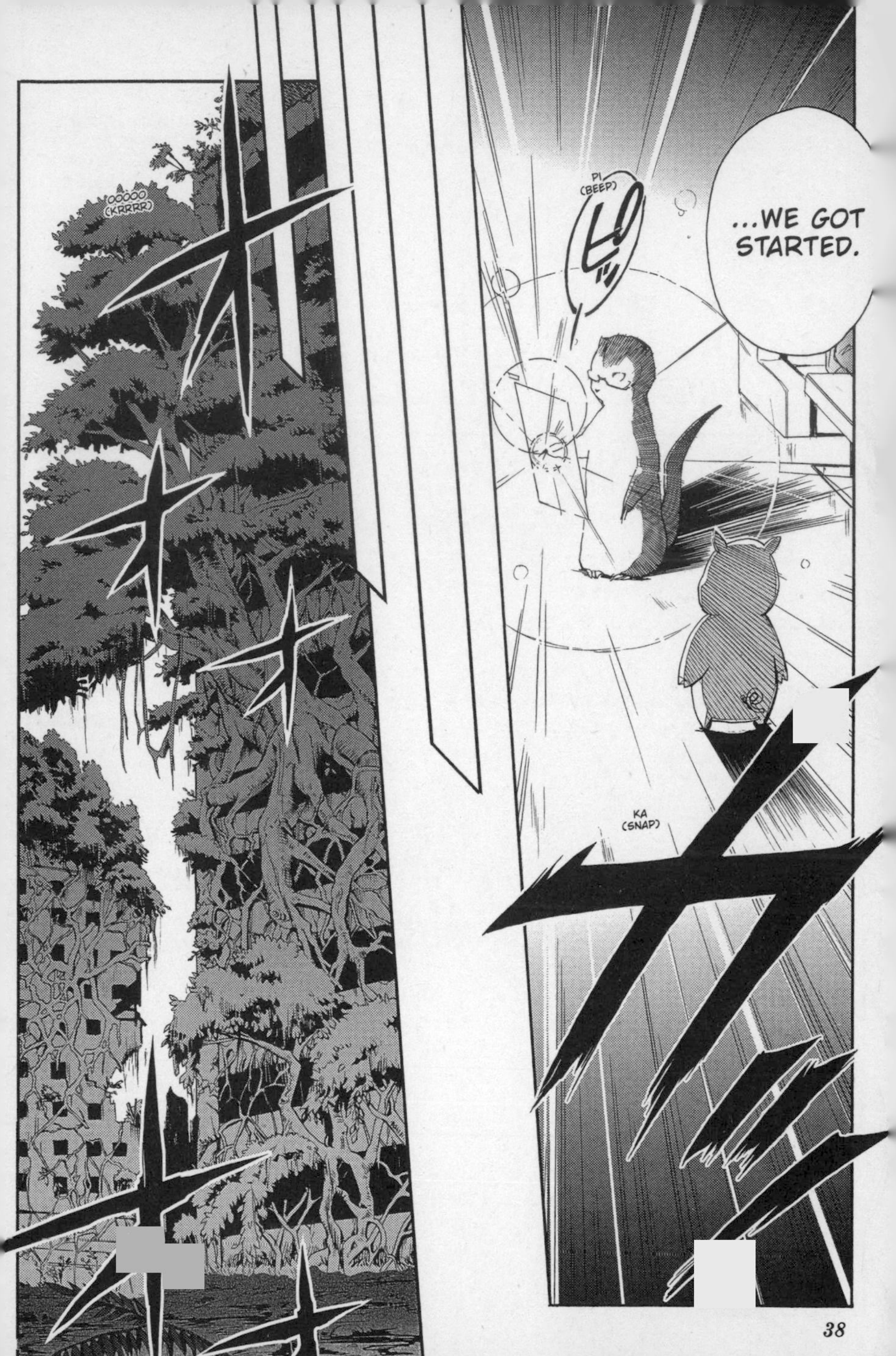
...WE GOT STARTED.
PI (BEEP)
KA (SNAP)
OOOOO (KRRRR)

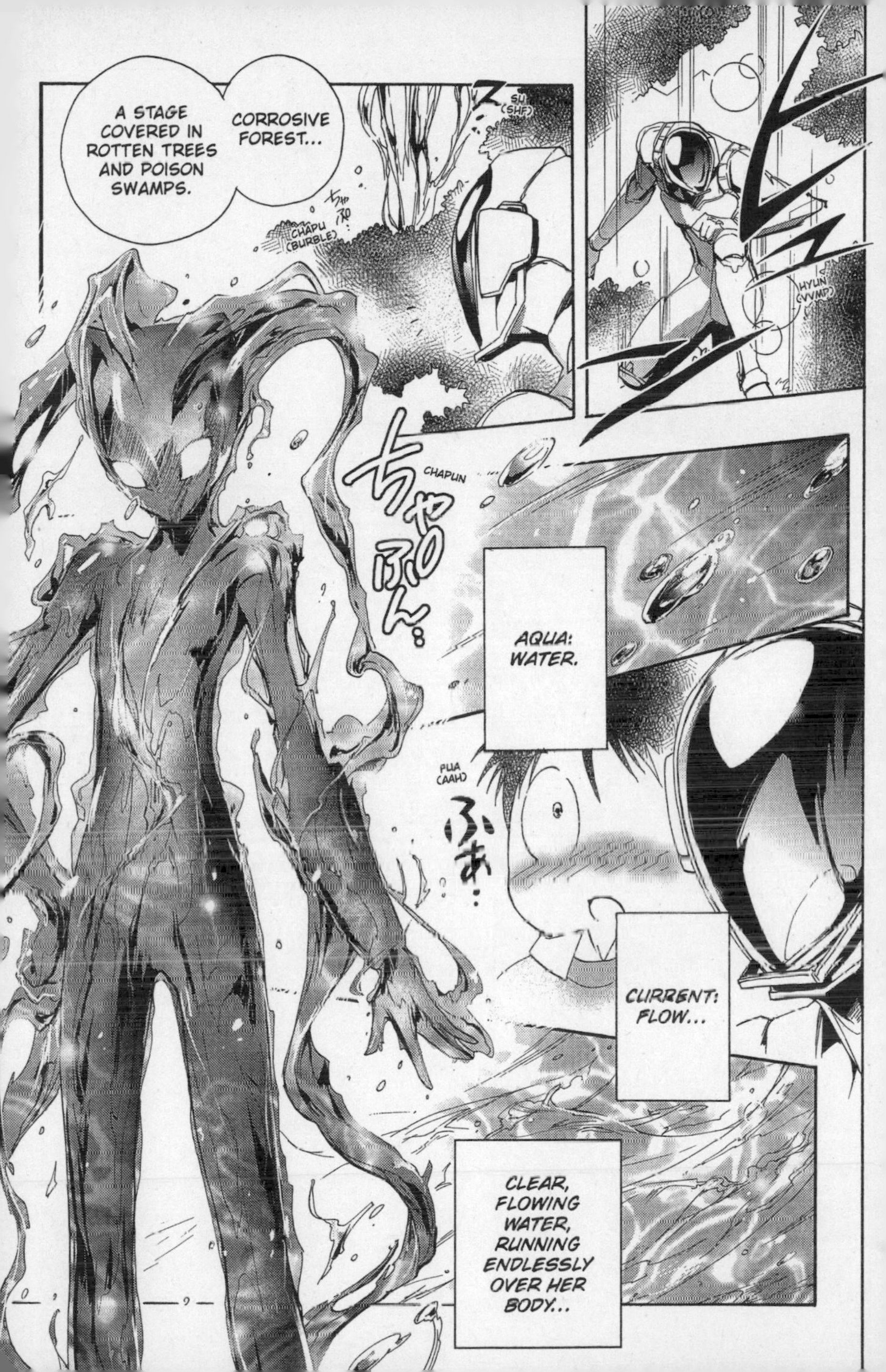

HYUN (VVMP)
SH (SHF)
CORROSIVE FOREST...
A STAGE COVERED IN ROTTEN TREES AND POISON SWAMPS.
CHAPU (BURBLE)
ちゃぷん
CHAPUN
AQUA: WATER.
ふぁ
PUA (AAH)
CURRENT: FLOW...
CLEAR, FLOWING WATER, RUNNING ENDLESSLY OVER HER BODY...

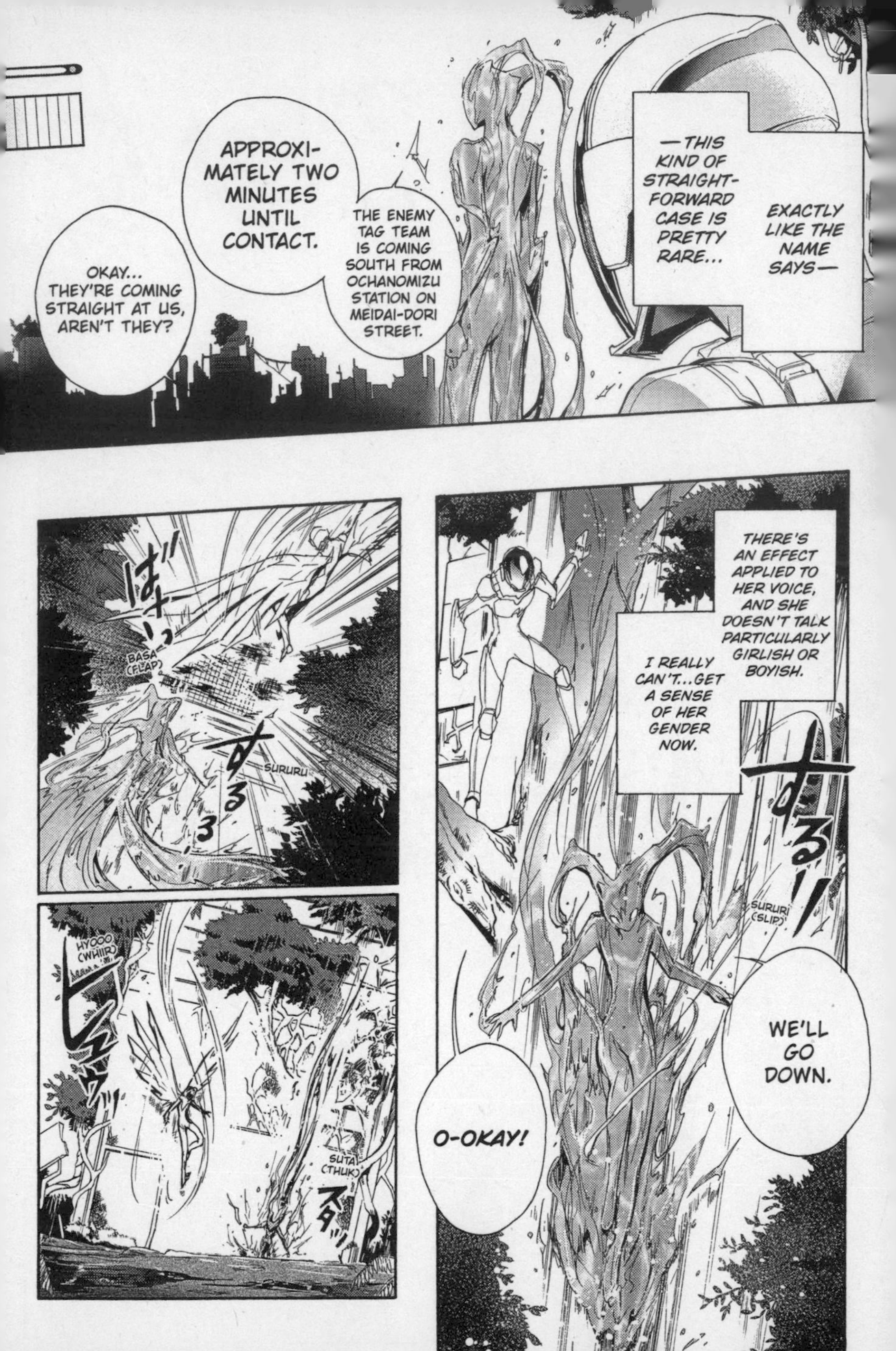
EXACTLY LIKE THE NAME SAYS—
—THIS KIND OF STRAIGHT-FORWARD CASE IS PRETTY RARE...
THE ENEMY TAG TEAM IS COMING SOUTH FROM OCHANOMIZU STATION ON MEIDAI-DORI STREET.
APPROXI-MATELY TWO MINUTES UNTIL CONTACT.
OKAY... THEY'RE COMING STRAIGHT AT US, AREN'T THEY?
THERE'S AN EFFECT APPLIED TO HER VOICE, AND SHE DOESN'T TALK PARTICULARLY GIRLISH OR BOYISH.
I REALLY CAN'T...GET A SENSE OF HER GENDER NOW.
SURURI (SLIP)
WE'LL GO DOWN.
O-OKAY!
BASA (FLAP)
SURURU
HYOOO (WHIIR)
SUTA (THUK)

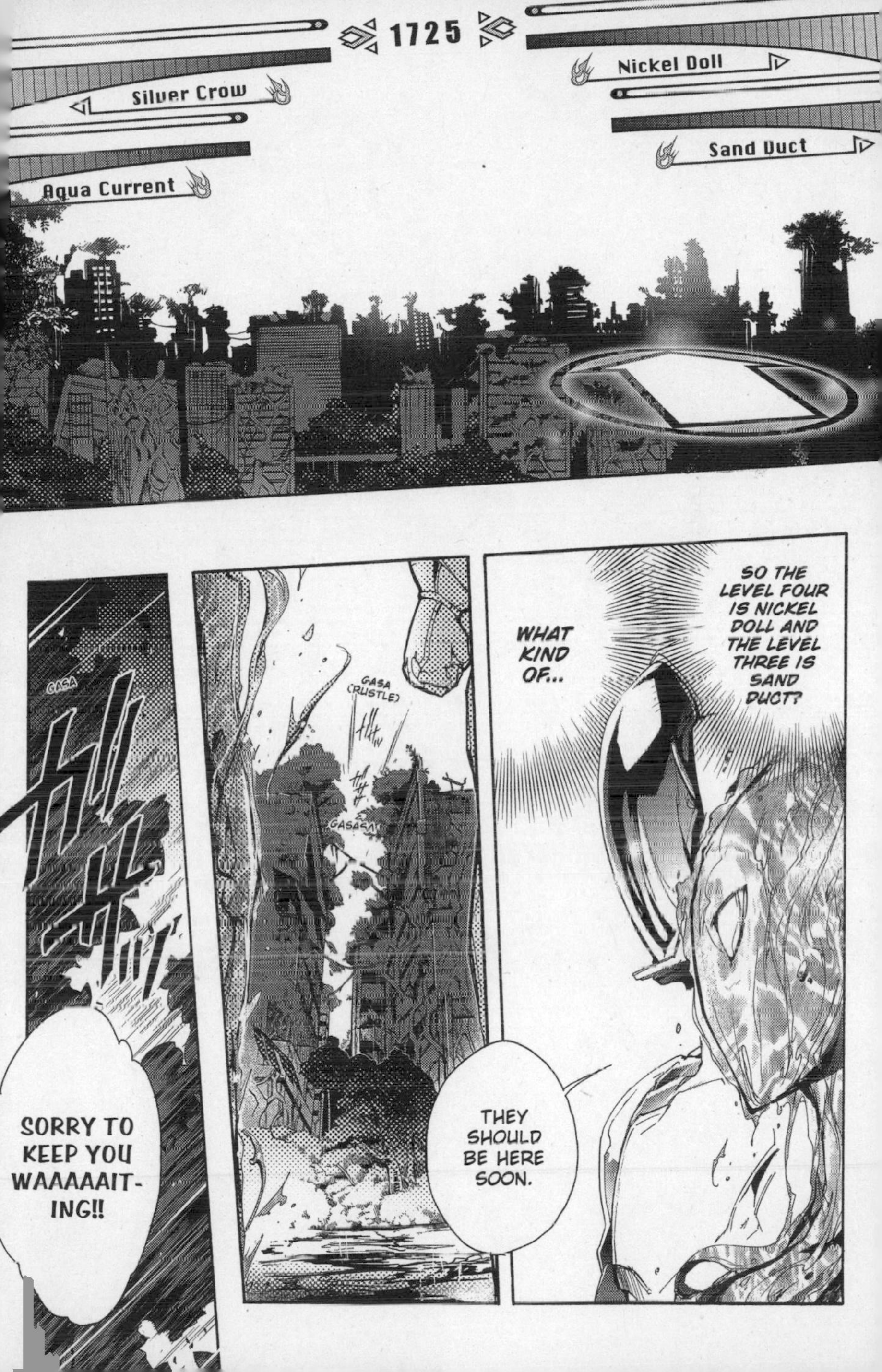
1725
Nickel Doll
Sand Duct
Silver Crow
Aqua Current
SO THE LEVEL FOUR IS NICKEL DOLL AND THE LEVEL THREE IS SAND DUCT?
WHAT KIND OF...
THEY SHOULD BE HERE SOON.
GASA (RUSTLE)
GASASA
GASA
SORRY TO KEEP YOU WAAAAAIT-ING!!

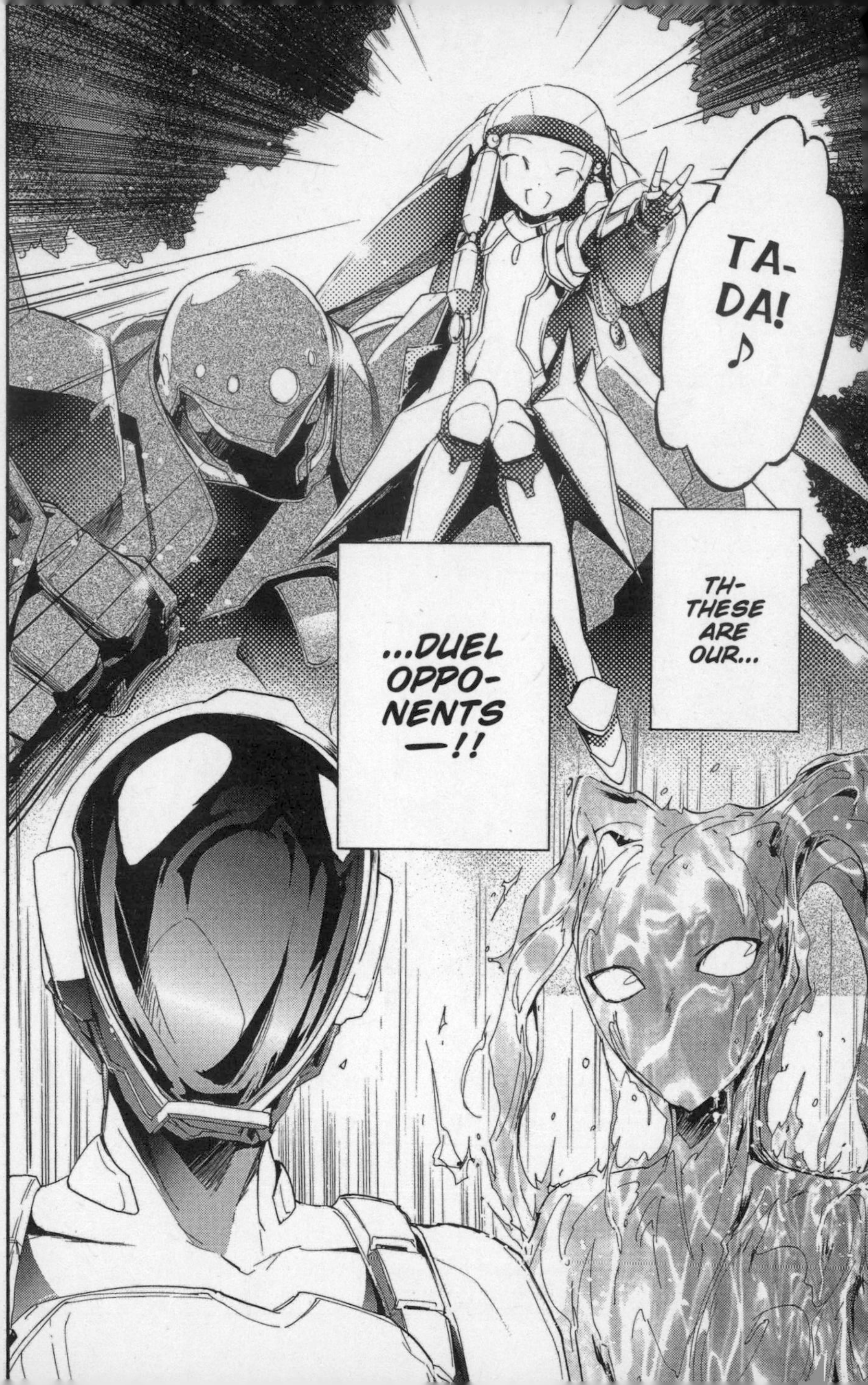
TA-DA! ♪
TH-THESE ARE OUR...
...DUEL OPPONENTS—!!

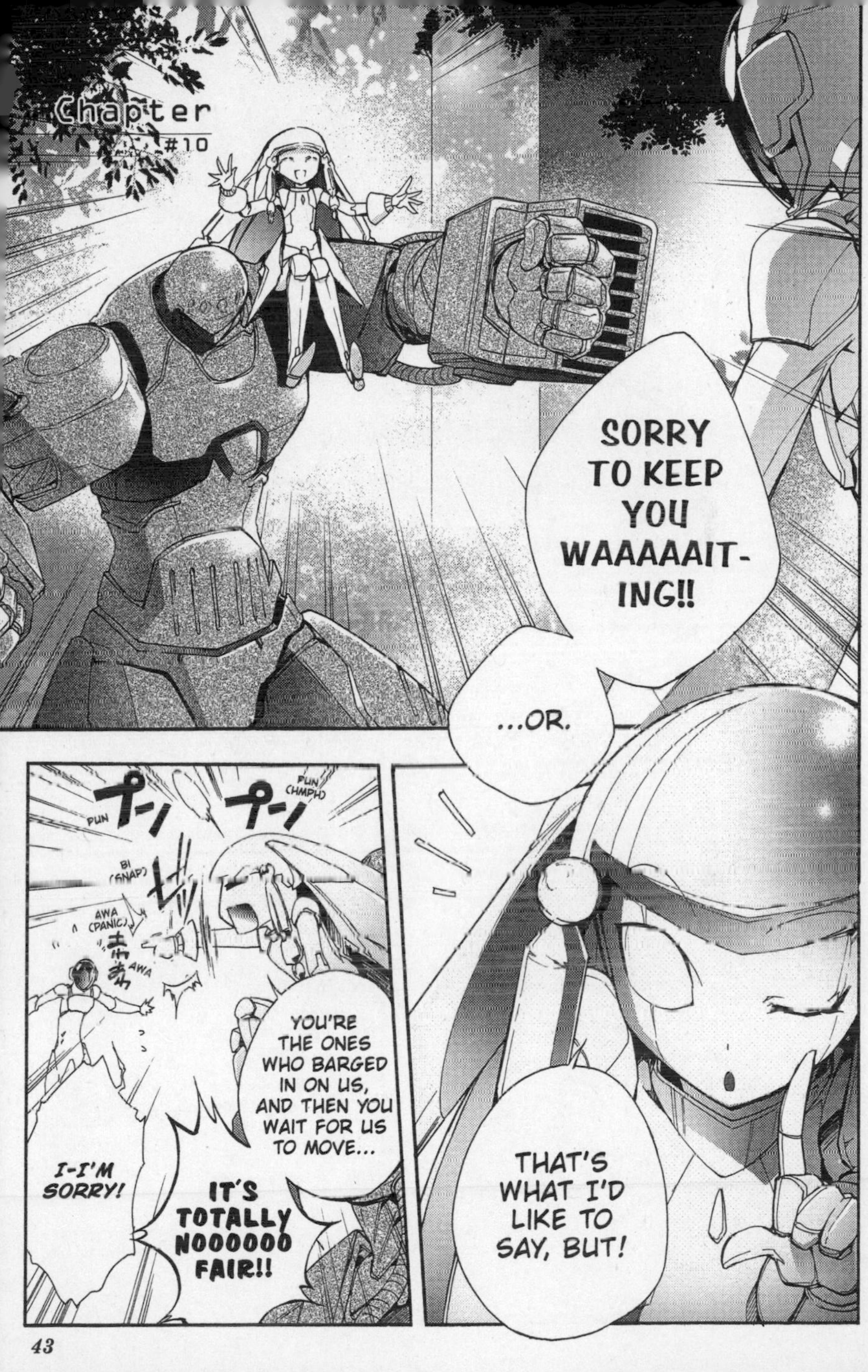
Chapter #10
SORRY TO KEEP YOU WAAAAAIT-ING!!
...OR.
THAT'S WHAT I'D LIKE TO SAY, BUT!
PUN (HMPH)
PUN
BI (SNAP)
AWA (PANIC)
AWA
YOU'RE THE ONES WHO BARGED IN ON US, AND THEN YOU WAIT FOR US TO MOVE...
IT'S TOTALLY NOOOOOO FAIR!!
I-I'M SORRY!

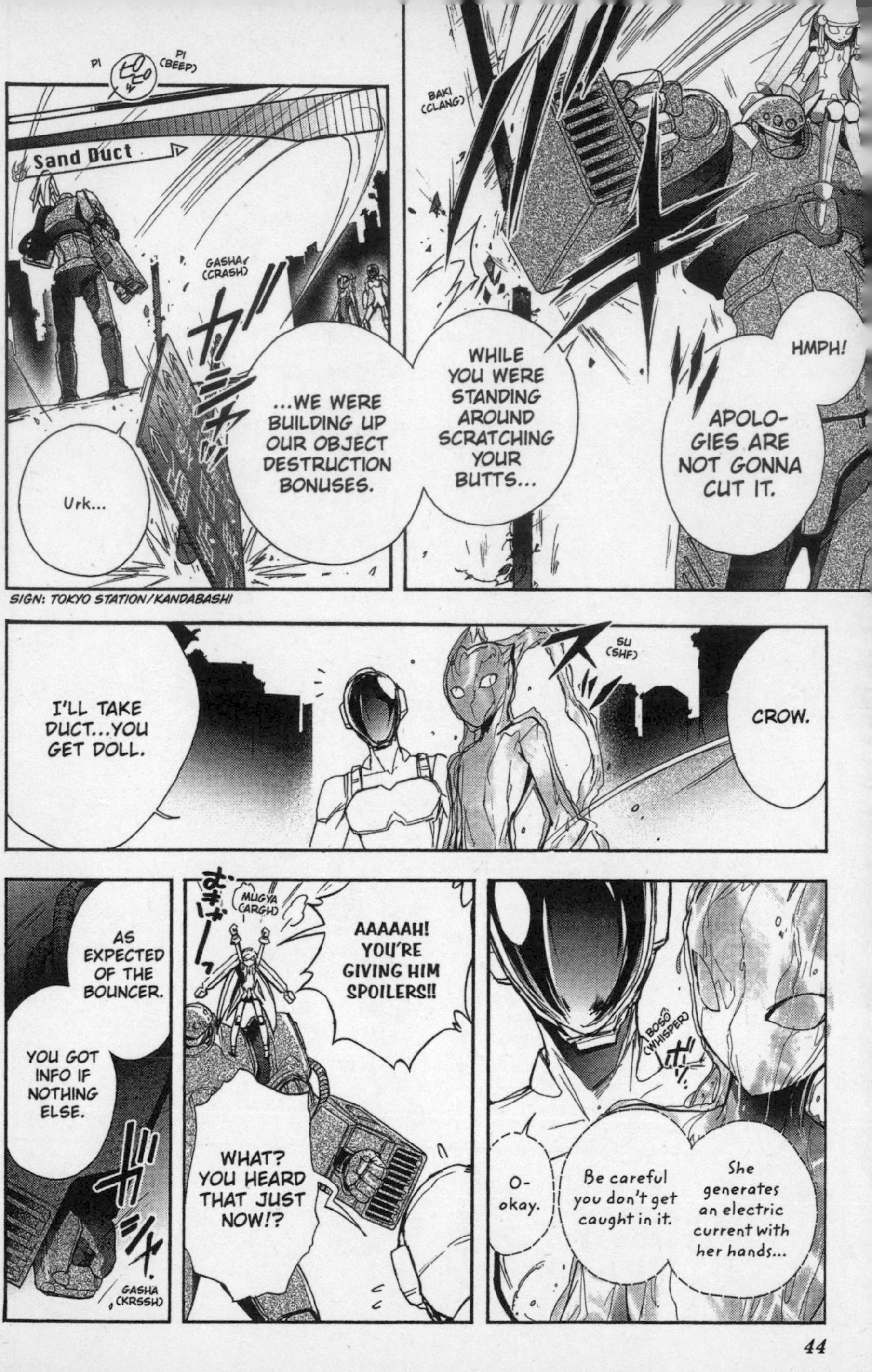
BAKI (CLANG)
HMPH!
APOLOGIES ARE NOT GONNA CUT IT.
WHILE YOU WERE STANDING AROUND SCRATCHING YOUR BUTTS...
...WE WERE BUILDING UP OUR OBJECT DESTRUCTION BONUSES.
PI PI (BEEP)
Sand Duct
GASHA (CRASH)
Urk...
SIGN: TOKYO STATION/KANDABASHI
SU (SHF)
CROW.
I'LL TAKE DUCT...YOU GET DOLL.
BOSÔ (WHISPER)
She generates an electric current with her hands...
Be careful you don't get caught in it.
O-okay.
MUGYA (ARGH)
AAAAAH! YOU'RE GIVING HIM SPOILERS!!
WHAT? YOU HEARD THAT JUST NOW!?
AS EXPECTED OF THE BOUNCER.
YOU GOT INFO IF NOTHING ELSE.
GASHA (KRSSH)

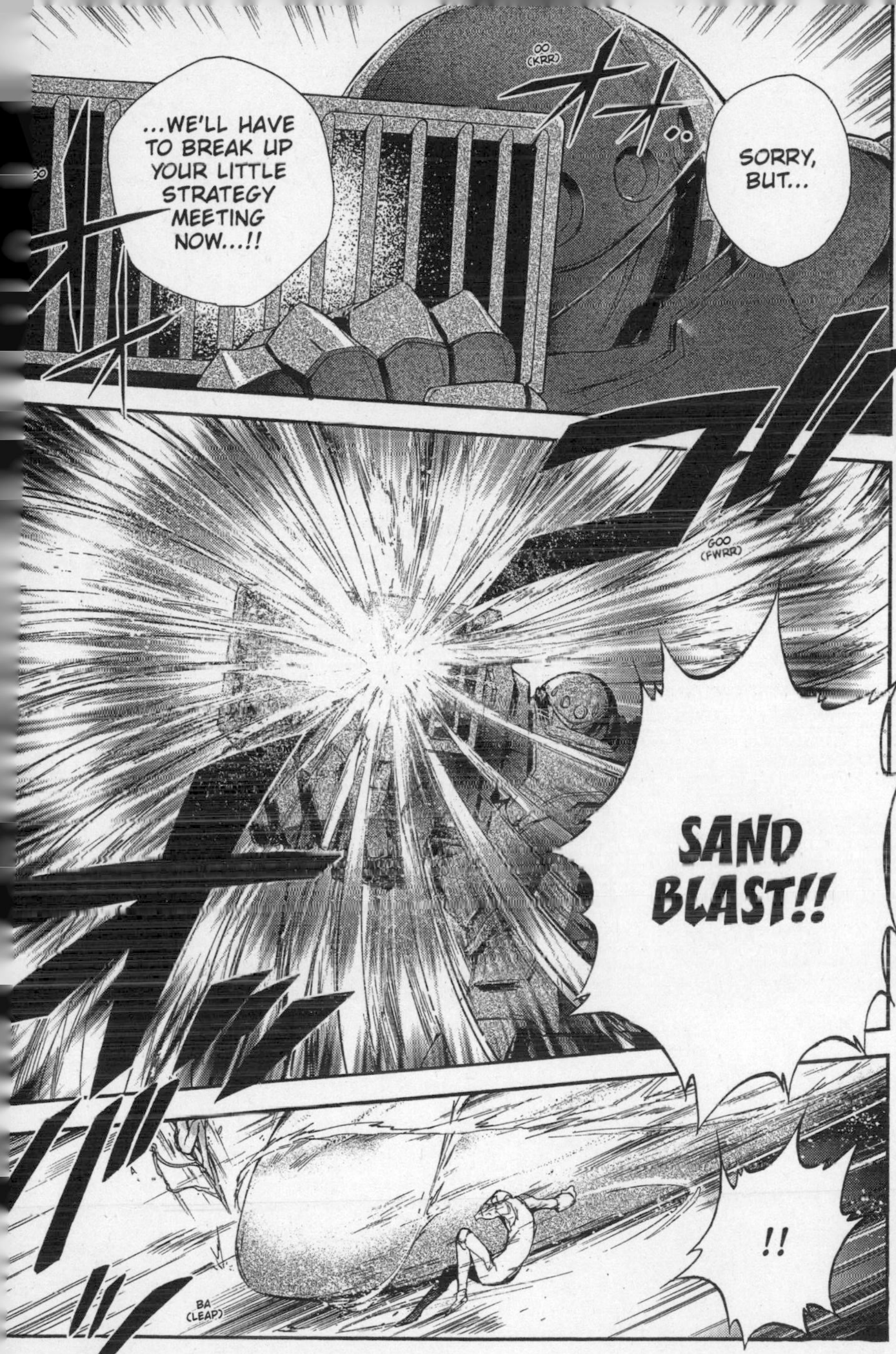
OO (KRR)
SORRY, BUT...
...WE'LL HAVE TO BREAK UP YOUR LITTLE STRATEGY MEETING NOW...!!
GOO (FWRR)
SAND BLAST!!
!!
BA (LEAP)

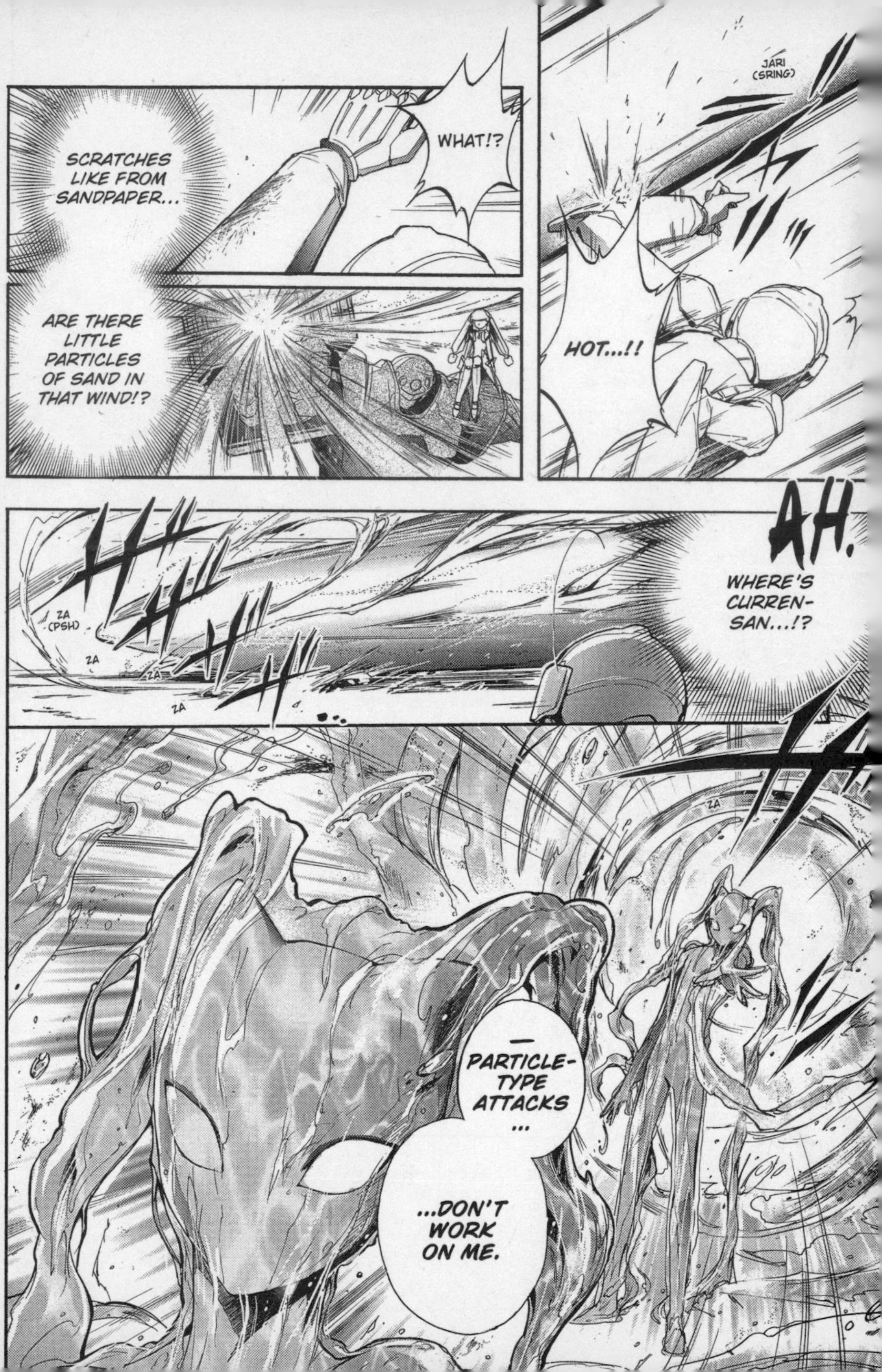
JARI (SRING)
HOT...!!
WHAT!?
SCRATCHES LIKE FROM SANDPAPER...
ARE THERE LITTLE PARTICLES OF SAND IN THAT WIND!?
AH.
WHERE'S CURREN-SAN...!?
ZA (PSH)
ZA
ZA
ZA
ZA
—PARTICLE-TYPE ATTACKS...
...DON'T WORK ON ME.

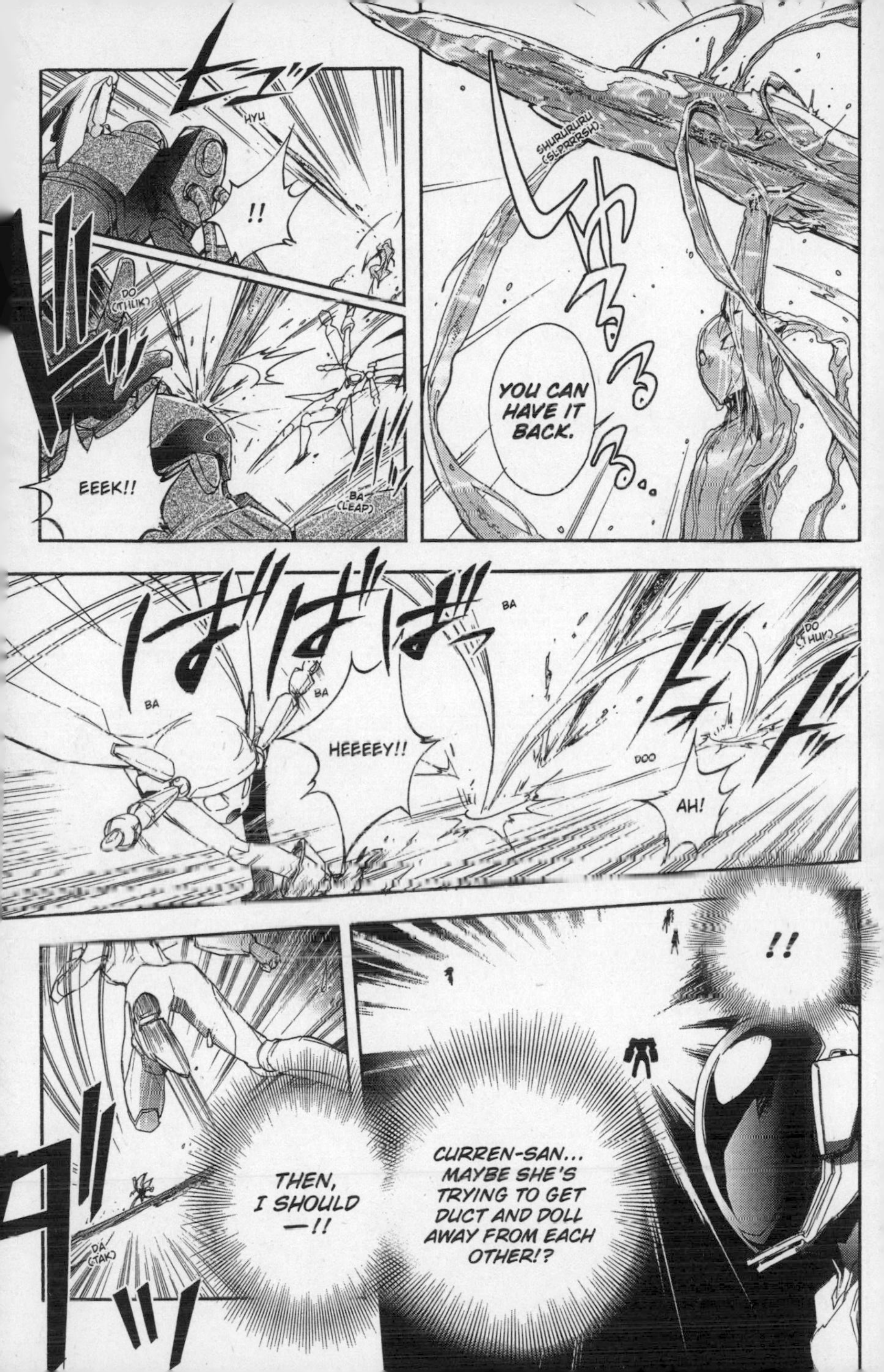
SHURURURU (SLPRRRSH)
YOU CAN HAVE IT BACK.
HYU
!!
DO (THLIK)
EEEK!!
BA (LEAP)
DO (THUK)
DOO
AH!
BA
HEEEEY!!
BA
BA
!!
CURREN-SAN... MAYBE SHE'S TRYING TO GET DUCT AND DOLL AWAY FROM EACH OTHER!?
THEN, I SHOULD —!!
DA (TAK)

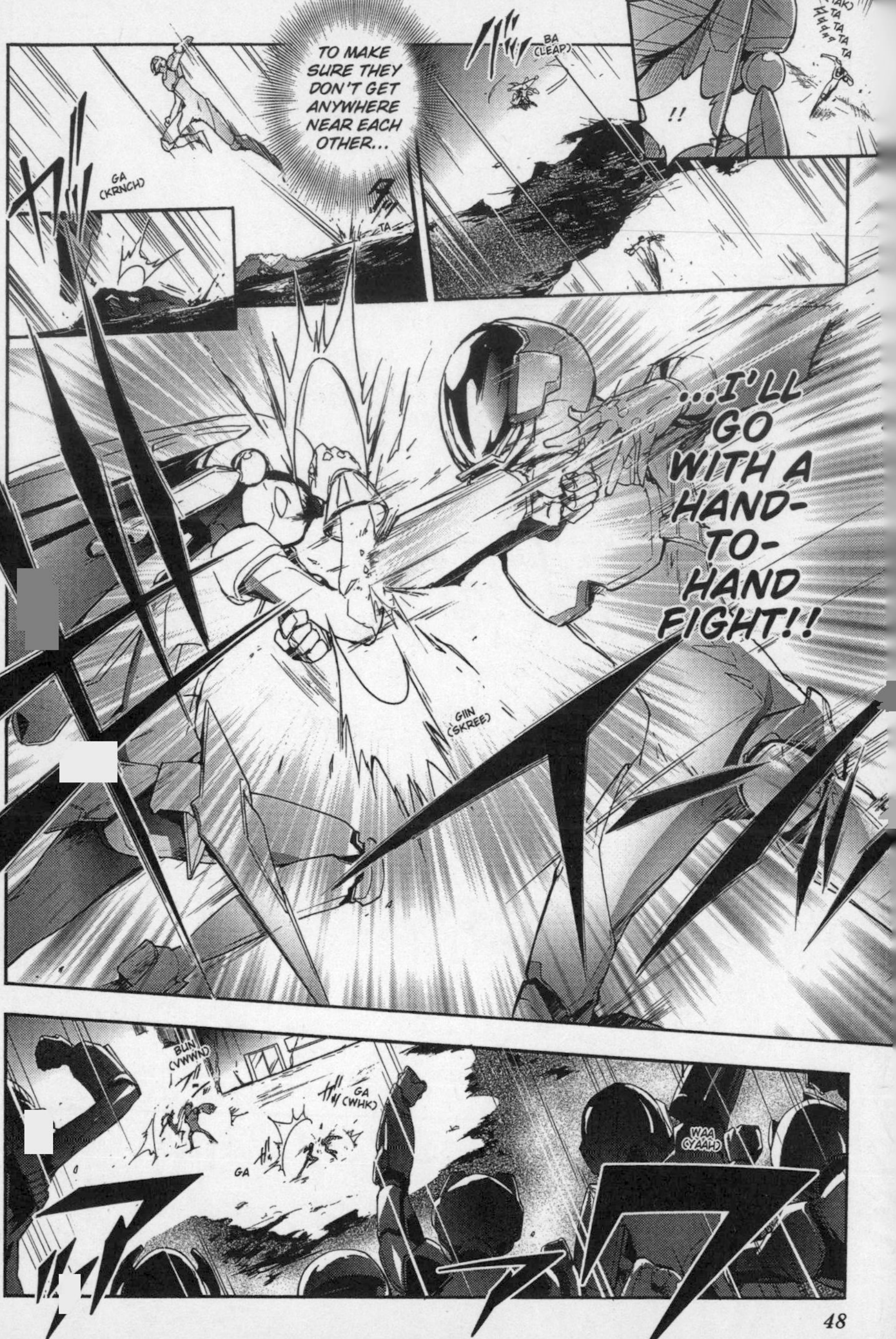
TA (TAK) TA TA TA TA
!!
BA (LEAP)
TO MAKE SURE THEY DON'T GET ANYWHERE NEAR EACH OTHER...
TA
GA (KRNCH)
...I'LL GO WITH A HAND-TO-HAND FIGHT!!
GIIN (SKREE)
WAA (YAAH)
GA (WHK)
BUN (VWWN)
GA

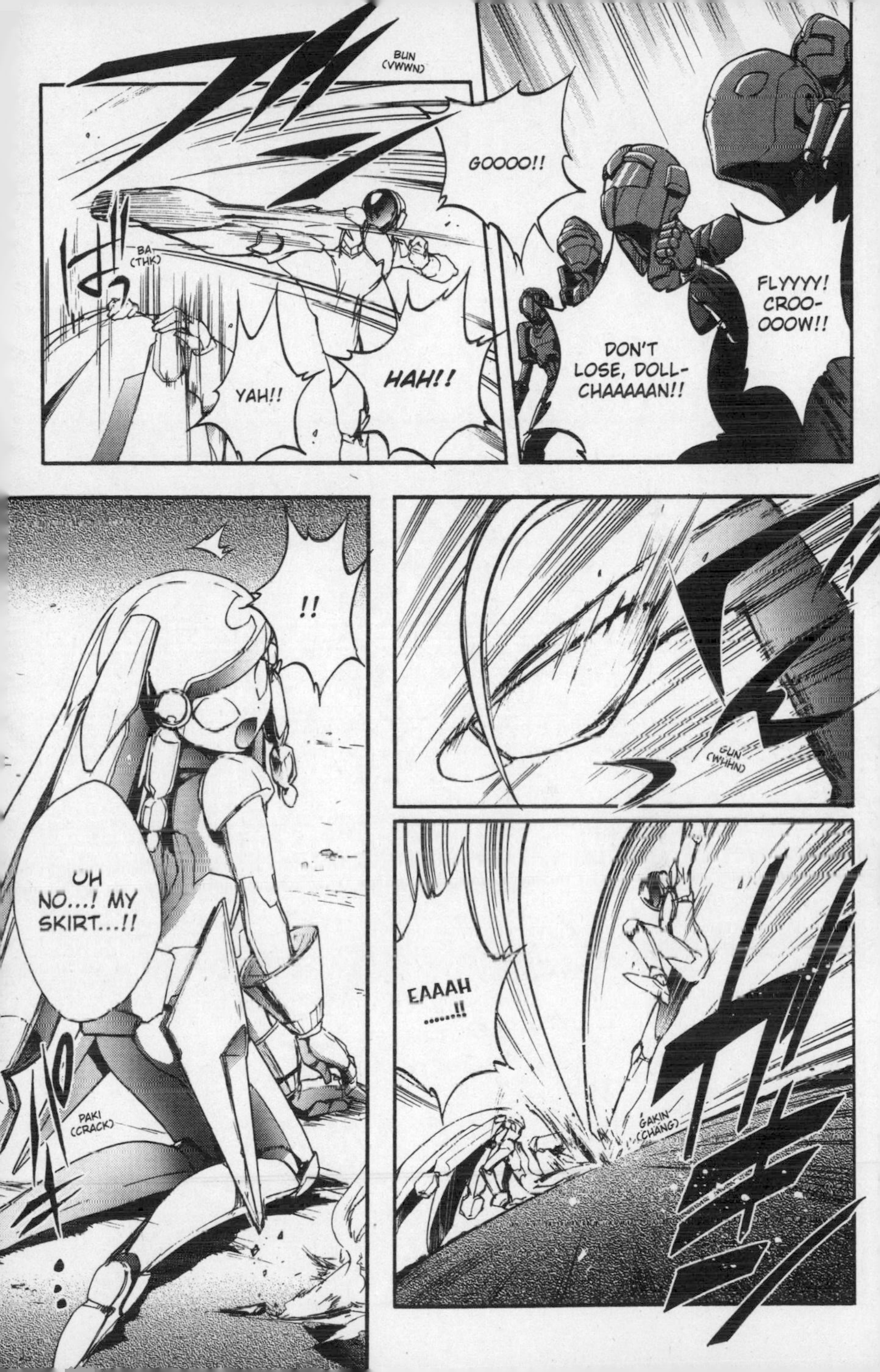
FLYYYY! CROOOOOW!!
DON'T LOSE, DOLL-CHAAAAAN!!
BUN (VWWN)
GOOOO!!
HAH!!
YAH!!
BA (THK)
GUN (WHHN)
EAAAH ......!!
GAKIN (CHANG)
!!
UH NO...! MY SKIRT...!!
PAKI (CRACK)

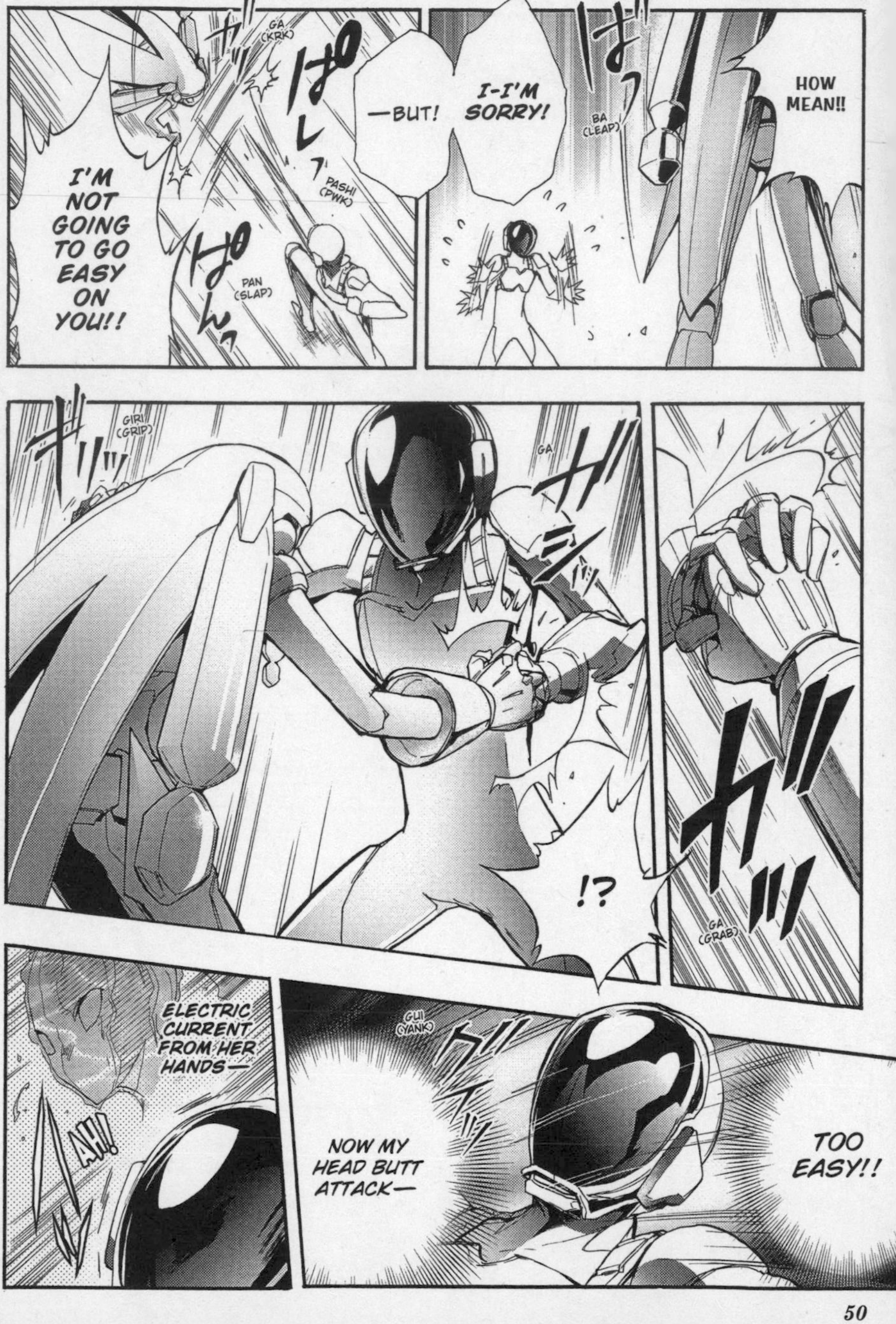
HOW MEAN!!
BA (LEAP)
I-I'M SORRY!
—BUT!
GA (KRK)
PASHI (PWK)
PAN (SLAP)
I'M NOT GOING TO GO EASY ON YOU!!
GA (GRAB)
GIRI (GRIP)
GA
!?
GUI (YANK)
TOO EASY!!
NOW MY HEAD BUTT ATTACK—
ELECTRIC CURRENT FROM HER HANDS—
AH!!

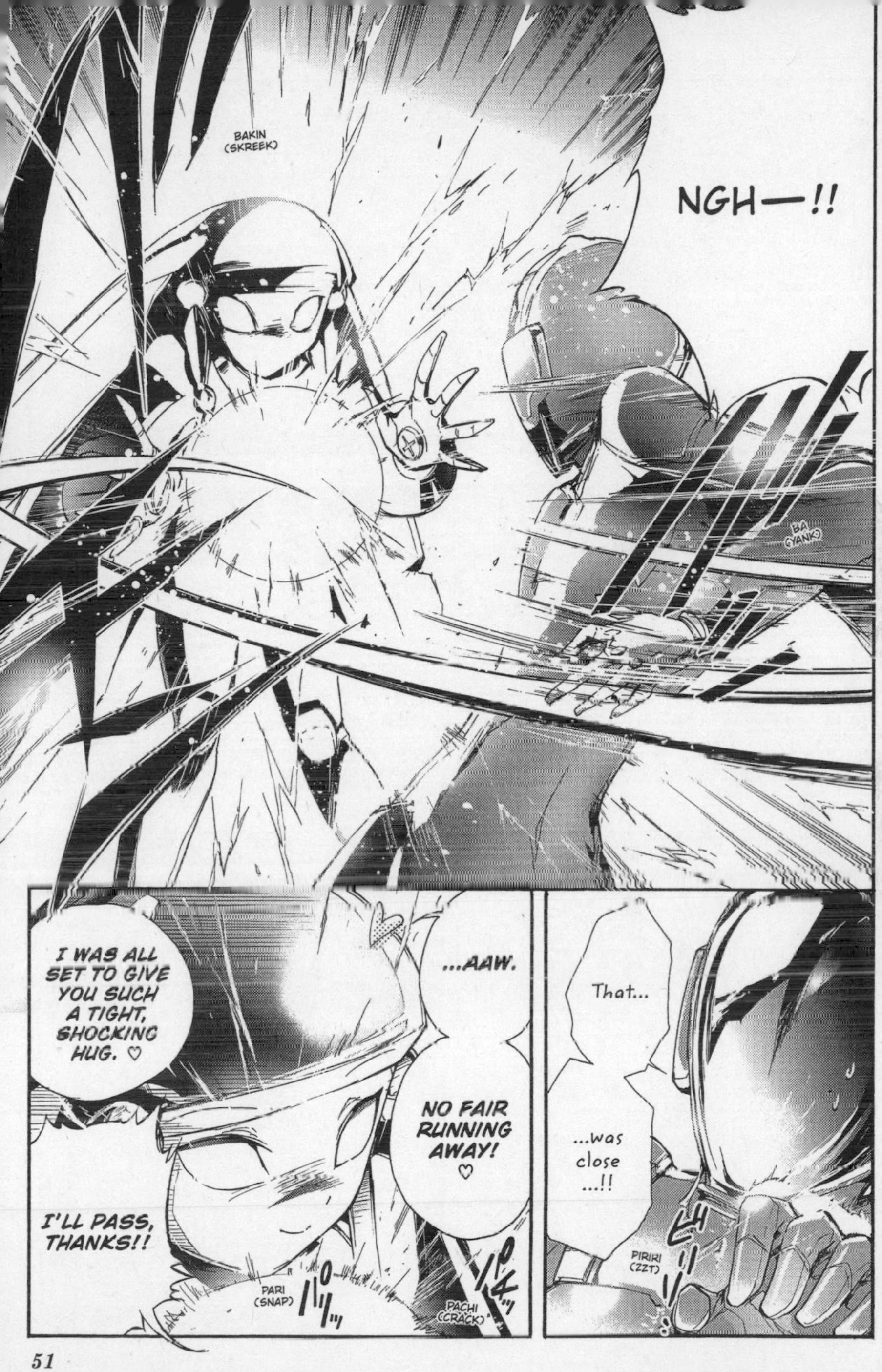
NGH—!!
BAKIN (SKREEK)
BA (YANK)
That...
...was close ...!!
PIRIRI (ZZT)
...AAW.
I WAS ALL SET TO GIVE YOU SUCH A TIGHT, SHOCKING HUG. ♡
NO FAIR RUNNING AWAY! ♡
I'LL PASS, THANKS!!
PACHI (CRACK)
PARI (SNAP)

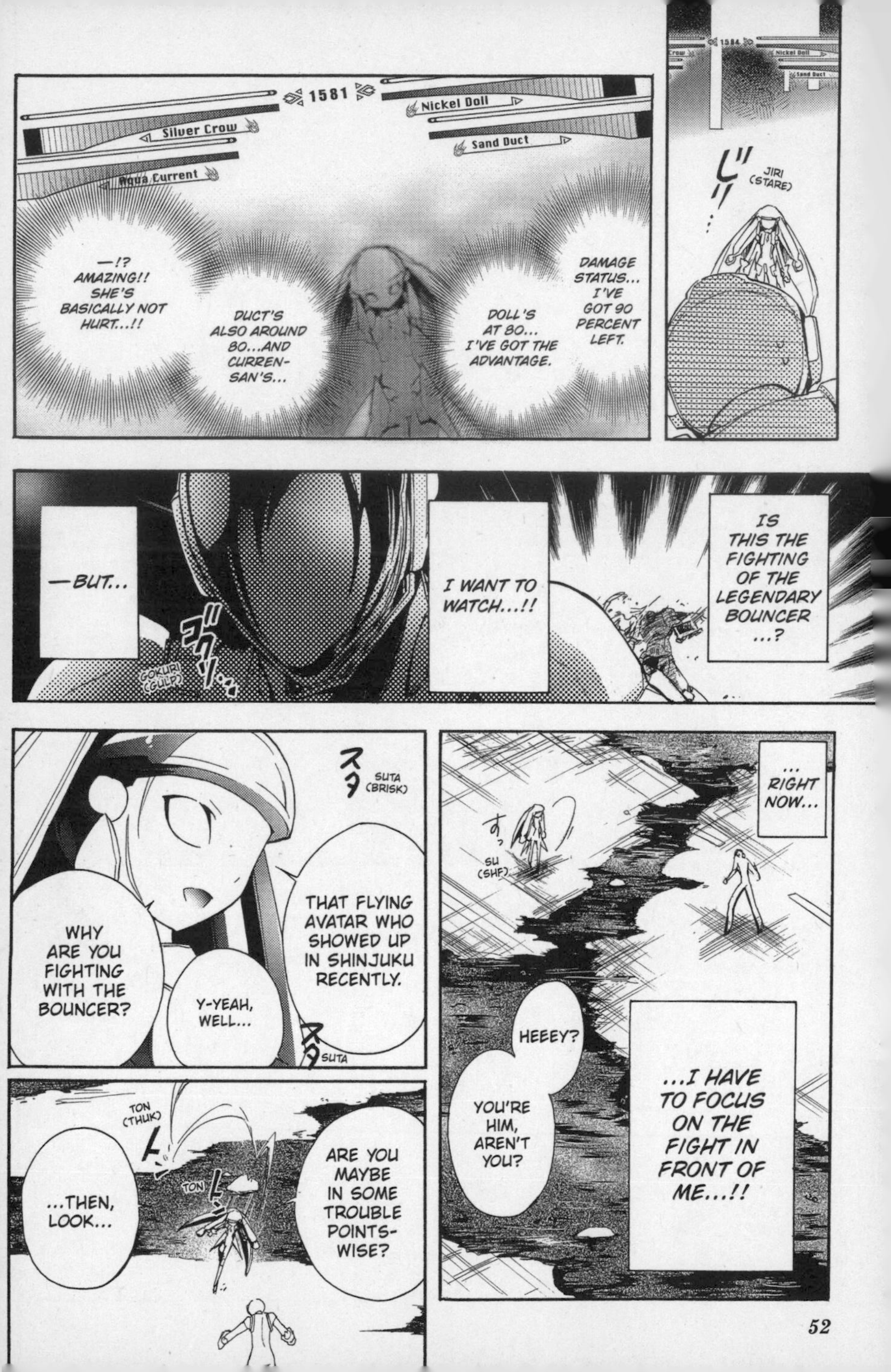

1584
Crow
Nickel Doll
Sand Duct
JIRI (STARE)
1581
Nickel Doll
Silver Crow
Sand Duct
Aqua Current
DAMAGE STATUS... I'VE GOT 90 PERCENT LEFT.
DOLL'S AT 80... I'VE GOT THE ADVANTAGE.
DUCT'S ALSO AROUND 80...AND CURREN-SAN'S...
—!? AMAZING!! SHE'S BASICALLY NOT HURT...!!
IS THIS THE FIGHTING OF THE LEGENDARY BOUNCER ...?
I WANT TO WATCH...!!
GOKURI (GULP)
—BUT...
... RIGHT NOW...
SU (SHF)
HEEEY?
YOU'RE HIM, AREN'T YOU?
...I HAVE TO FOCUS ON THE FIGHT IN FRONT OF ME...!!
SUTA (BRISK)
THAT FLYING AVATAR WHO SHOWED UP IN SHINJUKU RECENTLY.
WHY ARE YOU FIGHTING WITH THE BOUNCER?
Y-YEAH, WELL...
SUTA
ARE YOU MAYBE IN SOME TROUBLE POINTS-WISE?
TON (THUK)
TON
...THEN, LOOK...

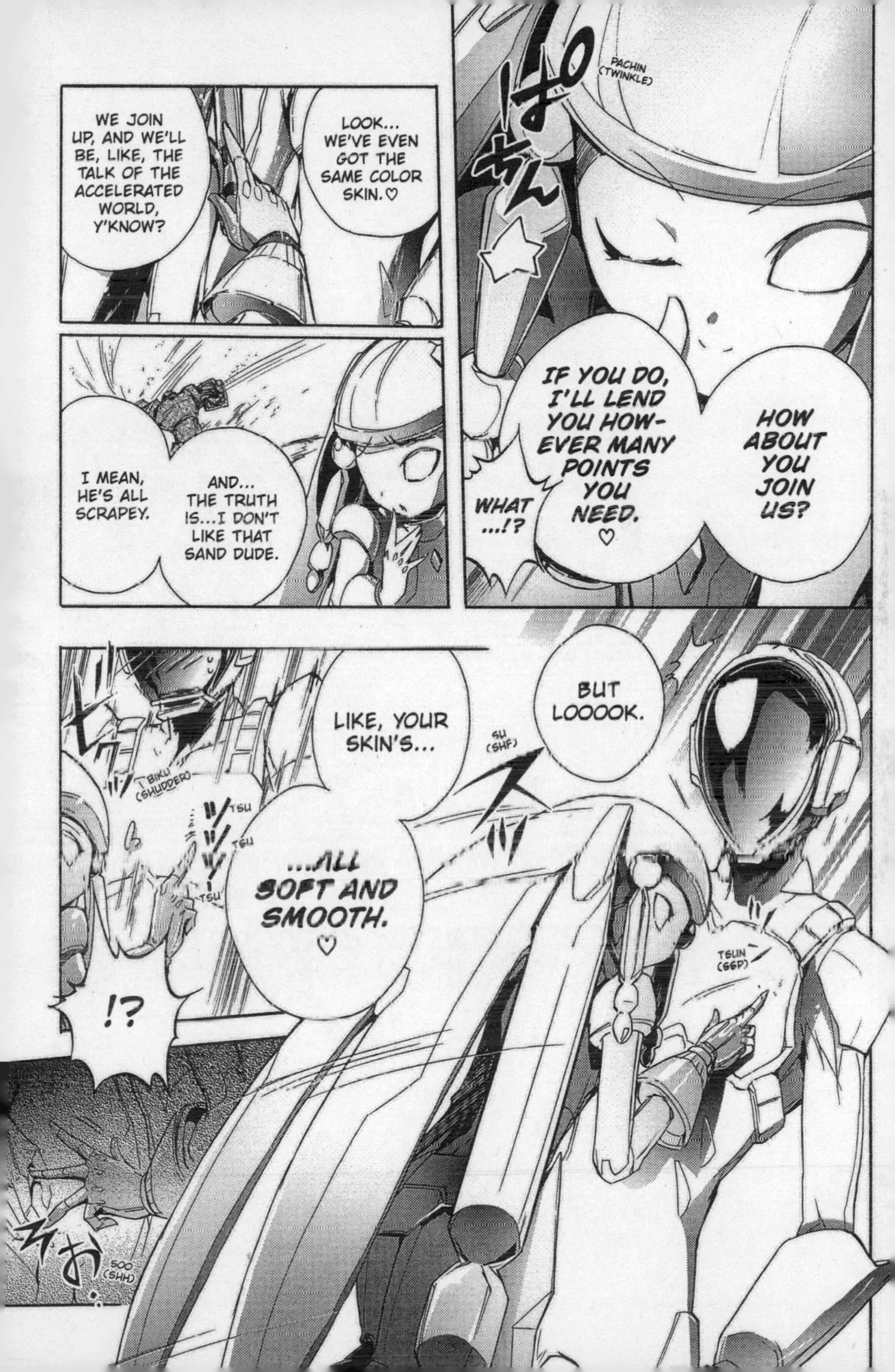
PACHIN (TWINKLE)
HOW ABOUT YOU JOIN US?
IF YOU DO, I'LL LEND YOU HOW-EVER MANY POINTS YOU NEED. ♡
WHAT ...!?
LOOK... WE'VE EVEN GOT THE SAME COLOR SKIN. ♡
WE JOIN UP, AND WE'LL BE, LIKE, THE TALK OF THE ACCELERATED WORLD, Y'KNOW?
AND... THE TRUTH IS...I DON'T LIKE THAT SAND DUDE.
I MEAN, HE'S ALL SCRAPEY.
BUT LOOOOK.
SU (SHF)
LIKE, YOUR SKIN'S...
...ALL SOFT AND SMOOTH. ♡
TSUN (SSP)
TSU
TSU
TSU
BIKU (SHUDDER)
!?
SOO (SHH)

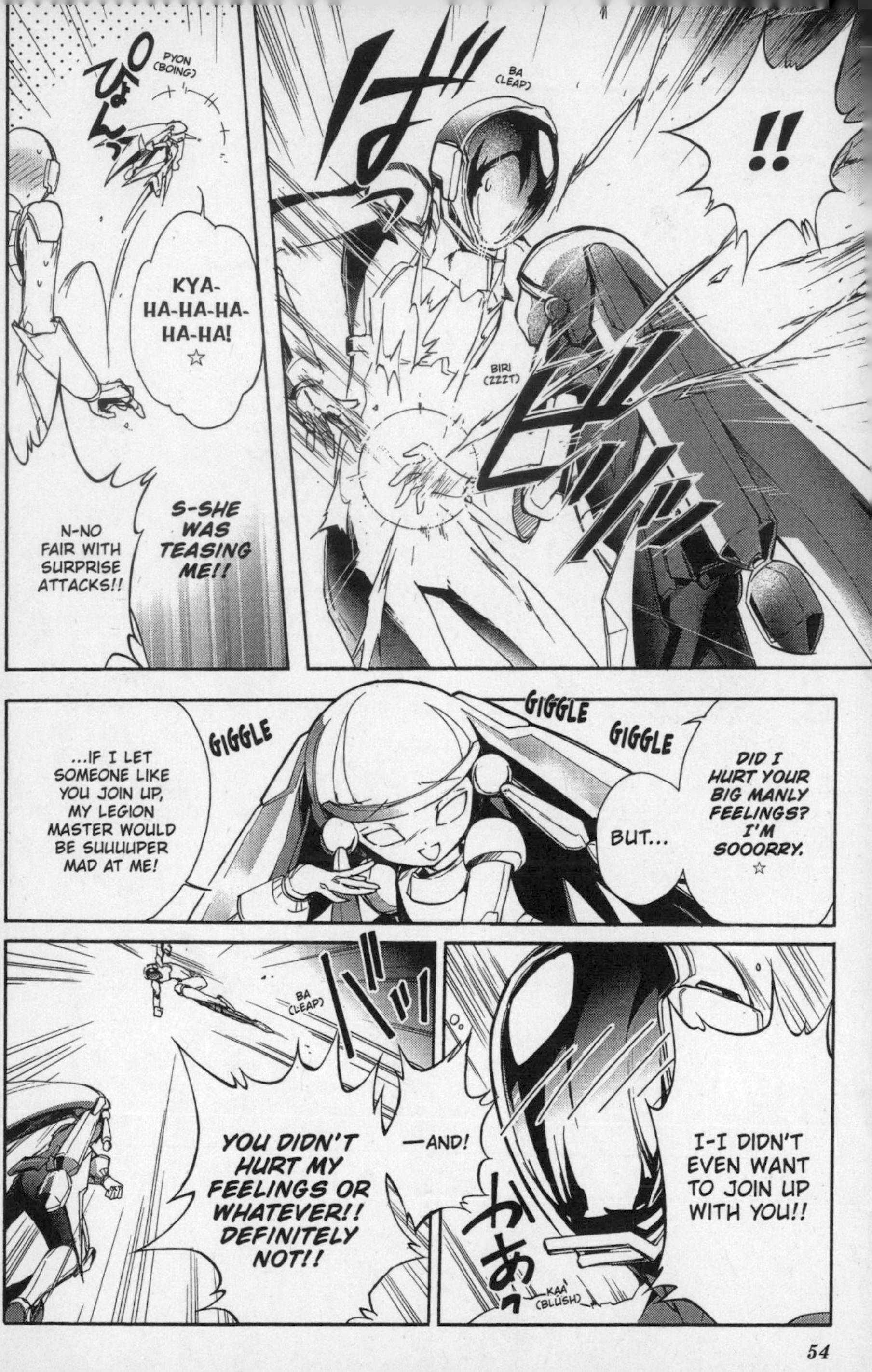
BA (LEAP)
!!
BIRI (ZZZT)
PYON (BOING)
KYA-HA-HA-HA-HA-HA! ☆
S-SHE WAS TEASING ME!!
N-NO FAIR WITH SURPRISE ATTACKS!!
DID I HURT YOUR BIG MANLY FEELINGS? I'M SOOORRY. ☆
GIGGLE
GIGGLE
BUT...
GIGGLE
...IF I LET SOMEONE LIKE YOU JOIN UP, MY LEGION MASTER WOULD BE SUUUUPER MAD AT ME!
I-I DIDN'T EVEN WANT TO JOIN UP WITH YOU!!
KAA (BLUSH)
—AND!
BA (LEAP)
YOU DIDN'T HURT MY FEELINGS OR WHATEVER!! DEFINITELY NOT!!

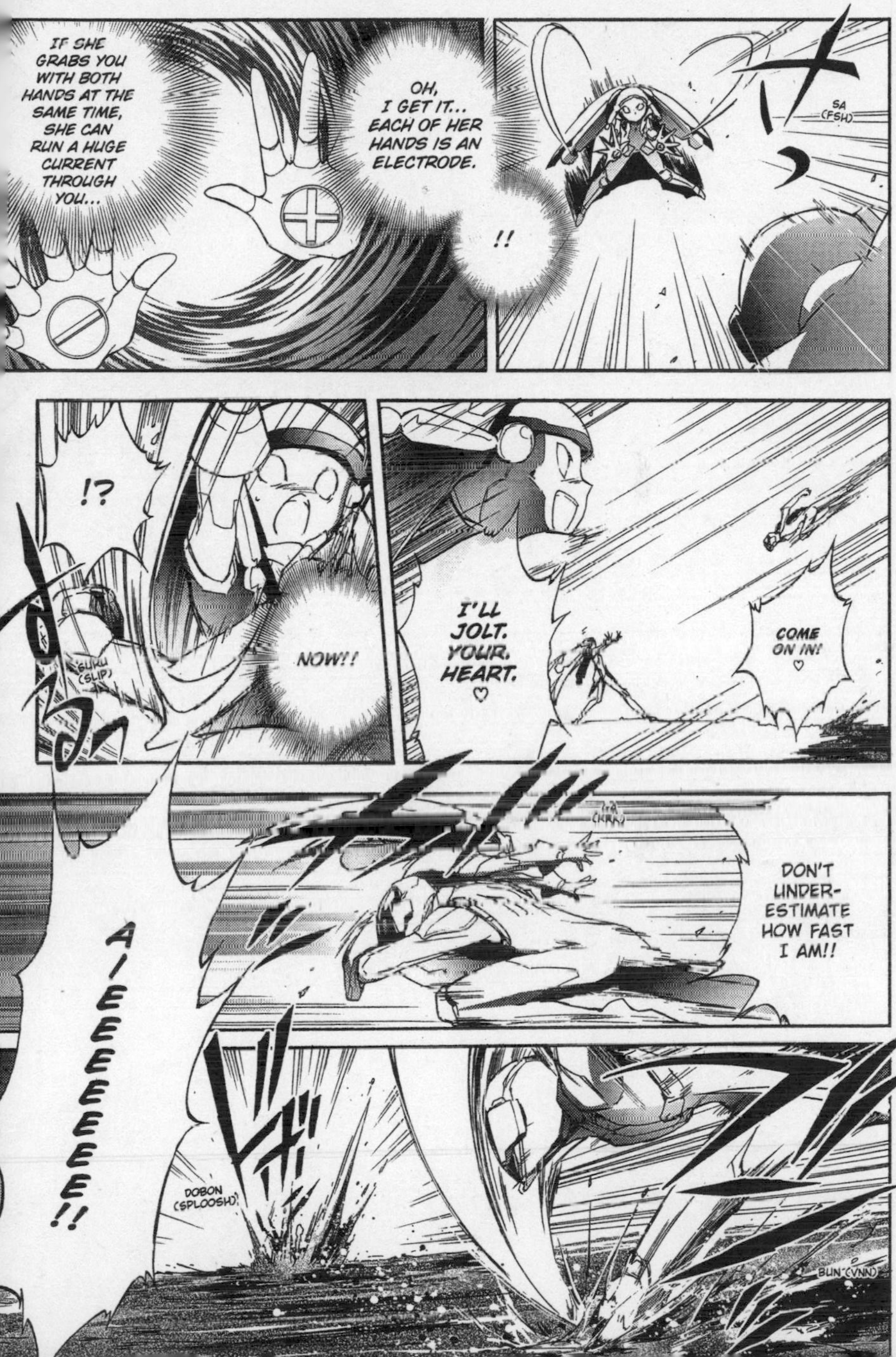
SA (FSH)
OH, I GET IT... EACH OF HER HANDS IS AN ELECTRODE.
IF SHE GRABS YOU WITH BOTH HANDS AT THE SAME TIME, SHE CAN RUN A HUGE CURRENT THROUGH YOU...
!!
COME ON IN! ♡
I'LL JOLT. YOUR. HEART. ♡
!?
NOW!!
SUKU (SLIP)
DON'T UNDER-ESTIMATE HOW FAST I AM!!
BUN (VNN)
DOBON (SPLOOSH)
AIEEEEEEEEEE!!

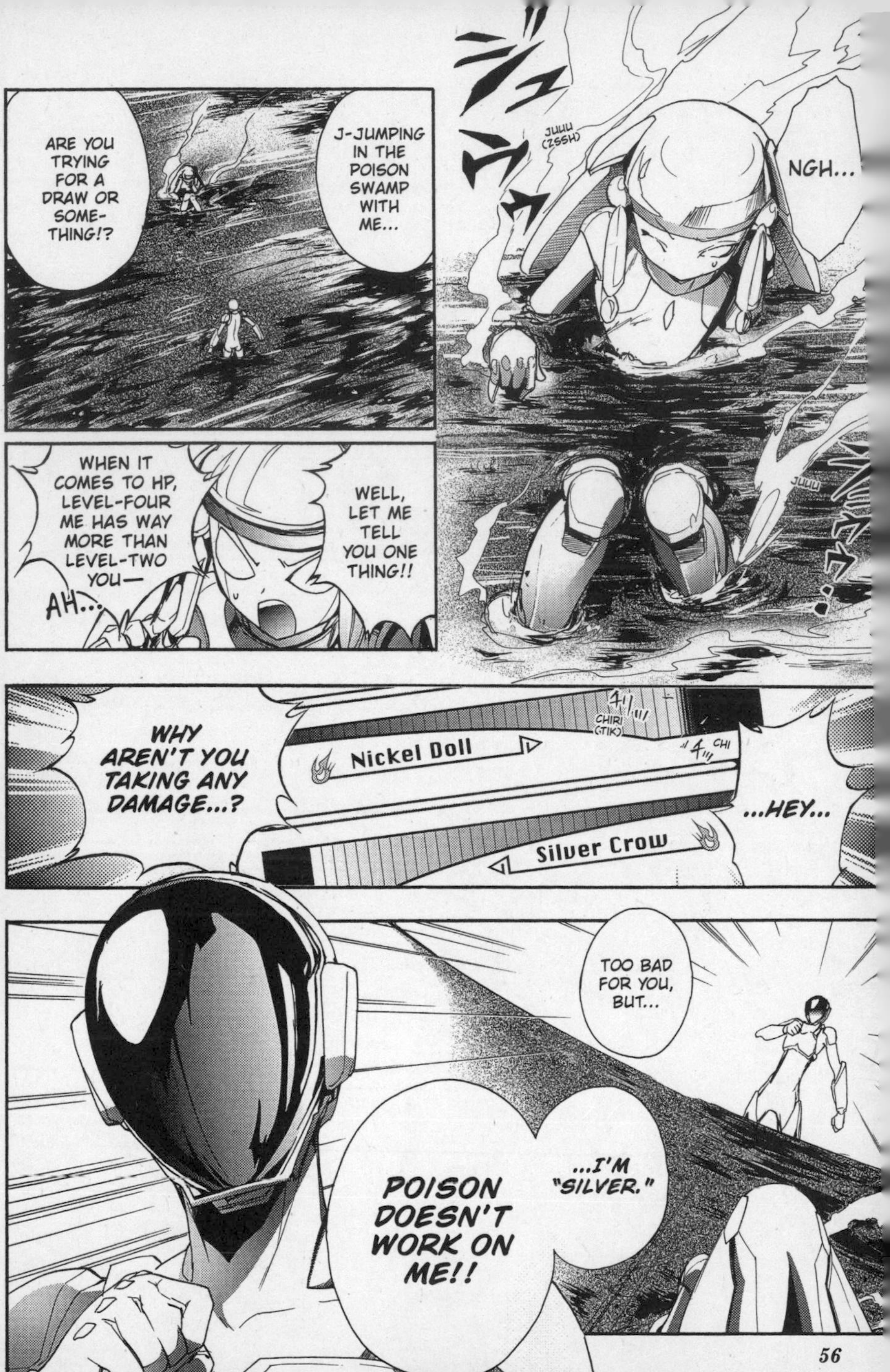
JUUU (ZSSH)
NGH...
JUUU
J-JUMPING IN THE POISON SWAMP WITH ME...
ARE YOU TRYING FOR A DRAW OR SOME-THING!?
WELL, LET ME TELL YOU ONE THING!!
WHEN IT COMES TO HP, LEVEL-FOUR ME HAS WAY MORE THAN LEVEL-TWO YOU—
AH...
...HEY...
CHI
CHIRI (TIK)
Nickel Doll
Silver Crow
WHY AREN'T YOU TAKING ANY DAMAGE...?
TOO BAD FOR YOU, BUT...
...I'M "SILVER."
POISON DOESN'T WORK ON ME!!

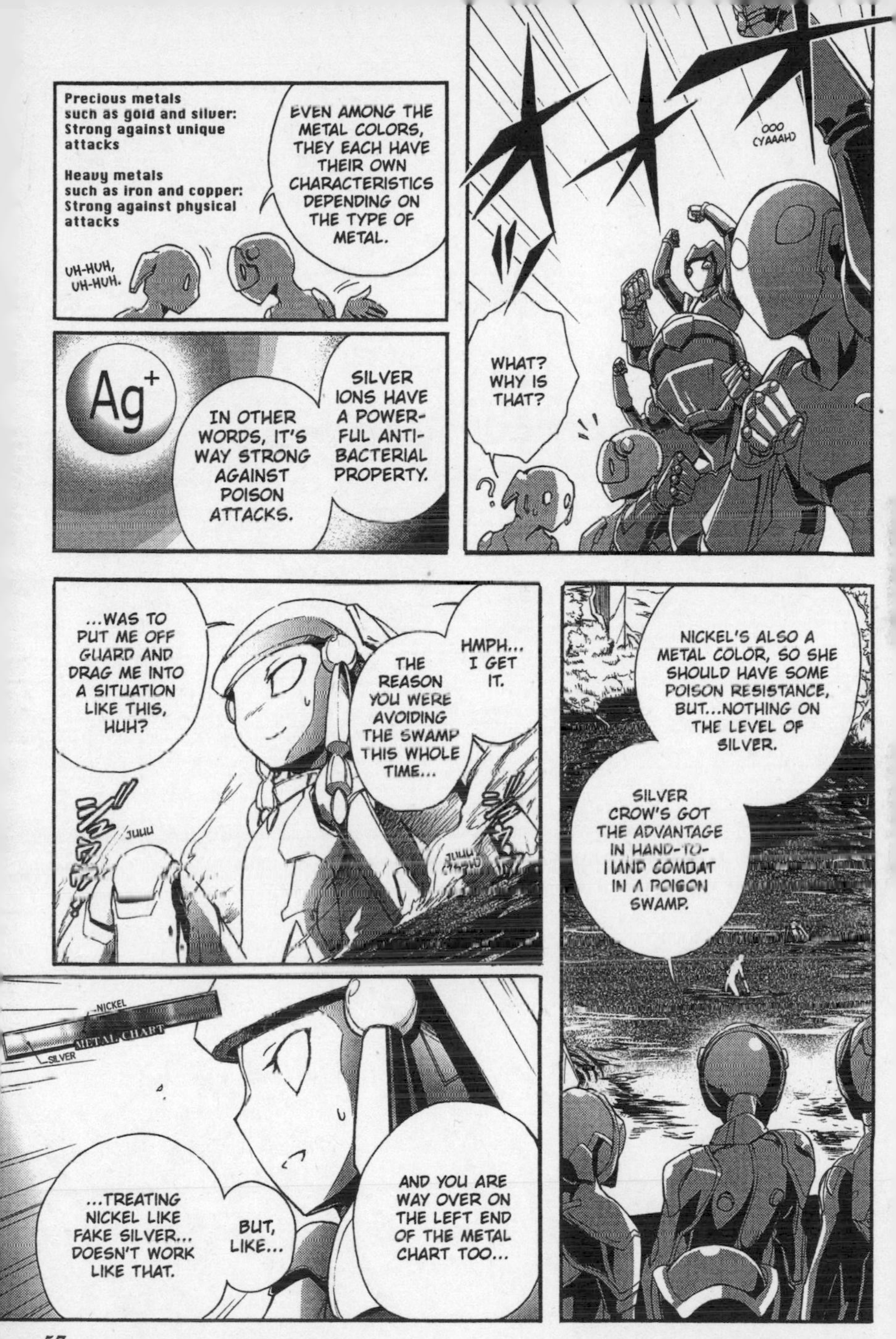
OOO
(YAAAH)
WHAT? WHY IS THAT?
EVEN AMONG THE METAL COLORS, THEY EACH HAVE THEIR OWN CHARACTERISTICS DEPENDING ON THE TYPE OF METAL.
Precious metals such as gold and silver: Strong against unique attacks
Heavy metals such as iron and copper: Strong against physical attacks
UH-HUH, UH-HUH.
SILVER IONS HAVE A POWERFUL ANTI-BACTERIAL PROPERTY.
IN OTHER WORDS, IT'S WAY STRONG AGAINST POISON ATTACKS.
Ag^+
NICKEL'S ALSO A METAL COLOR, SO SHE SHOULD HAVE SOME POISON RESISTANCE, BUT...NOTHING ON THE LEVEL OF SILVER.
SILVER CROW'S GOT THE ADVANTAGE IN HAND-TO-HAND COMBAT IN A POISON SWAMP.
HMPH... I GET IT.
THE REASON YOU WERE AVOIDING THE SWAMP THIS WHOLE TIME...
...WAS TO PUT ME OFF GUARD AND DRAG ME INTO A SITUATION LIKE THIS, HUH?
JUUU
JUUU
AND YOU ARE WAY OVER ON THE LEFT END OF THE METAL CHART TOO...
BUT, LIKE...
...TREATING NICKEL LIKE FAKE SILVER... DOESN'T WORK LIKE THAT.
NICKEL
METAL CHART
SILVER

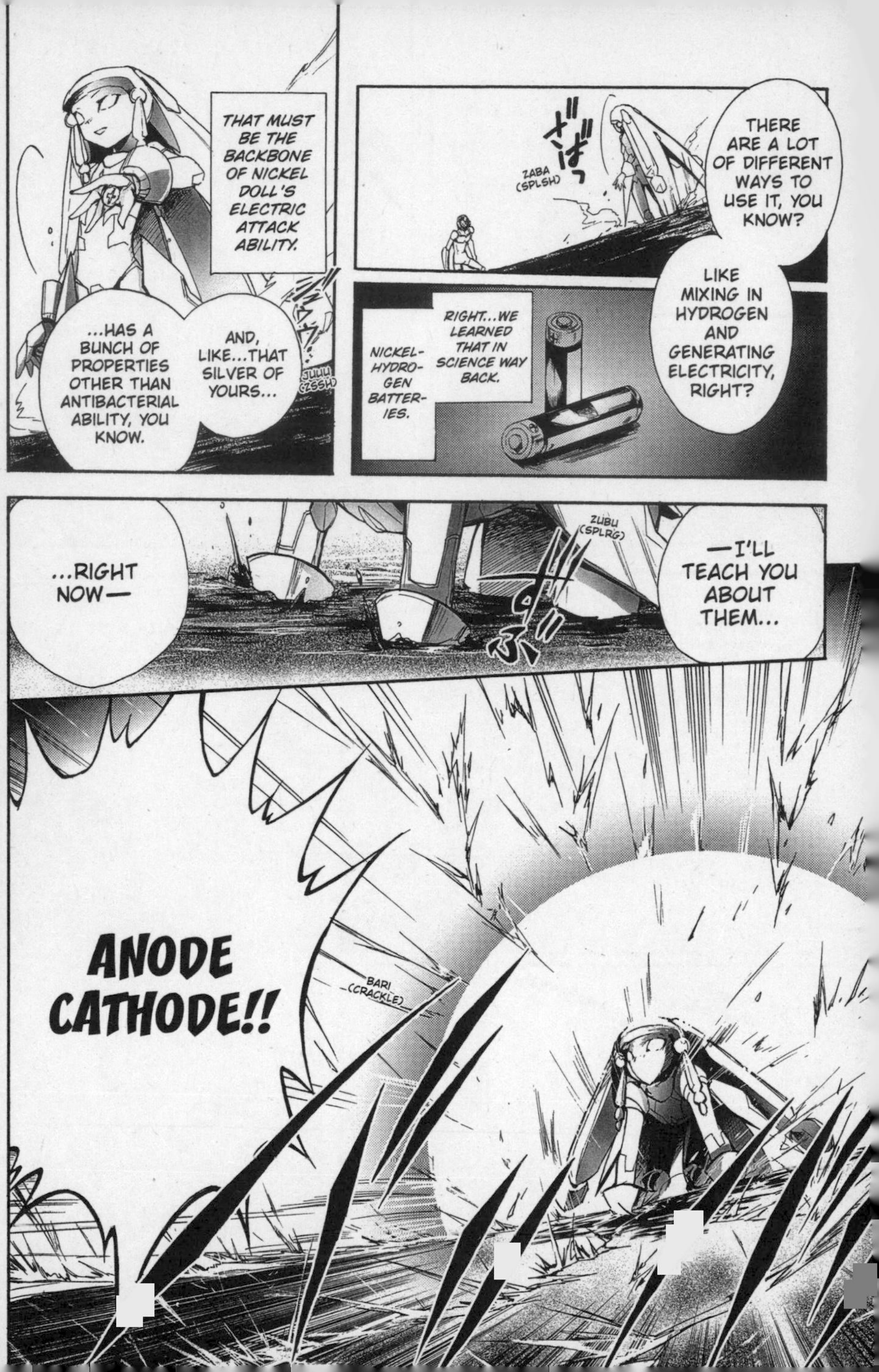
THERE ARE A LOT OF DIFFERENT WAYS TO USE IT, YOU KNOW?
ZABA (SPLSH)
LIKE MIXING IN HYDROGEN AND GENERATING ELECTRICITY, RIGHT?
RIGHT...WE LEARNED THAT IN SCIENCE WAY BACK.
NICKEL-HYDROGEN BATTERIES.
THAT MUST BE THE BACKBONE OF NICKEL DOLL'S ELECTRIC ATTACK ABILITY.
AND, LIKE...THAT SILVER OF YOURS...
...HAS A BUNCH OF PROPERTIES OTHER THAN ANTIBACTERIAL ABILITY, YOU KNOW.
JUUU (ZSSH)
—I'LL TEACH YOU ABOUT THEM...
ZUBU (SPLRG)
...RIGHT NOW—
BARI (CRACKLE)
ANODE CATHODE!!

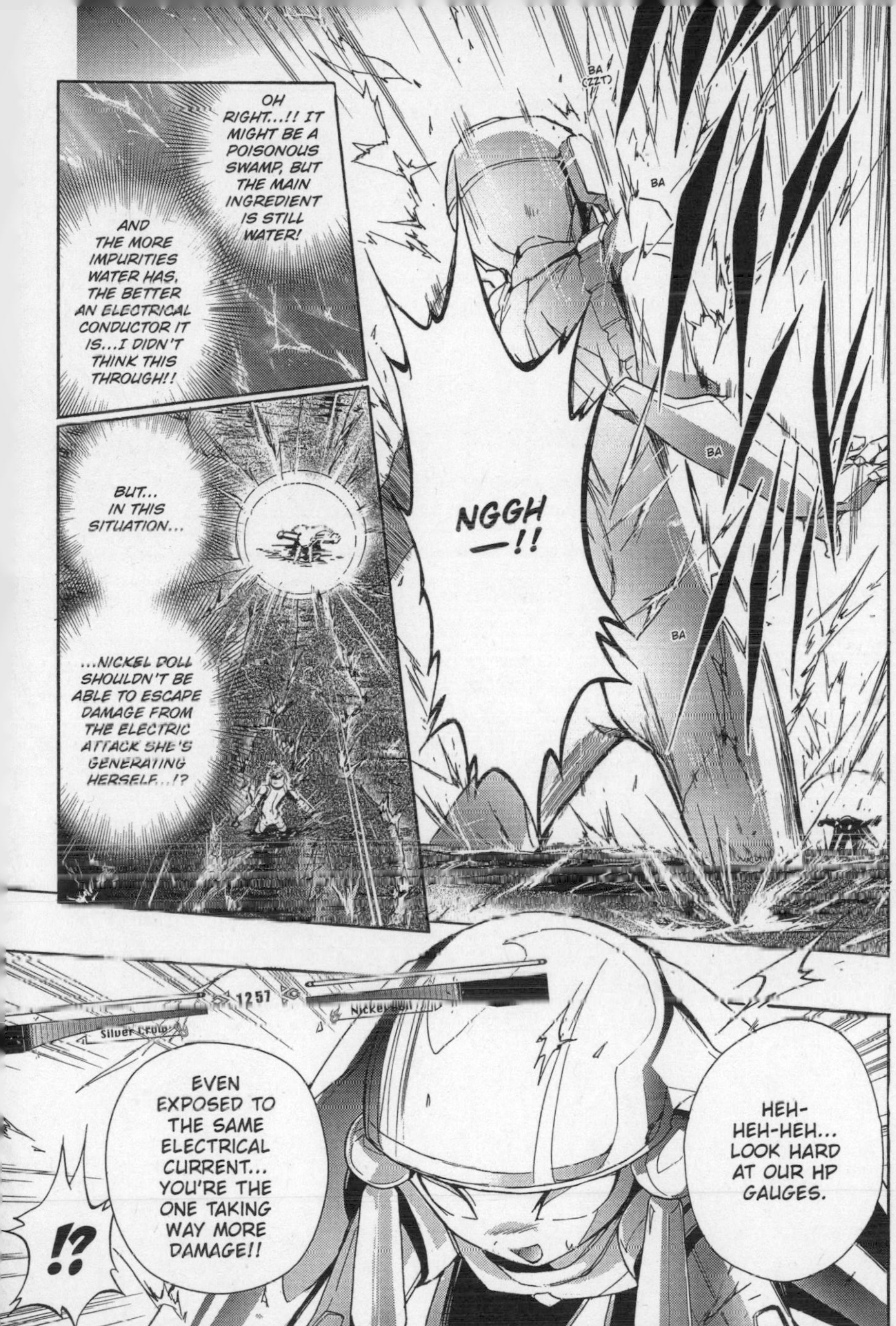
BA (ZZZT)
BA
BA
NGGH—!!
BA
OH RIGHT...!! IT MIGHT BE A POISONOUS SWAMP, BUT THE MAIN INGREDIENT IS STILL WATER!
AND THE MORE IMPURITIES WATER HAS, THE BETTER AN ELECTRICAL CONDUCTOR IT IS...I DIDN'T THINK THIS THROUGH!!
BUT... IN THIS SITUATION...
...NICKEL DOLL SHOULDN'T BE ABLE TO ESCAPE DAMAGE FROM THE ELECTRIC ATTACK SHE'S GENERATING HERSELF...!?
1257
HEH-HEH-HEH... LOOK HARD AT OUR HP GAUGES.
EVEN EXPOSED TO THE SAME ELECTRICAL CURRENT... YOU'RE THE ONE TAKING WAY MORE DAMAGE!!
!?

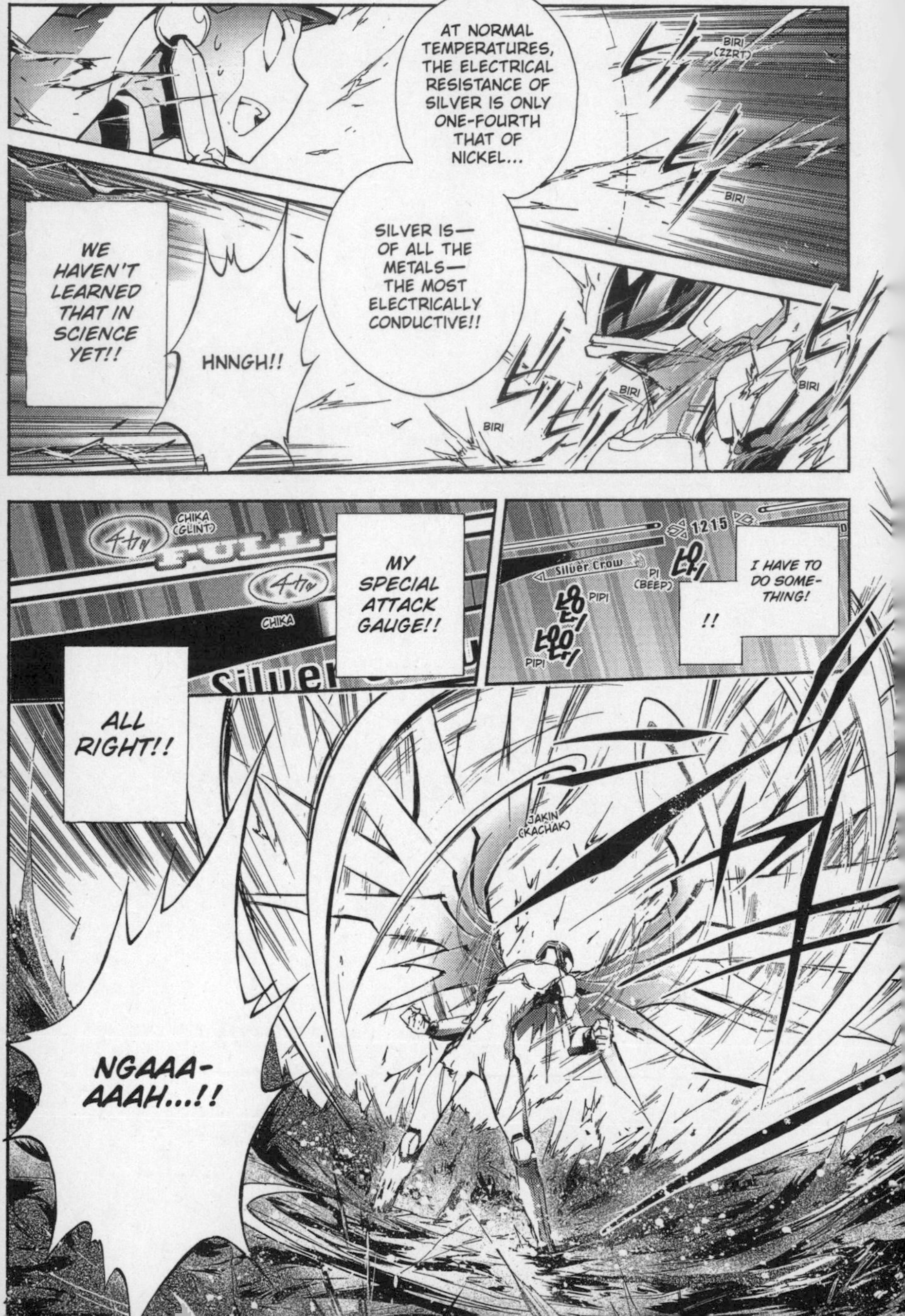
BIRI (ZZRT)
AT NORMAL TEMPERATURES, THE ELECTRICAL RESISTANCE OF SILVER IS ONLY ONE-FOURTH THAT OF NICKEL...
BIRI
SILVER IS— OF ALL THE METALS— THE MOST ELECTRICALLY CONDUCTIVE!!
BIRI
BIRI
BIRI
HNNGH!!
WE HAVEN'T LEARNED THAT IN SCIENCE YET!!
1215
Silver Crow
PI (BEEP)
PIPI
PIPI
I HAVE TO DO SOME-THING!
!!
MY SPECIAL ATTACK GAUGE!!
CHIKA (GLINT)
FULL
CHIKA
JAKIN (KACHAK)
ALL RIGHT!!
NGAAA-AAAH...!!

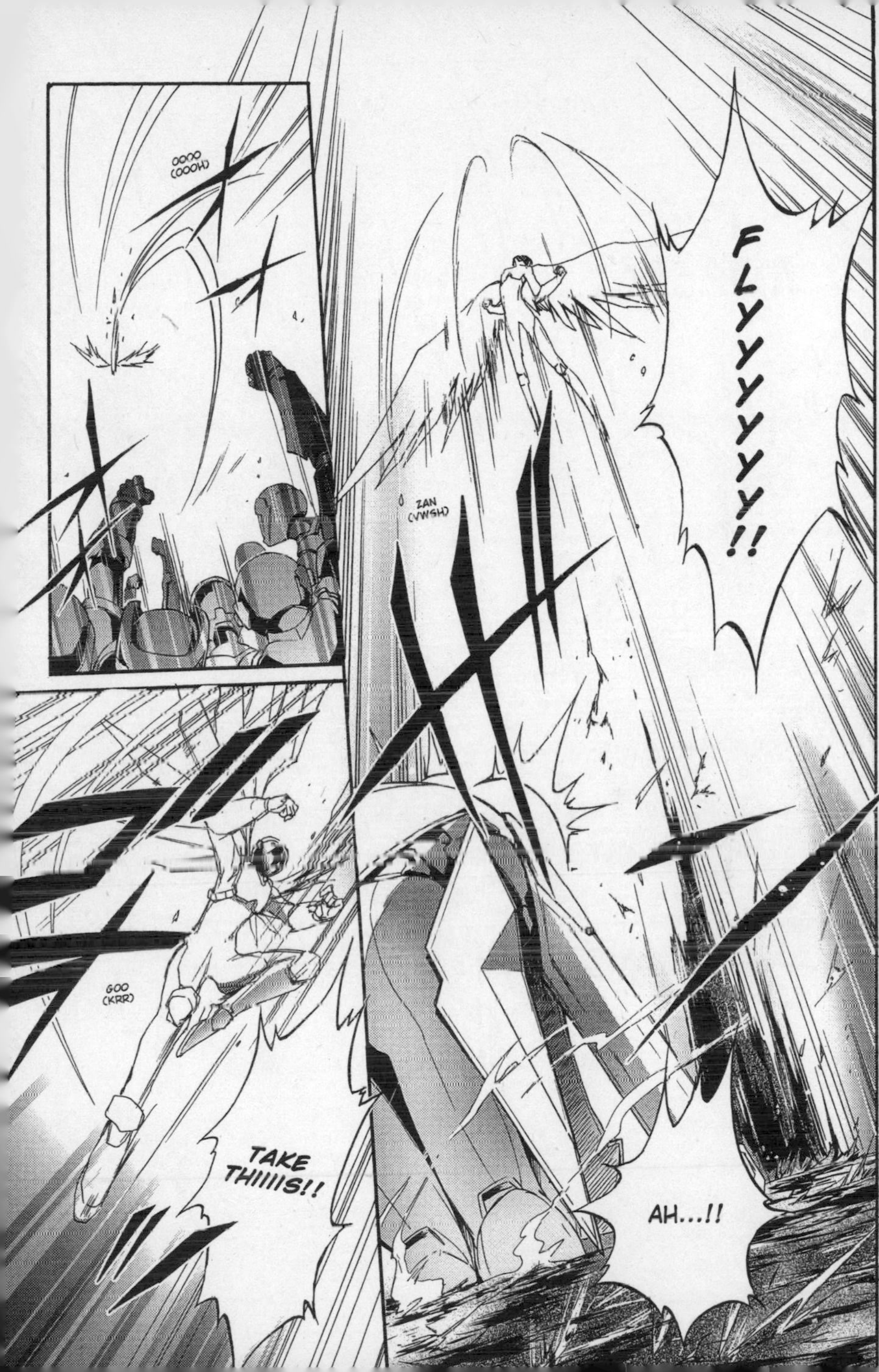
FLYYYYYY!!
ZAN (VWSH)
AH...!!
OOOO (OOOH)
GOO (KRR)
TAKE THIIIIS!!

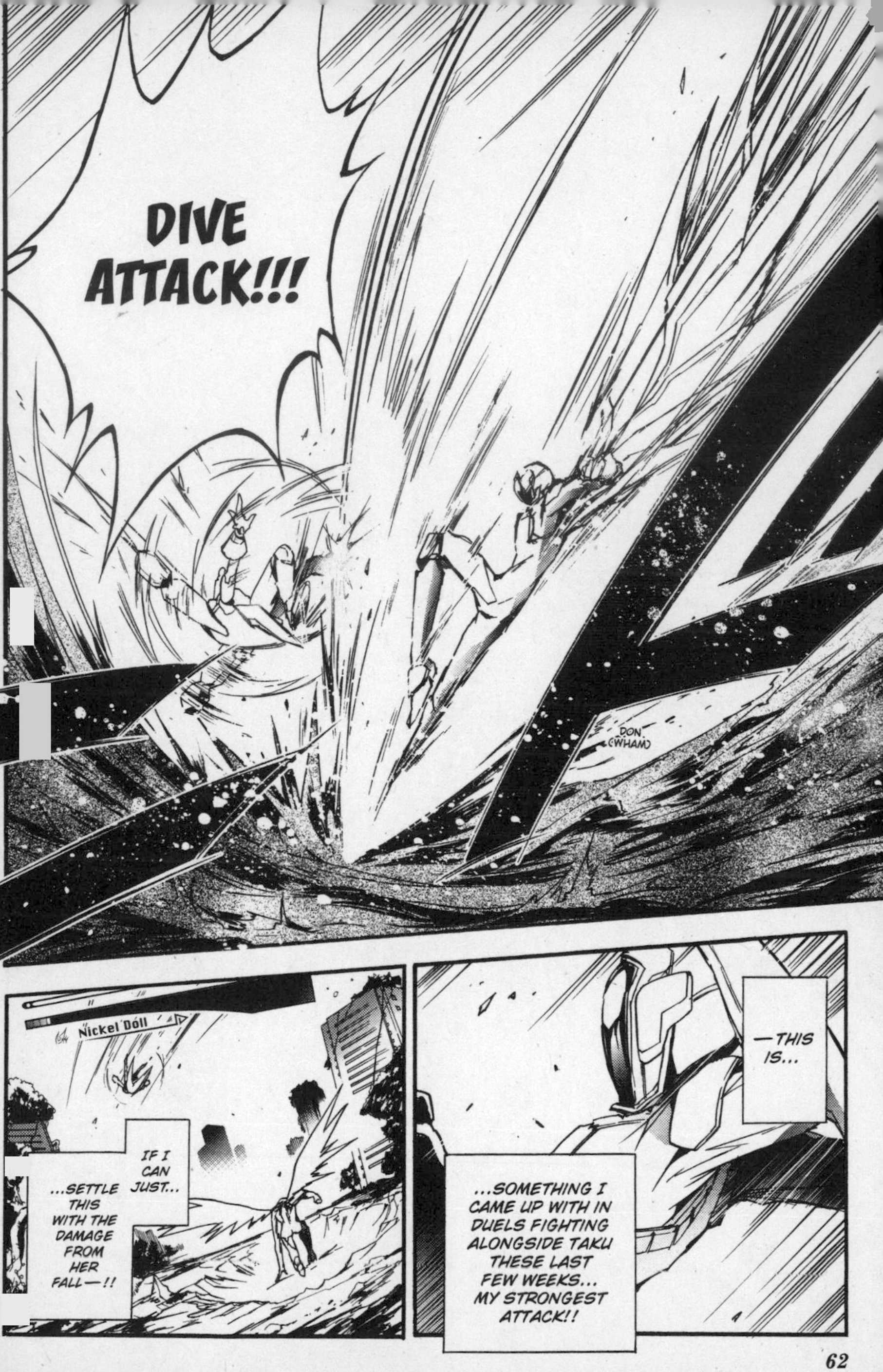
DIVE ATTACK!!!
DON (WHAM)
—THIS IS...
...SOMETHING I CAME UP WITH IN DUELS FIGHTING ALONGSIDE TAKU THESE LAST FEW WEEKS... MY STRONGEST ATTACK!!
Nickel Doll
IF I CAN JUST...
...SETTLE THIS WITH THE DAMAGE FROM HER FALL—!!

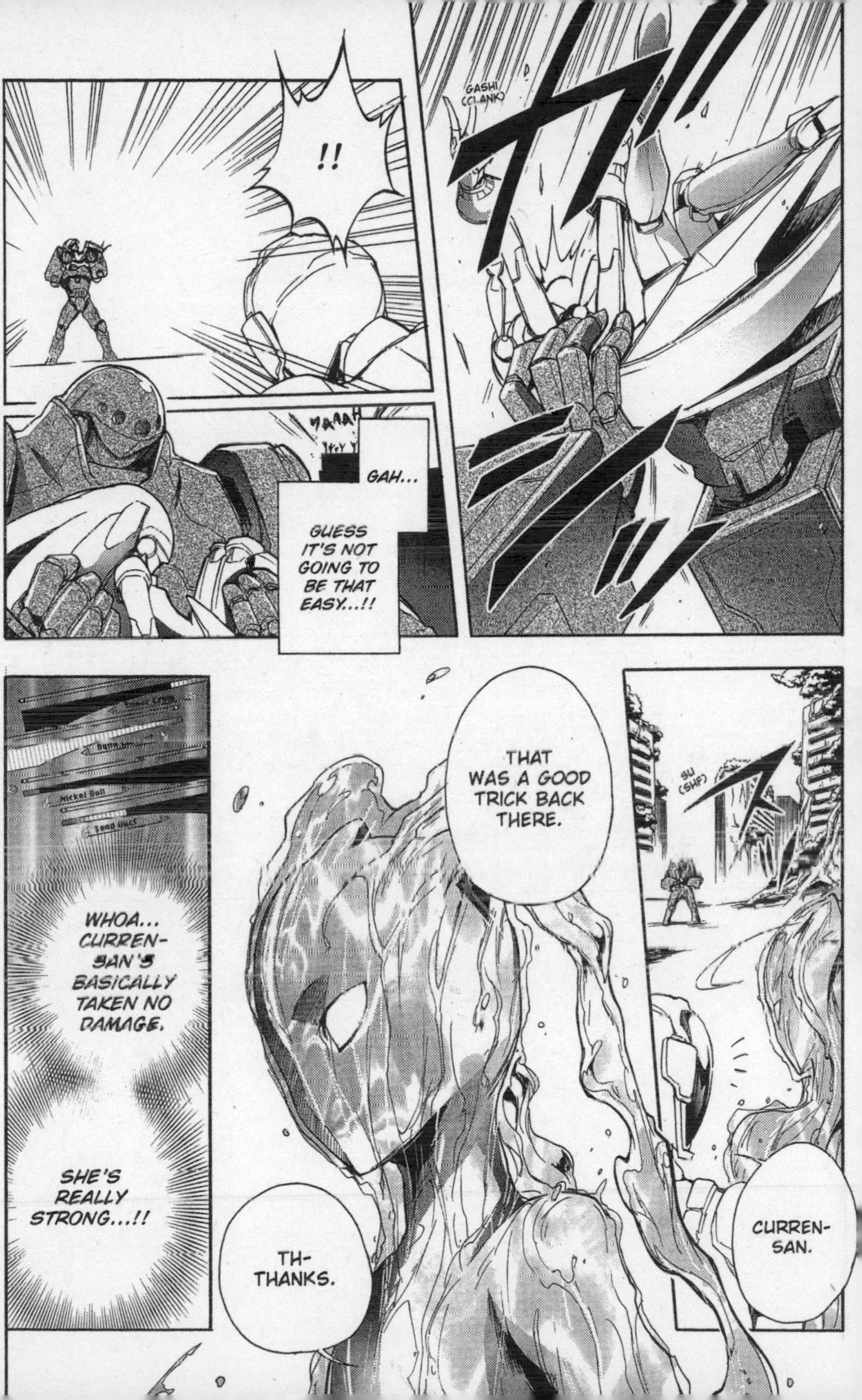
GASHI (CLANK)
!!
GAH...
GUESS IT'S NOT GOING TO BE THAT EASY...!!
SU (SHF)
CURREN-SAN.
THAT WAS A GOOD TRICK BACK THERE.
TH- THANKS.
WHOA... CURREN-SAN'S BASICALLY TAKEN NO DAMAGE.
SHE'S REALLY STRONG...!!

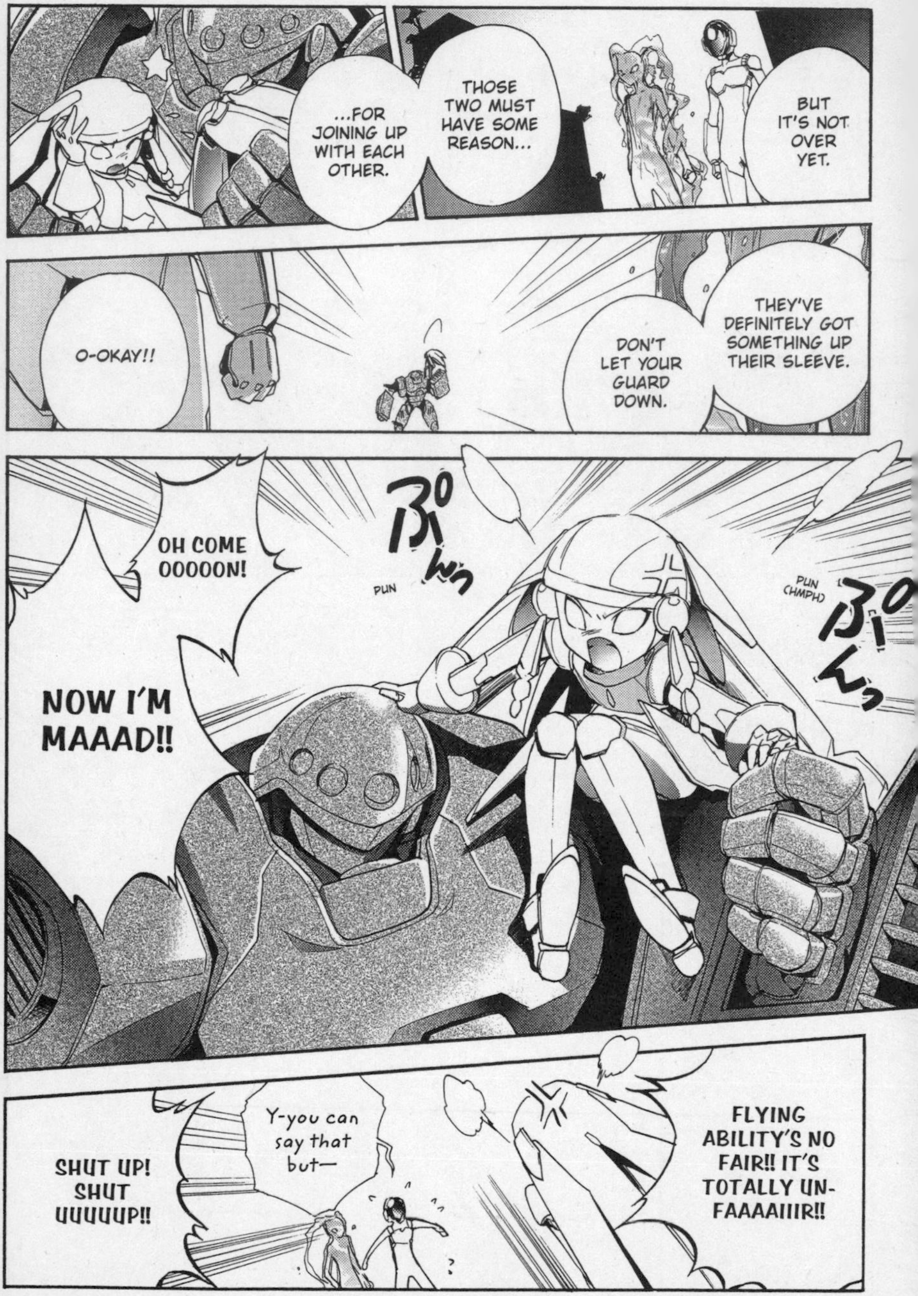

BUT IT'S NOT OVER YET.
THOSE TWO MUST HAVE SOME REASON...
...FOR JOINING UP WITH EACH OTHER.
THEY'VE DEFINITELY GOT SOMETHING UP THEIR SLEEVE.
DON'T LET YOUR GUARD DOWN.
O-OKAY!!
PUN (HMPH)
PUN
OH COME OOOOON!
NOW I'M MAAAD!!
FLYING ABILITY'S NO FAIR!! IT'S TOTALLY UN-FAAAAIIIR!!
Y-you can say that but—
SHUT UP! SHUT UUUUUP!!

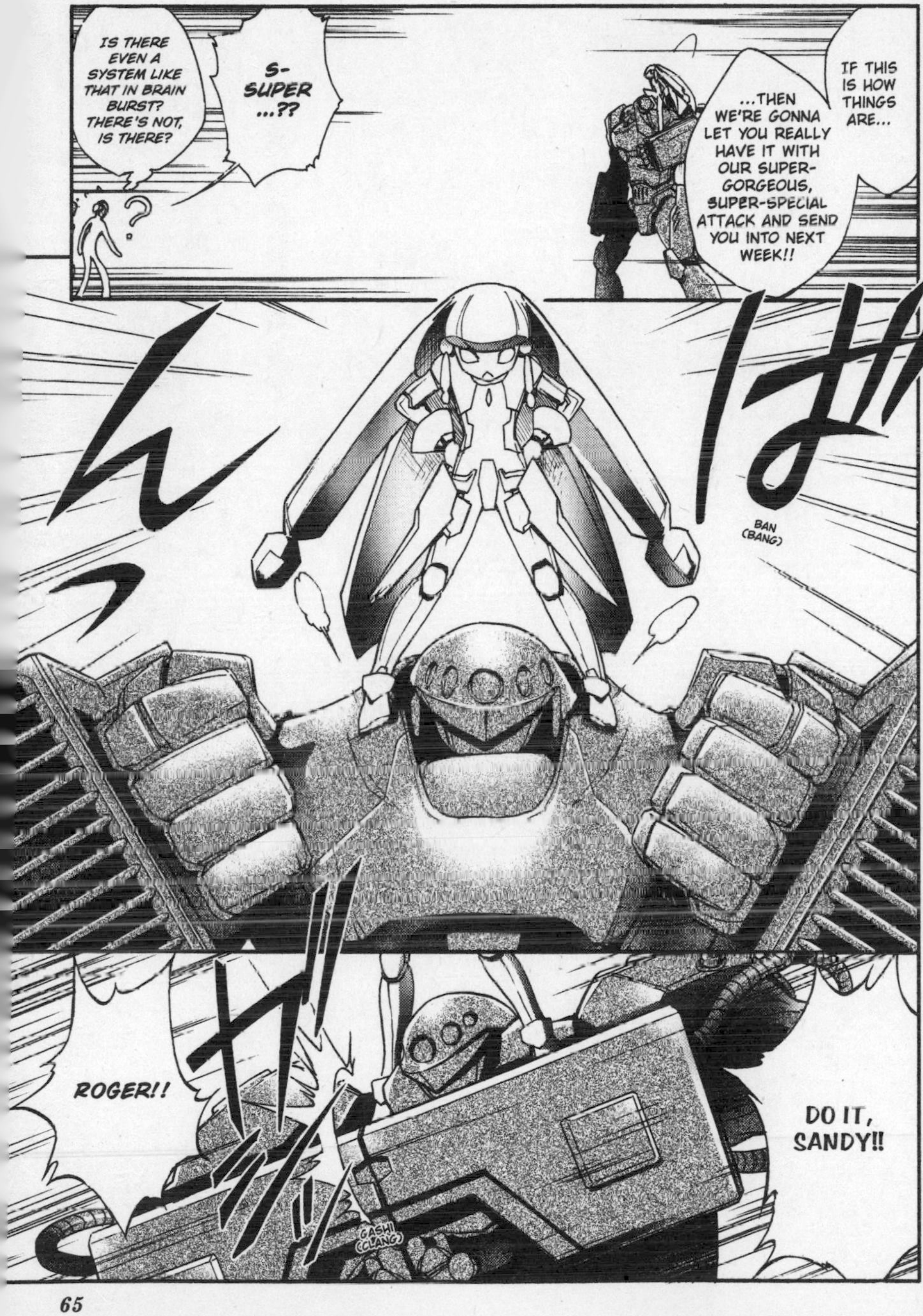
IF THIS IS HOW THINGS ARE...
...THEN WE'RE GONNA LET YOU REALLY HAVE IT WITH OUR SUPER-GORGEOUS, SUPER-SPECIAL ATTACK AND SEND YOU INTO NEXT WEEK!!
S-SUPER ...??
IS THERE EVEN A SYSTEM LIKE THAT IN BRAIN BURST? THERE'S NOT, IS THERE?
BAN (BANG)
DO IT, SANDY!!
ROGER!!
GASHI (CLANG)

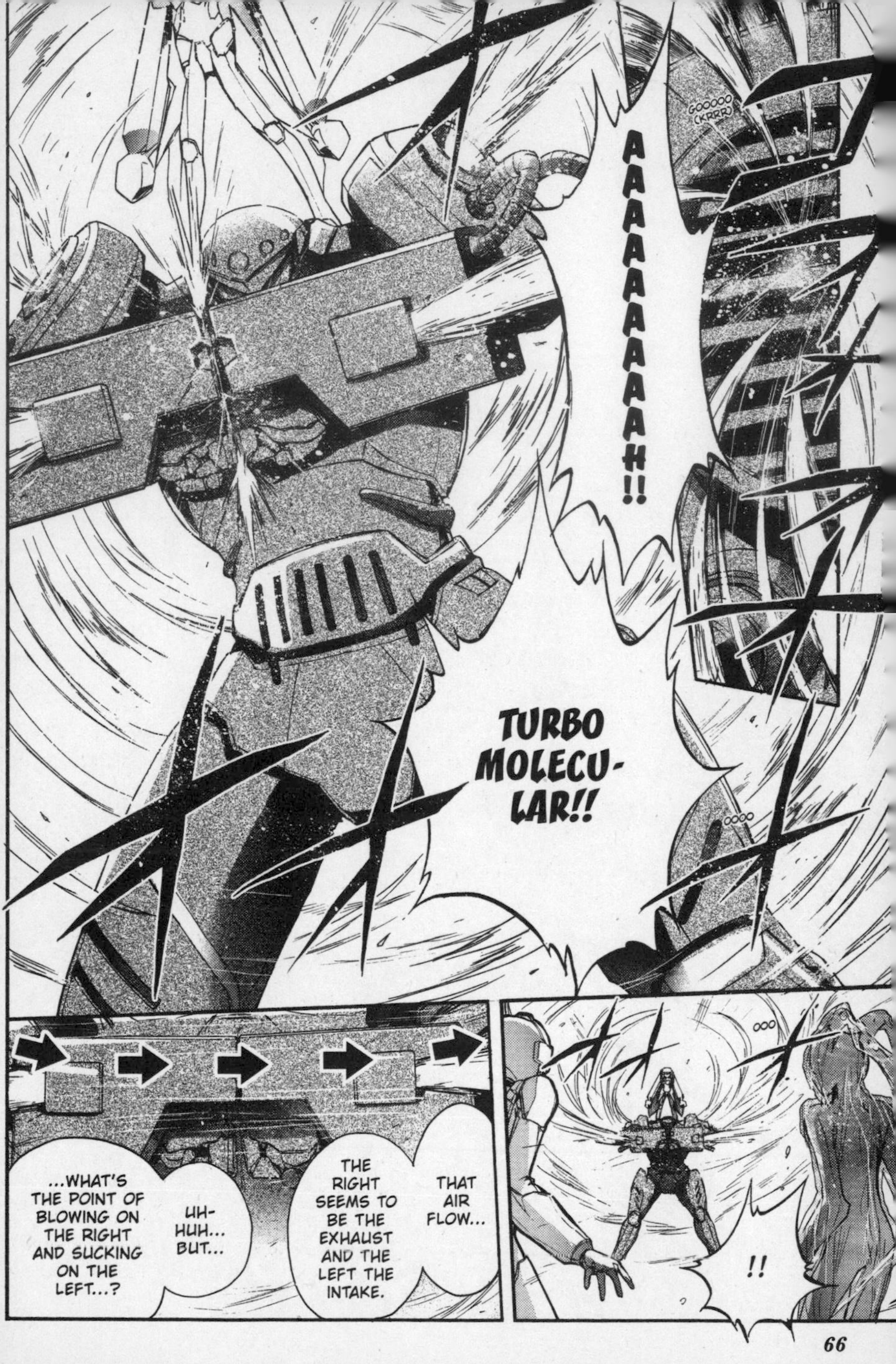
GOOOOO (KRRR)
AAAAAAAAAAAH!!
TURBO MOLECULAR!!
!!
THAT AIR FLOW...
THE RIGHT SEEMS TO BE THE EXHAUST AND THE LEFT THE INTAKE.
UH-HUH... BUT...
...WHAT'S THE POINT OF BLOWING ON THE RIGHT AND SUCKING ON THE LEFT...?

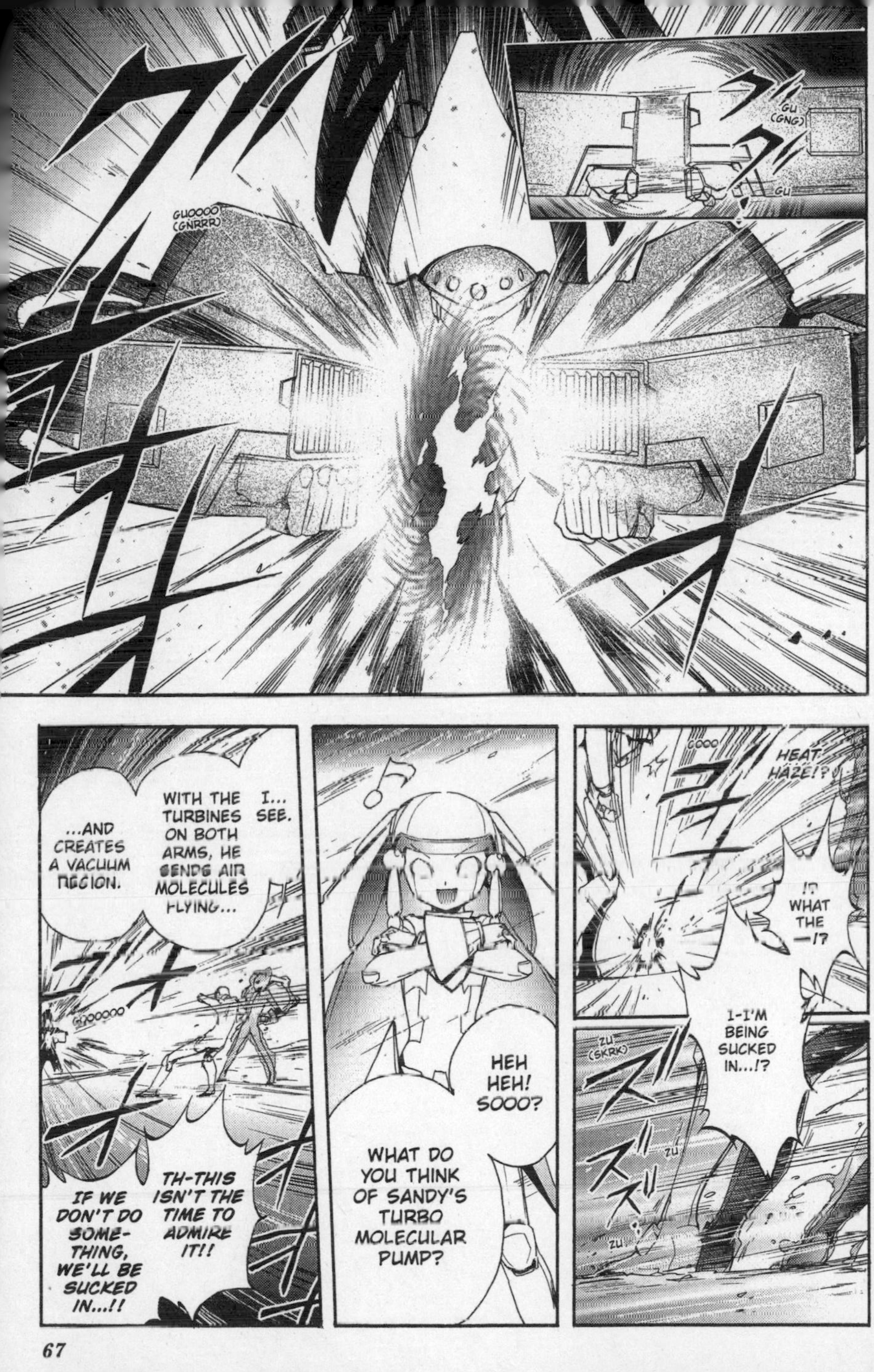
GU (GNG)
GU
GUOOOO (GNRRR)
GOOO
HEAT HAZE!?
!? WHAT THE —!?
I-I'M BEING SUCKED IN...!?
ZU (SKRK)
ZU
ZU
HEH HEH! SOOO?
WHAT DO YOU THINK OF SANDY'S TURBO MOLECULAR PUMP?
I... SEE.
WITH THE TURBINES ON BOTH ARMS, HE SENDS AIR MOLECULES FLYING...
...AND CREATES A VACUUM REGION.
GOOOOOO
TH-THIS ISN'T THE TIME TO ADMIRE IT!!
IF WE DON'T DO SOME-THING, WE'LL BE SUCKED IN...!!

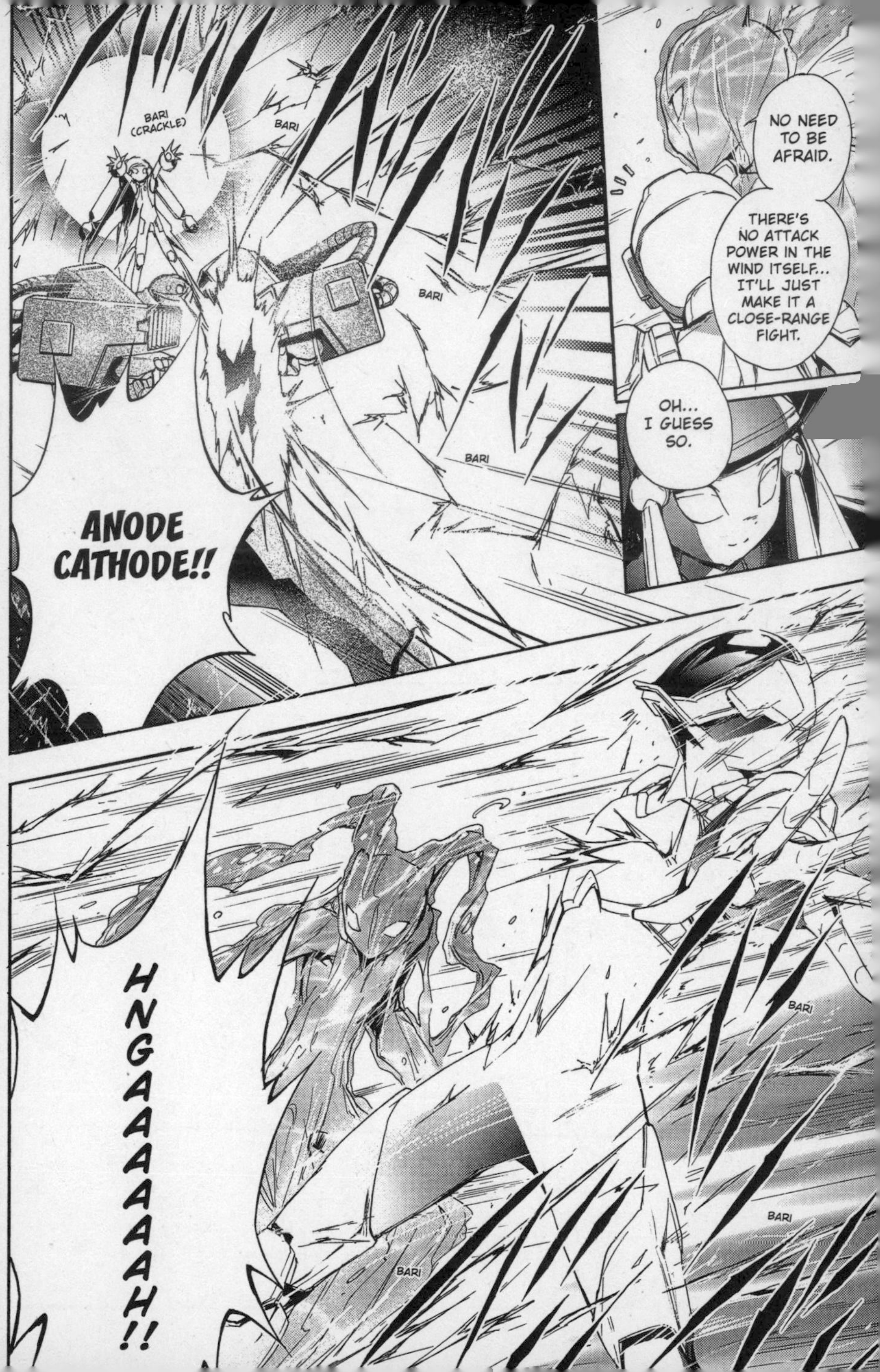
NO NEED TO BE AFRAID.
THERE'S NO ATTACK POWER IN THE WIND ITSELF... IT'LL JUST MAKE IT A CLOSE-RANGE FIGHT.
OH... I GUESS SO.
BARI (CRACKLE)
BARI
BARI
BARI
ANODE CATHODE!!
BARI
BARI
BARI
HNGAAAAAAH!!

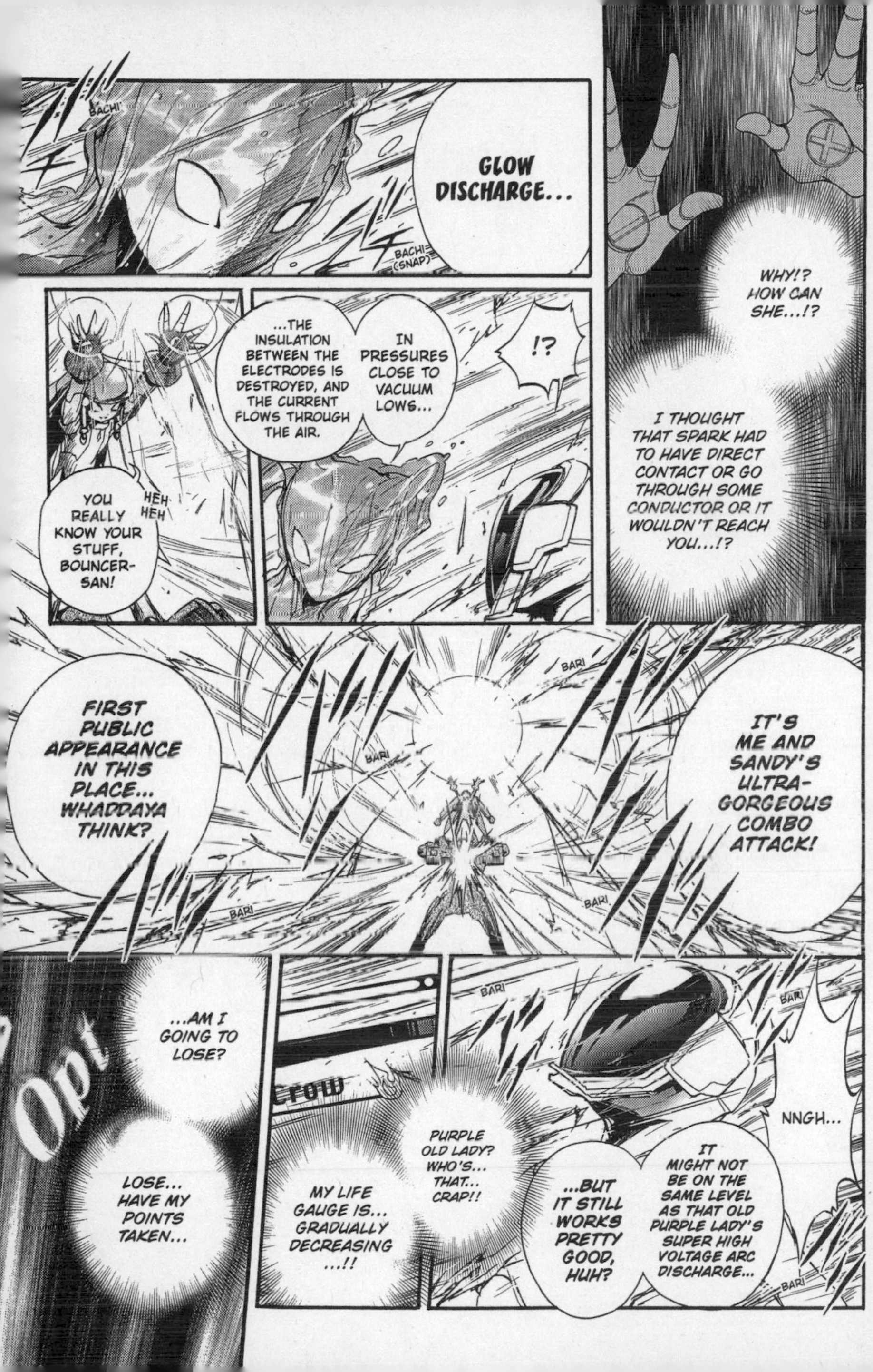

WHY!? HOW CAN SHE...!?
I THOUGHT THAT SPARK HAD TO HAVE DIRECT CONTACT OR GO THROUGH SOME CONDUCTOR OR IT WOULDN'T REACH YOU...!?
BACHI
GLOW DISCHARGE...
BACHI (SNAP)
!?
IN PRESSURES CLOSE TO VACUUM LOWS...
...THE INSULATION BETWEEN THE ELECTRODES IS DESTROYED, AND THE CURRENT FLOWS THROUGH THE AIR.
HEH HEH
YOU REALLY KNOW YOUR STUFF, BOUNCER-SAN!
BARI
IT'S ME AND SANDY'S ULTRA-GORGEOUS COMBO ATTACK!
BARI
FIRST PUBLIC APPEARANCE IN THIS PLACE... WHADDAYA THINK?
BARI
BARI
BARI
BARI
NNGH...
IT MIGHT NOT BE ON THE SAME LEVEL AS THAT OLD PURPLE LADY'S SUPER HIGH VOLTAGE ARC DISCHARGE...
...BUT IT STILL WORKS PRETTY GOOD, HUH?
BARI
BARI
Crow
PURPLE OLD LADY? WHO'S... THAT... CRAP!!
MY LIFE GAUGE IS... GRADUALLY DECREASING ...!!
Opt
...AM I GOING TO LOSE?
LOSE... HAVE MY POINTS TAKEN...

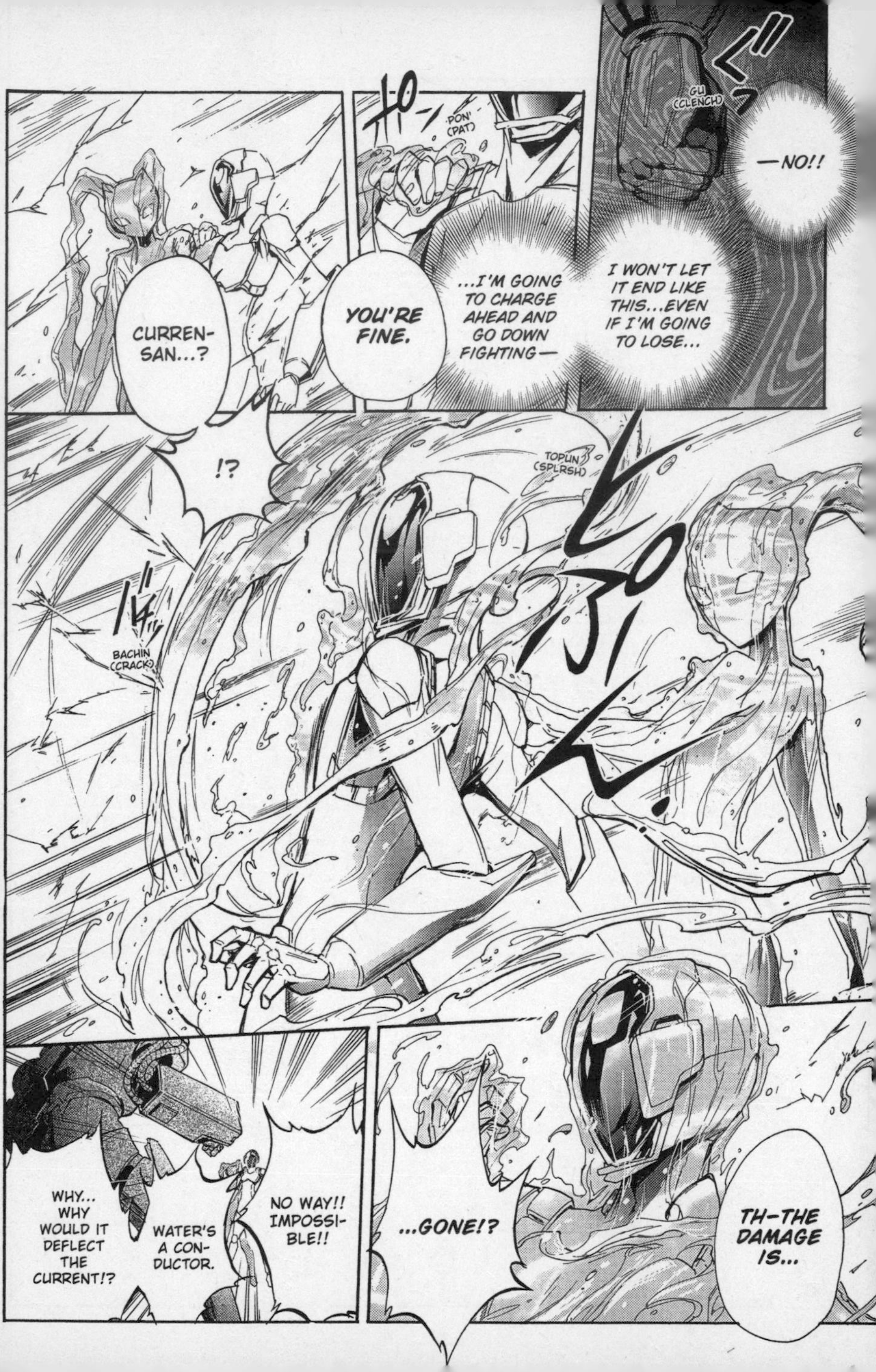
GU (CLENCH)
—NO!!
I WON'T LET IT END LIKE THIS...EVEN IF I'M GOING TO LOSE...
PON' (PAT)
...I'M GOING TO CHARGE AHEAD AND GO DOWN FIGHTING—
YOU'RE FINE.
CURREN-SAN...?
TOPUN (SPLRSH)
!?
BACHIN (CRACK)
TH-THE DAMAGE IS...
...GONE!?
NO WAY!! IMPOSSI-BLE!!
WATER'S A CON-DUCTOR.
WHY... WHY WOULD IT DEFLECT THE CURRENT!?

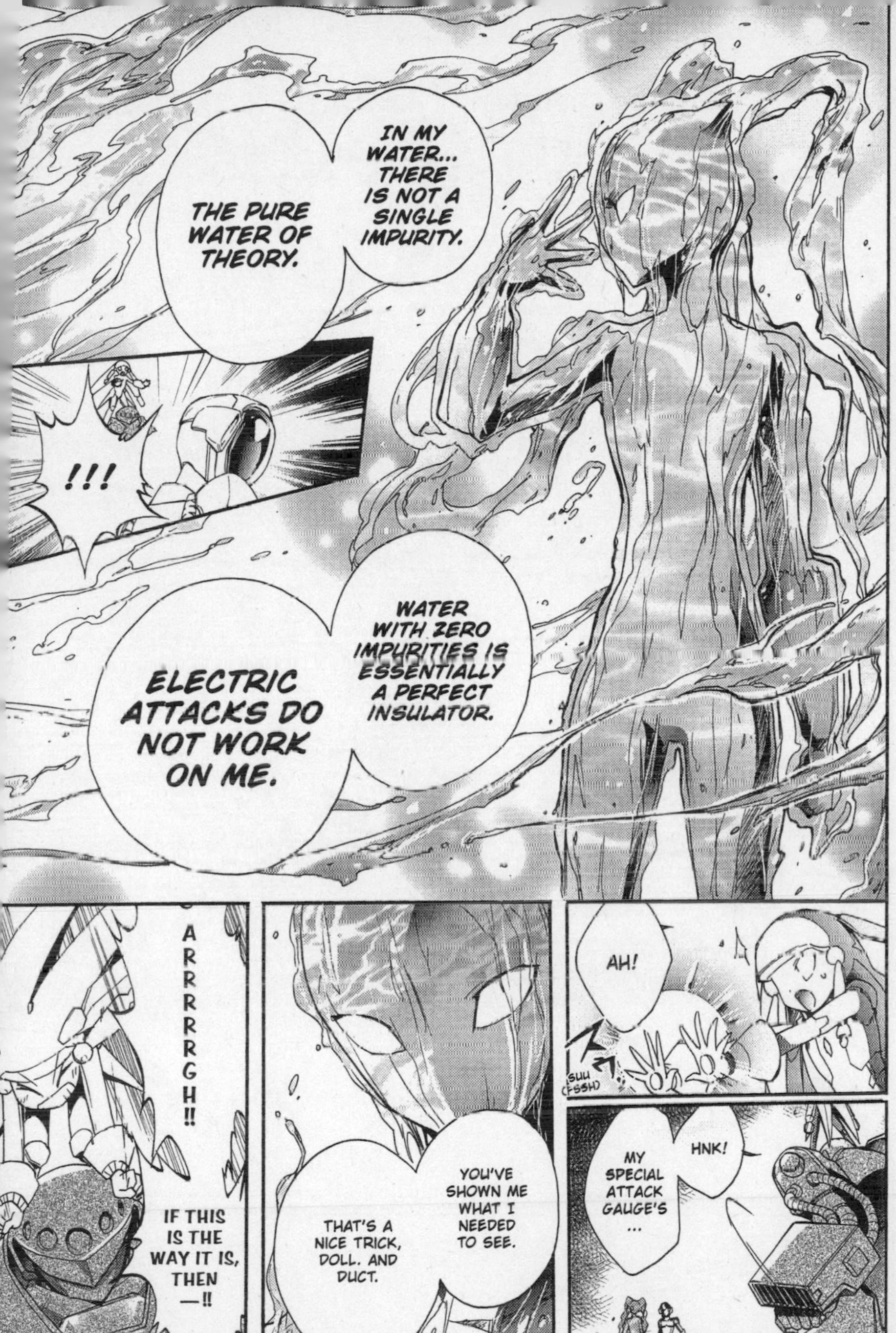

IN MY WATER... THERE IS NOT A SINGLE IMPURITY.
THE PURE WATER OF THEORY.
!!!
WATER WITH ZERO IMPURITIES IS ESSENTIALLY A PERFECT INSULATOR.
ELECTRIC ATTACKS DO NOT WORK ON ME.
AH!
SUU (FSSH)
HNK!
MY SPECIAL ATTACK GAUGE'S ...
YOU'VE SHOWN ME WHAT I NEEDED TO SEE.
THAT'S A NICE TRICK, DOLL. AND DUCT.
ARRRRRGH!!
IF THIS IS THE WAY IT IS, THEN —!!

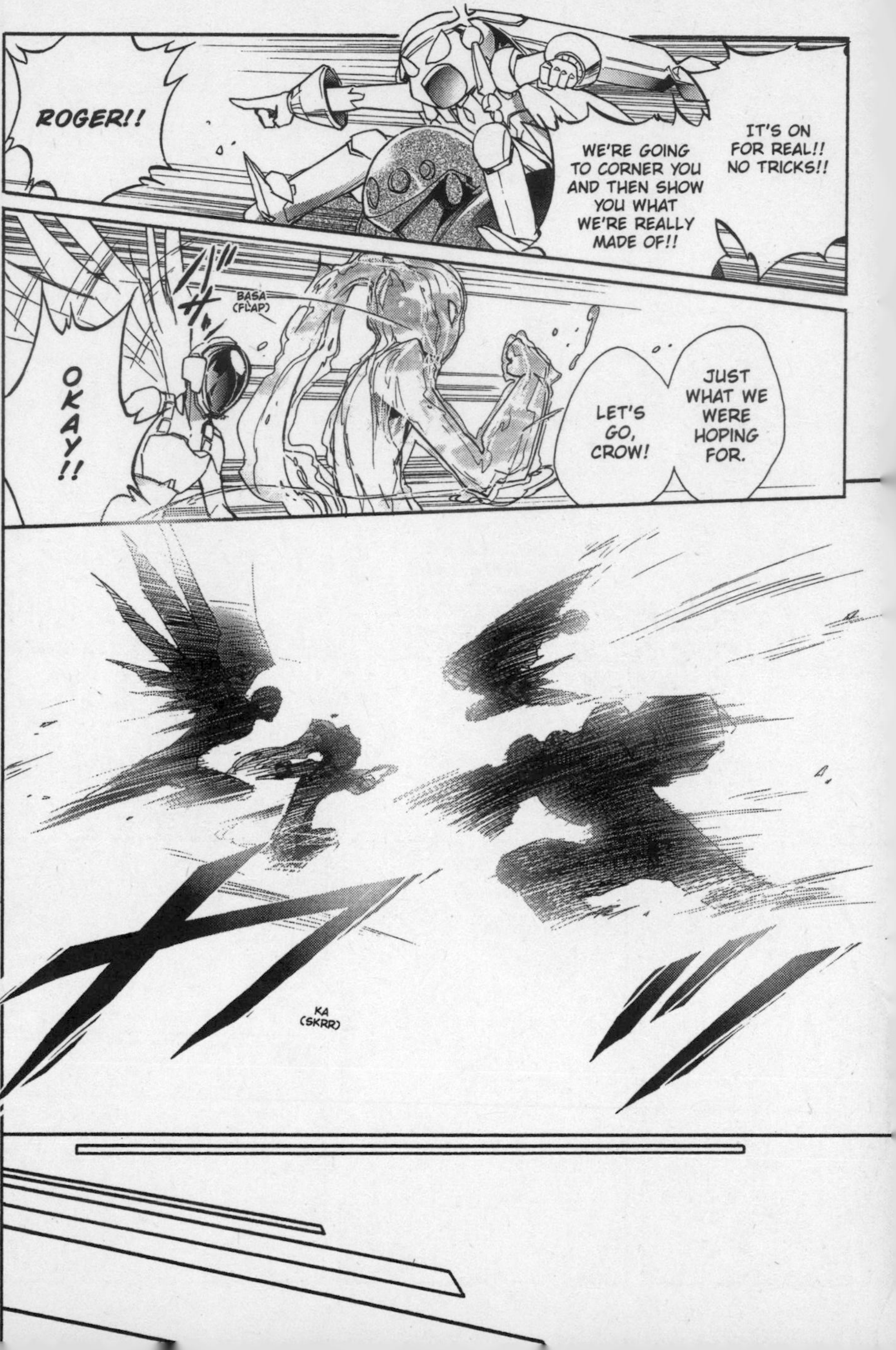
IT'S ON FOR REAL!! NO TRICKS!!
WE'RE GOING TO CORNER YOU AND THEN SHOW YOU WHAT WE'RE REALLY MADE OF!!
ROGER!!
JUST WHAT WE WERE HOPING FOR.
LET'S GO, CROW!
BASA (FLAP)
OKAY!!
KA (SKRR)

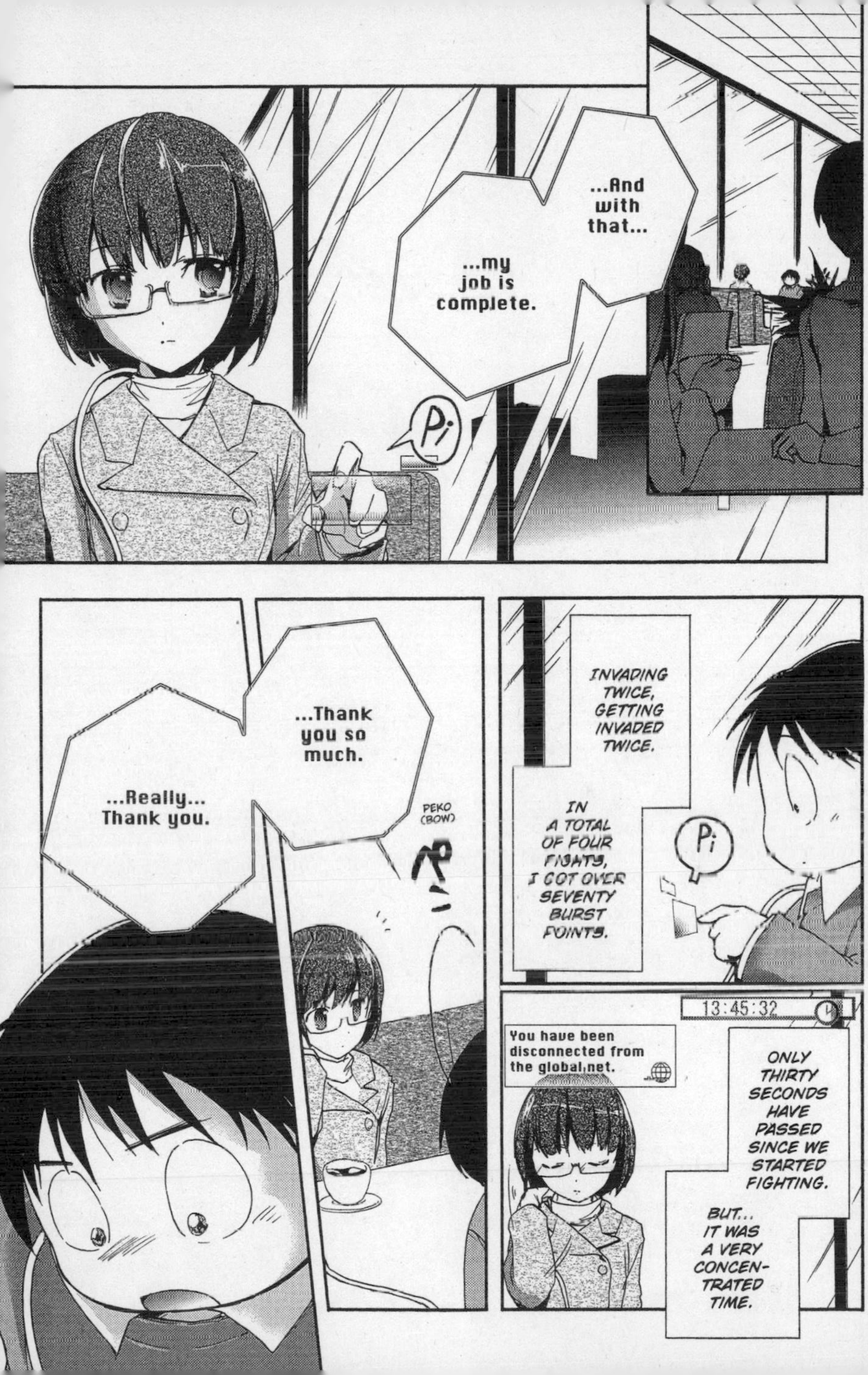

...And with that...
...my job is complete.
Pi
INVADING TWICE, GETTING INVADED TWICE.
IN A TOTAL OF FOUR FIGHTS, I GOT OVER SEVENTY BURST POINTS.
Pi
13:45:32
You have been disconnected from the global net.
ONLY THIRTY SECONDS HAVE PASSED SINCE WE STARTED FIGHTING.
BUT... IT WAS A VERY CONCENTRATED TIME.
...Thank you so much.
...Really... Thank you.
PEKO (BOW)

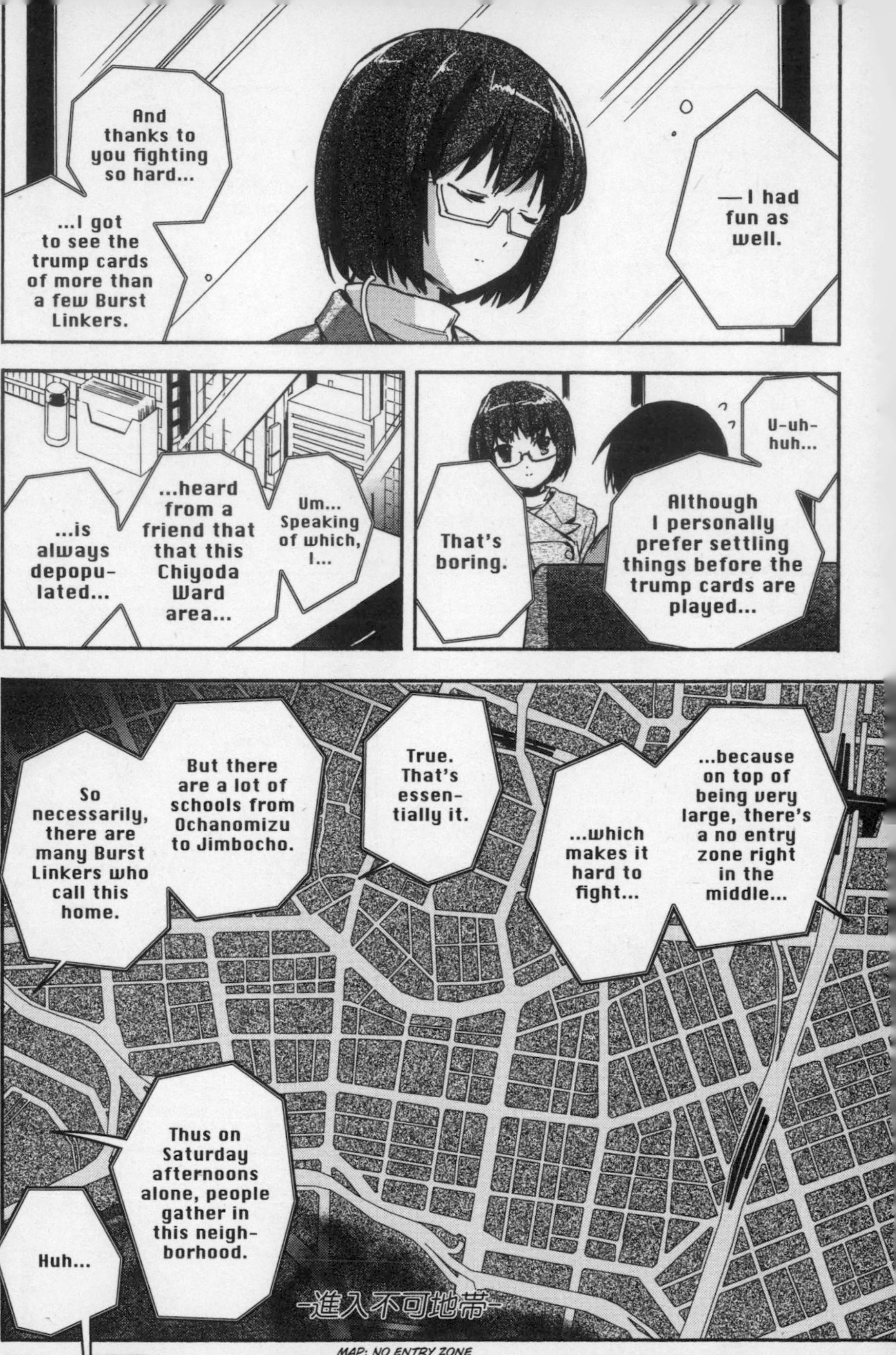
—I had fun as well.
And thanks to you fighting so hard...
...I got to see the trump cards of more than a few Burst Linkers.
U-uh-huh...
Although I personally prefer settling things before the trump cards are played...
That's boring.
Um... Speaking of which, I...
...heard from a friend that that this Chiyoda Ward area...
...is always depopulated...
...because on top of being very large, there's a no entry zone right in the middle...
...which makes it hard to fight...
True. That's essentially it.
But there are a lot of schools from Ochanomizu to Jimbocho.
So necessarily, there are many Burst Linkers who call this home.
Thus on Saturday afternoons alone, people gather in this neighborhood.
Huh...
—進入不可地帯—
MAP: NO ENTRY ZONE

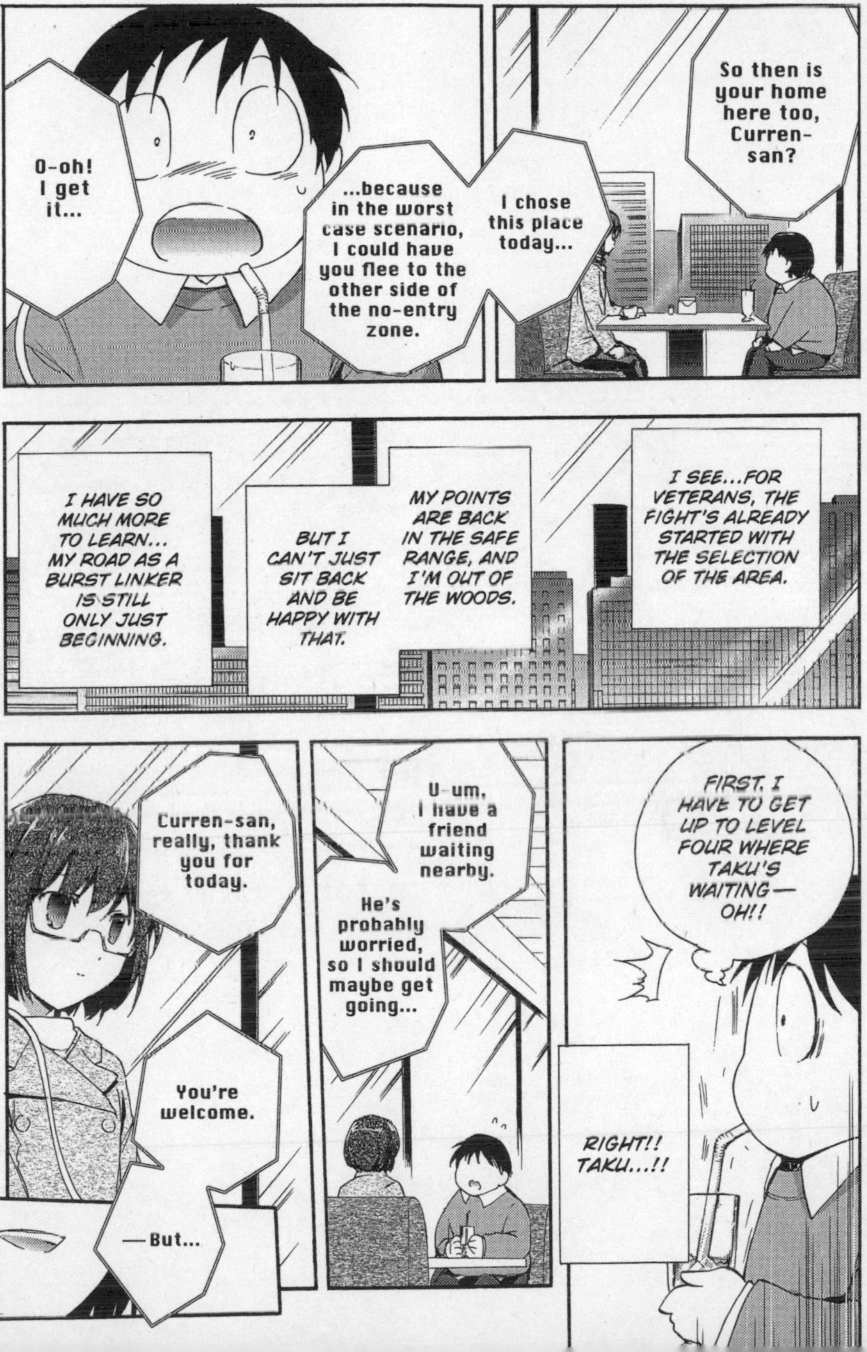
So then is your home here too, Curren-san?
I chose this place today...
...because in the worst case scenario, I could have you flee to the other side of the no-entry zone.
O-oh! I get it...
I SEE...FOR VETERANS, THE FIGHT'S ALREADY STARTED WITH THE SELECTION OF THE AREA.
MY POINTS ARE BACK IN THE SAFE RANGE, AND I'M OUT OF THE WOODS.
BUT I CAN'T JUST SIT BACK AND BE HAPPY WITH THAT.
I HAVE SO MUCH MORE TO LEARN... MY ROAD AS A BURST LINKER IS STILL ONLY JUST BEGINNING.
FIRST, I HAVE TO GET UP TO LEVEL FOUR WHERE TAKU'S WAITING—OH!!
RIGHT!! TAKU...!!
U-um, I have a friend waiting nearby.
He's probably worried, so I should maybe get going...
Curren-san, really, thank you for today.
You're welcome.
—But...

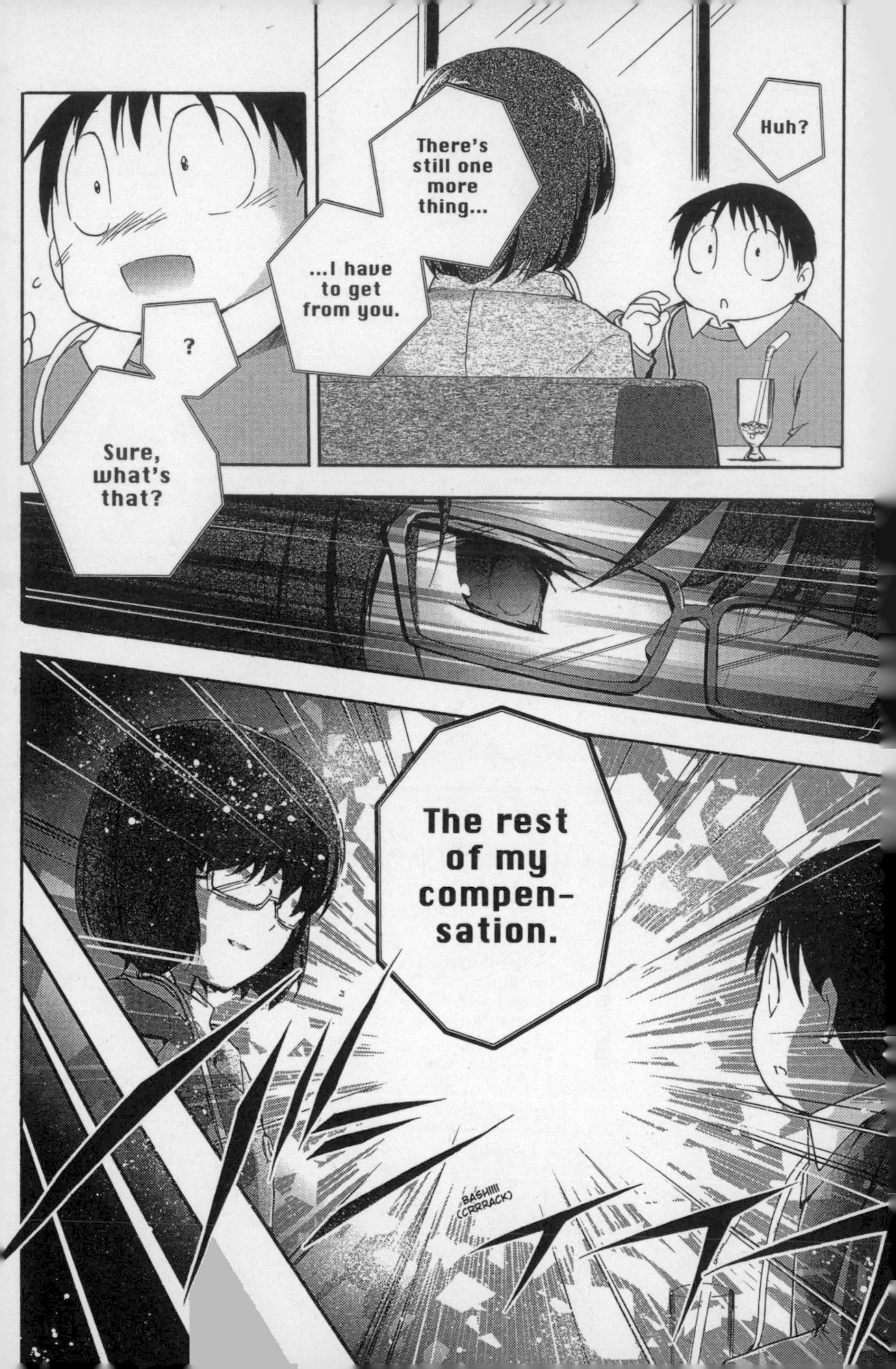
Huh?
There's still one more thing...
...I have to get from you.
?
Sure, what's that?
The rest of my compensation.
BASHIIIII (CRRRACK)

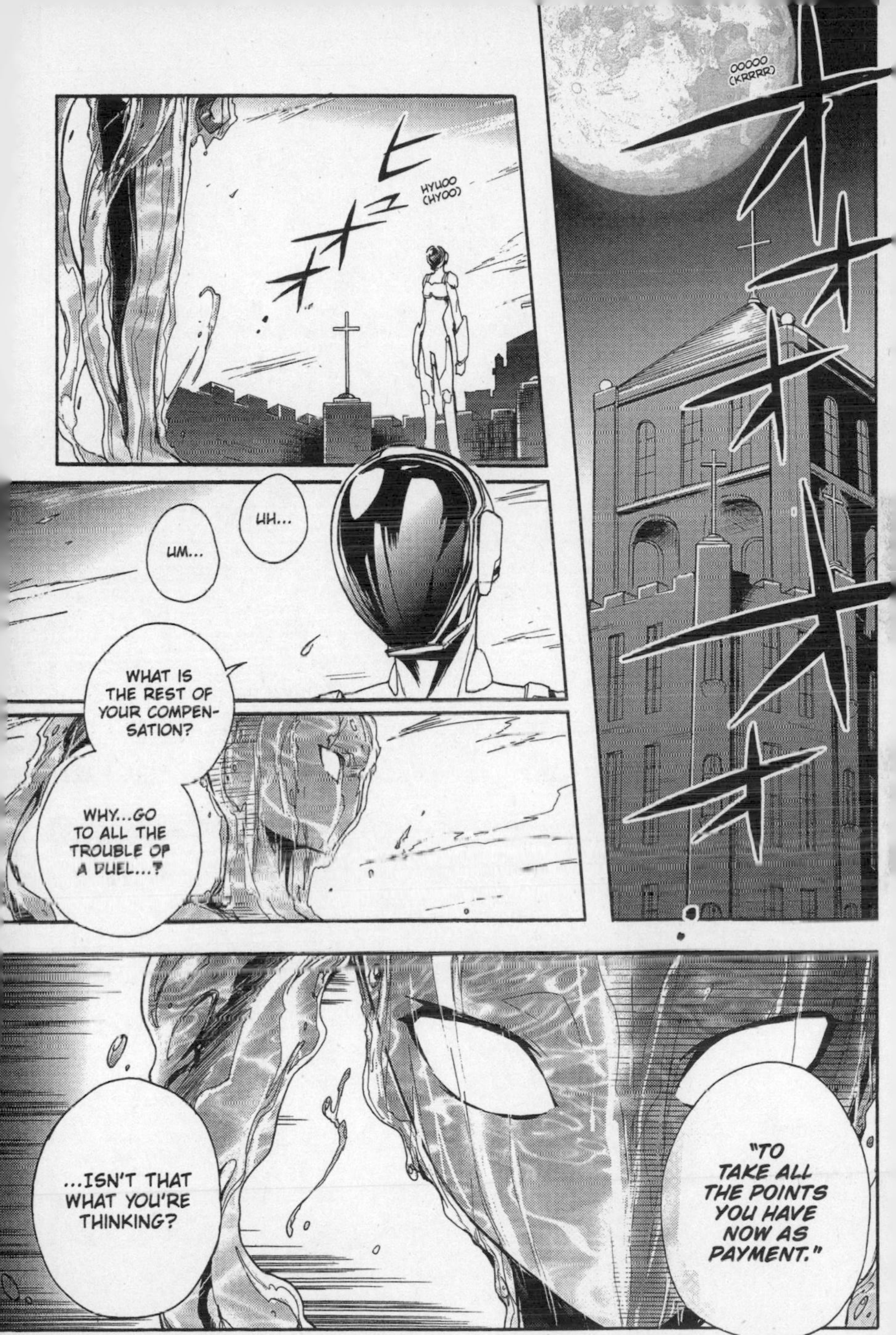

OOOOO (KRRRR)
HYUOO (HYOO)
UH...
UM...
WHAT IS THE REST OF YOUR COMPENSATION?
WHY...GO TO ALL THE TROUBLE OF A DUEL...?
"TO TAKE ALL THE POINTS YOU HAVE NOW AS PAYMENT."
...ISN'T THAT WHAT YOU'RE THINKING?

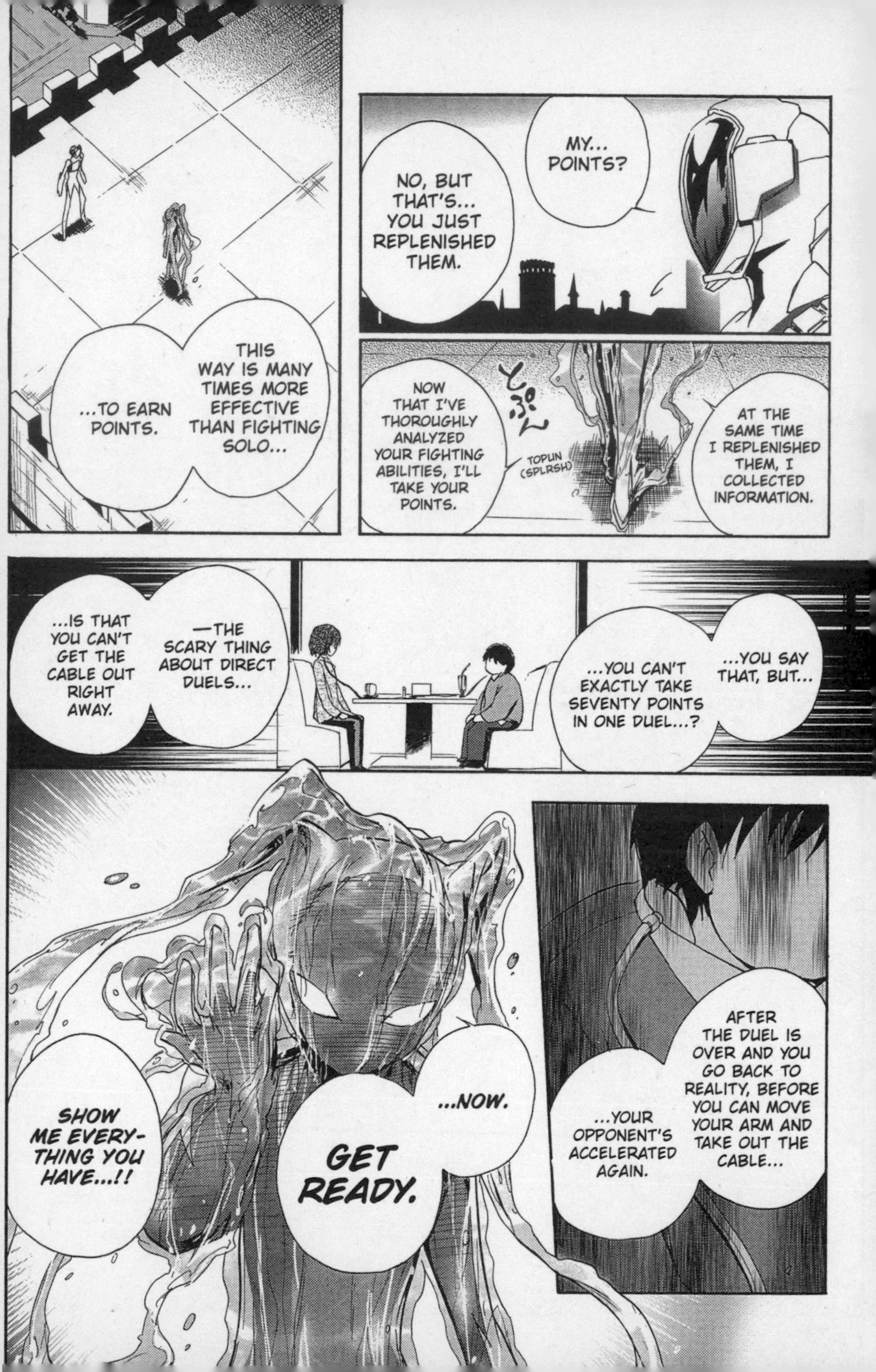
MY... POINTS?
NO, BUT THAT'S... YOU JUST REPLENISHED THEM.
AT THE SAME TIME I REPLENISHED THEM, I COLLECTED INFORMATION.
とぷん
TOPUN (SPLRSH)
NOW THAT I'VE THOROUGHLY ANALYZED YOUR FIGHTING ABILITIES, I'LL TAKE YOUR POINTS.
THIS WAY IS MANY TIMES MORE EFFECTIVE THAN FIGHTING SOLO...
...TO EARN POINTS.
...YOU SAY THAT, BUT...
...YOU CAN'T EXACTLY TAKE SEVENTY POINTS IN ONE DUEL...?
—THE SCARY THING ABOUT DIRECT DUELS...
...IS THAT YOU CAN'T GET THE CABLE OUT RIGHT AWAY.
AFTER THE DUEL IS OVER AND YOU GO BACK TO REALITY, BEFORE YOU CAN MOVE YOUR ARM AND TAKE OUT THE CABLE...
...YOUR OPPONENT'S ACCELERATED AGAIN.
...NOW.
GET READY.
SHOW ME EVERY-THING YOU HAVE...!!

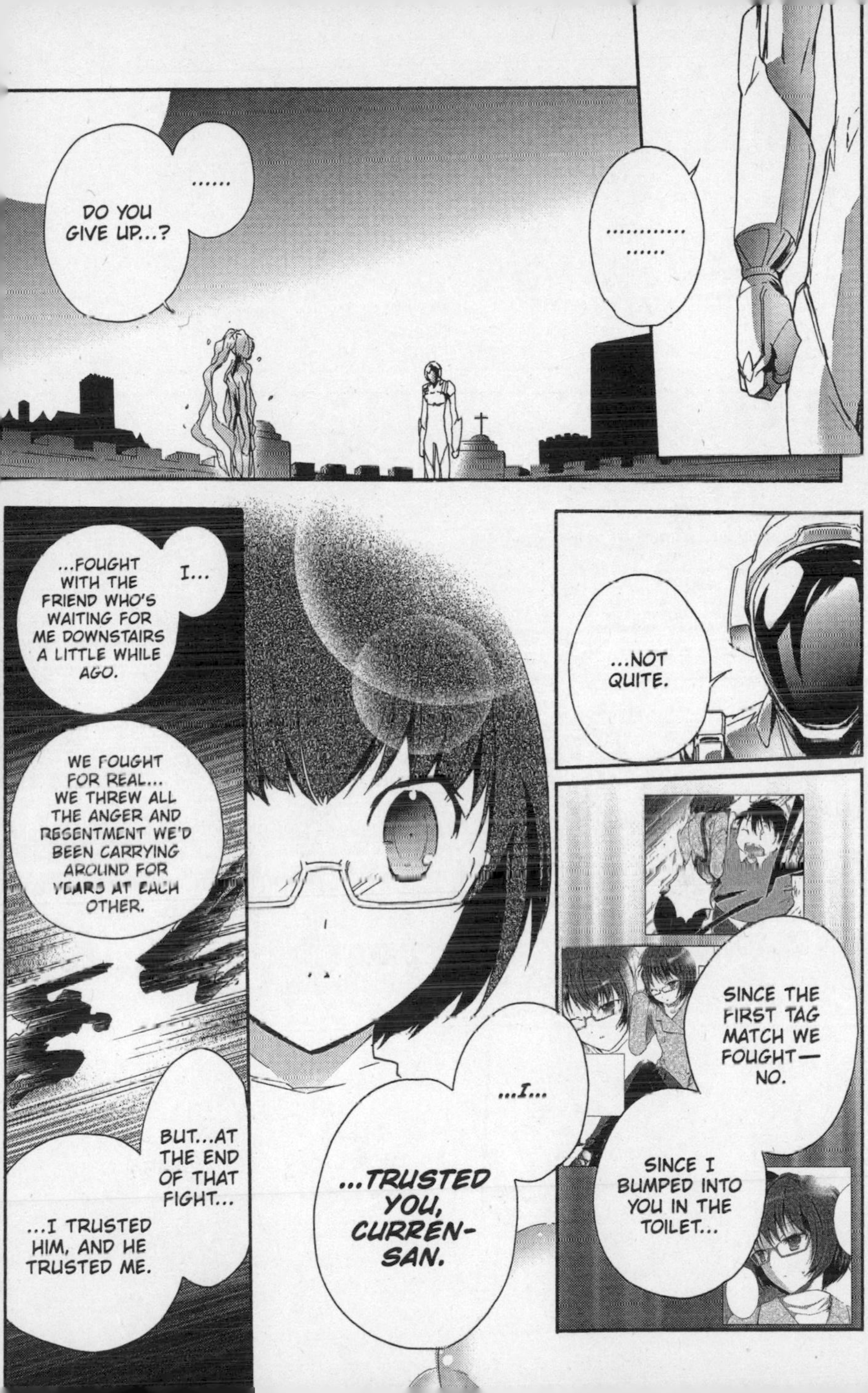

....
...... DO YOU GIVE UP...?
...NOT QUITE.
SINCE THE FIRST TAG MATCH WE FOUGHT— NO.
SINCE I BUMPED INTO YOU IN THE TOILET...
...I...
...TRUSTED YOU, CURREN-SAN.
I...
...FOUGHT WITH THE FRIEND WHO'S WAITING FOR ME DOWNSTAIRS A LITTLE WHILE AGO.
WE FOUGHT FOR REAL... WE THREW ALL THE ANGER AND RESENTMENT WE'D BEEN CARRYING AROUND FOR YEARS AT EACH OTHER.
BUT...AT THE END OF THAT FIGHT...
...I TRUSTED HIM, AND HE TRUSTED ME.

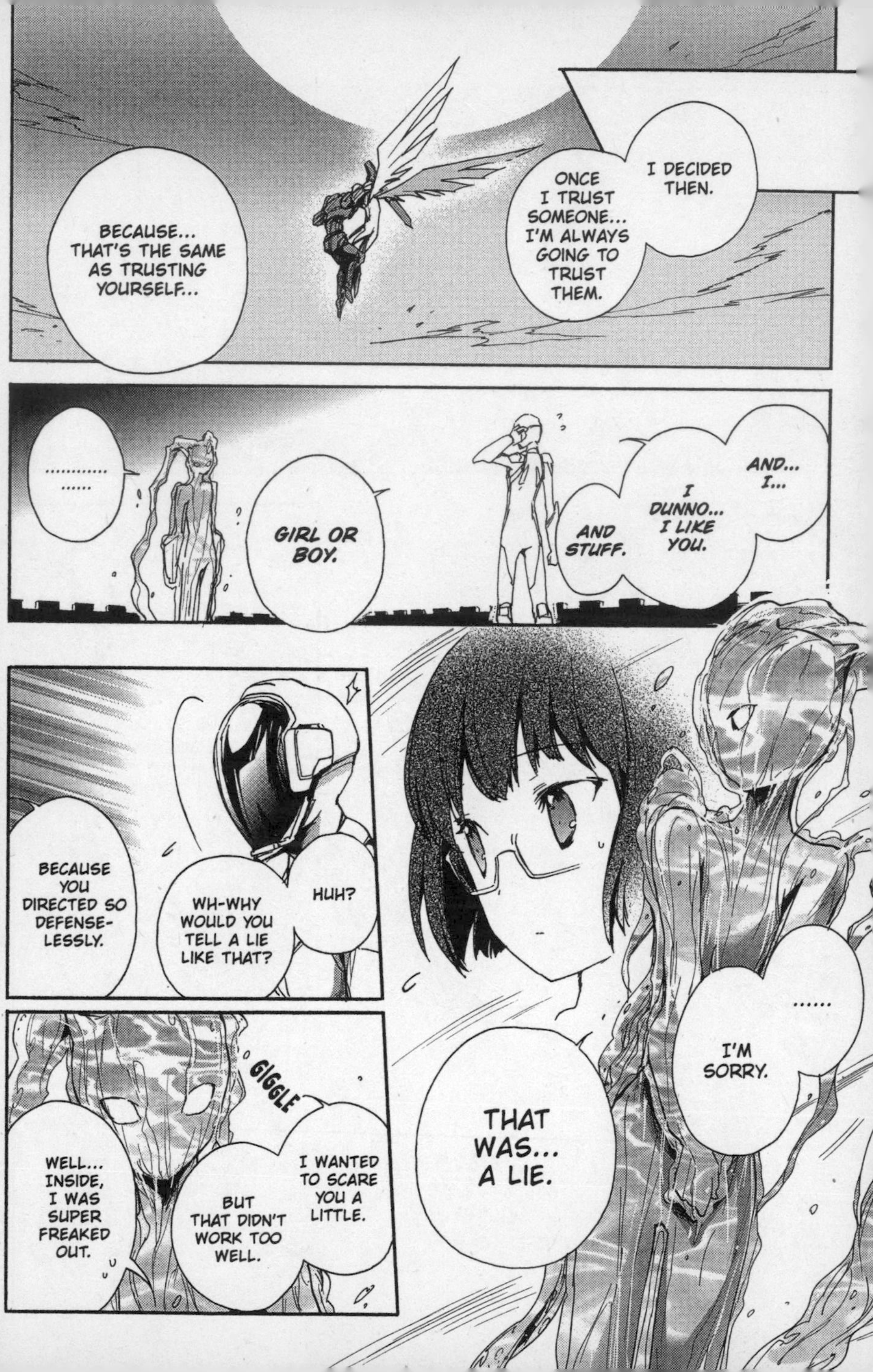
I DECIDED THEN.
ONCE I TRUST SOMEONE... I'M ALWAYS GOING TO TRUST THEM.
BECAUSE... THAT'S THE SAME AS TRUSTING YOURSELF...
AND... I...
I DUNNO... I LIKE YOU.
AND STUFF.
GIRL OR BOY.
....
...... I'M SORRY.
THAT WAS... A LIE.
HUH?
WH-WHY WOULD YOU TELL A LIE LIKE THAT?
BECAUSE YOU DIRECTED SO DEFENSE-LESSLY.
I WANTED TO SCARE YOU A LITTLE.
GIGGLE
BUT THAT DIDN'T WORK TOO WELL.
WELL... INSIDE, I WAS SUPER FREAKED OUT.

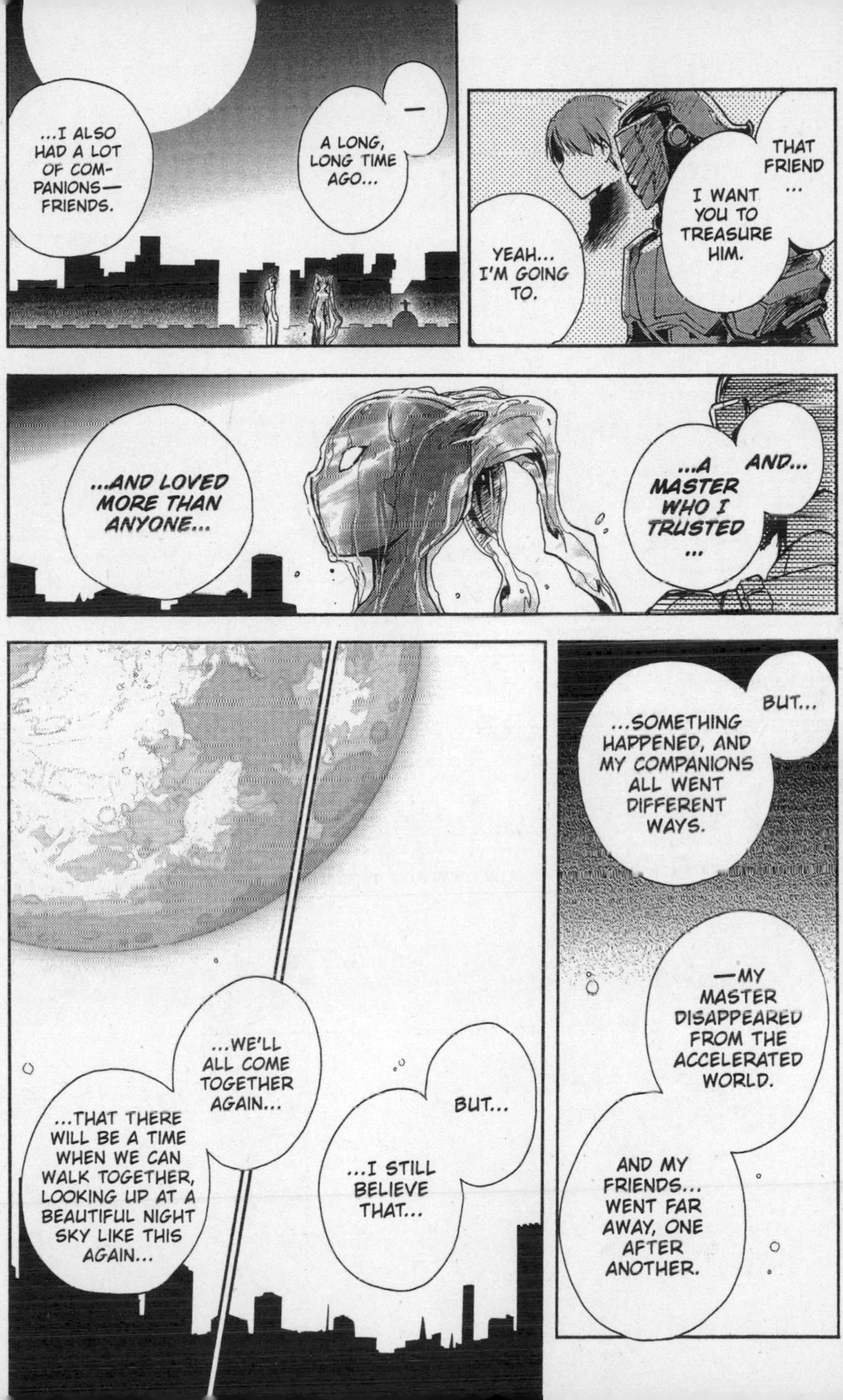
THAT FRIEND...
I WANT YOU TO TREASURE HIM.
YEAH... I'M GOING TO.
—
A LONG, LONG TIME AGO...
...I ALSO HAD A LOT OF COMPANIONS—FRIENDS.
AND...
...A MASTER WHO I TRUSTED...
...AND LOVED MORE THAN ANYONE...
BUT...
...SOMETHING HAPPENED, AND MY COMPANIONS ALL WENT DIFFERENT WAYS.
—MY MASTER DISAPPEARED FROM THE ACCELERATED WORLD.
AND MY FRIENDS... WENT FAR AWAY, ONE AFTER ANOTHER.
BUT...
...I STILL BELIEVE THAT...
...WE'LL ALL COME TOGETHER AGAIN...
...THAT THERE WILL BE A TIME WHEN WE CAN WALK TOGETHER, LOOKING UP AT A BEAUTIFUL NIGHT SKY LIKE THIS AGAIN...

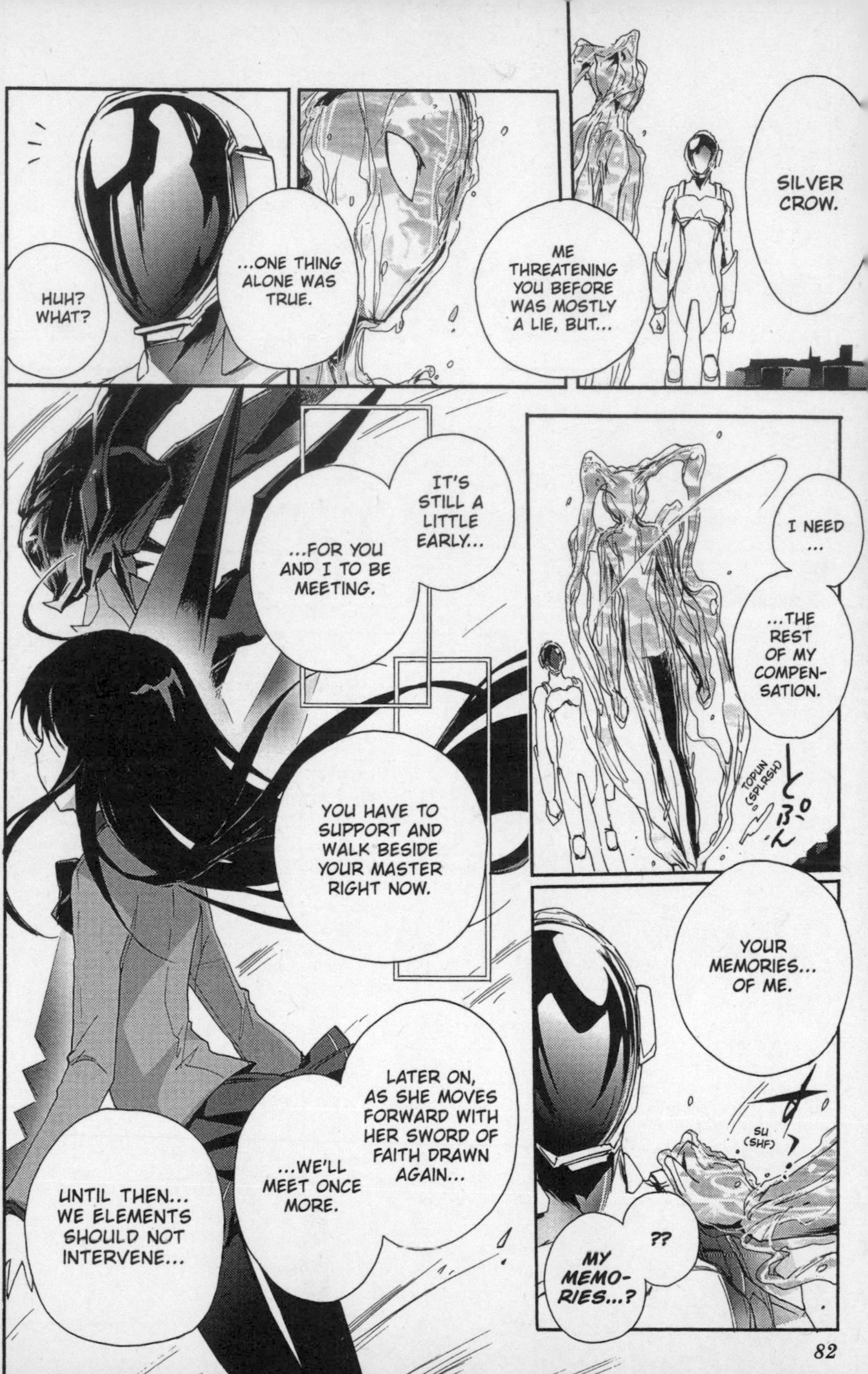
SILVER CROW.
ME THREATENING YOU BEFORE WAS MOSTLY A LIE, BUT...
...ONE THING ALONE WAS TRUE.
HUH? WHAT?
I NEED ...
...THE REST OF MY COMPENSATION.
とぷん
TOPUN (SPLASH)
YOUR MEMORIES... OF ME.
すっ
SU (SHF)
??
MY MEMO-RIES...?
IT'S STILL A LITTLE EARLY...
...FOR YOU AND I TO BE MEETING.
YOU HAVE TO SUPPORT AND WALK BESIDE YOUR MASTER RIGHT NOW.
LATER ON, AS SHE MOVES FORWARD WITH HER SWORD OF FAITH DRAWN AGAIN...
...WE'LL MEET ONCE MORE.
UNTIL THEN... WE ELEMENTS SHOULD NOT INTERVENE...

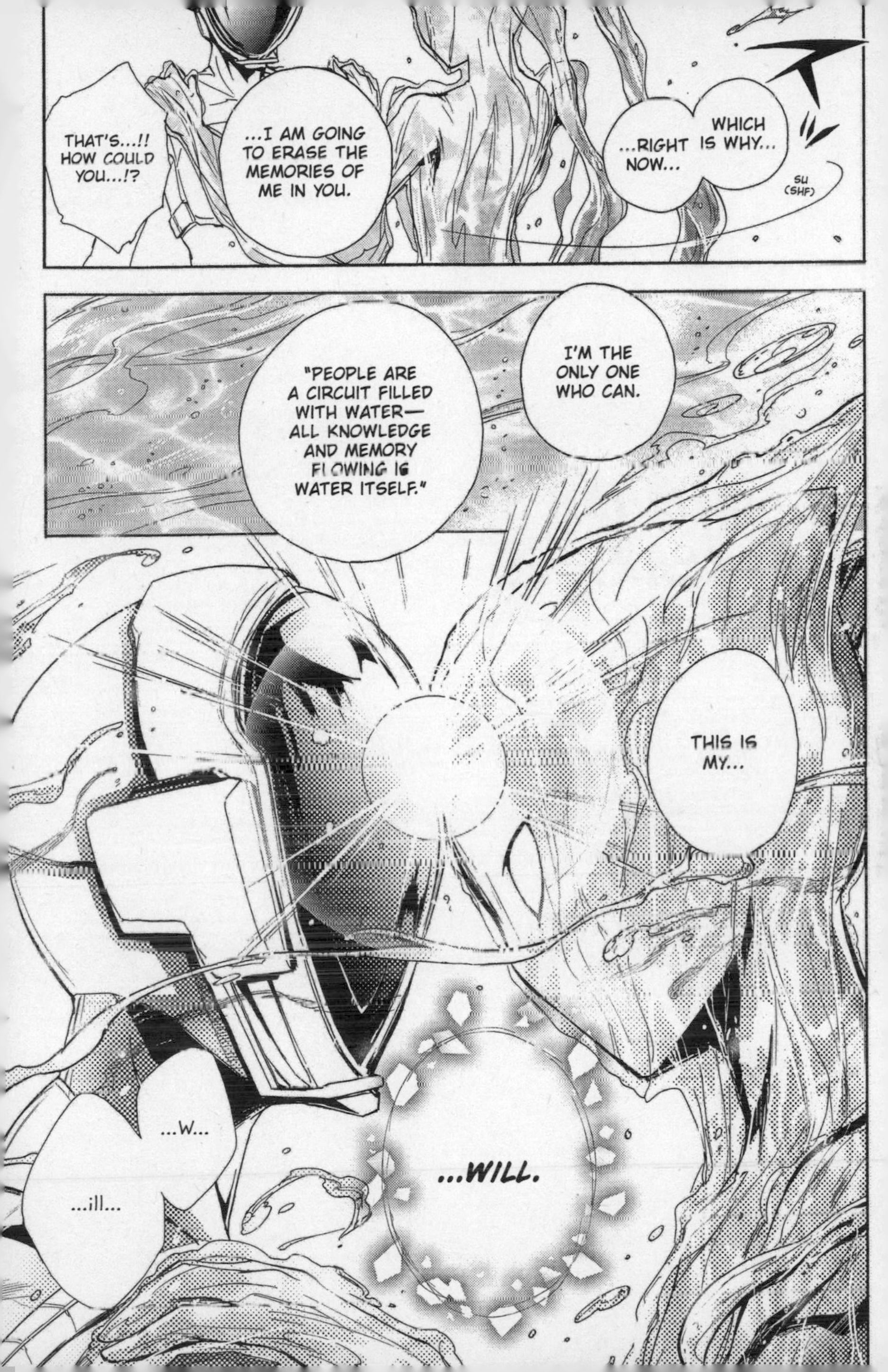
SU (SHF)
WHICH IS WHY...
...RIGHT NOW...
...I AM GOING TO ERASE THE MEMORIES OF ME IN YOU.
THAT'S...!! HOW COULD YOU...!?
I'M THE ONLY ONE WHO CAN.
"PEOPLE ARE A CIRCUIT FILLED WITH WATER— ALL KNOWLEDGE AND MEMORY FLOWING IS WATER ITSELF."
THIS IS MY...
...WILL.
...W...
...ill...

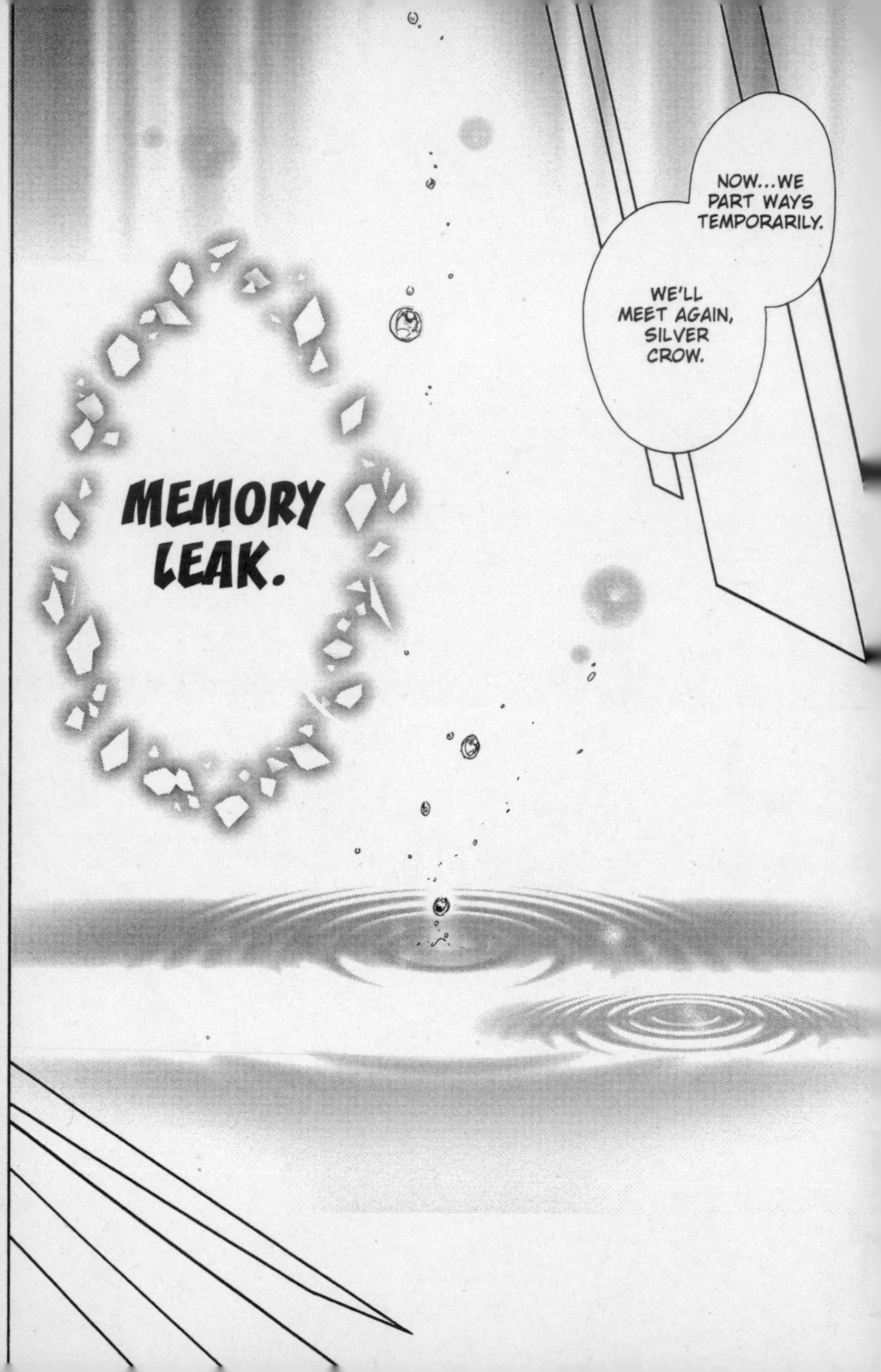
NOW...WE PART WAYS TEMPORARILY.
WE'LL MEET AGAIN, SILVER CROW.
MEMORY LEAK.

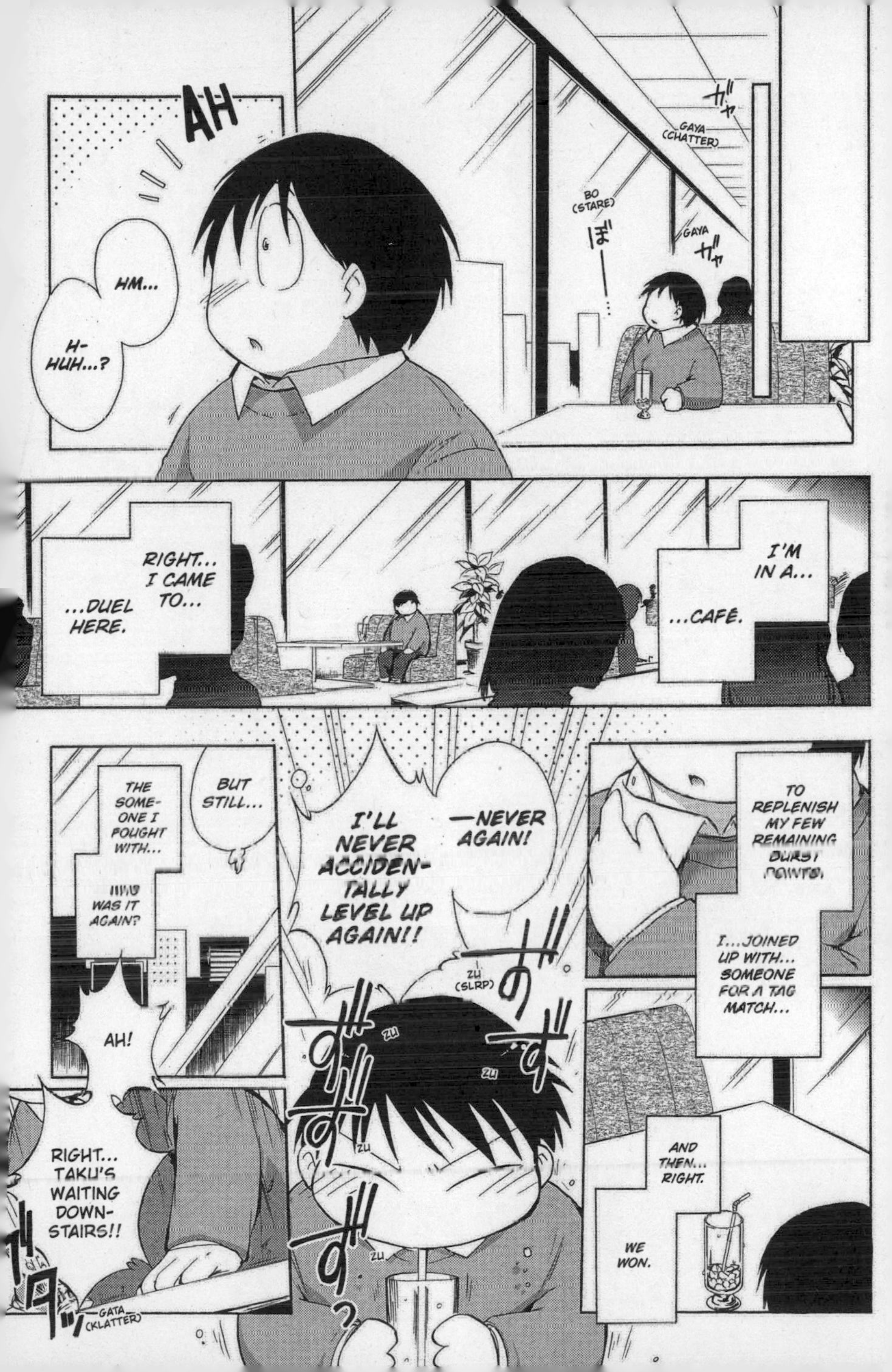
GAYA (CHATTER)
BO (STARE)
GAYA
AH
HM...
H-HUH...?
I'M IN A... ...CAFÉ.
RIGHT... I CAME TO... ...DUEL HERE.
TO REPLENISH MY FEW REMAINING BURST POINTS,
I...JOINED UP WITH... SOMEONE FOR A TAG MATCH...
AND THEN... RIGHT.
WE WON.
—NEVER AGAIN!
I'LL NEVER ACCIDENTALLY LEVEL UP AGAIN!!
ZU (SLRP)
ZU
ZU
ZU
ZU
BUT STILL...
THE SOMEONE I FOUGHT WITH...
WHO WAS IT AGAIN?
AH!
RIGHT... TAKU'S WAITING DOWNSTAIRS!!
GATA (KLATTER)

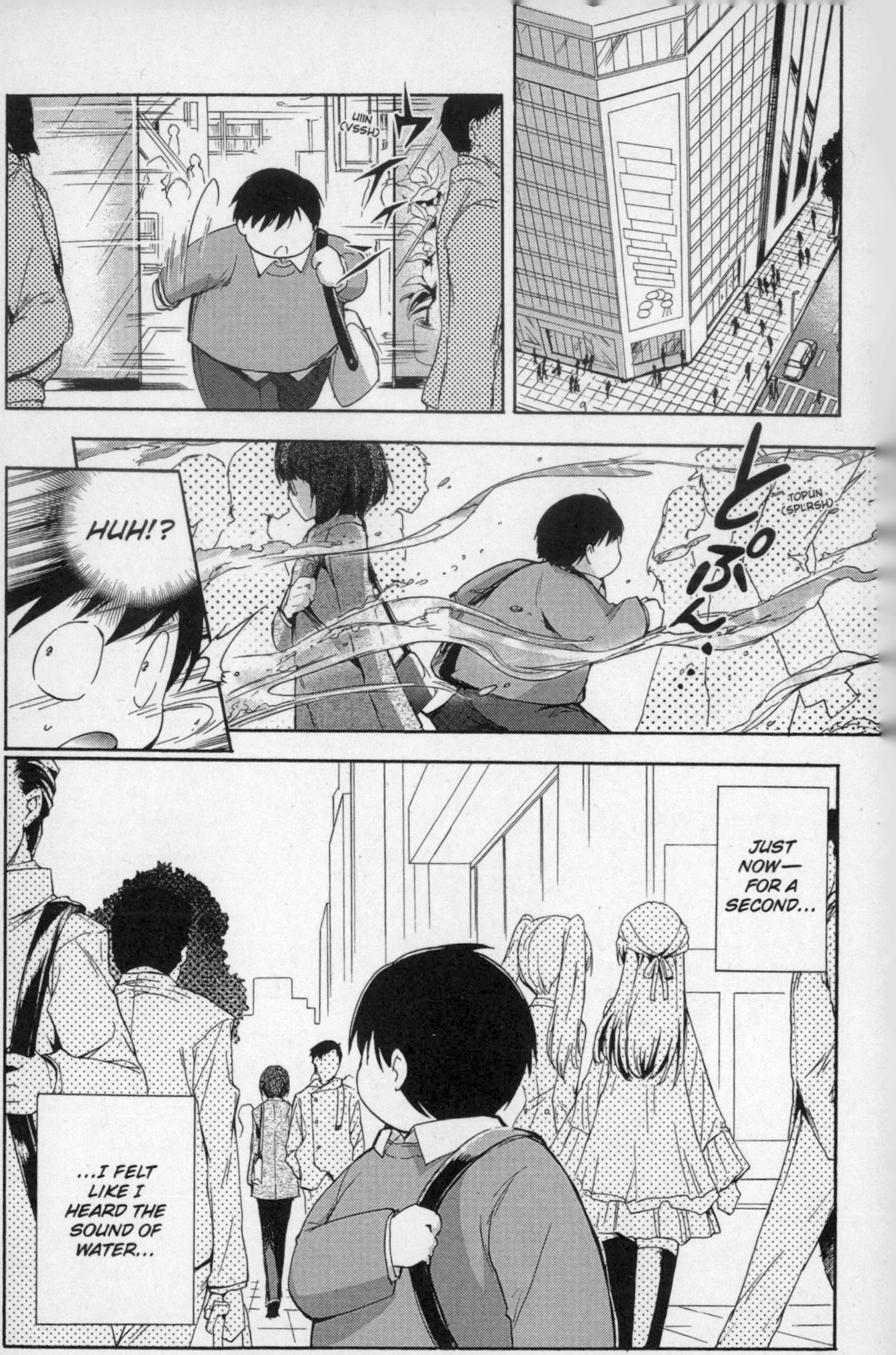
UIIN (VSSH)
とぷん
TOPUN (SPLRSH)
HUH!?
JUST NOW— FOR A SECOND...
...I FELT LIKE I HEARD THE SOUND OF WATER...

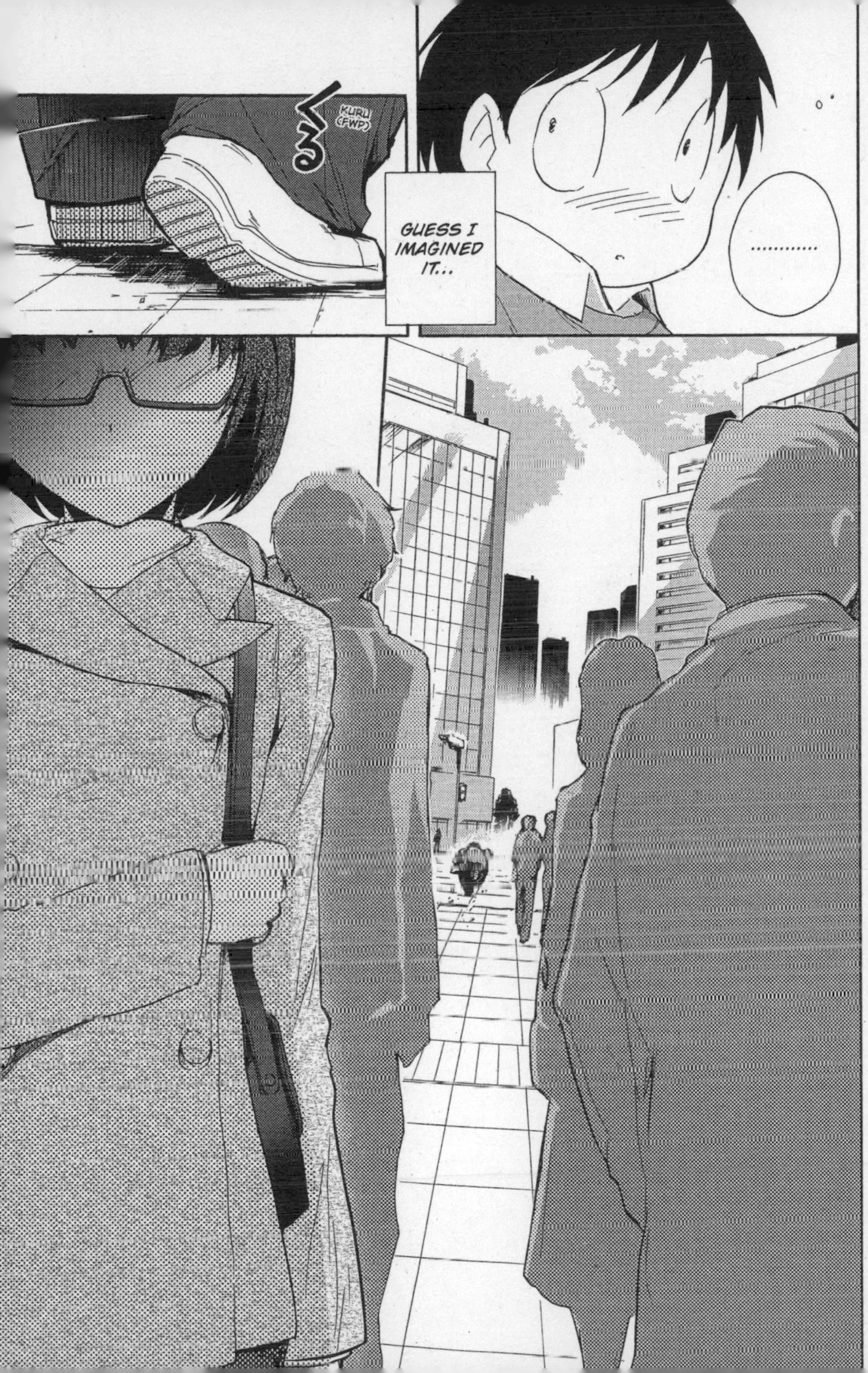
....
GUESS I IMAGINED IT...
くる
KURU (FWP)

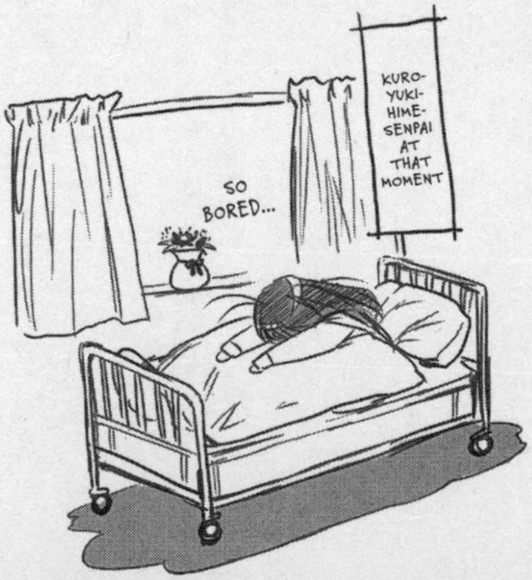
KURO-YUKI-HIME-SENPAI AT THAT MOMENT
SO BORED...

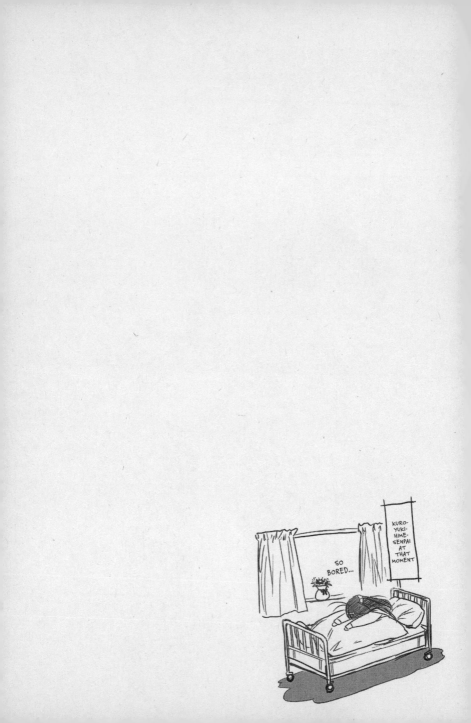

Chapter
#11

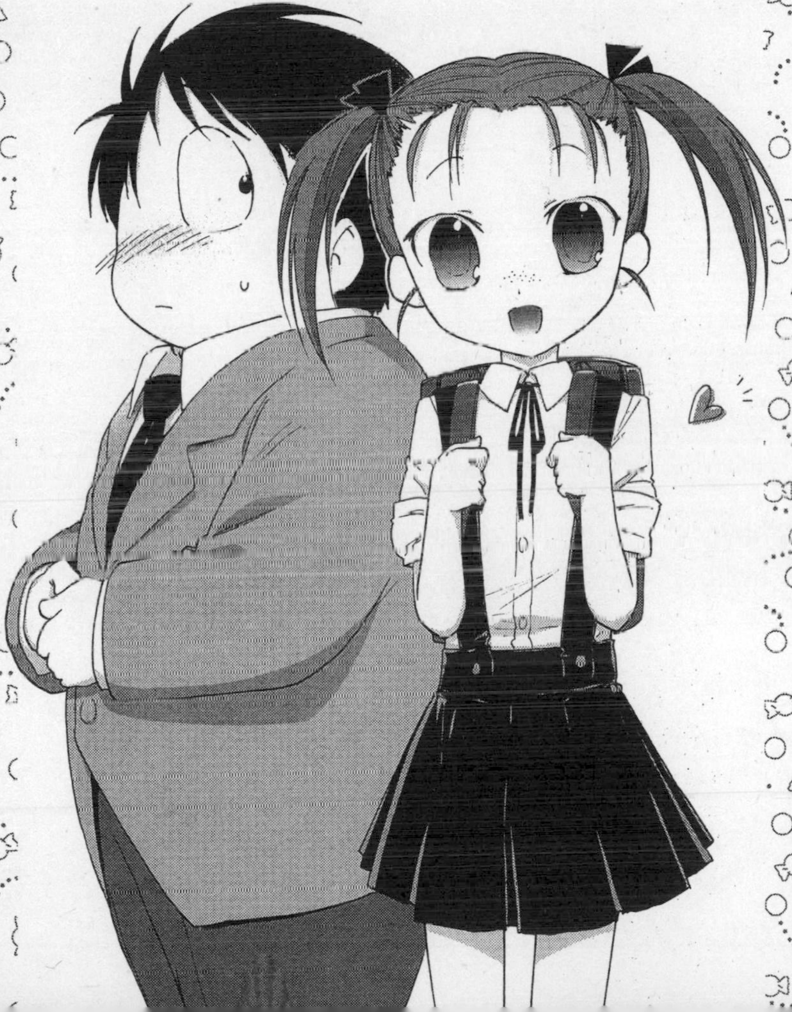

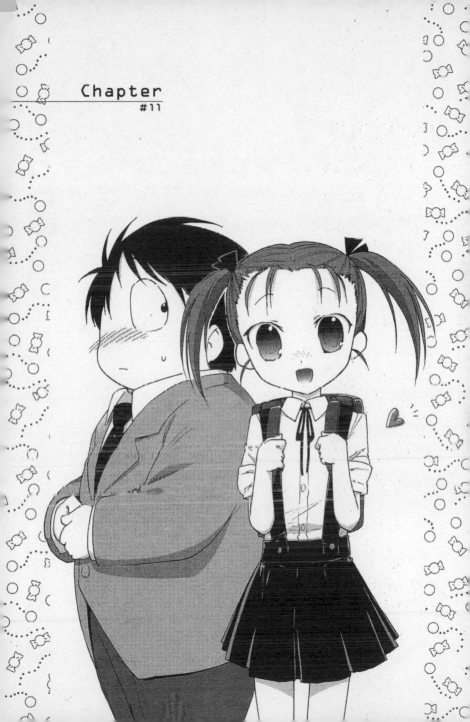

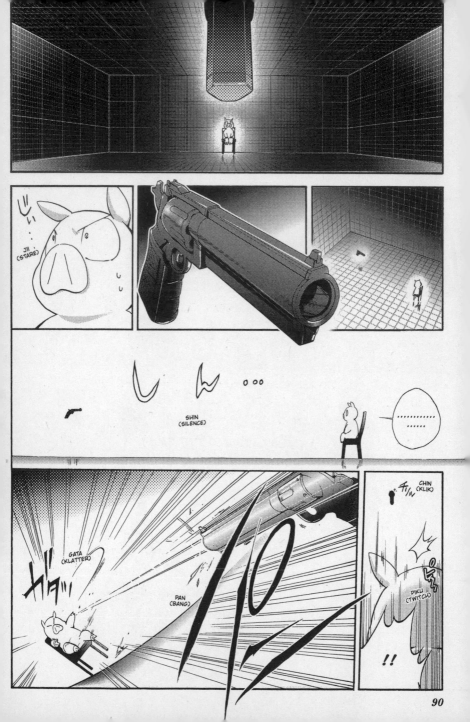

JII
(STARE)

SHIN
(SILENCE)

....
......

CHIN
(KLIK)

GATA
(KLATTER)

PAN
(BANG)

PIKU
(TWITCH)

!!

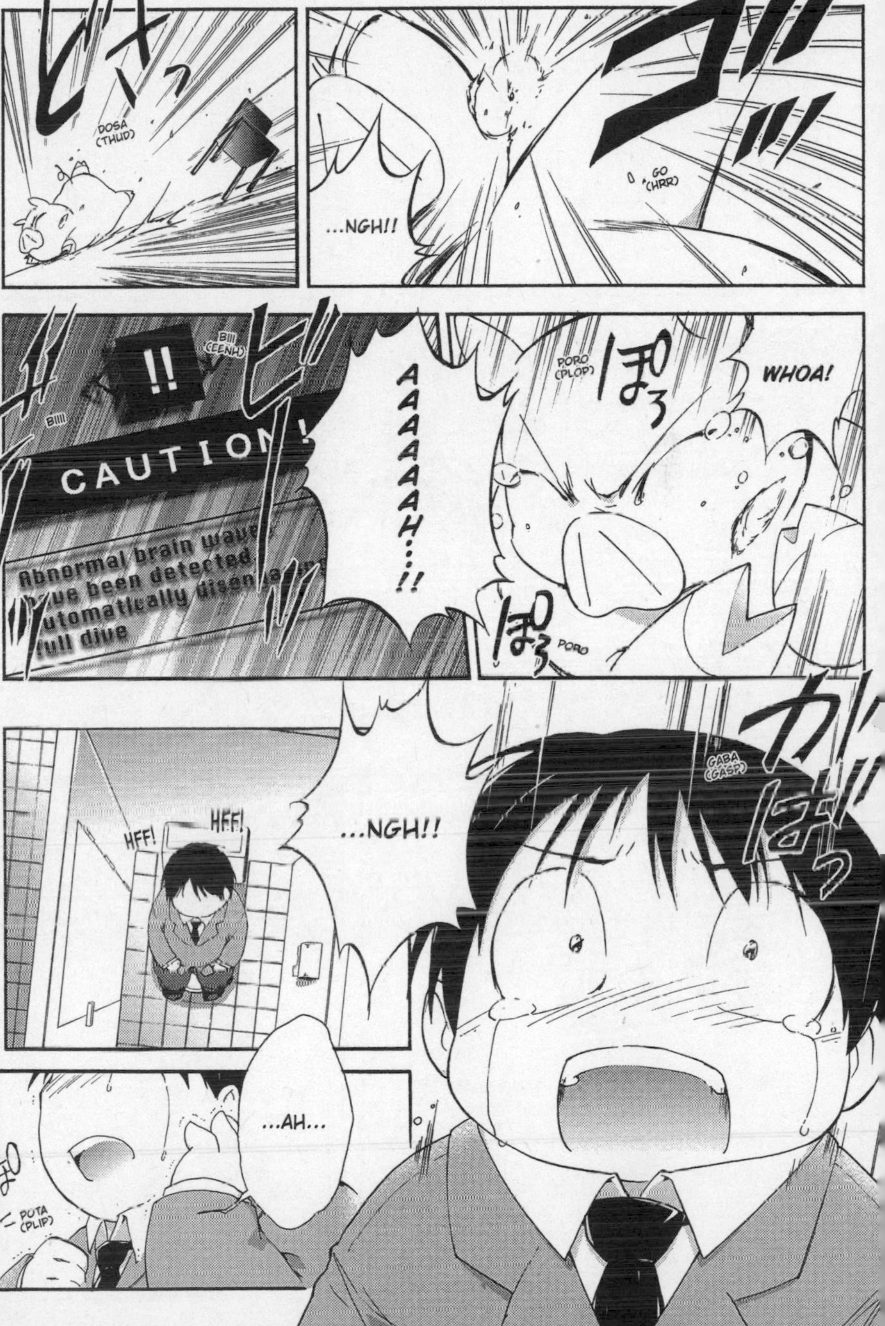
GO
(HRR)
...NGH!!
DOSA
(THUD)
PORO
(PLOP)
WHOA!
AAAAAAAH...!!
PORO
BIII
(EENH)
!!
BIII
CAUTION!
Abnormal brain wave
have been detected
automatically disen
full dive
GABA
(GASP)
...NGH!!
HFF!
HFF!
...AH...
POTA
(PLIP)

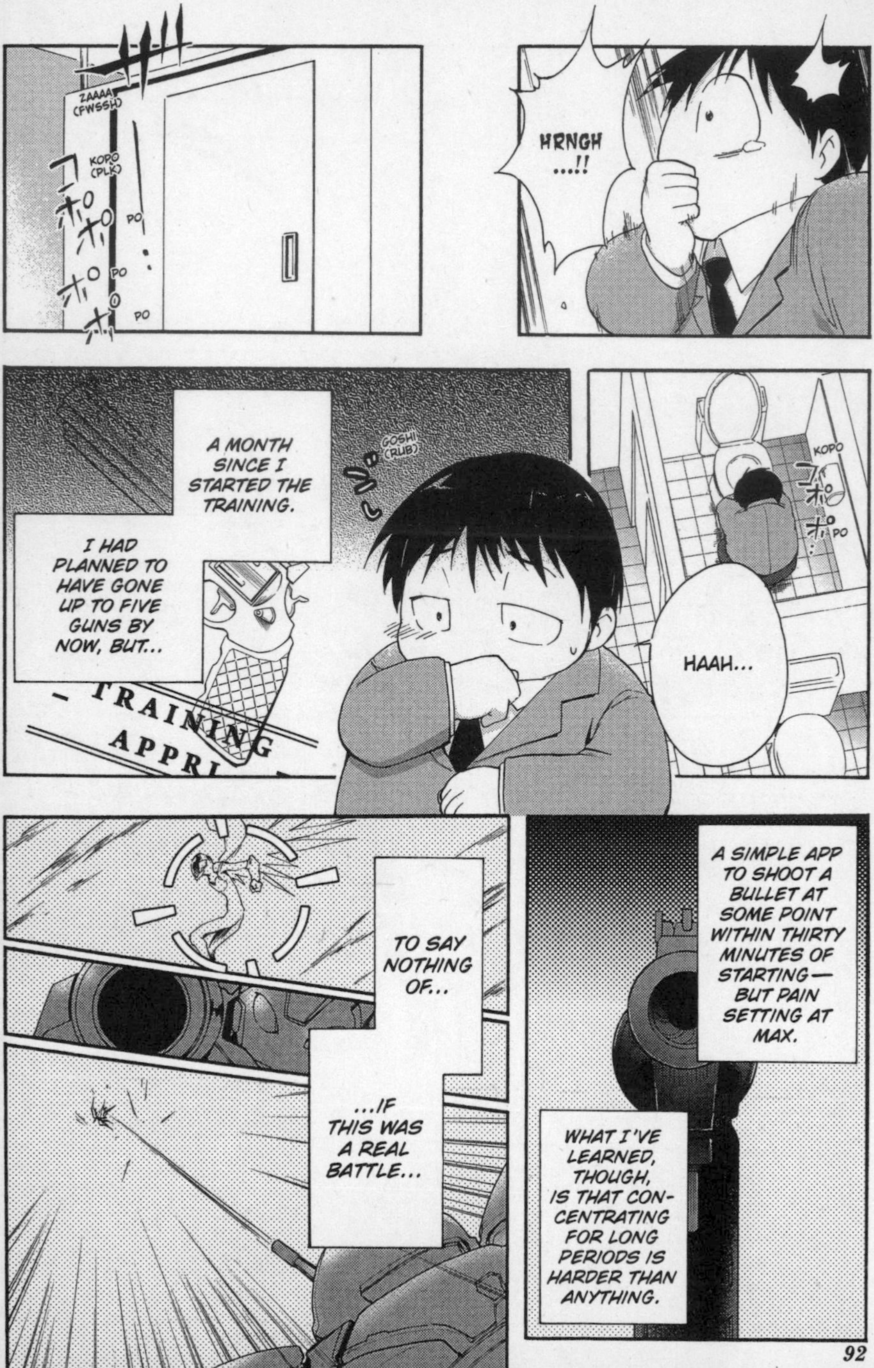
HRNGH ...!!
ZAAAA (FWSSH)
KOPO (PLK)
PO
PO
PO
KOPO
PO
HAAH...
GOSHI (RUB)
A MONTH SINCE I STARTED THE TRAINING.
I HAD PLANNED TO HAVE GONE UP TO FIVE GUNS BY NOW, BUT...
TRAINING
A SIMPLE APP TO SHOOT A BULLET AT SOME POINT WITHIN THIRTY MINUTES OF STARTING—BUT PAIN SETTING AT MAX.
WHAT I'VE LEARNED, THOUGH, IS THAT CON-CENTRATING FOR LONG PERIODS IS HARDER THAN ANYTHING.
TO SAY NOTHING OF...
...IF THIS WAS A REAL BATTLE...

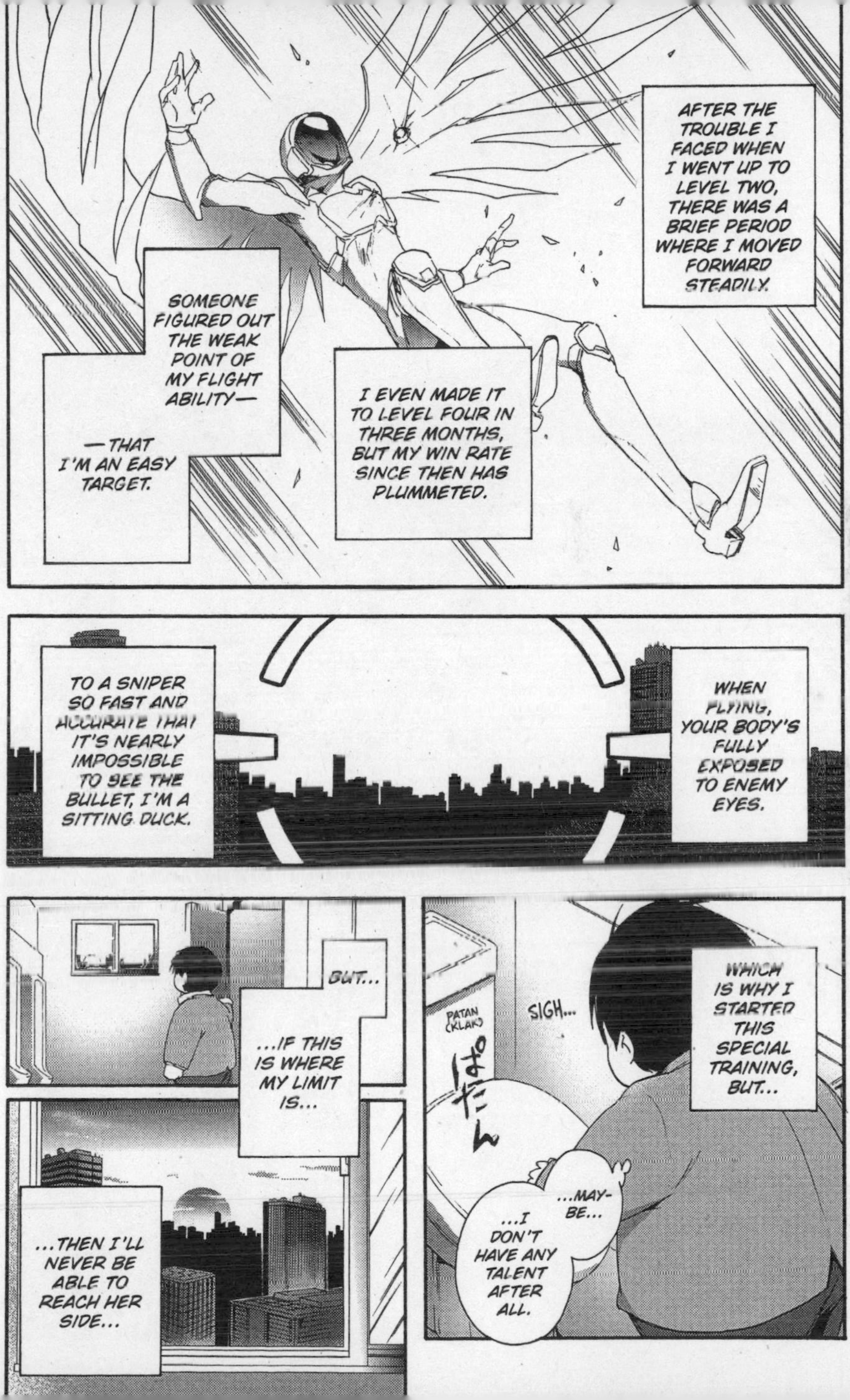
AFTER THE TROUBLE I FACED WHEN I WENT UP TO LEVEL TWO, THERE WAS A BRIEF PERIOD WHERE I MOVED FORWARD STEADILY.
I EVEN MADE IT TO LEVEL FOUR IN THREE MONTHS, BUT MY WIN RATE SINCE THEN HAS PLUMMETED.
SOMEONE FIGURED OUT THE WEAK POINT OF MY FLIGHT ABILITY—
—THAT I'M AN EASY TARGET.
WHEN FLYING, YOUR BODY'S FULLY EXPOSED TO ENEMY EYES.
TO A SNIPER SO FAST AND ACCURATE THAT IT'S NEARLY IMPOSSIBLE TO SEE THE BULLET, I'M A SITTING DUCK.
WHICH IS WHY I STARTED THIS SPECIAL TRAINING, BUT...
SIGH...
PATAN (KLAK)
...MAY-BE...
...I DON'T HAVE ANY TALENT AFTER ALL.
BUT...
...IF THIS IS WHERE MY LIMIT IS...
...THEN I'LL NEVER BE ABLE TO REACH HER SIDE...

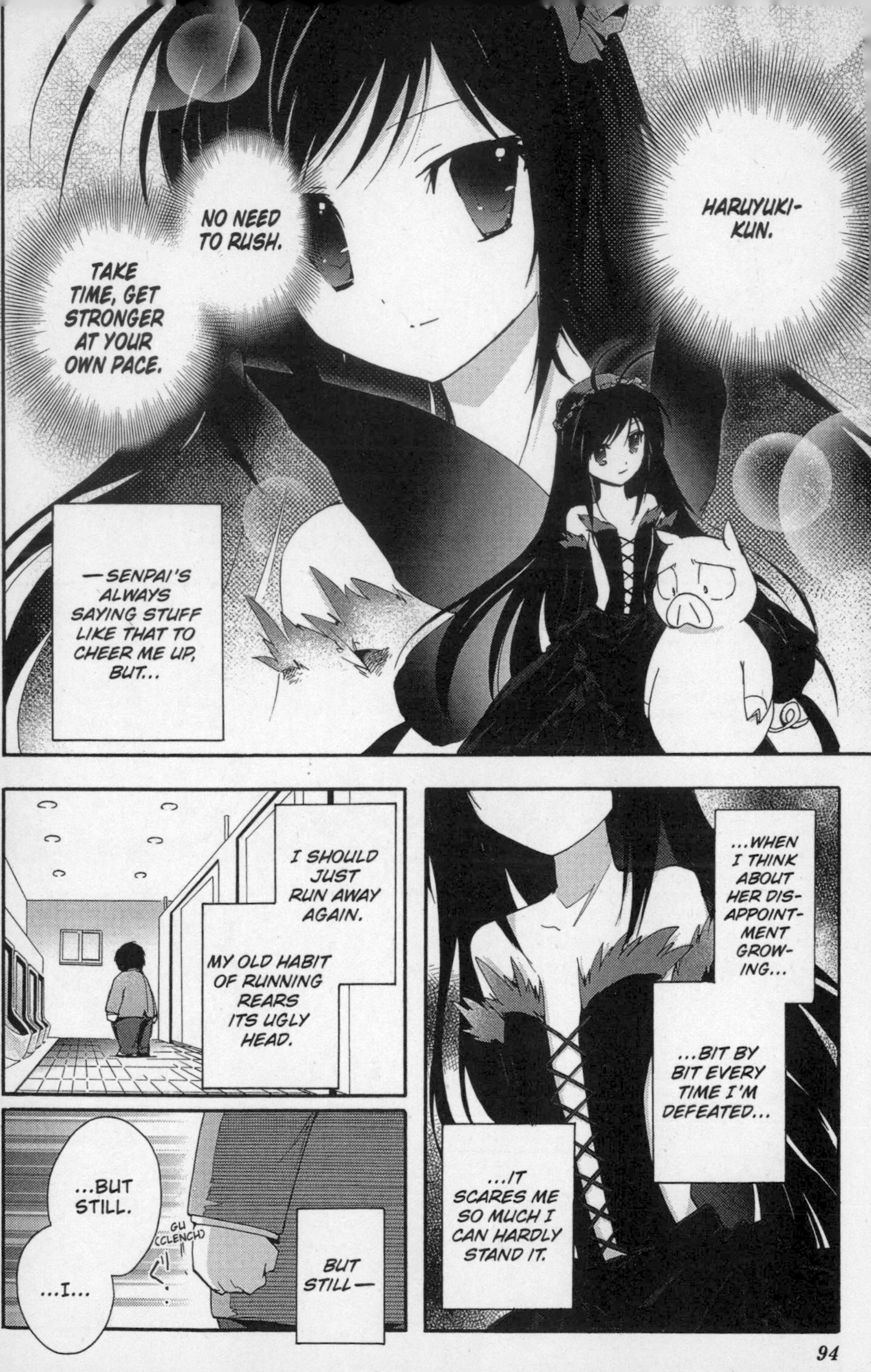
HARUYUKI-KUN.
NO NEED TO RUSH.
TAKE TIME, GET STRONGER AT YOUR OWN PACE.
—SENPAI'S ALWAYS SAYING STUFF LIKE THAT TO CHEER ME UP, BUT...
...WHEN I THINK ABOUT HER DIS-APPOINTMENT GROWING...
...BIT BY BIT EVERY TIME I'M DEFEATED...
...IT SCARES ME SO MUCH I CAN HARDLY STAND IT.
I SHOULD JUST RUN AWAY AGAIN.
MY OLD HABIT OF RUNNING REARS ITS UGLY HEAD.
BUT STILL—
GU (CLENCH)
...BUT STILL.
...I...

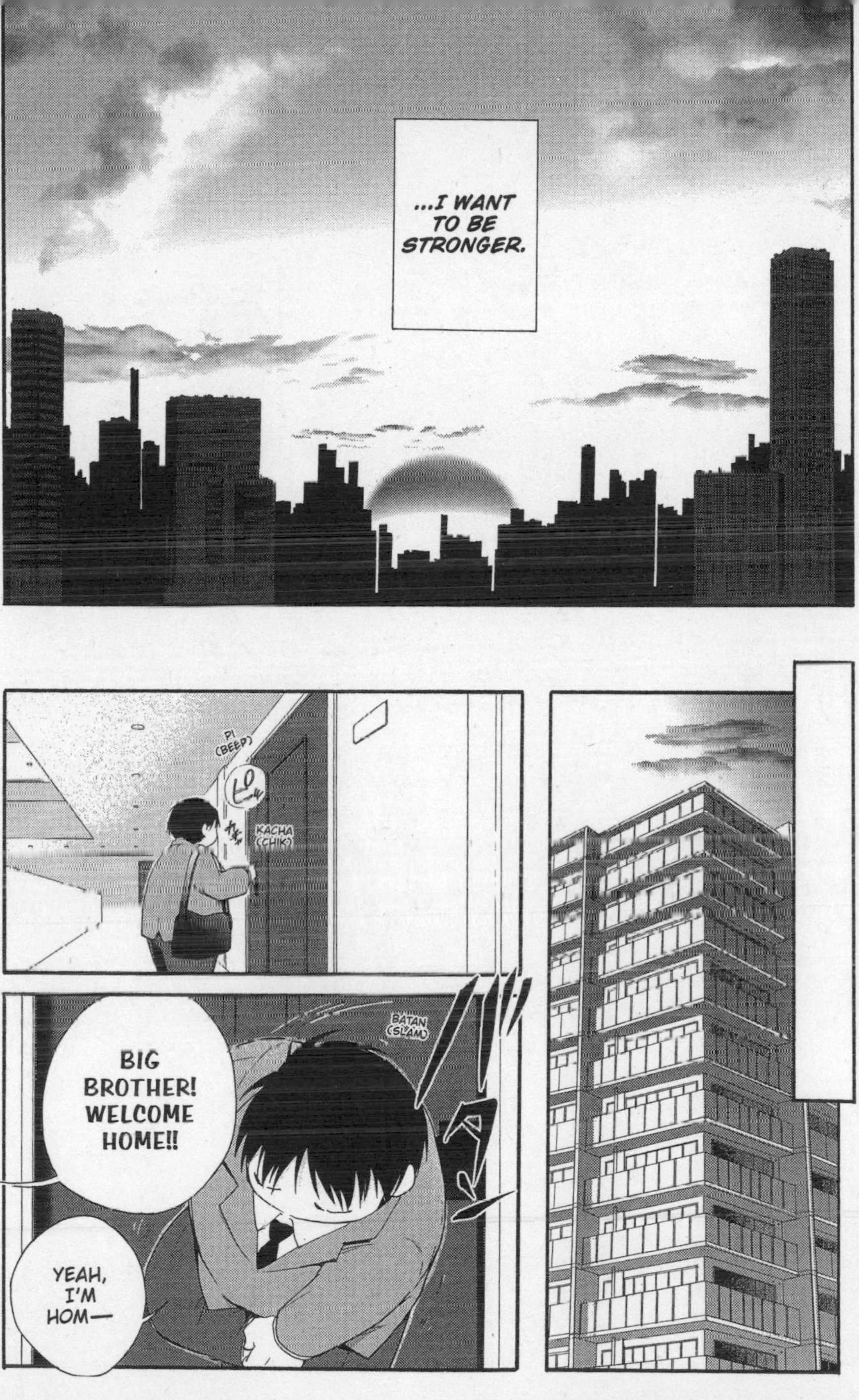
...I WANT TO BE STRONGER.
PI (BEEP)
KACHA (CHIK)
BATAN (SLAM)
BIG BROTHER! WELCOME HOME!!
YEAH, I'M HOM—

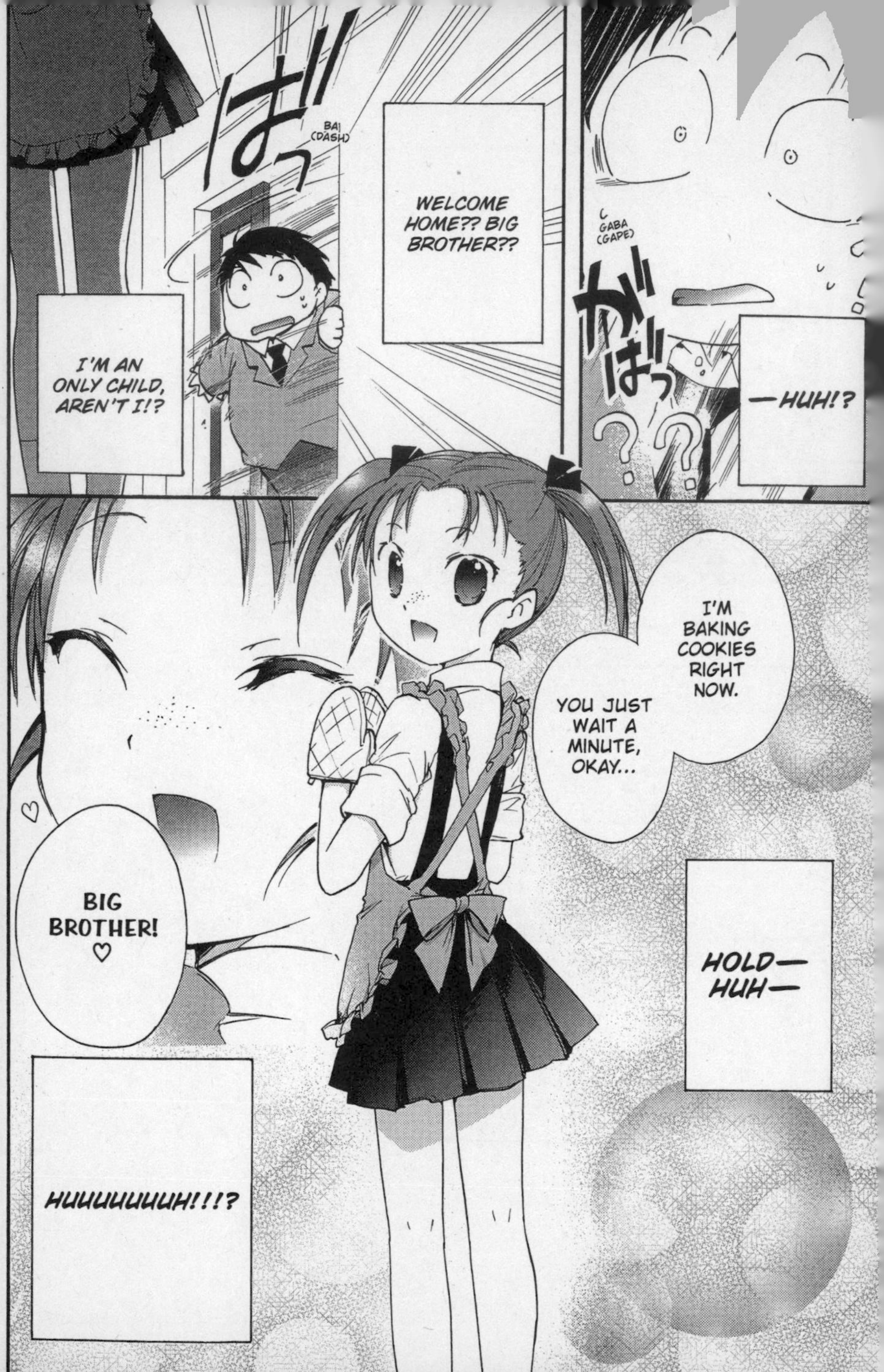
GABA (GAPE)
—HUH!?
WELCOME HOME?? BIG BROTHER??
BA! (DASH)
I'M AN ONLY CHILD, AREN'T I!?
I'M BAKING COOKIES RIGHT NOW.
YOU JUST WAIT A MINUTE, OKAY...
HOLD— HUH—
BIG BROTHER! ♡
HUUUUUUUH!!!?

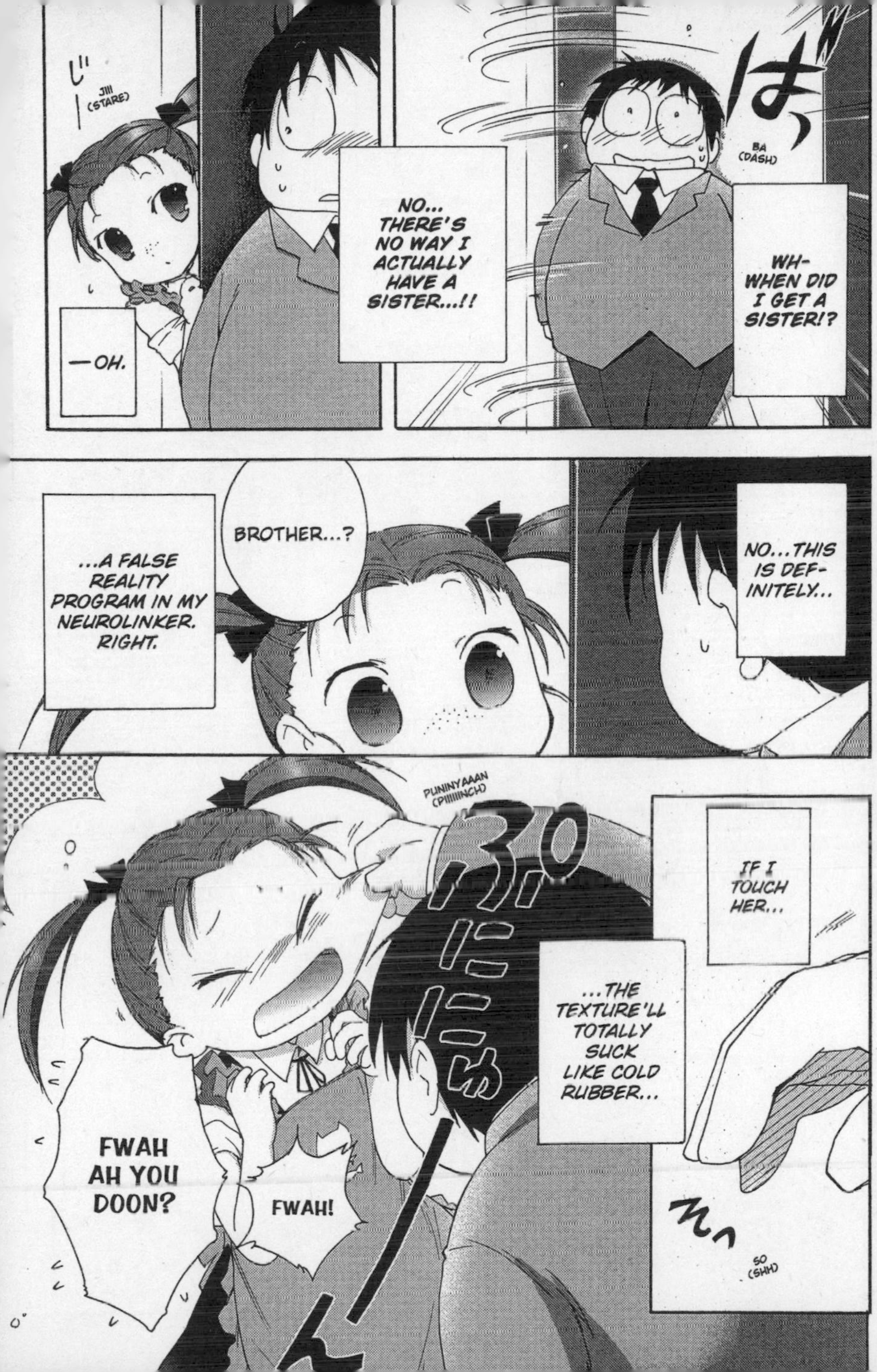
BA (DASH)
WH- WHEN DID I GET A SISTER!?
NO... THERE'S NO WAY I ACTUALLY HAVE A SISTER...!!
JIII (STARE)
—OH.
NO...THIS IS DEF- INITELY...
BROTHER...?
...A FALSE REALITY PROGRAM IN MY NEUROLINKER. RIGHT.
IF I TOUCH HER...
...THE TEXTURE'LL TOTALLY SUCK LIKE COLD RUBBER...
SO (SHH)
PUNINYAAAN (PIIIIIINCH)
FWAH!
FWAH AH YOU DOON?

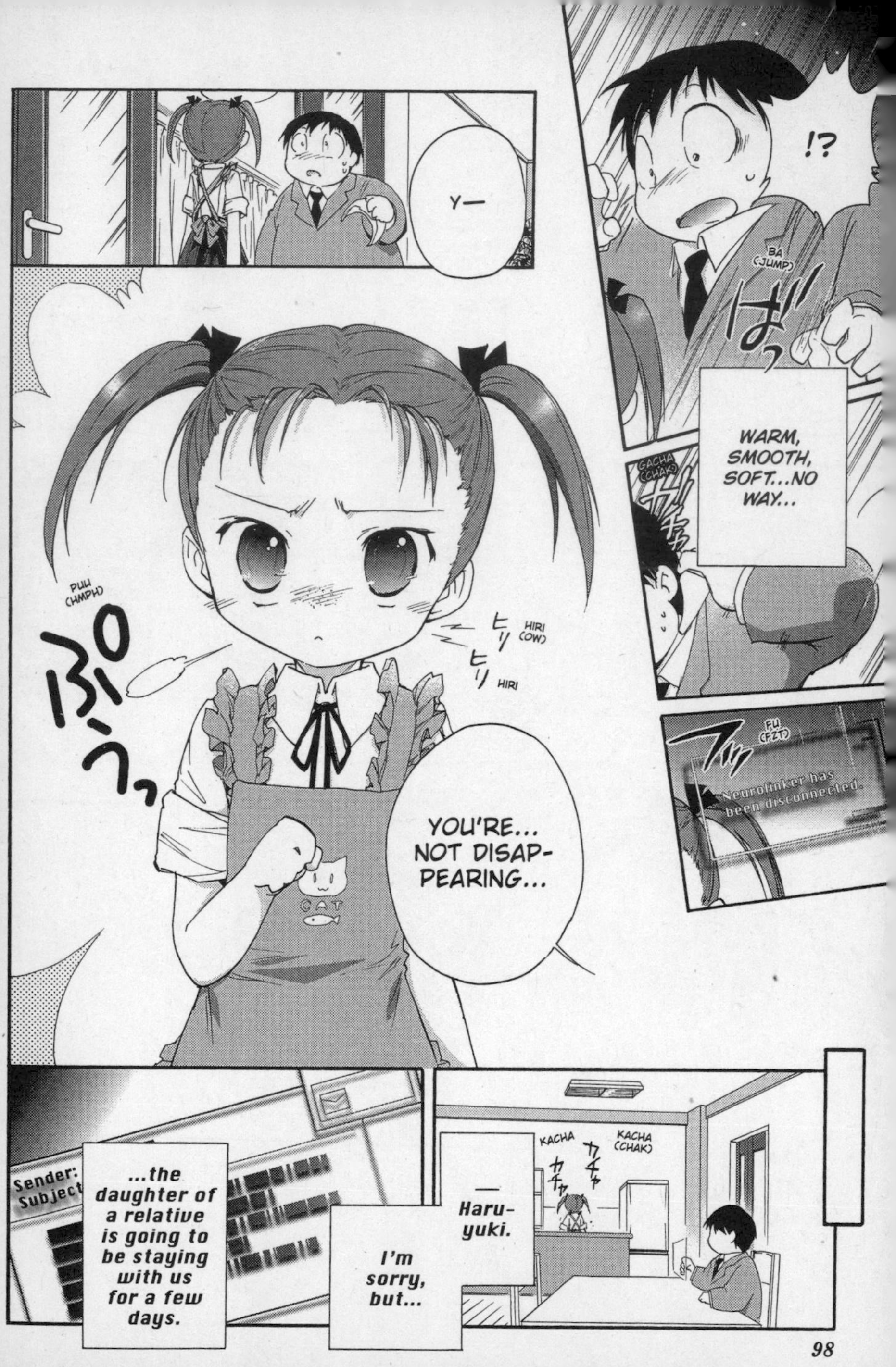
!?
BA (JUMP)
ばっ
GACHA (CHAK)
WARM, SMOOTH, SOFT...NO WAY...
FU (FZT)
フッ
Neurolinker has been disconnected.
Y—
PUU (HMPH)
ぷぅっ
HIRI (OW)
ヒリ
ヒリ
HIRI
YOU'RE... NOT DISAP-PEARING...
KACHA (CHAK)
カチャ
KACHA
カチャ
—Haru-yuki.
I'm sorry, but...
...the daughter of a relative is going to be staying with us for a few days.
Sender:
Subject

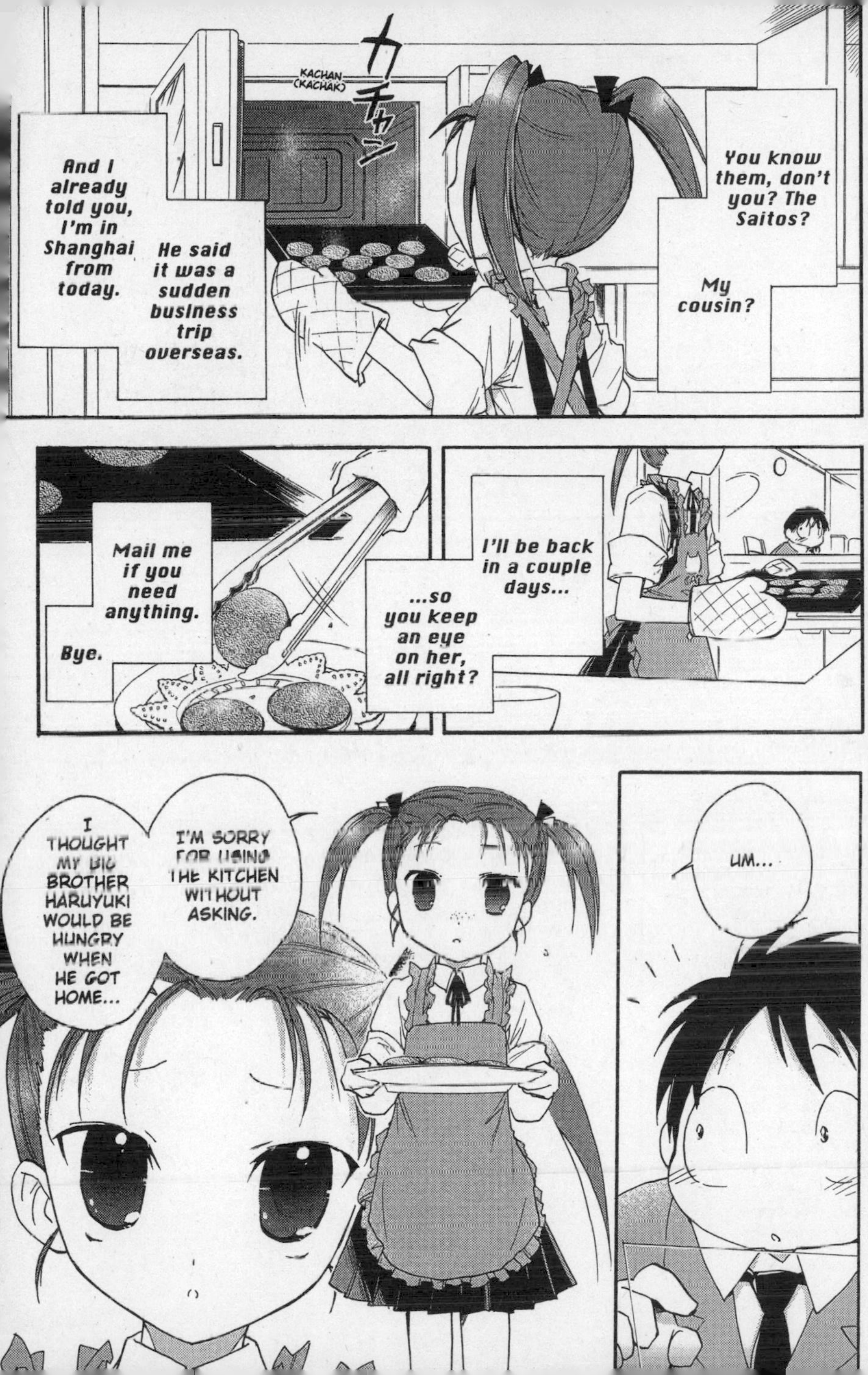
You know them, don't you? The Saitos?
My cousin?
KACHAN (KACHAK)
He said it was a sudden business trip overseas.
And I already told you, I'm in Shanghai from today.
I'll be back in a couple days...
...so you keep an eye on her, all right?
Mail me if you need anything.
Bye.
UM...
I'M SORRY FOR USING THE KITCHEN WITHOUT ASKING.
I THOUGHT MY BIG BROTHER HARUYUKI WOULD BE HUNGRY WHEN HE GOT HOME...

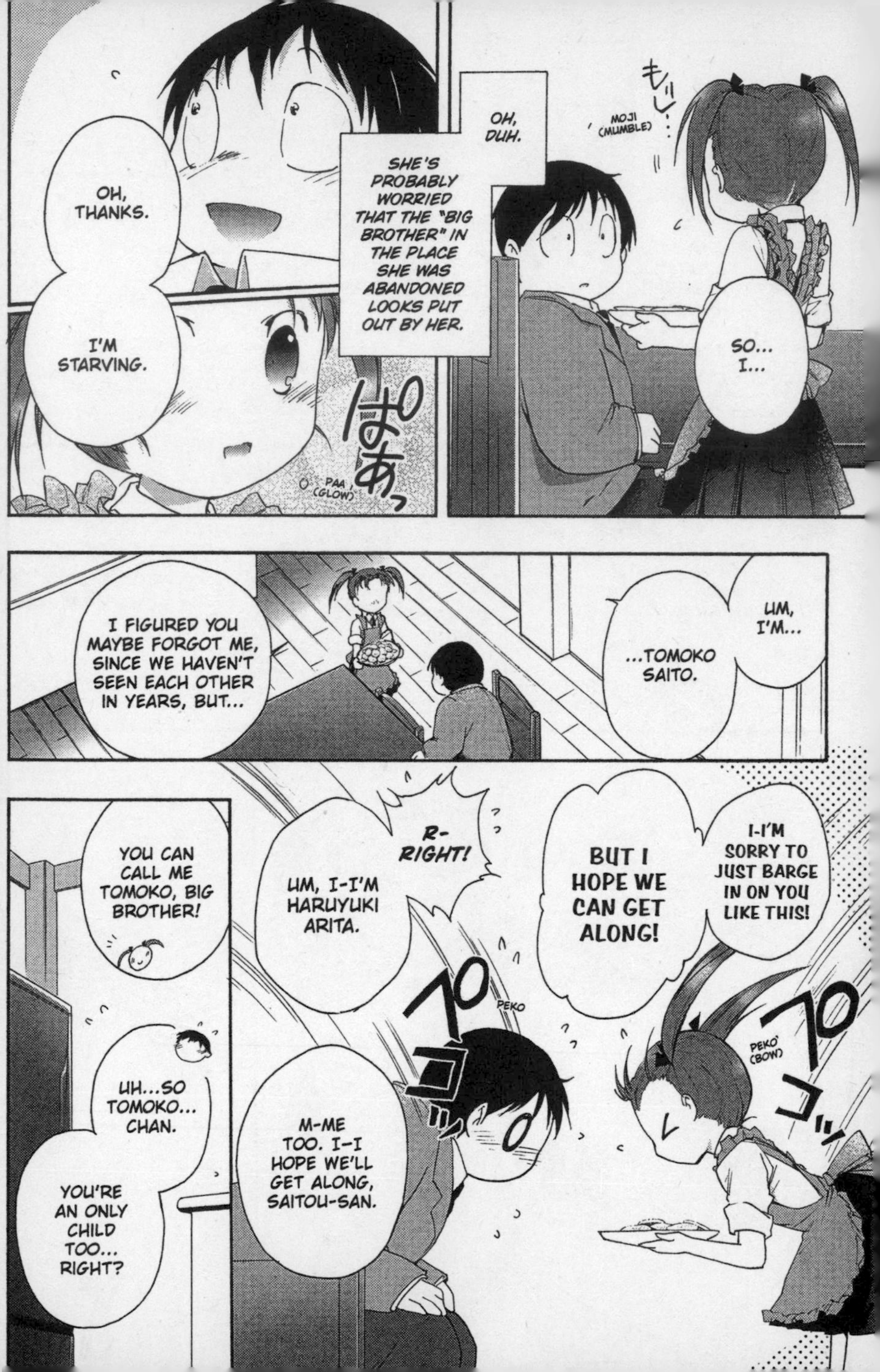
MOJI (MUMBLE)
SO... I...
OH, DUH.
SHE'S PROBABLY WORRIED THAT THE "BIG BROTHER" IN THE PLACE SHE WAS ABANDONED LOOKS PUT OUT BY HER.
OH, THANKS.
I'M STARVING.
ぱあっ
PAA (GLOW)
UM, I'M...
...TOMOKO SAITO.
I FIGURED YOU MAYBE FORGOT ME, SINCE WE HAVEN'T SEEN EACH OTHER IN YEARS, BUT...
I-I'M SORRY TO JUST BARGE IN ON YOU LIKE THIS!
BUT I HOPE WE CAN GET ALONG!
PEKO (BOW)
R- RIGHT!
UM, I-I'M HARUYUKI ARITA.
PEKO
M-ME TOO. I-I HOPE WE'LL GET ALONG, SAITOU-SAN.
YOU CAN CALL ME TOMOKO, BIG BROTHER!
UH...SO TOMOKO... CHAN.
YOU'RE AN ONLY CHILD TOO... RIGHT?

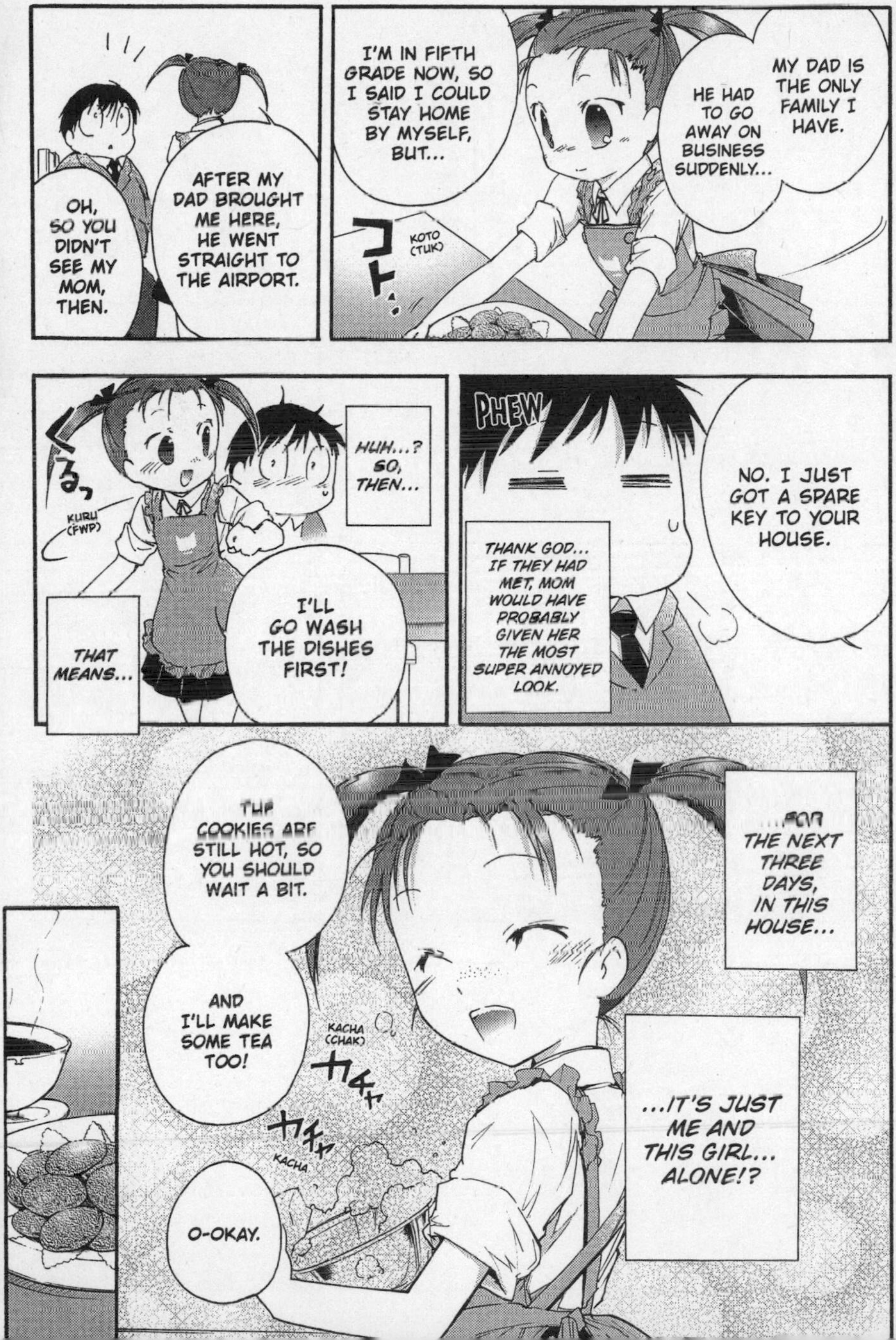
MY DAD IS THE ONLY FAMILY I HAVE.
HE HAD TO GO AWAY ON BUSINESS SUDDENLY...
I'M IN FIFTH GRADE NOW, SO I SAID I COULD STAY HOME BY MYSELF, BUT...
KOTO (TUK)
AFTER MY DAD BROUGHT ME HERE, HE WENT STRAIGHT TO THE AIRPORT.
OH, SO YOU DIDN'T SEE MY MOM, THEN.
PHEW
NO. I JUST GOT A SPARE KEY TO YOUR HOUSE.
THANK GOD... IF THEY HAD MET, MOM WOULD HAVE PROBABLY GIVEN HER THE MOST SUPER ANNOYED LOOK.
HUH...? SO, THEN...
KURU (FWP)
I'LL GO WASH THE DISHES FIRST!
THAT MEANS...
...FOR THE NEXT THREE DAYS, IN THIS HOUSE...
THE COOKIES ARE STILL HOT, SO YOU SHOULD WAIT A BIT.
AND I'LL MAKE SOME TEA TOO!
KACHA (CHAK)
KACHA
...IT'S JUST ME AND THIS GIRL... ALONE!?
O-OKAY.

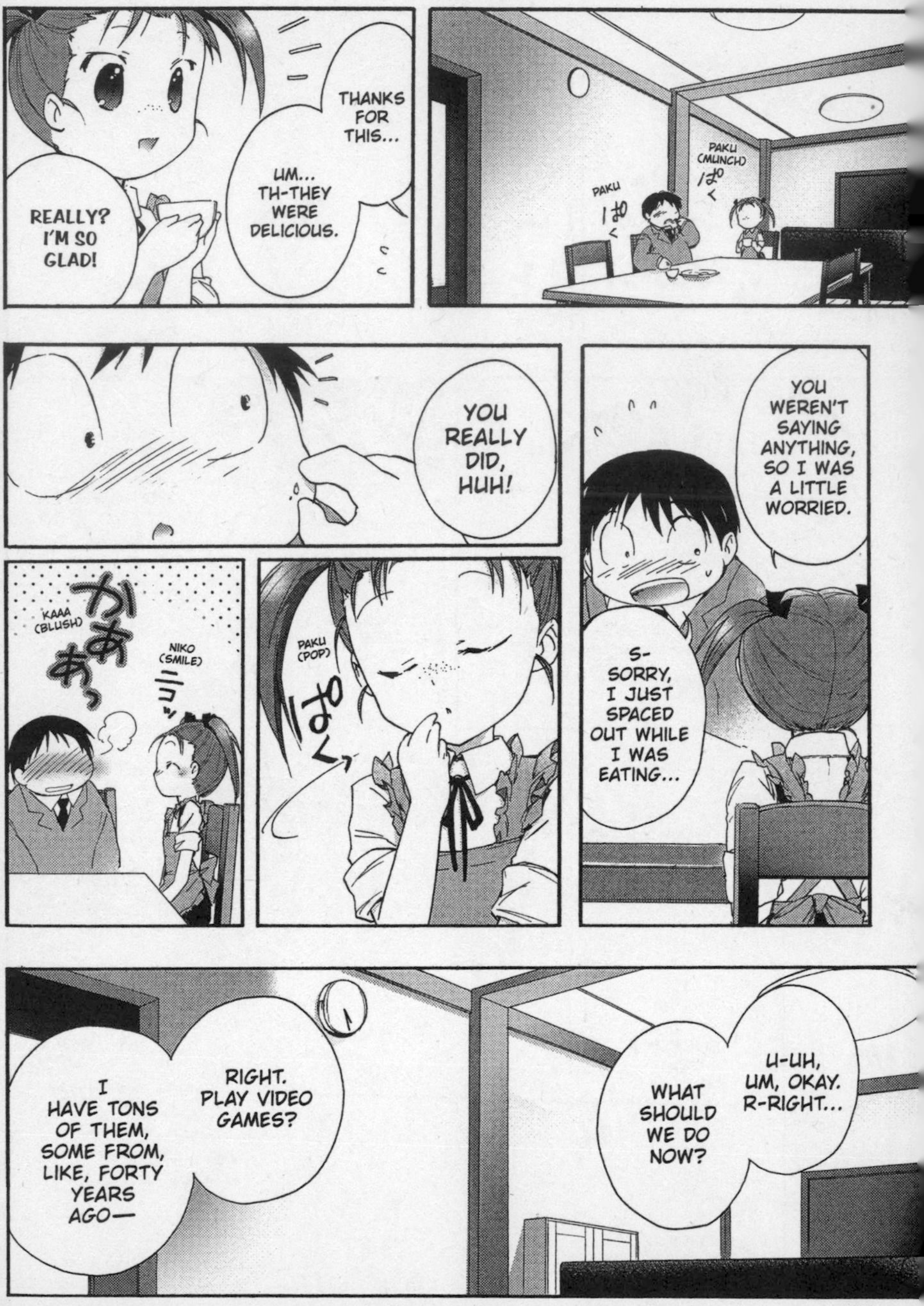
PAKU (MUNCH)
ぱく
PAKU
ぱく
THANKS FOR THIS...
UM... TH-THEY WERE DELICIOUS.
REALLY? I'M SO GLAD!
YOU WEREN'T SAYING ANYTHING, SO I WAS A LITTLE WORRIED.
S-SORRY, I JUST SPACED OUT WHILE I WAS EATING...
YOU REALLY DID, HUH!
PAKU (POP)
ぱく
NIKO (SMILE)
ニコッ
KAAA (BLUSH)
かあああっ
U-UH, UM, OKAY. R-RIGHT...
WHAT SHOULD WE DO NOW?
RIGHT. PLAY VIDEO GAMES?
I HAVE TONS OF THEM, SOME FROM, LIKE, FORTY YEARS AGO—

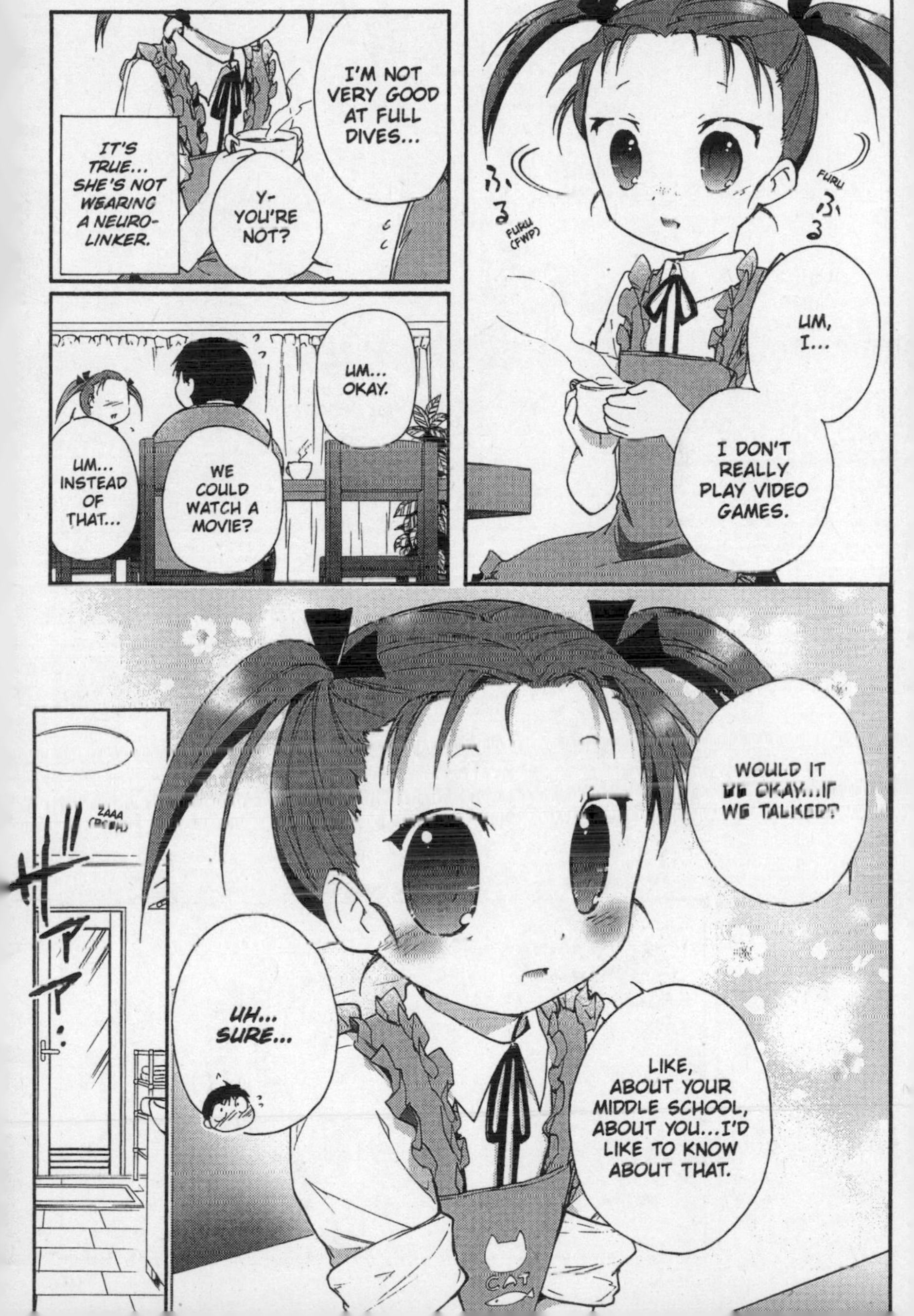
FURU (FWP)
FURU
UM, I...
I DON'T REALLY PLAY VIDEO GAMES.
I'M NOT VERY GOOD AT FULL DIVES...
Y-YOU'RE NOT?
IT'S TRUE... SHE'S NOT WEARING A NEURO-LINKER.
UM... OKAY.
WE COULD WATCH A MOVIE?
UM... INSTEAD OF THAT...
WOULD IT BE OKAY...IF WE TALKED?
LIKE, ABOUT YOUR MIDDLE SCHOOL, ABOUT YOU...I'D LIKE TO KNOW ABOUT THAT.
UH... SURE...
ZAAA

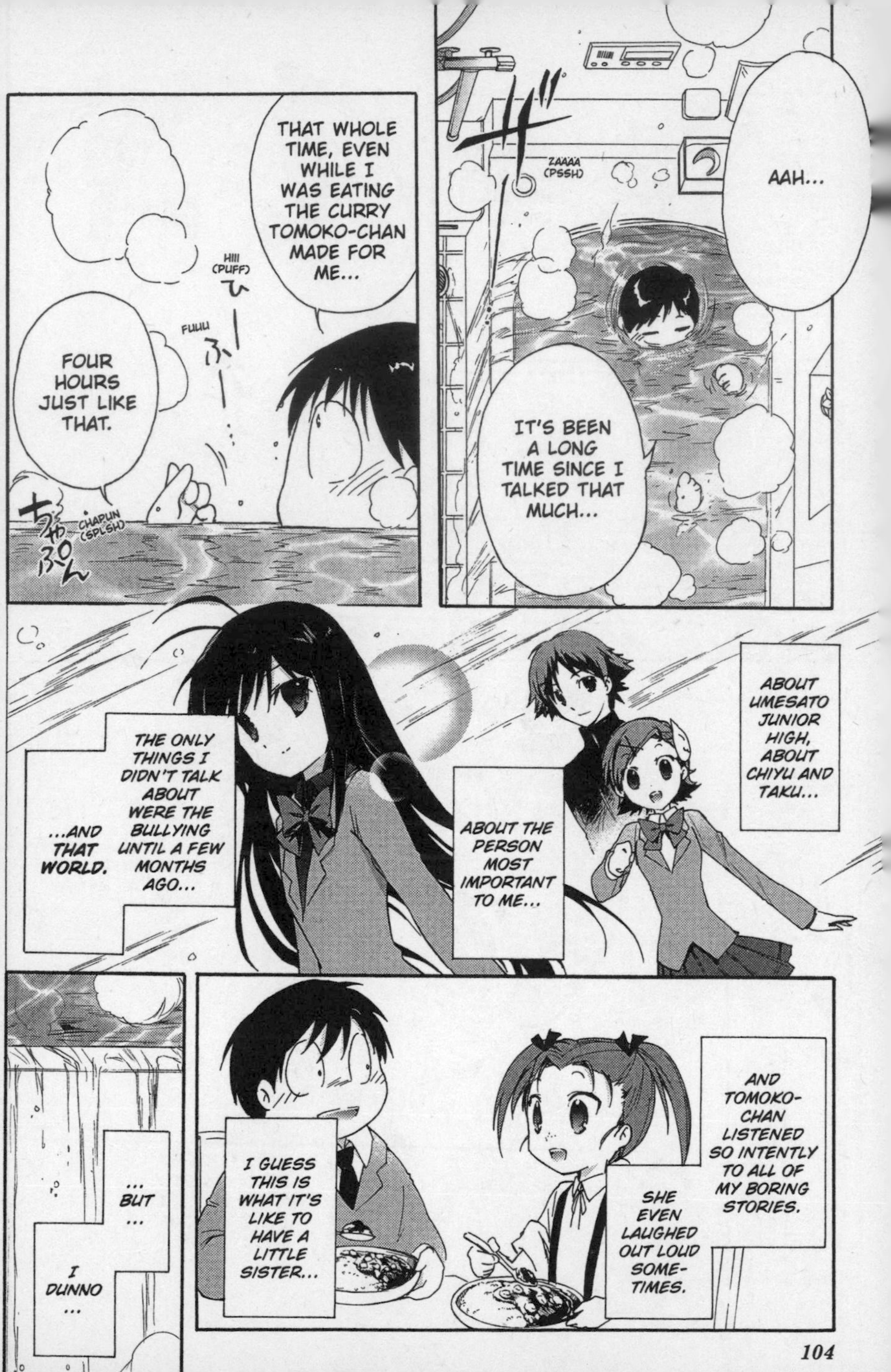
AAH...
ZAAAA (PSSH)
IT'S BEEN A LONG TIME SINCE I TALKED THAT MUCH...
THAT WHOLE TIME, EVEN WHILE I WAS EATING THE CURRY TOMOKO-CHAN MADE FOR ME...
HIII (PUFF)
FUUU
FOUR HOURS JUST LIKE THAT.
CHAPUN (SPLSH)
ABOUT UMESATO JUNIOR HIGH, ABOUT CHIYU AND TAKU...
ABOUT THE PERSON MOST IMPORTANT TO ME...
THE ONLY THINGS I DIDN'T TALK ABOUT WERE THE BULLYING UNTIL A FEW MONTHS AGO...
...AND THAT WORLD.
AND TOMOKO-CHAN LISTENED SO INTENTLY TO ALL OF MY BORING STORIES.
SHE EVEN LAUGHED OUT LOUD SOMETIMES.
I GUESS THIS IS WHAT IT'S LIKE TO HAVE A LITTLE SISTER...
...BUT...
I DUNNO...

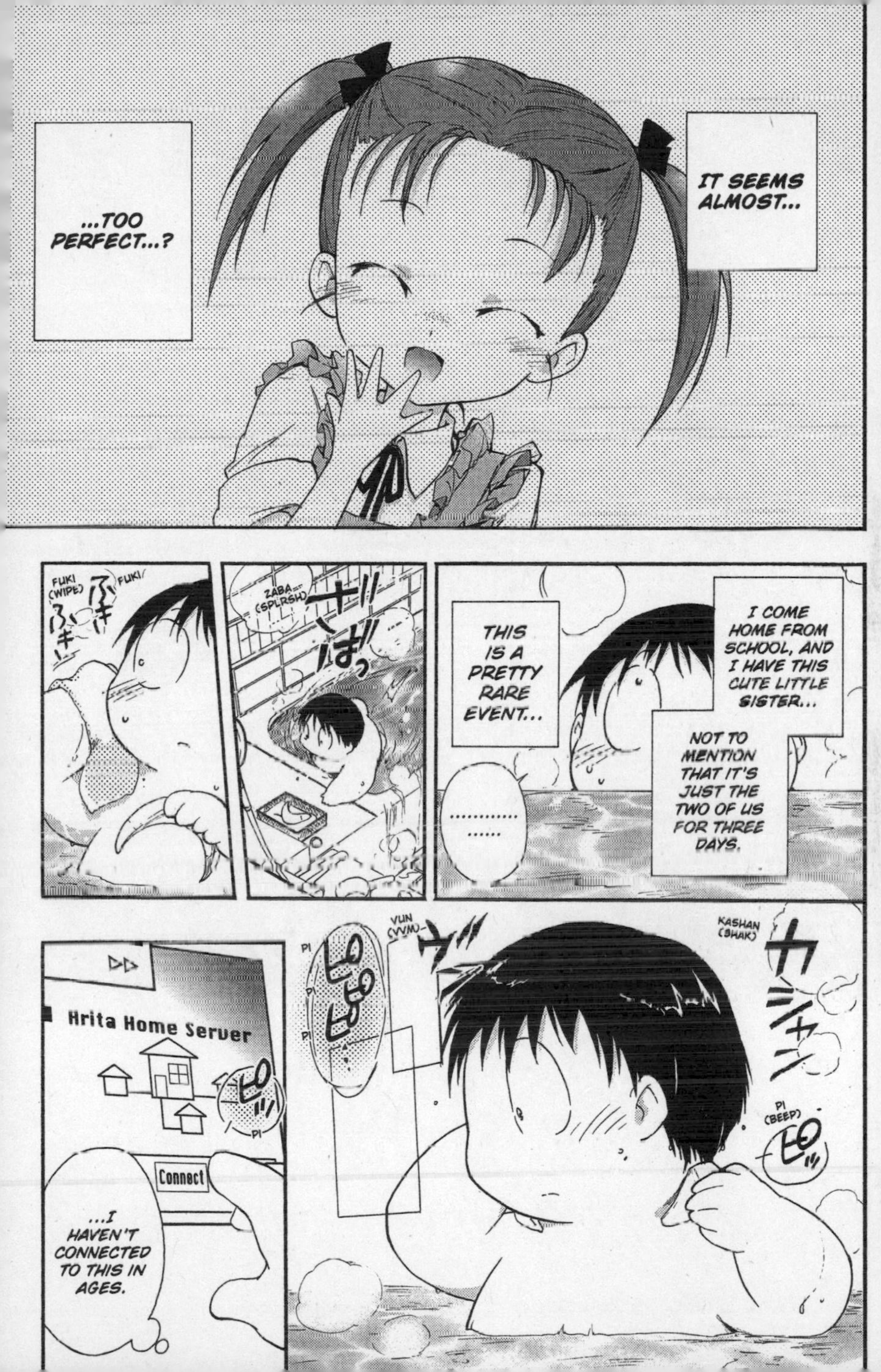
IT SEEMS ALMOST...
...TOO PERFECT...?
I COME HOME FROM SCHOOL, AND I HAVE THIS CUTE LITTLE SISTER...
NOT TO MENTION THAT IT'S JUST THE TWO OF US FOR THREE DAYS.
THIS IS A PRETTY RARE EVENT...
....
ZABA (SPLASH)
FUKI (WIPE)
FUKI
KASHAN (SHAK)
PI (BEEP)
VUN (VVVM)
PI
PI
PI
Hrita Home Server
PI
Connect
...I HAVEN'T CONNECTED TO THIS IN AGES.

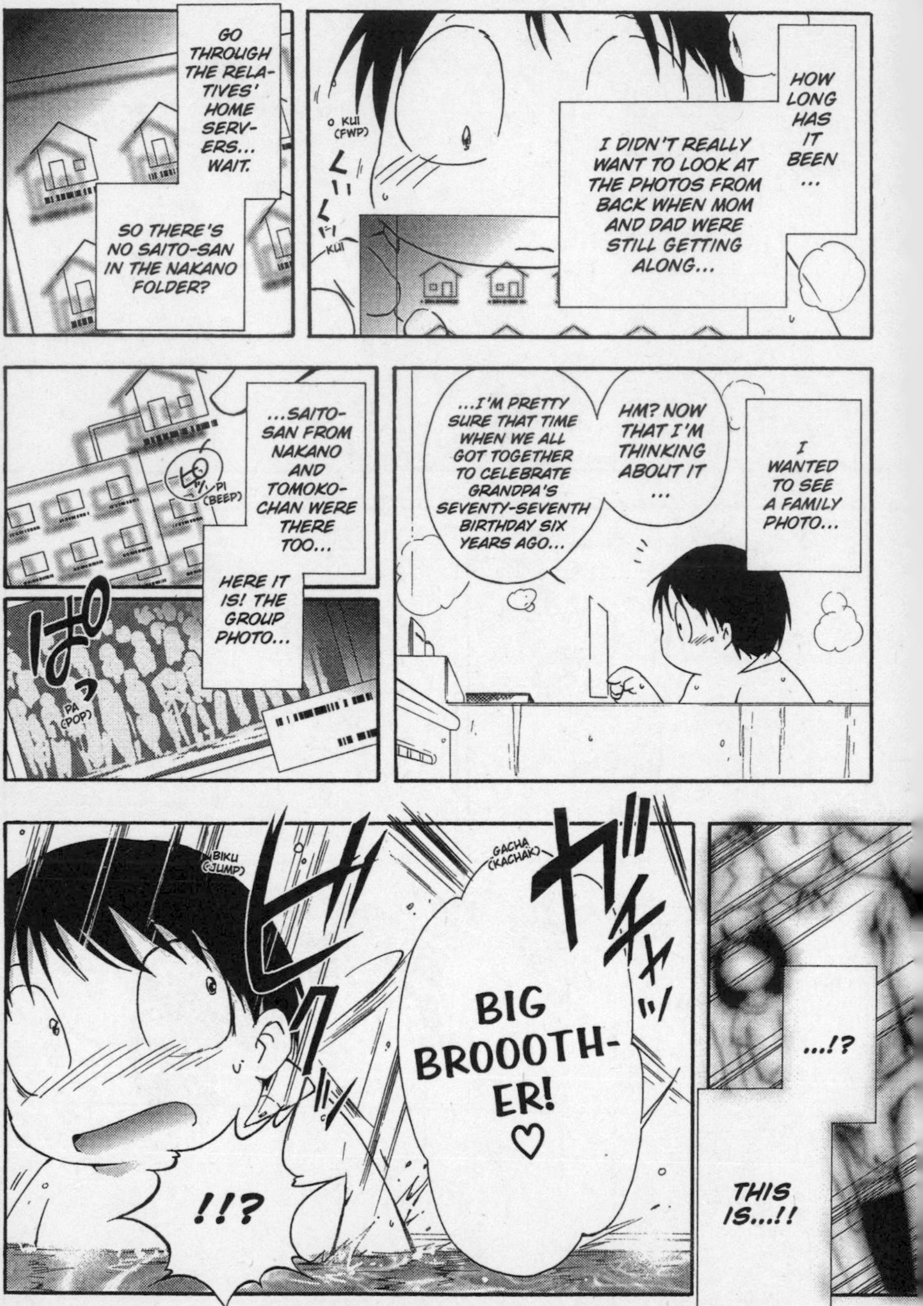
HOW LONG HAS IT BEEN...
I DIDN'T REALLY WANT TO LOOK AT THE PHOTOS FROM BACK WHEN MOM AND DAD WERE STILL GETTING ALONG...
KUI (FWP)
KUI
GO THROUGH THE RELATIVES' HOME SERVERS... WAIT.
SO THERE'S NO SAITO-SAN IN THE NAKANO FOLDER?
I WANTED TO SEE A FAMILY PHOTO...
HM? NOW THAT I'M THINKING ABOUT IT...
...I'M PRETTY SURE THAT TIME WHEN WE ALL GOT TOGETHER TO CELEBRATE GRANDPA'S SEVENTY-SEVENTH BIRTHDAY SIX YEARS AGO...
...SAITO-SAN FROM NAKANO AND TOMOKO-CHAN WERE THERE TOO...
PI (BEEP)
HERE IT IS! THE GROUP PHOTO...
PA (POP)
...!?
THIS IS...!!
GACHA (KACHAK)
BIG BROOOTHER! ♡
BIKU (JUMP)
!!?

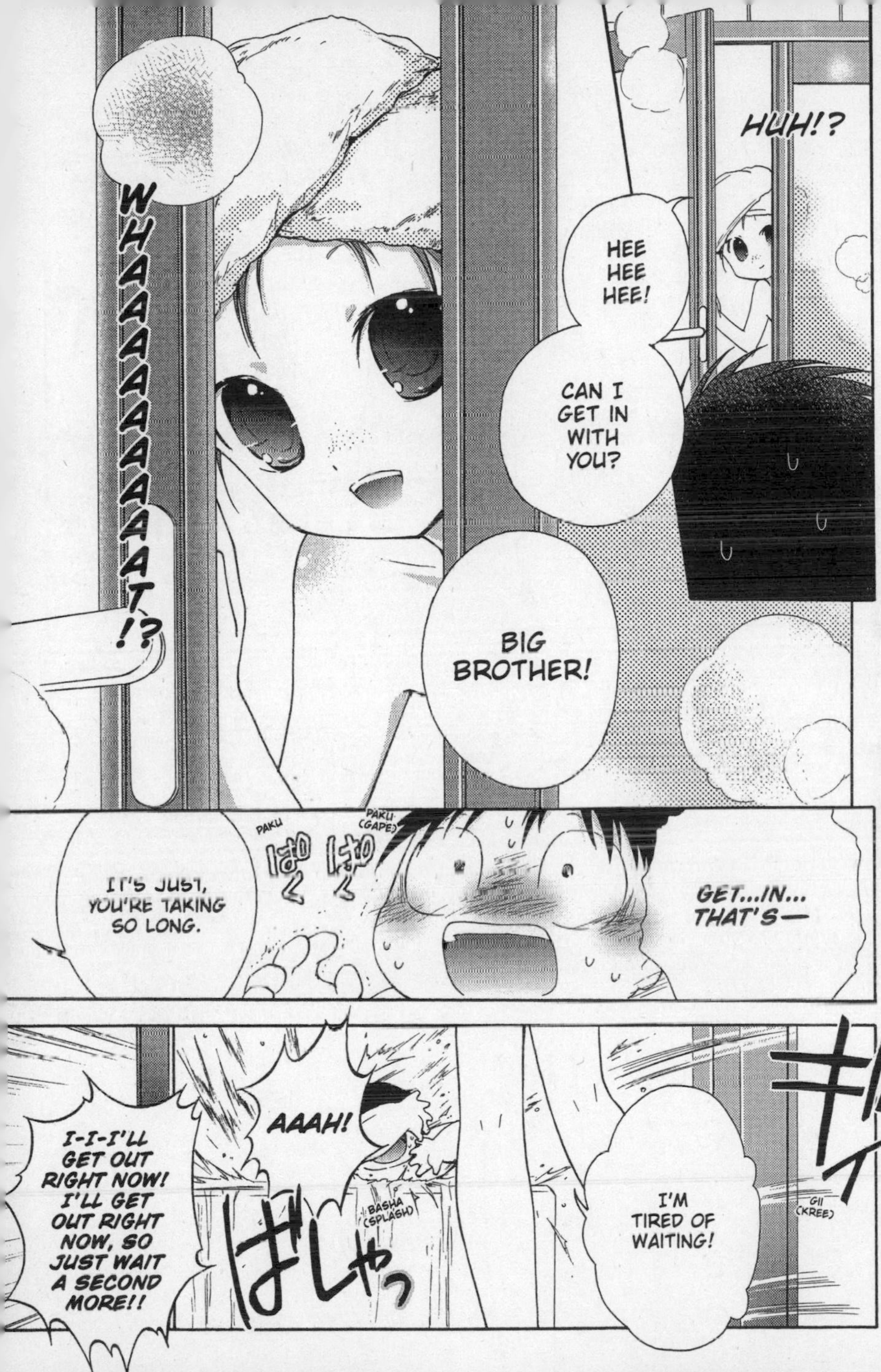
HUH!?
HEE HEE HEE!
CAN I GET IN WITH YOU?
BIG BROTHER!
WHAAAAAAAAAAAT!?
GET...IN... THAT'S—
PAKU (GAPE)
ぱく
PAKU
ぱく
IT'S JUST, YOU'RE TAKING SO LONG.
ギィ
GII (KREE)
I'M TIRED OF WAITING!
AAAH!
ばしゃっ
BASHA (SPLASH)
I-I-I'LL GET OUT RIGHT NOW! I'LL GET OUT RIGHT NOW, SO JUST WAIT A SECOND MORE!!

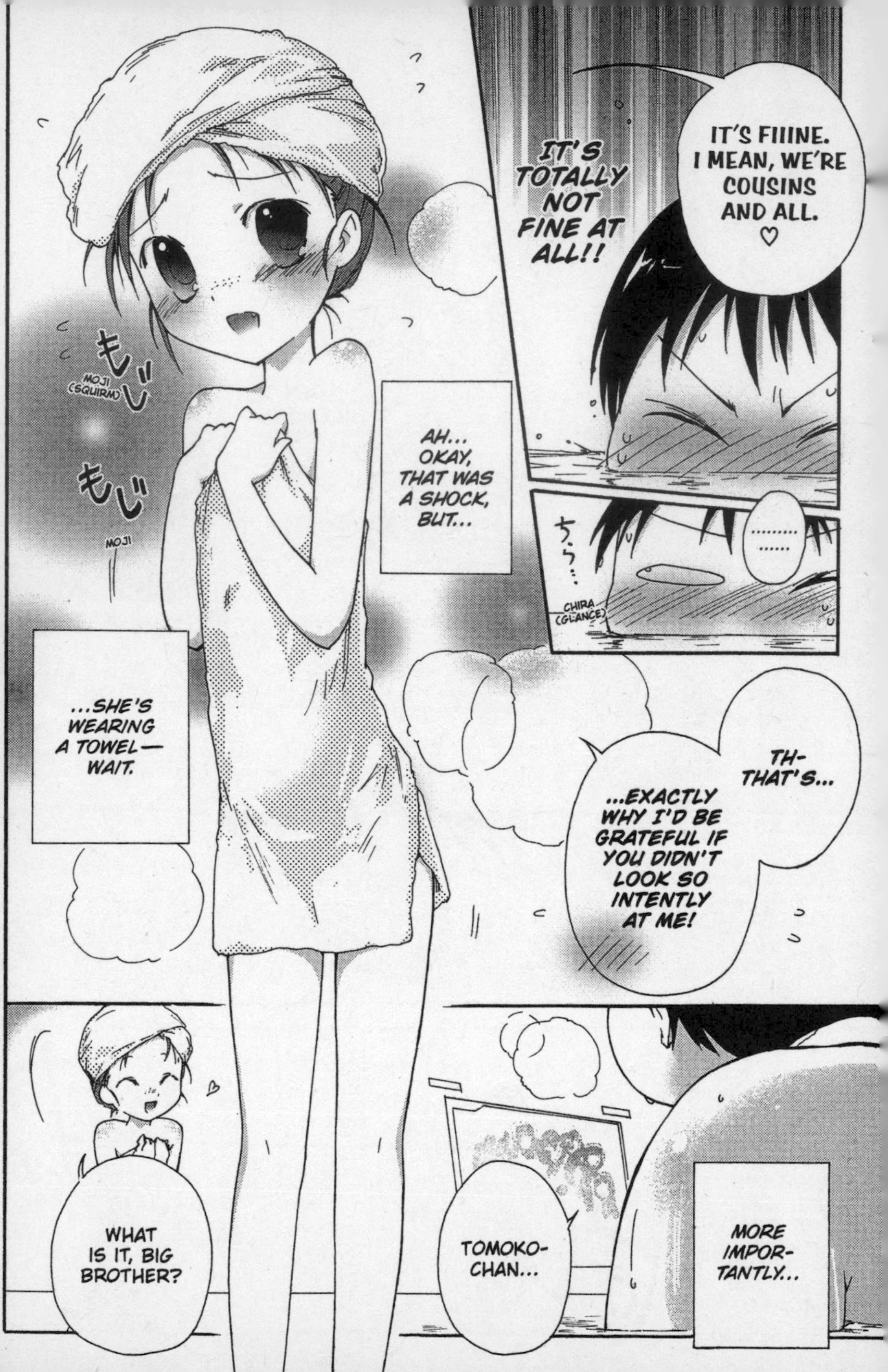
IT'S FIIINE. I MEAN, WE'RE COUSINS AND ALL. ♡
IT'S TOTALLY NOT FINE AT ALL!!
....
......
ちら…
CHIRA (GLANCE)
AH... OKAY, THAT WAS A SHOCK, BUT...
...SHE'S WEARING A TOWEL— WAIT.
もじ
MOJI (SQUIRM)
もじ
MOJI
TH- THAT'S...
...EXACTLY WHY I'D BE GRATEFUL IF YOU DIDN'T LOOK SO INTENTLY AT ME!
MORE IMPOR-TANTLY...
TOMOKO-CHAN...
WHAT IS IT, BIG BROTHER?

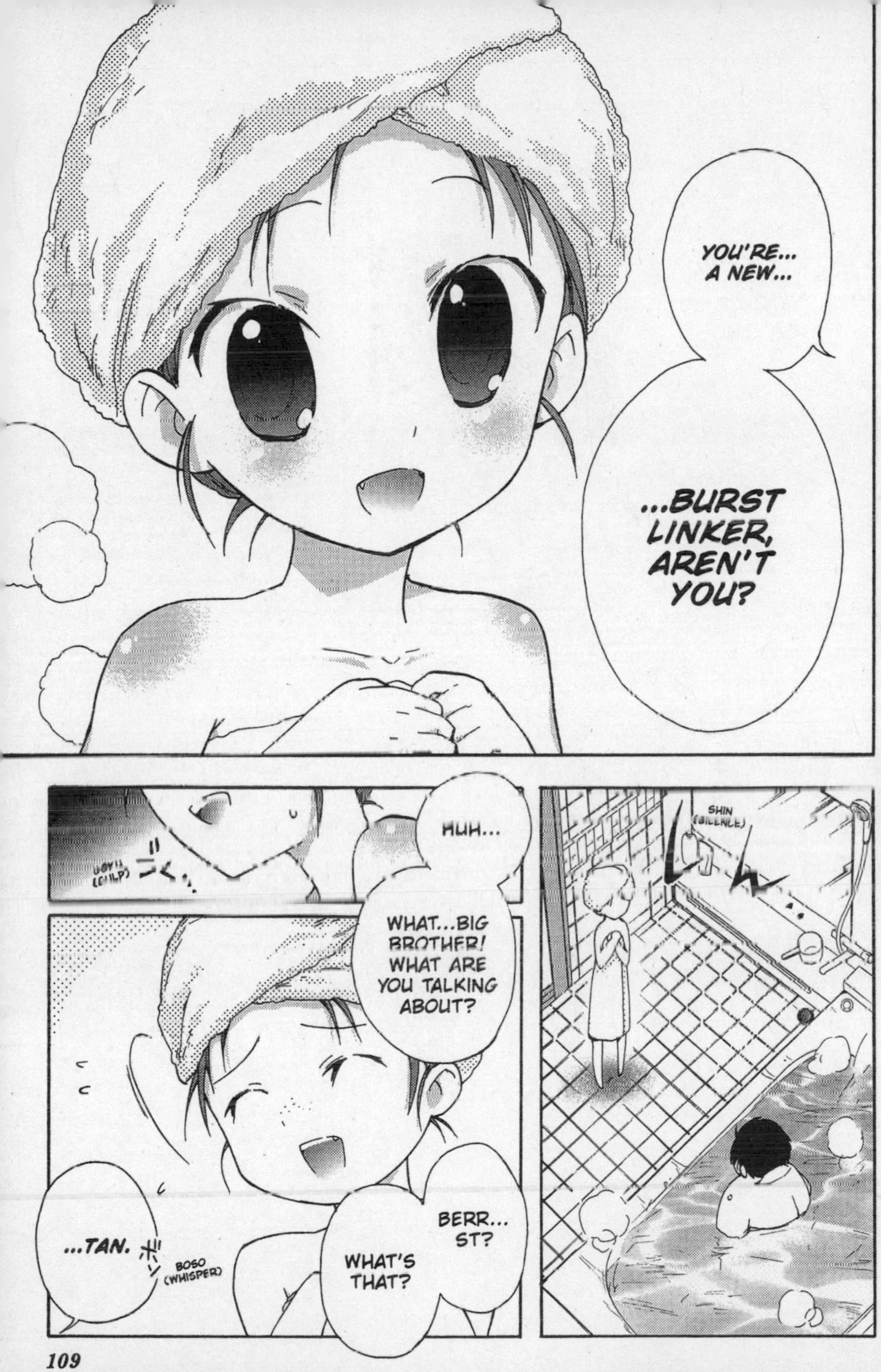
YOU'RE... A NEW...
...BURST LINKER, AREN'T YOU?
SHIN (SILENCE)
HUH...
(GULP)
WHAT...BIG BROTHER! WHAT ARE YOU TALKING ABOUT?
BERR... ST?
WHAT'S THAT?
...TAN.
BOSO (WHISPER)

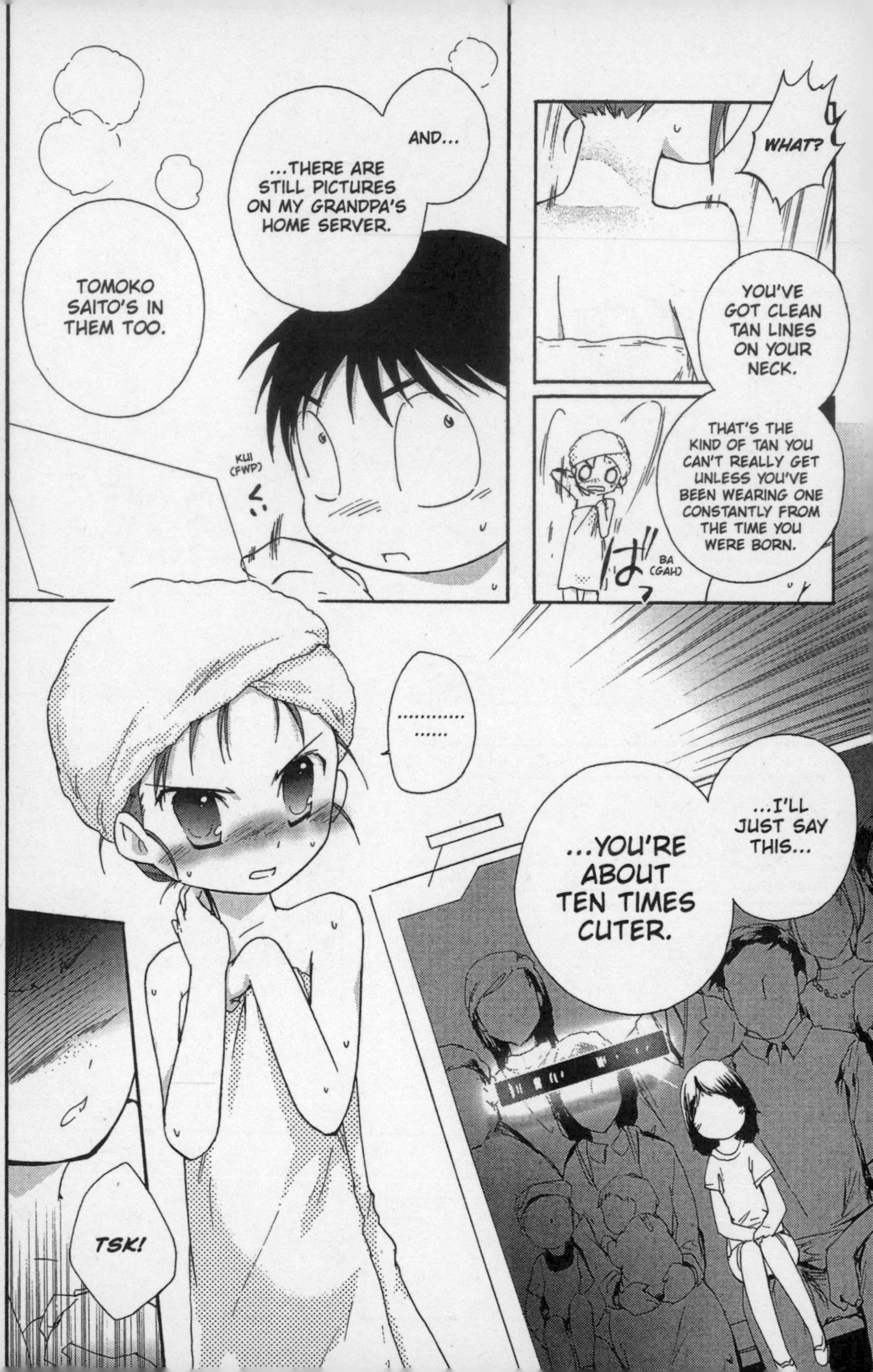
WHAT?
YOU'VE GOT CLEAN TAN LINES ON YOUR NECK.
THAT'S THE KIND OF TAN YOU CAN'T REALLY GET UNLESS YOU'VE BEEN WEARING ONE CONSTANTLY FROM THE TIME YOU WERE BORN.
BA (GAH)
AND...
...THERE ARE STILL PICTURES ON MY GRANDPA'S HOME SERVER.
TOMOKO SAITO'S IN THEM TOO.
KUI (FWP)
...I'LL JUST SAY THIS...
...YOU'RE ABOUT TEN TIMES CUTER.
....
TSK!

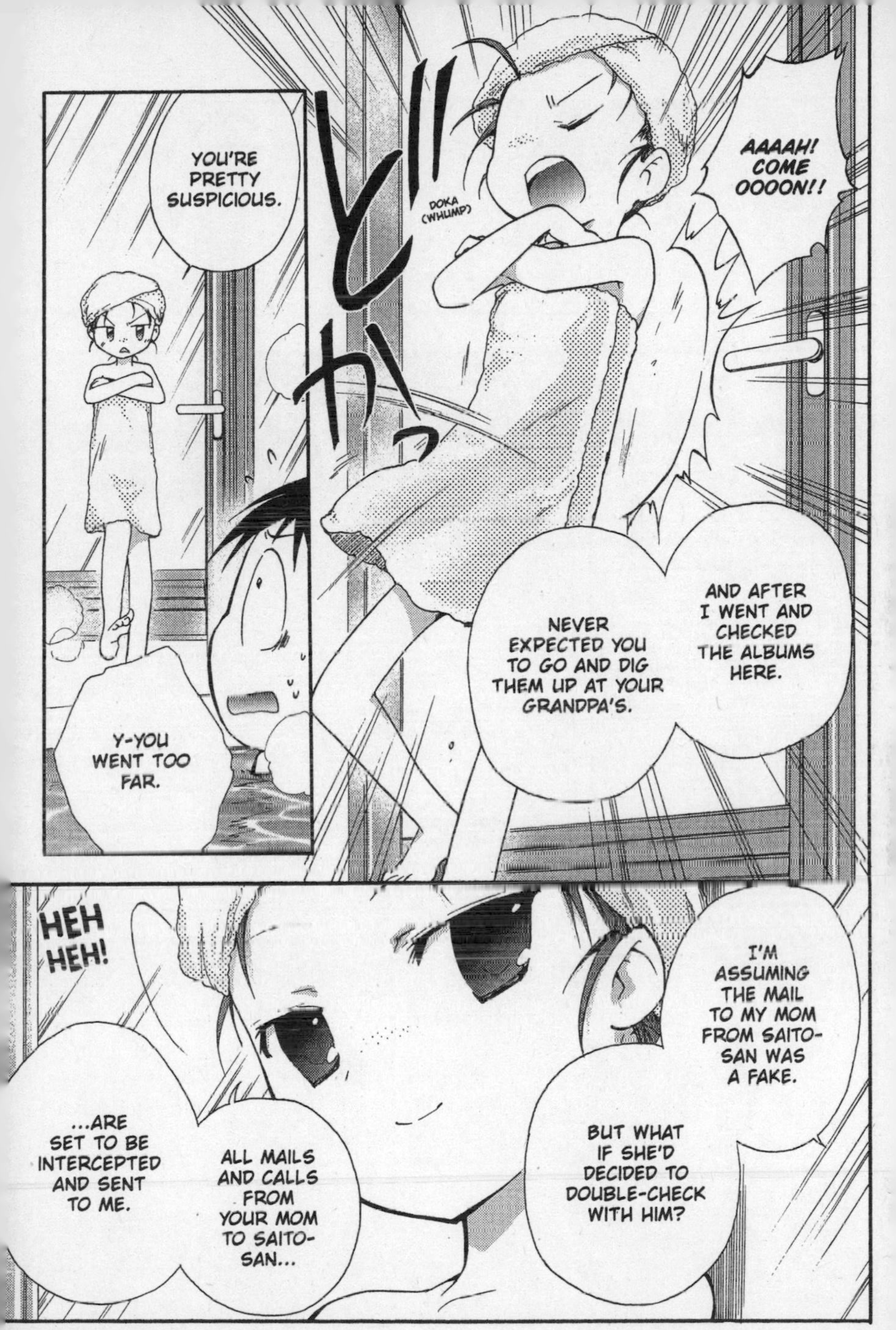
AAAAH! COME OOOON!!
DOKA (WHUMP)
AND AFTER I WENT AND CHECKED THE ALBUMS HERE.
NEVER EXPECTED YOU TO GO AND DIG THEM UP AT YOUR GRANDPA'S.
YOU'RE PRETTY SUSPICIOUS.
Y-YOU WENT TOO FAR.
I'M ASSUMING THE MAIL TO MY MOM FROM SAITO-SAN WAS A FAKE.
BUT WHAT IF SHE'D DECIDED TO DOUBLE-CHECK WITH HIM?
ALL MAILS AND CALLS FROM YOUR MOM TO SAITO-SAN...
...ARE SET TO BE INTERCEPTED AND SENT TO ME.
HEH HEH!

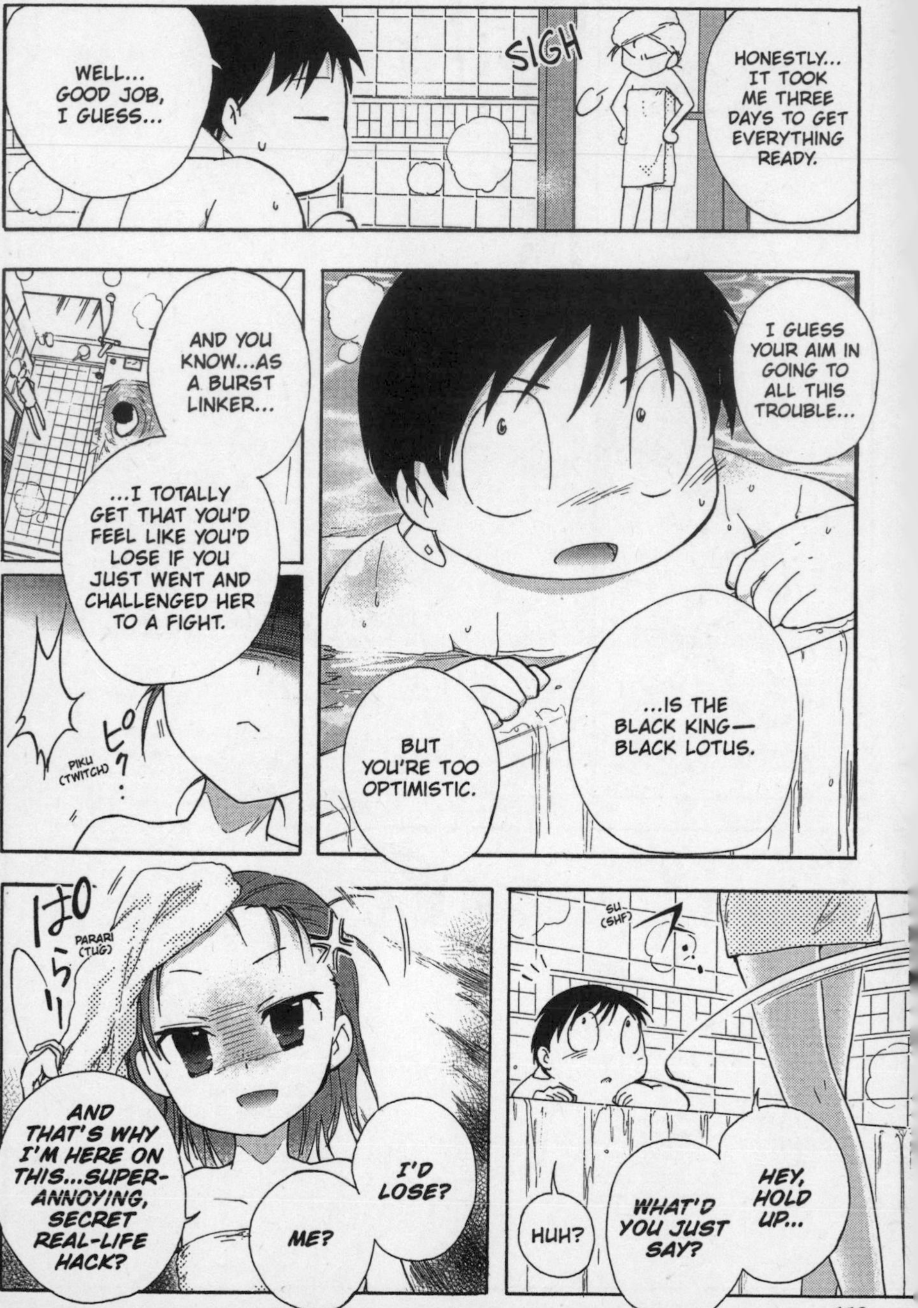

HONESTLY... IT TOOK ME THREE DAYS TO GET EVERYTHING READY.
SIGH
WELL... GOOD JOB, I GUESS...
I GUESS YOUR AIM IN GOING TO ALL THIS TROUBLE...
...IS THE BLACK KING—BLACK LOTUS.
BUT YOU'RE TOO OPTIMISTIC.
AND YOU KNOW...AS A BURST LINKER...
...I TOTALLY GET THAT YOU'D FEEL LIKE YOU'D LOSE IF YOU JUST WENT AND CHALLENGED HER TO A FIGHT.
ピク
PIKU (TWITCH)
SU (SHF)
HEY, HOLD UP...
WHAT'D YOU JUST SAY?
HUH?
はらり
PARARI (TUG)
I'D LOSE?
ME?
AND THAT'S WHY I'M HERE ON THIS...SUPER-ANNOYING, SECRET REAL-LIFE HACK?

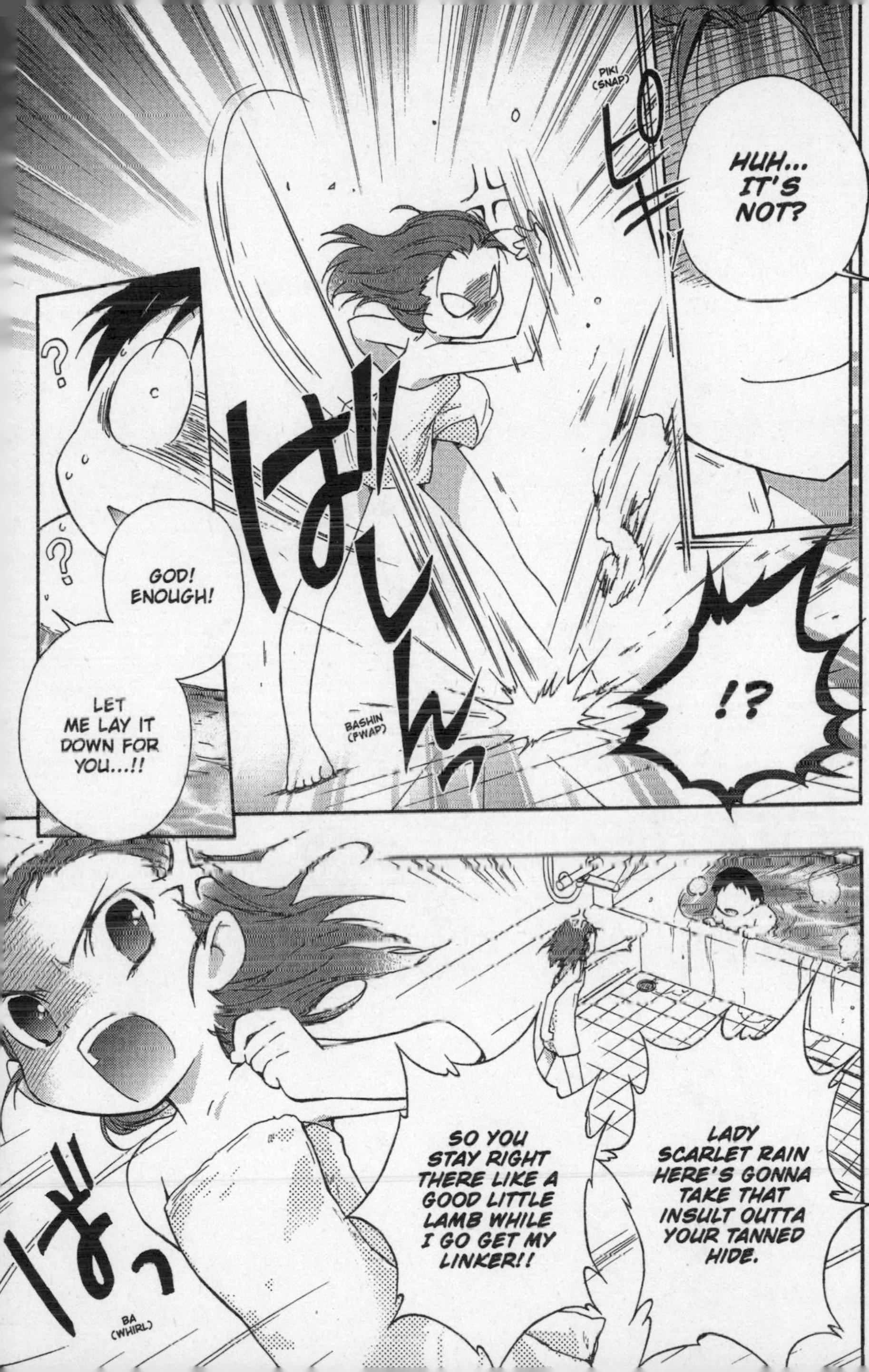
PIKI (SNAP)
HUH... IT'S NOT?
!?
ぱしんっ
BASHIN (PWAP)
GOD! ENOUGH!
LET ME LAY IT DOWN FOR YOU...!!
LADY SCARLET RAIN HERE'S GONNA TAKE THAT INSULT OUTTA YOUR TANNED HIDE.
SO YOU STAY RIGHT THERE LIKE A GOOD LITTLE LAMB WHILE I GO GET MY LINKER!!
ばっ
BA (WHIRL)

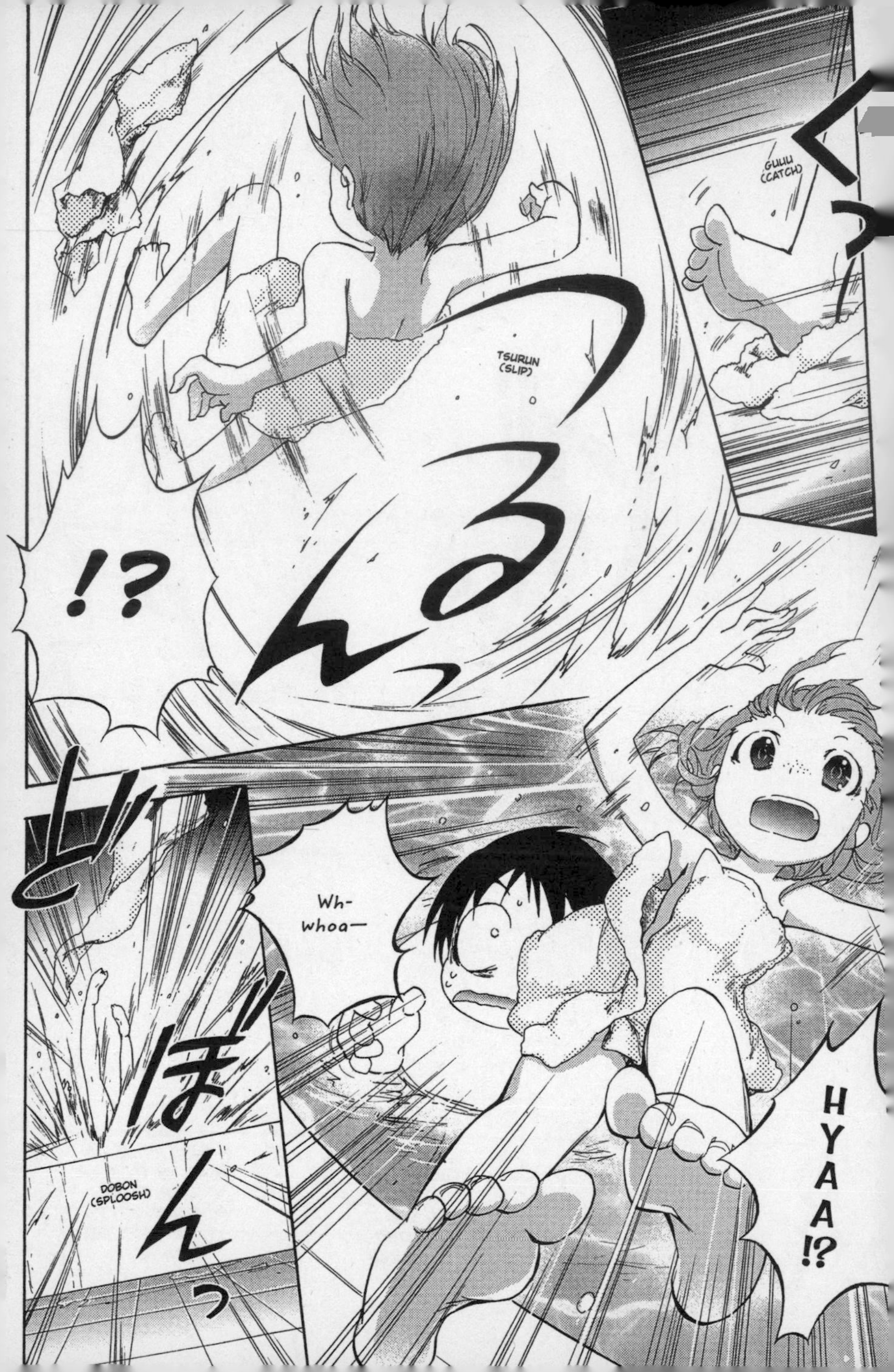
くっ
GUUU (CATCH)
つるんっ
TSURUN (SLIP)
!?
HYAA!?
Wh- whoa—
どぼんっ
DOBON (SPLOOSH)

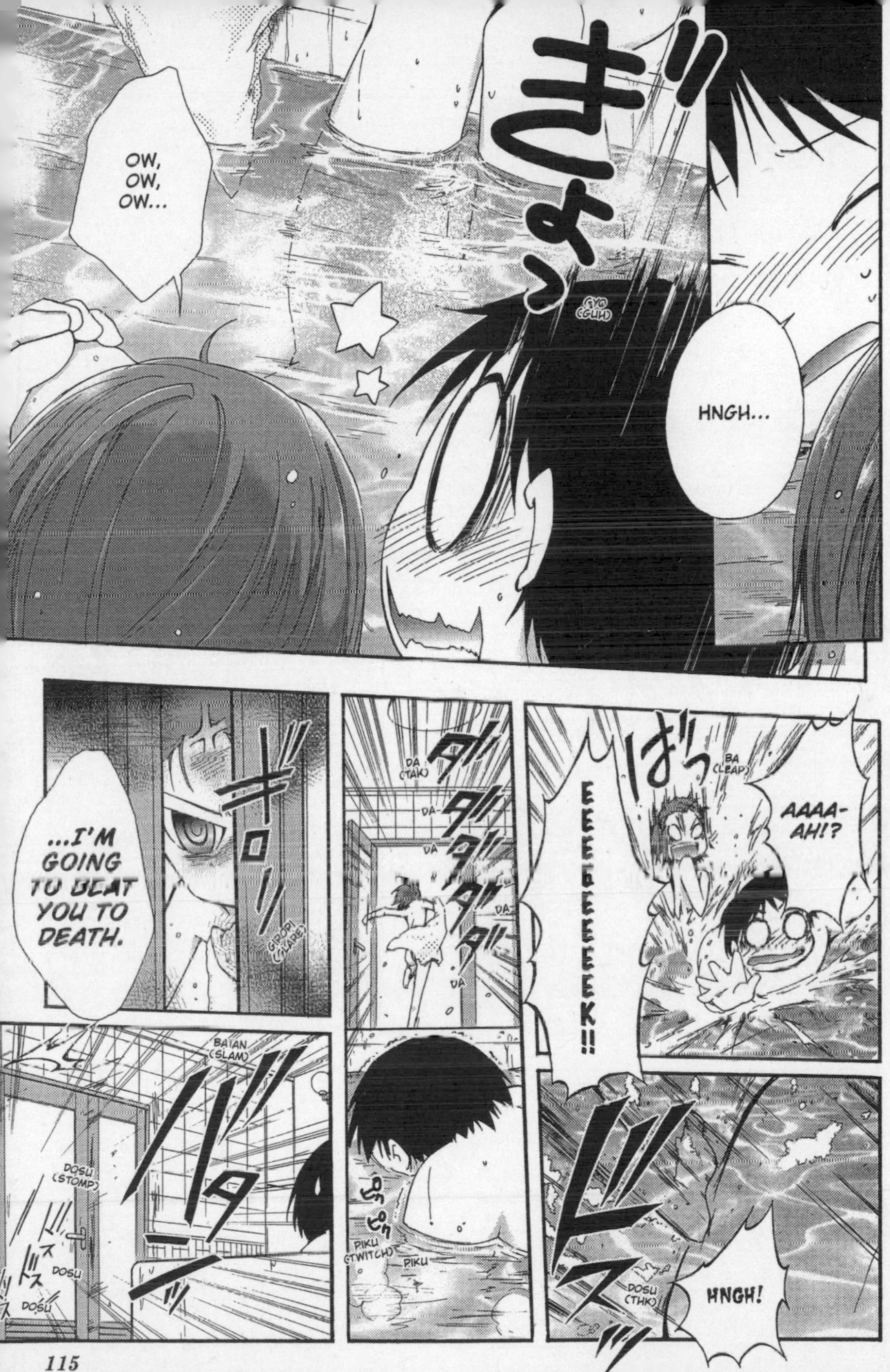
ぎょっ
GYO (GULP)
HNGH...
OW, OW, OW...
ばっ
BA (LEAP)
AAAA-AH!?
EEEEEEEEEK!!
DA (TAK)
DA-
DA
DA
DA
GIROPI (GLARE)
...I'M GOING TO BEAT YOU TO DEATH.
DOSU (THK)
HNGH!
PIKU (TWITCH)
PIKU
BATAN (SLAM)
DOSU (STOMP)
DOSU
DOSU

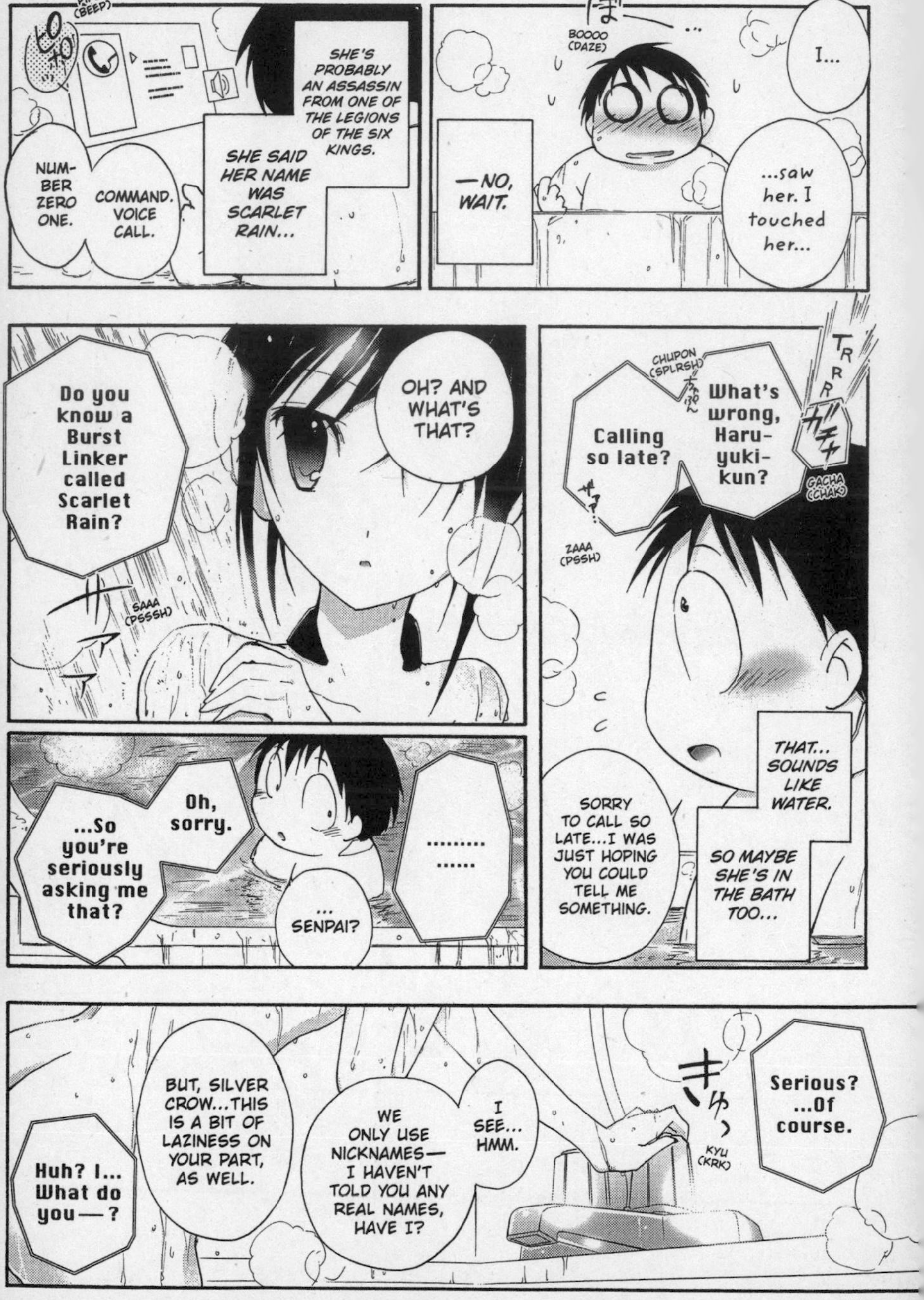
I...
...saw her. I touched her...
BOOOO (DAZE)
—NO, WAIT.
SHE'S PROBABLY AN ASSASSIN FROM ONE OF THE LEGIONS OF THE SIX KINGS.
SHE SAID HER NAME WAS SCARLET RAIN...
COMMAND. VOICE CALL.
PIPO (BEEP)
NUMBER ZERO ONE.
TRRR
GACHA (CHAK)
What's wrong, Haruyuki-kun?
CHUPON (SPLRSH)
Calling so late?
ZAAA (PSSH)
THAT... SOUNDS LIKE WATER.
SO MAYBE SHE'S IN THE BATH TOO...
SORRY TO CALL SO LATE...I WAS JUST HOPING YOU COULD TELL ME SOMETHING.
OH? AND WHAT'S THAT?
Do you know a Burst Linker called Scarlet Rain?
SAAA (PSSSH)
....
......
Oh, sorry.
... SENPAI?
...So you're seriously asking me that?
Serious? ...Of course.
KYU (KRK)
I SEE... HMM.
WE ONLY USE NICKNAMES—I HAVEN'T TOLD YOU ANY REAL NAMES, HAVE I?
BUT, SILVER CROW...THIS IS A BIT OF LAZINESS ON YOUR PART, AS WELL.
Huh? I... What do you—?

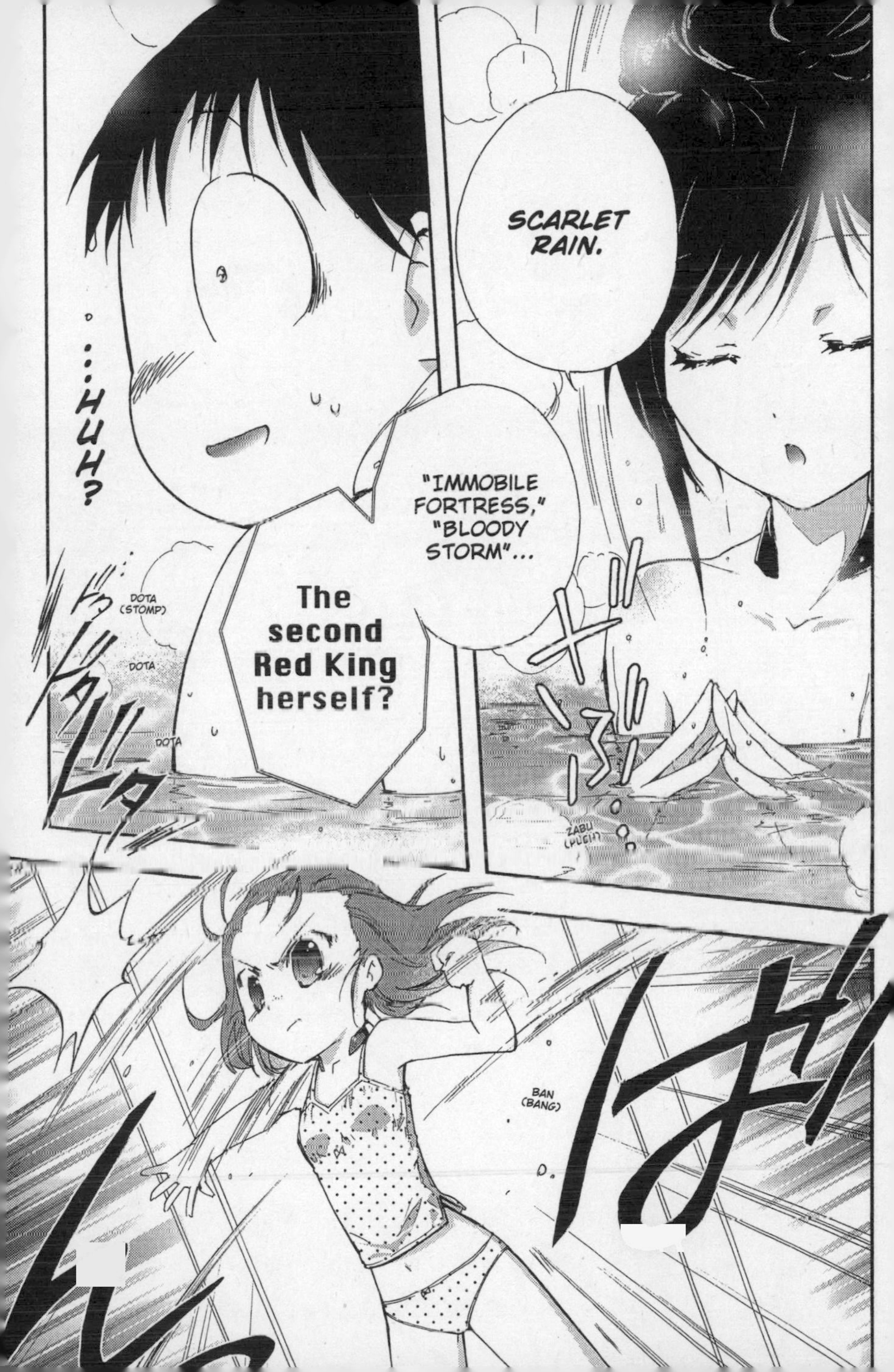
SCARLET RAIN.
"IMMOBILE FORTRESS," "BLOODY STORM"...
ZABU
The second Red King herself?
...HUH?
DOTA (STOMP)
DOTA
DOTA
BAN (BANG)

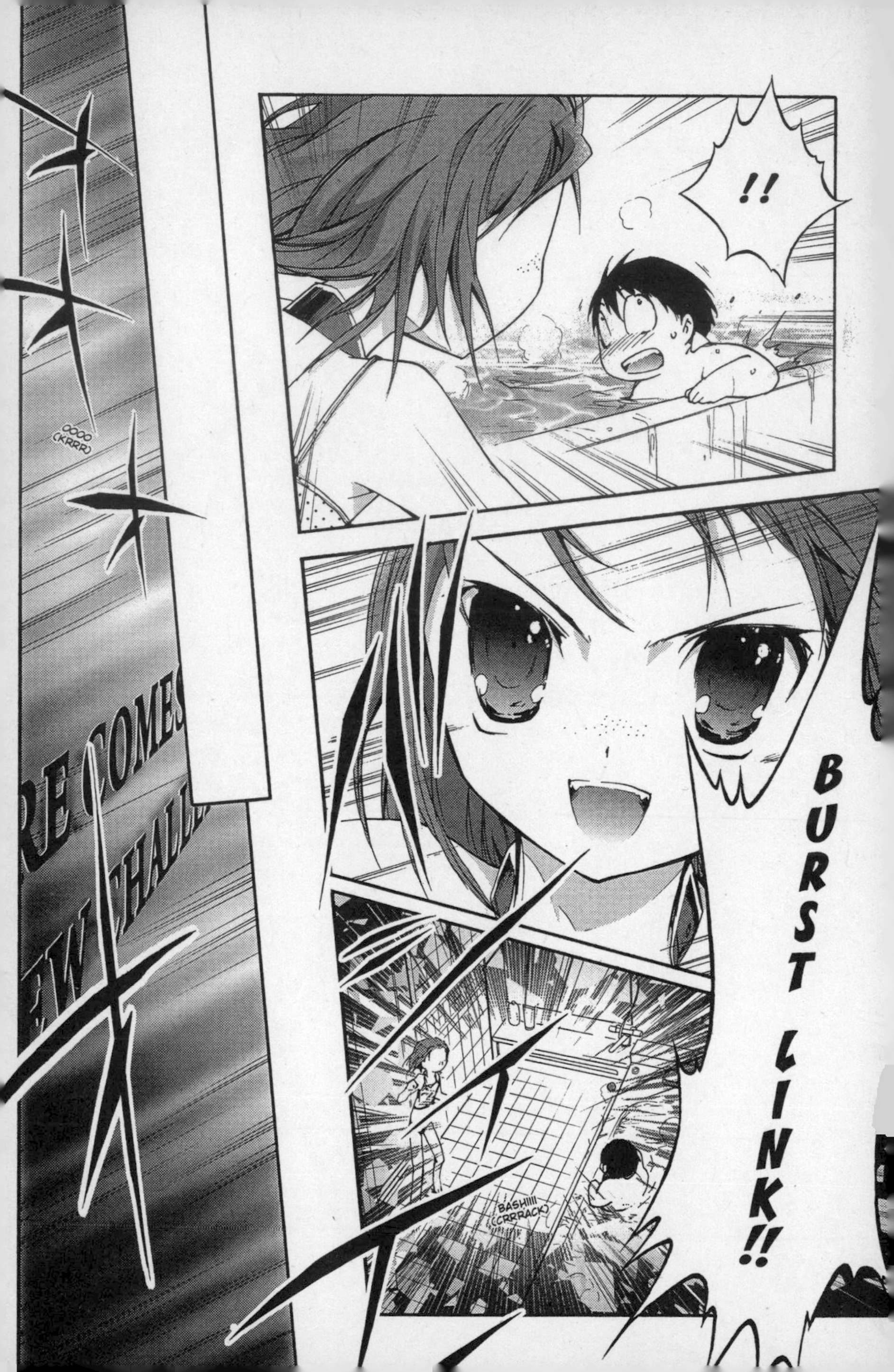
!!
BURST LINK!!
BASH!!!!!
(CRRRACK)
OOOO
(KRRR)
RE COMES
EW CHALL

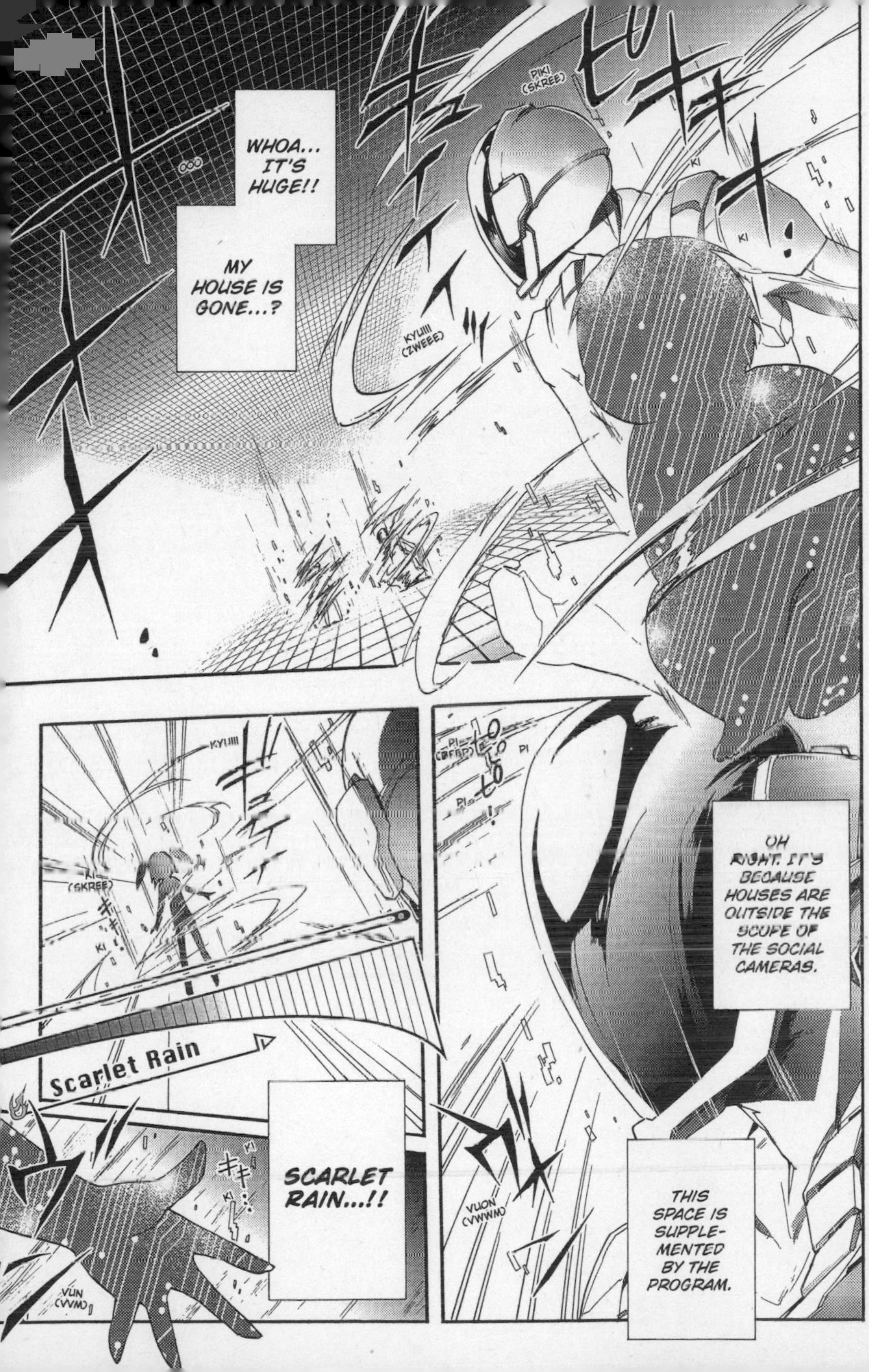
PIKI (SKREE)
WHOA... IT'S HUGE!!
KI
KI
MY HOUSE IS GONE...?
KYUIII (ZWEEE)
PI (BEEP)
PI
PI
OH RIGHT. IT'S BECAUSE HOUSES ARE OUTSIDE THE SCOPE OF THE SOCIAL CAMERAS.
THIS SPACE IS SUPPLEMENTED BY THE PROGRAM.
VUON (VWWM)
KYUIII
KI (SKREE)
KI
Scarlet Rain
SCARLET RAIN...!!
KI
KI
VUN (VVM)

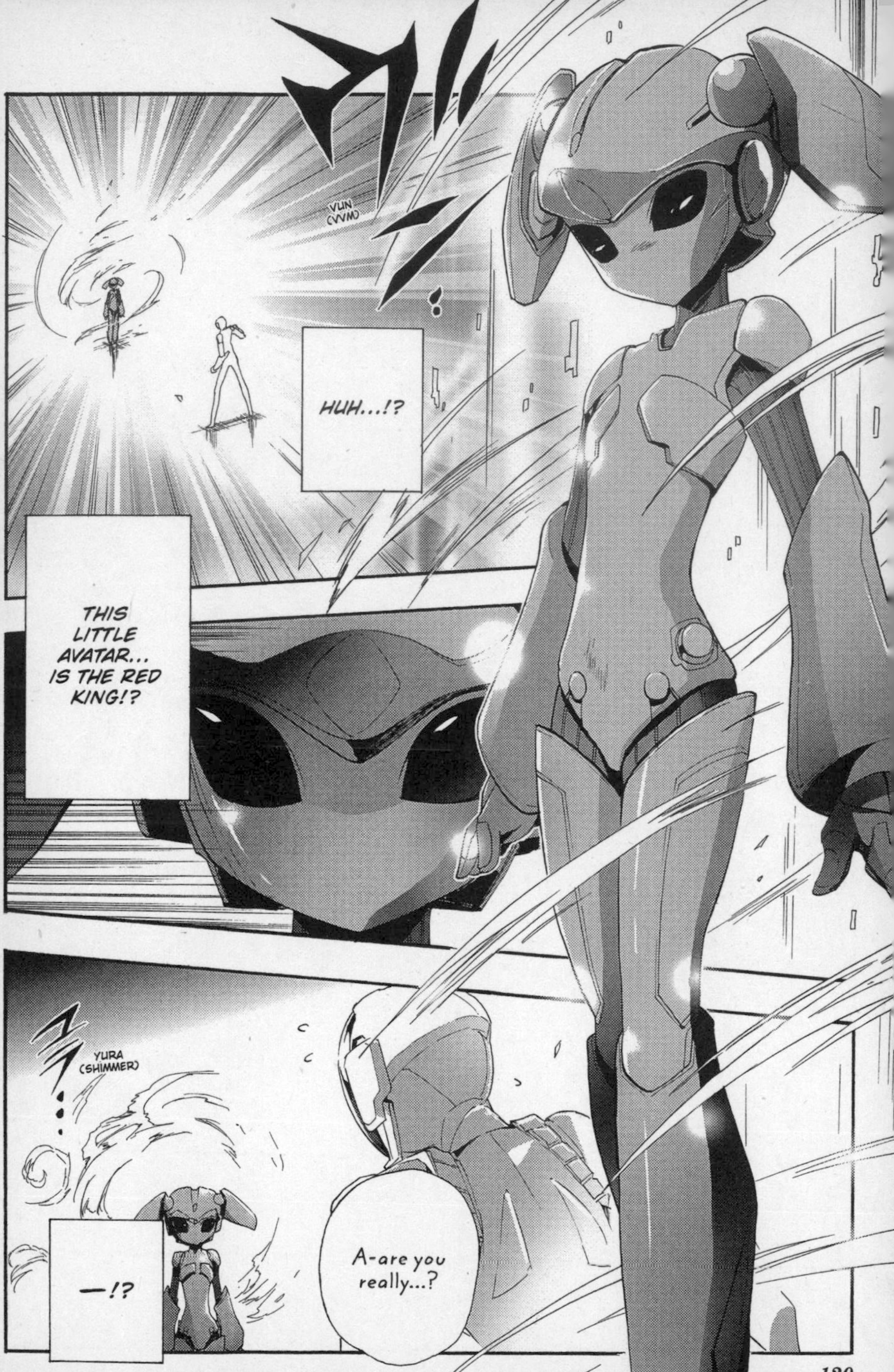
VUN (VVM)
HUH...!?
THIS LITTLE AVATAR... IS THE RED KING!?
A-are you really...?
YURA (SHIMMER)
—!?

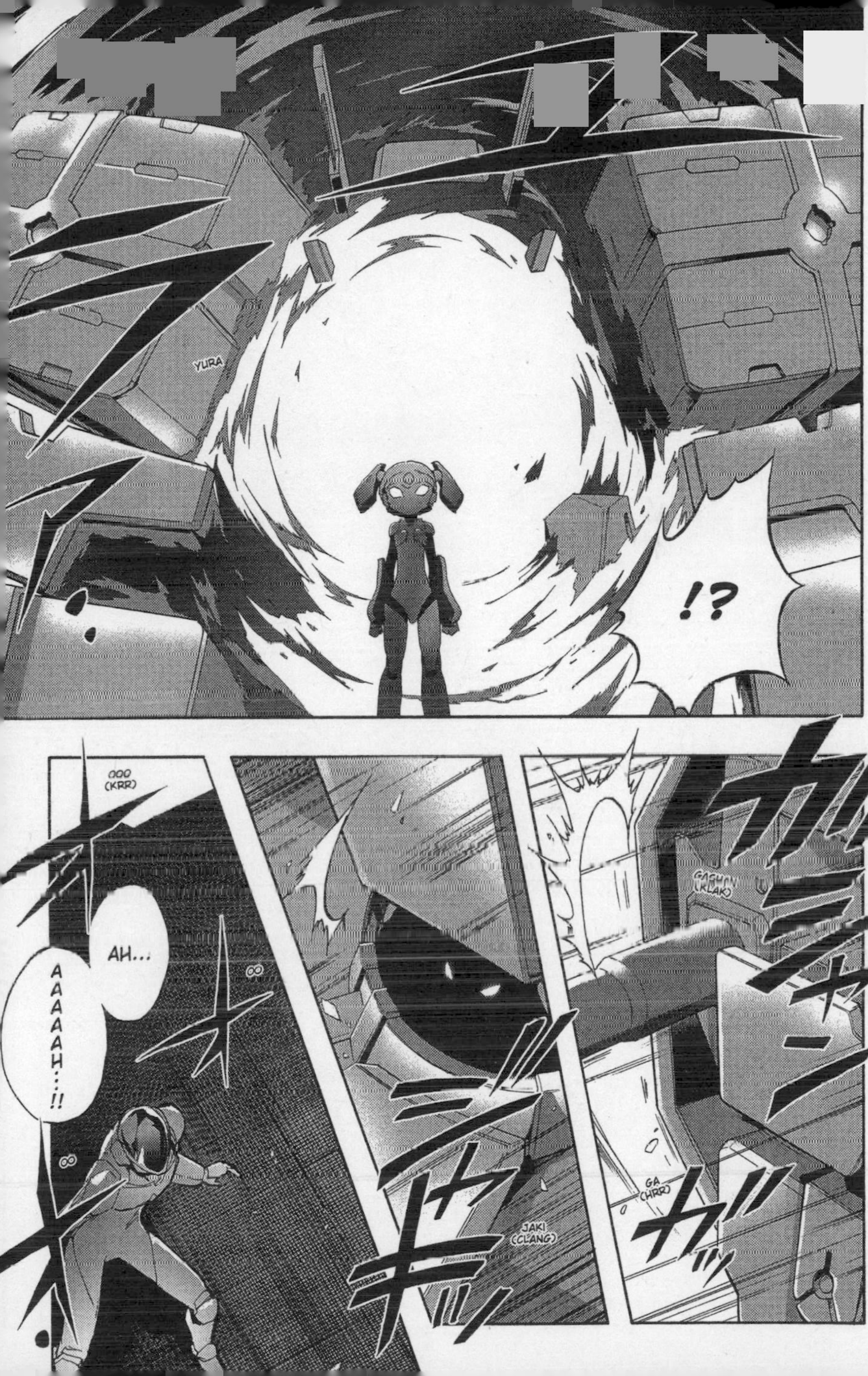
YURA
!?
GASHAN (KLAK)
GA (HRR)
JAKI (CLANG)
GGG (KRR)
AH...
AAAAAAH...!!

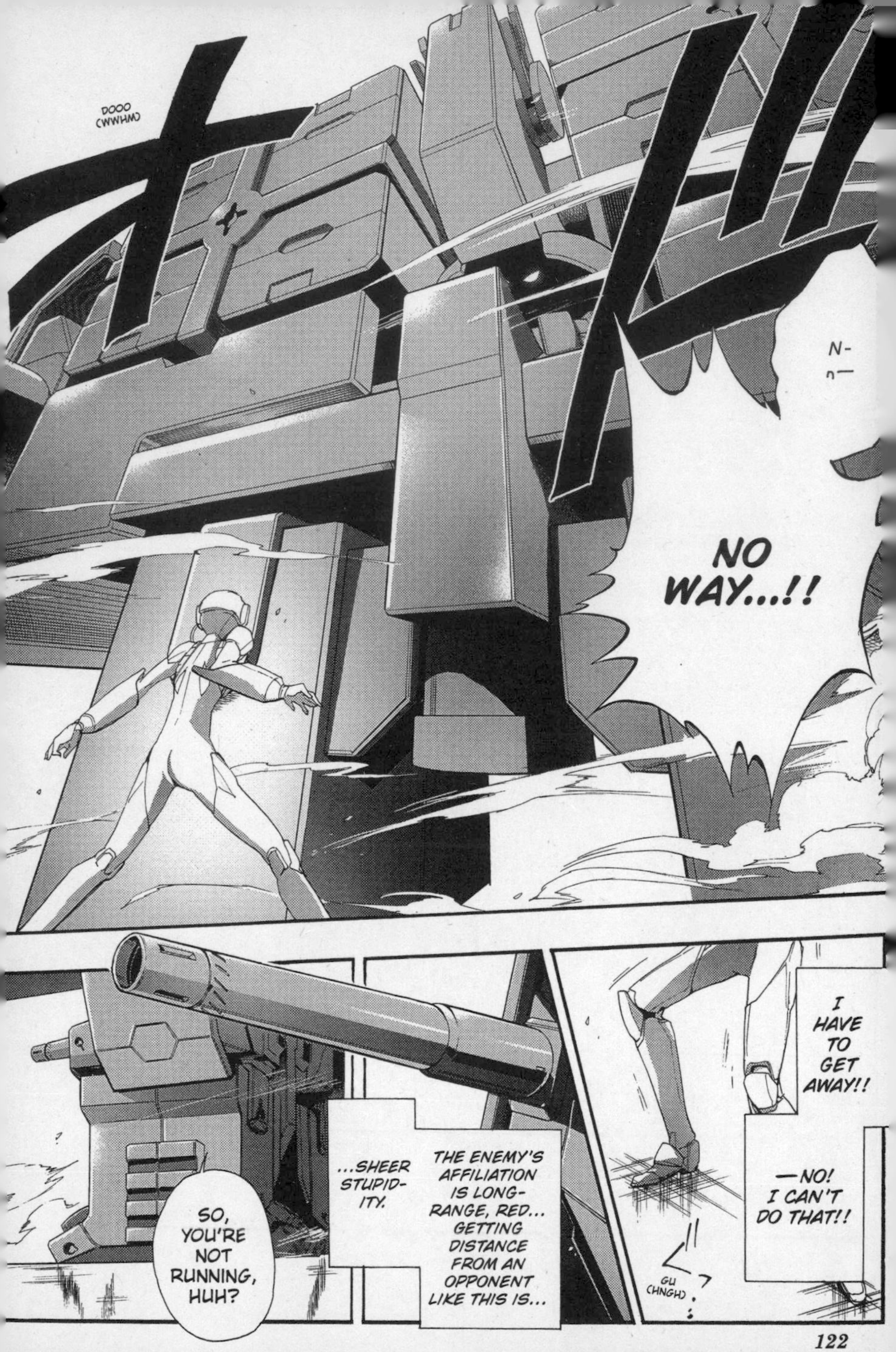
N-
n—
NO WAY...!!
DOOO (WWHM)
I HAVE TO GET AWAY!!
—NO! I CAN'T DO THAT!!
GU (HNGH)
THE ENEMY'S AFFILIATION IS LONG-RANGE, RED... GETTING DISTANCE FROM AN OPPONENT LIKE THIS IS...
...SHEER STUPID-ITY.
SO, YOU'RE NOT RUNNING, HUH?

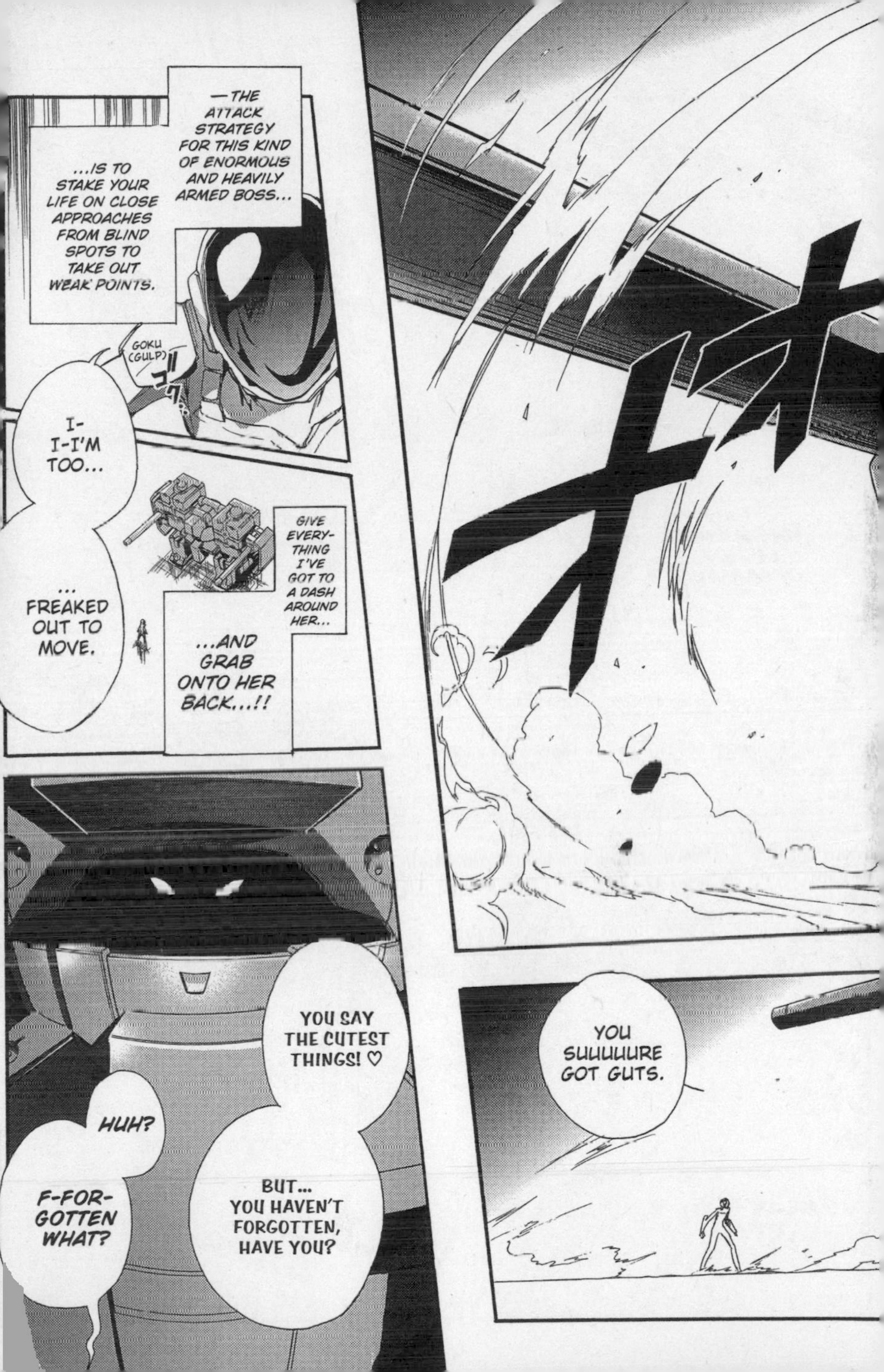
—THE ATTACK STRATEGY FOR THIS KIND OF ENORMOUS AND HEAVILY ARMED BOSS...
...IS TO STAKE YOUR LIFE ON CLOSE APPROACHES FROM BLIND SPOTS TO TAKE OUT WEAK POINTS.
GOKU (GULP)
I-I-I'M TOO...
...FREAKED OUT TO MOVE.
GIVE EVERYTHING I'VE GOT TO A DASH AROUND HER...
...AND GRAB ONTO HER BACK...!!
YOU SUUUUURE GOT GUTS.
YOU SAY THE CUTEST THINGS! ♡
HUH?
BUT... YOU HAVEN'T FORGOTTEN, HAVE YOU?
F-FORGOTTEN WHAT?

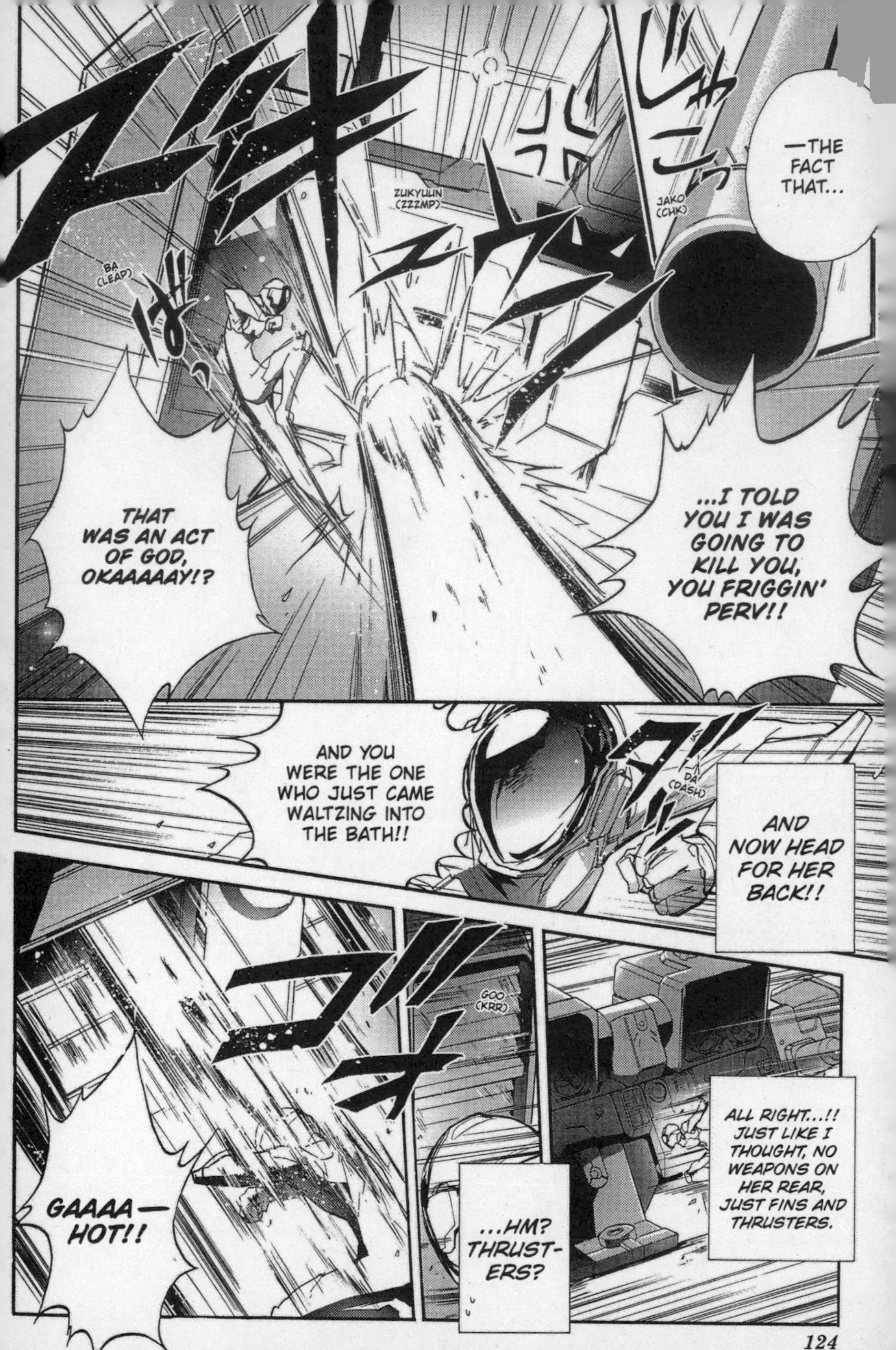
JAKO (CHK)
—THE FACT THAT...
...I TOLD YOU I WAS GOING TO KILL YOU, YOU FRIGGIN' PERV!!
ZUKYUUN (ZZZMP)
BA (LEAP)
THAT WAS AN ACT OF GOD, OKAAAAAY!?
AND NOW HEAD FOR HER BACK!!
DA (DASH)
AND YOU WERE THE ONE WHO JUST CAME WALTZING INTO THE BATH!!
ALL RIGHT...!! JUST LIKE I THOUGHT, NO WEAPONS ON HER REAR, JUST FINS AND THRUSTERS.
GOO (KRR)
...HM? THRUST-ERS?
GAAAA—HOT!!

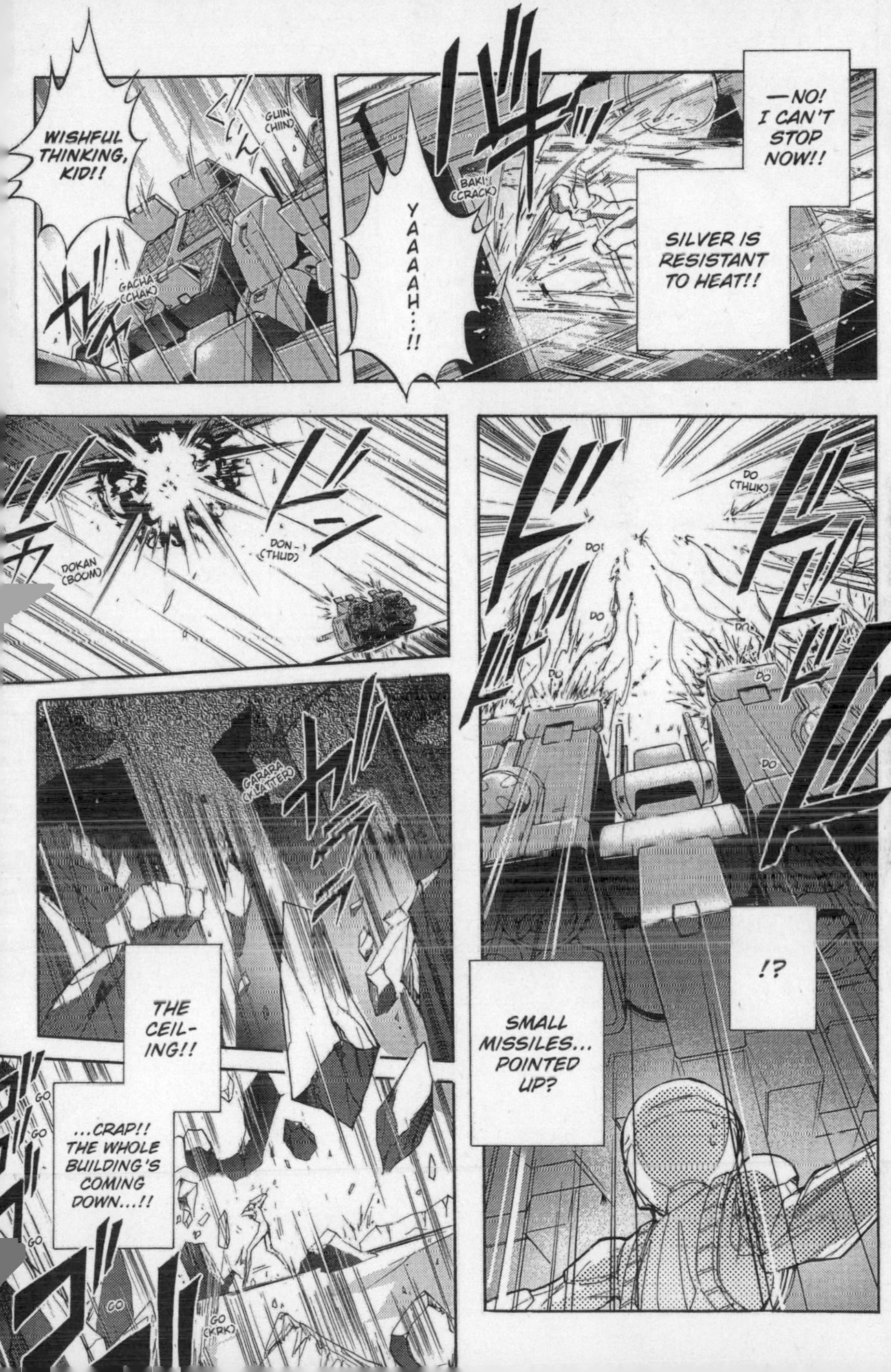
—NO! I CAN'T STOP NOW!!
BAKI (CRACK)
SILVER IS RESISTANT TO HEAT!!
YAAAAAH...!!
GUIN (HIIN)
WISHFUL THINKING, KID!!
GACHA (CHAK)
DO (THUK)
DO
DO
DO
DO
DO
DO
!?
SMALL MISSILES... POINTED UP?
DON (THUD)
DOKAN (BOOM)
GARARA (KLATTER)
THE CEIL-ING!!
...CRAP!! THE WHOLE BUILDING'S COMING DOWN...!!
GO
GO
GO
GO
GO (KRK)

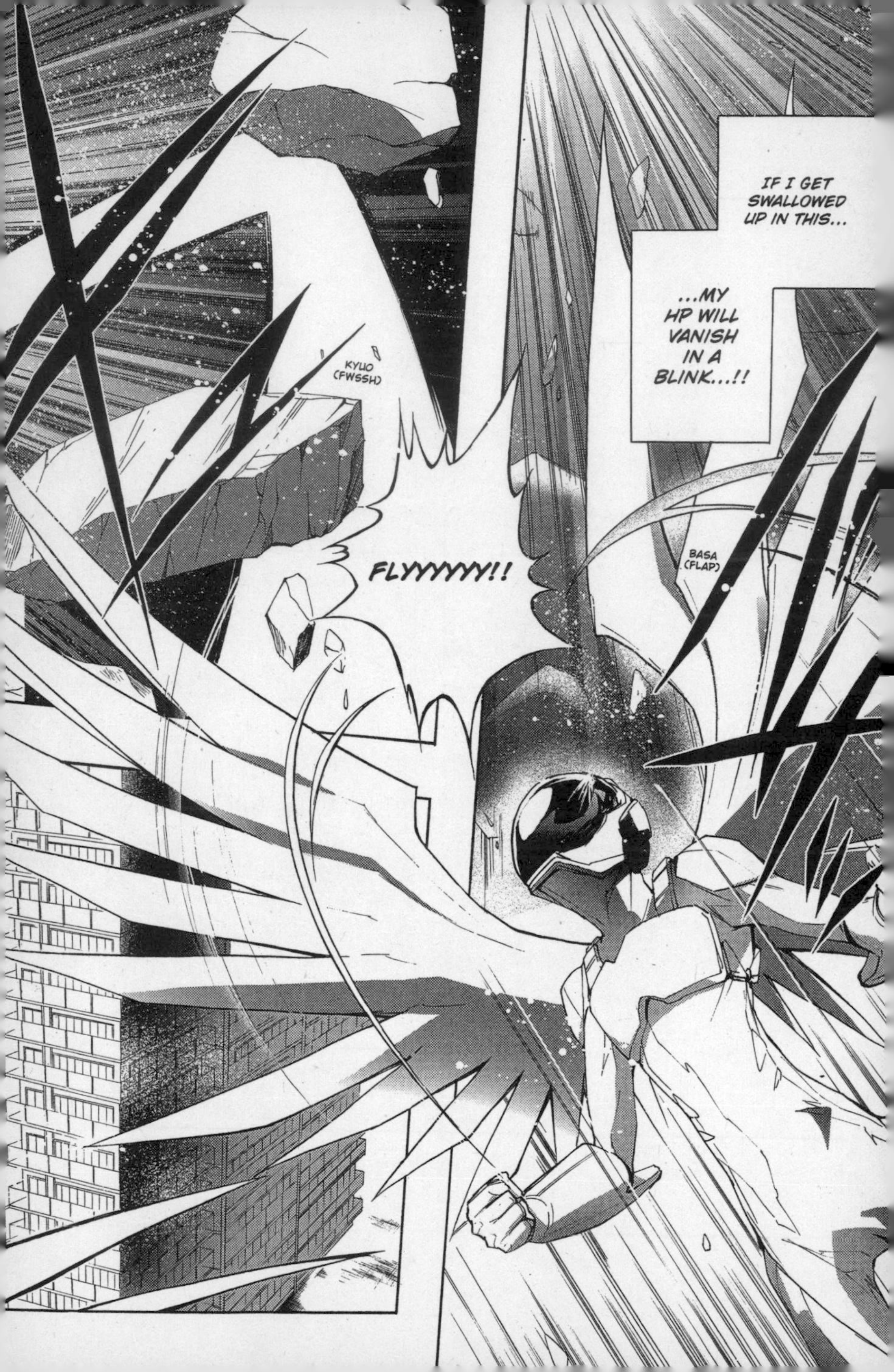
IF I GET SWALLOWED UP IN THIS...
...MY HP WILL VANISH IN A BLINK...!!
KYUO (FWSSH)
FLYYYYYY!!
BASA (FLAP)

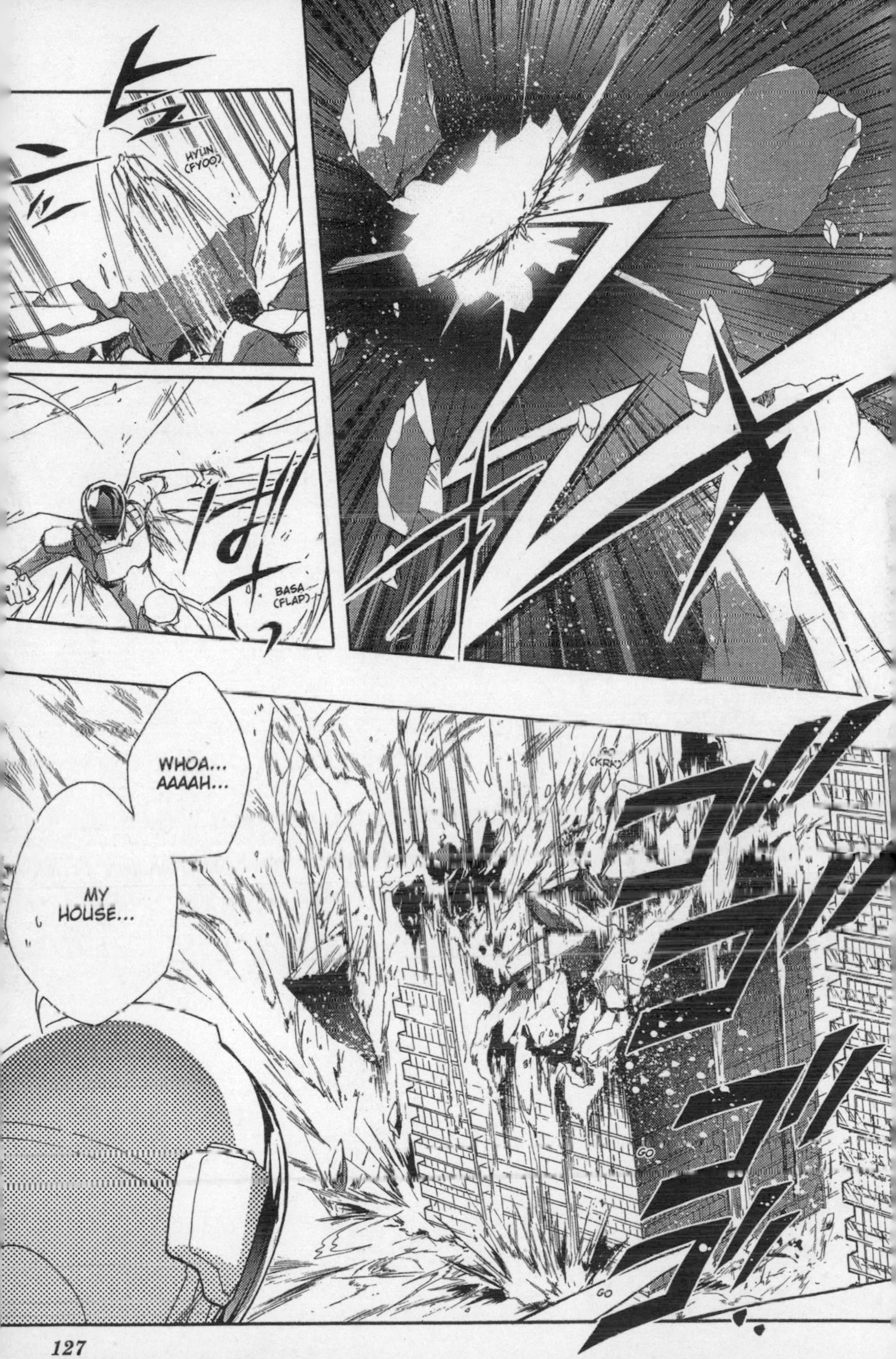
HYUN (FYOO)
BASA (FLAP)
WHOA... AAAAH...
MY HOUSE...
GO (KRK)
GO
GO
GO

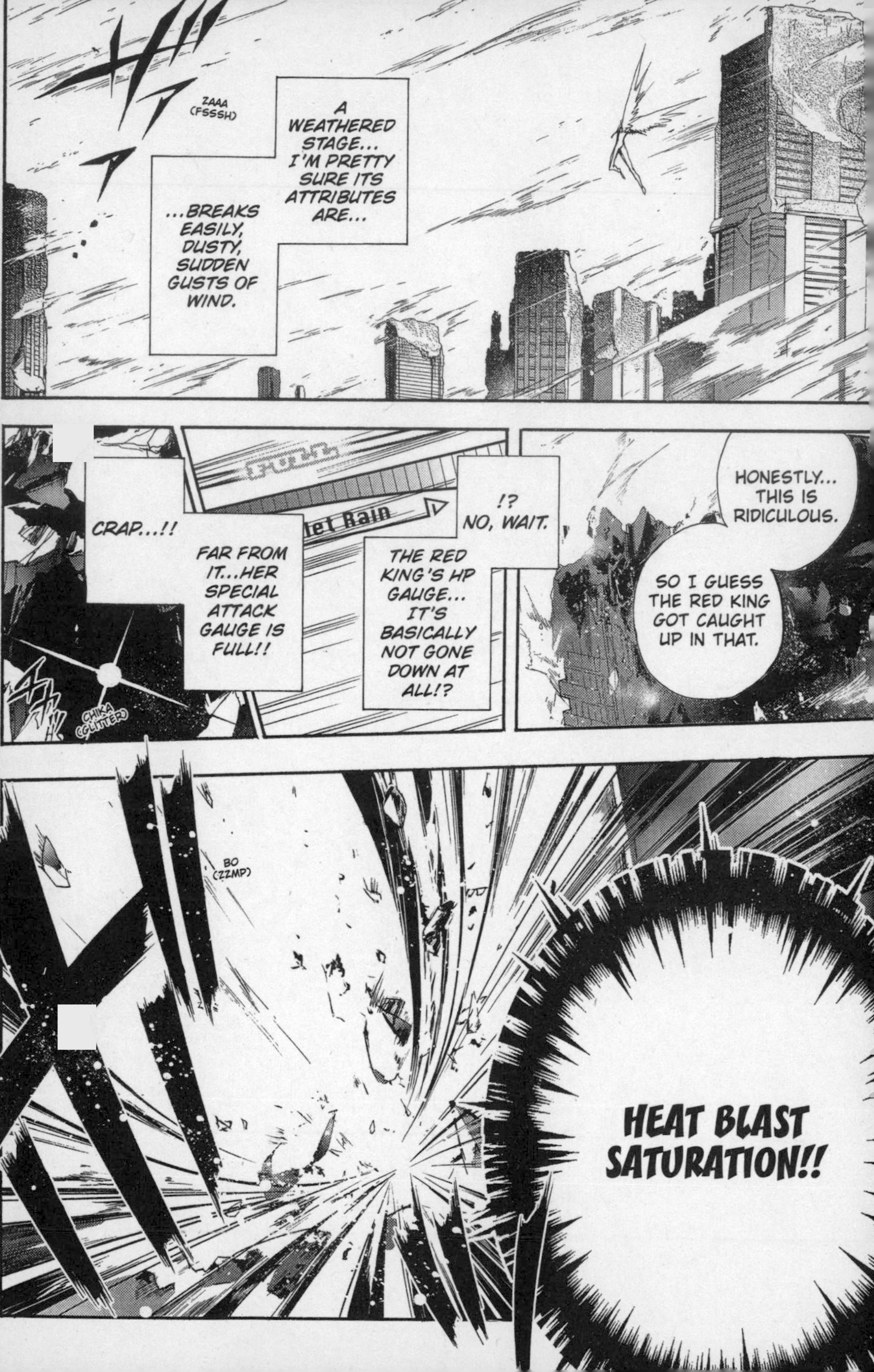
ZAAA (FSSSH)
A WEATHERED STAGE... I'M PRETTY SURE ITS ATTRIBUTES ARE...
...BREAKS EASILY, DUSTY, SUDDEN GUSTS OF WIND.
HONESTLY... THIS IS RIDICULOUS.
SO I GUESS THE RED KING GOT CAUGHT UP IN THAT.
!? NO, WAIT.
THE RED KING'S HP GAUGE... IT'S BASICALLY NOT GONE DOWN AT ALL!?
FULL
CRAP...!!
FAR FROM IT...HER SPECIAL ATTACK GAUGE IS FULL!!
CHIKA (GLITTER)
HEAT BLAST SATURATION!!
BO (ZZMP)

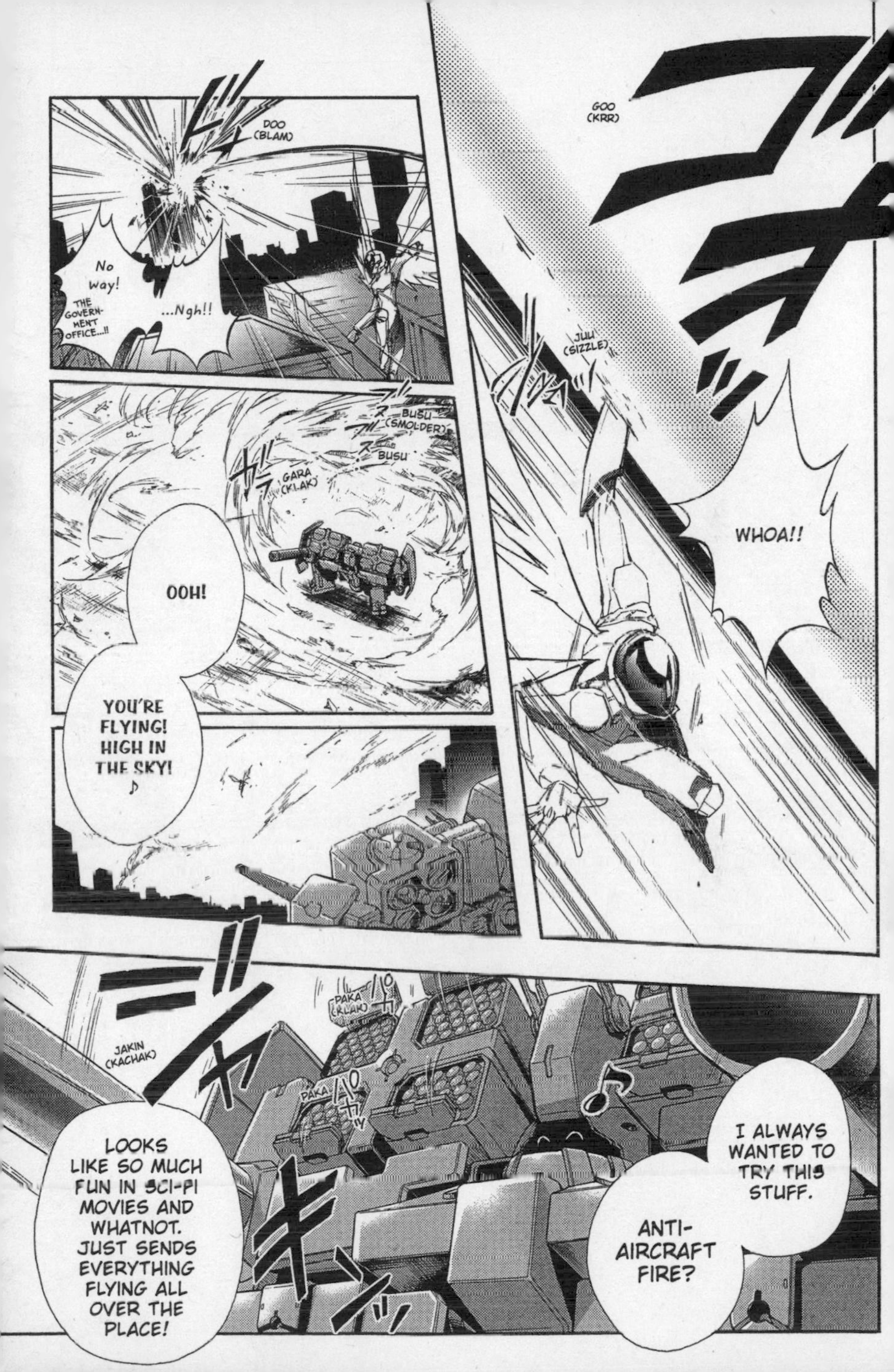
GOO (KRR)
JUU (SIZZLE)
WHOA!!
DOO (BLAM)
...Ngh!!
No way!
THE GOVERN-MENT OFFICE...!!
BUSU (SMOLDER)
BUSU
GARA (KLAK)
OOH!
YOU'RE FLYING! HIGH IN THE SKY! ♪
I ALWAYS WANTED TO TRY THIS STUFF.
ANTI-AIRCRAFT FIRE?
PAKA (KLAK)
PAKA
JAKIN (KACHAK)
LOOKS LIKE SO MUCH FUN IN SCI-FI MOVIES AND WHATNOT. JUST SENDS EVERYTHING FLYING ALL OVER THE PLACE!

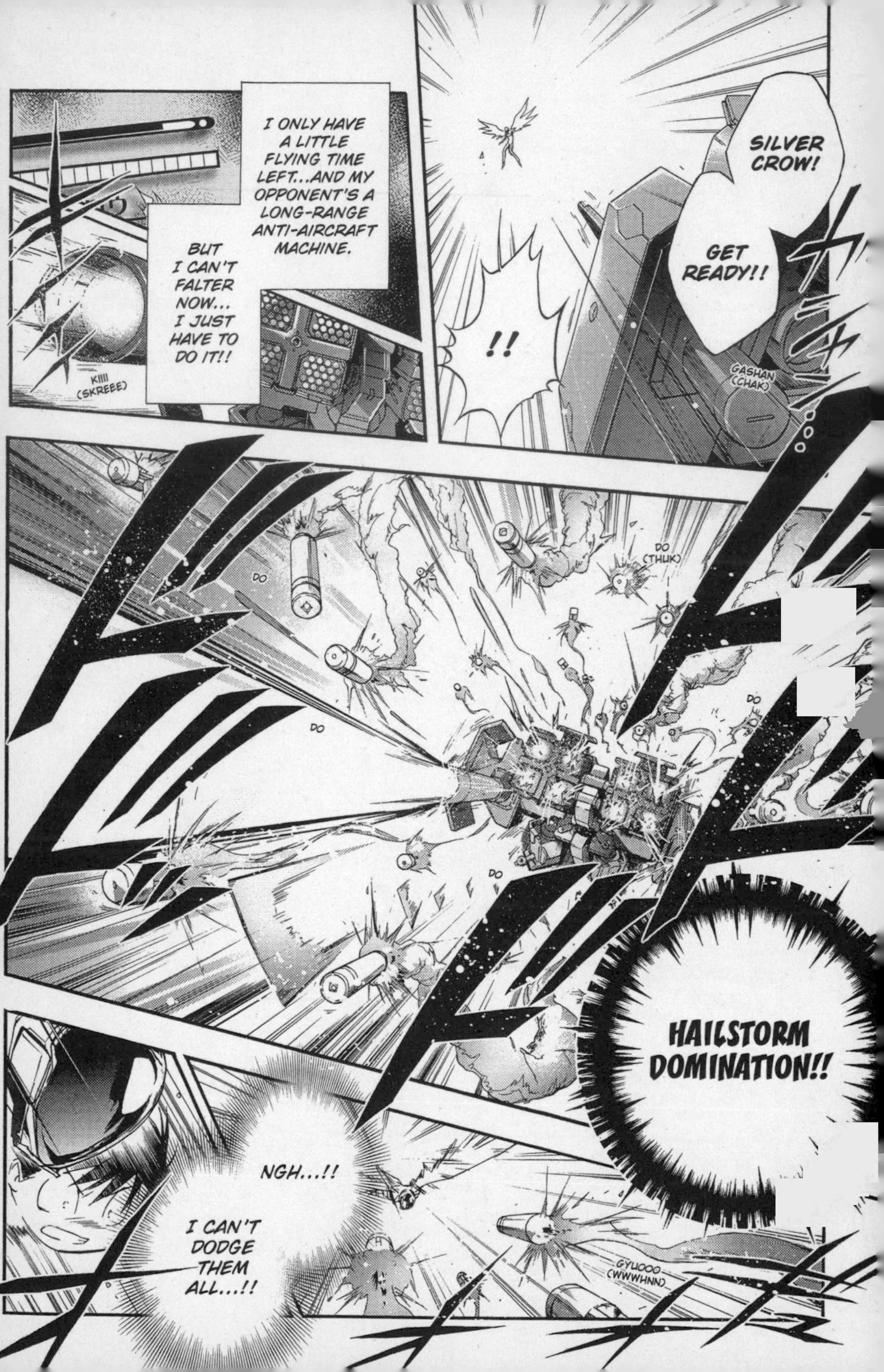
SILVER CROW!
GET READY!!
!!
GASHAN (CHAK)
I ONLY HAVE A LITTLE FLYING TIME LEFT...AND MY OPPONENT'S A LONG-RANGE ANTI-AIRCRAFT MACHINE.
BUT I CAN'T FALTER NOW... I JUST HAVE TO DO IT!!
KIIII (SKREEE)
DO (THUK)
DO
DO
DO
DO
HAILSTORM DOMINATION!!
NGH...!!
I CAN'T DODGE THEM ALL...!!
GYUOOO (WWWHNN)

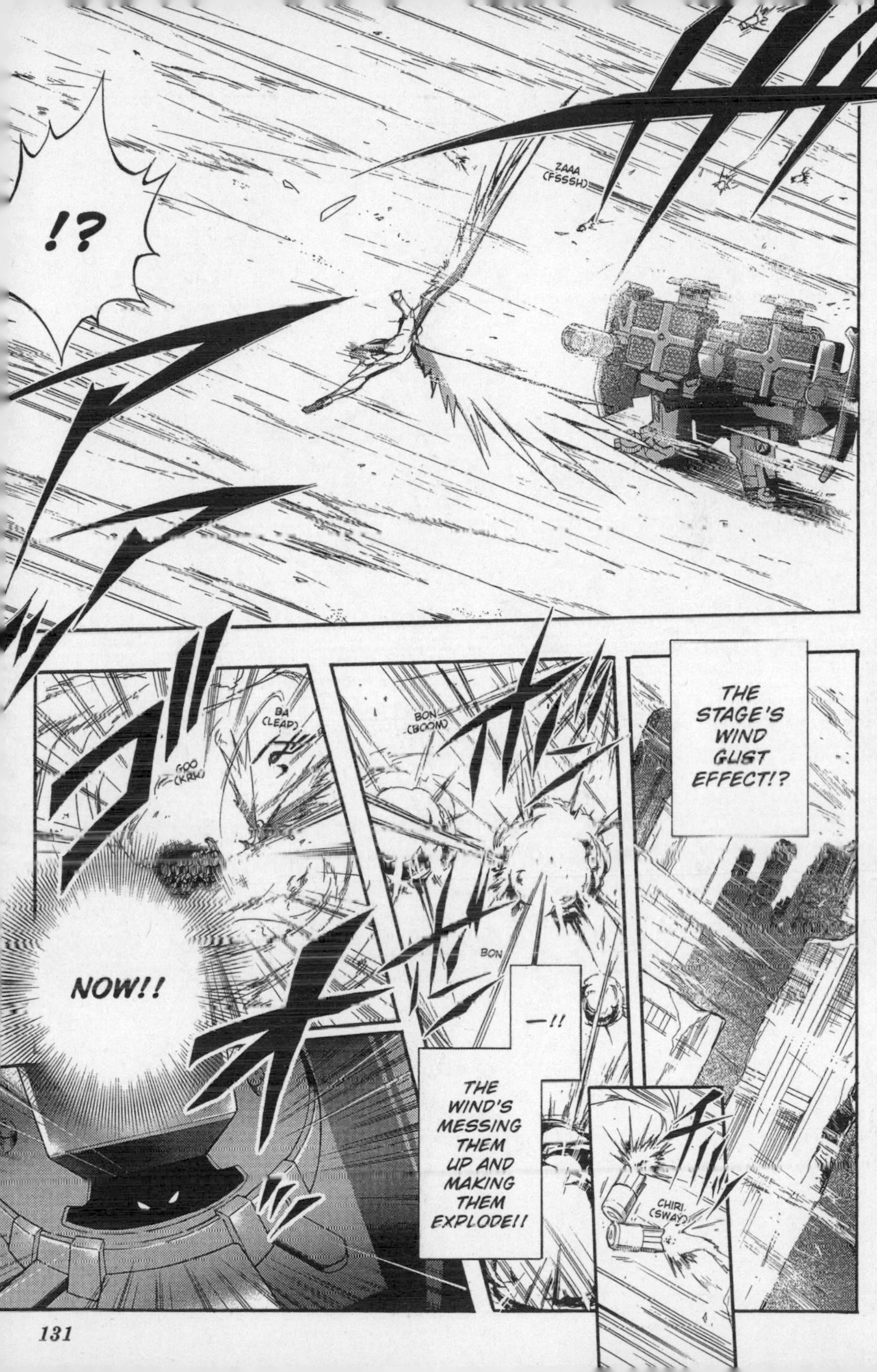
ZAAA
(FSSSH)
!?
THE STAGE'S WIND GUST EFFECT!?
THE WIND'S MESSING THEM UP AND MAKING THEM EXPLODE!!
CHIRI
(SWAY)
BON
(BOOM)
BON
—!!
BA
(LEAP)
GOO
(KRK)
NOW!!

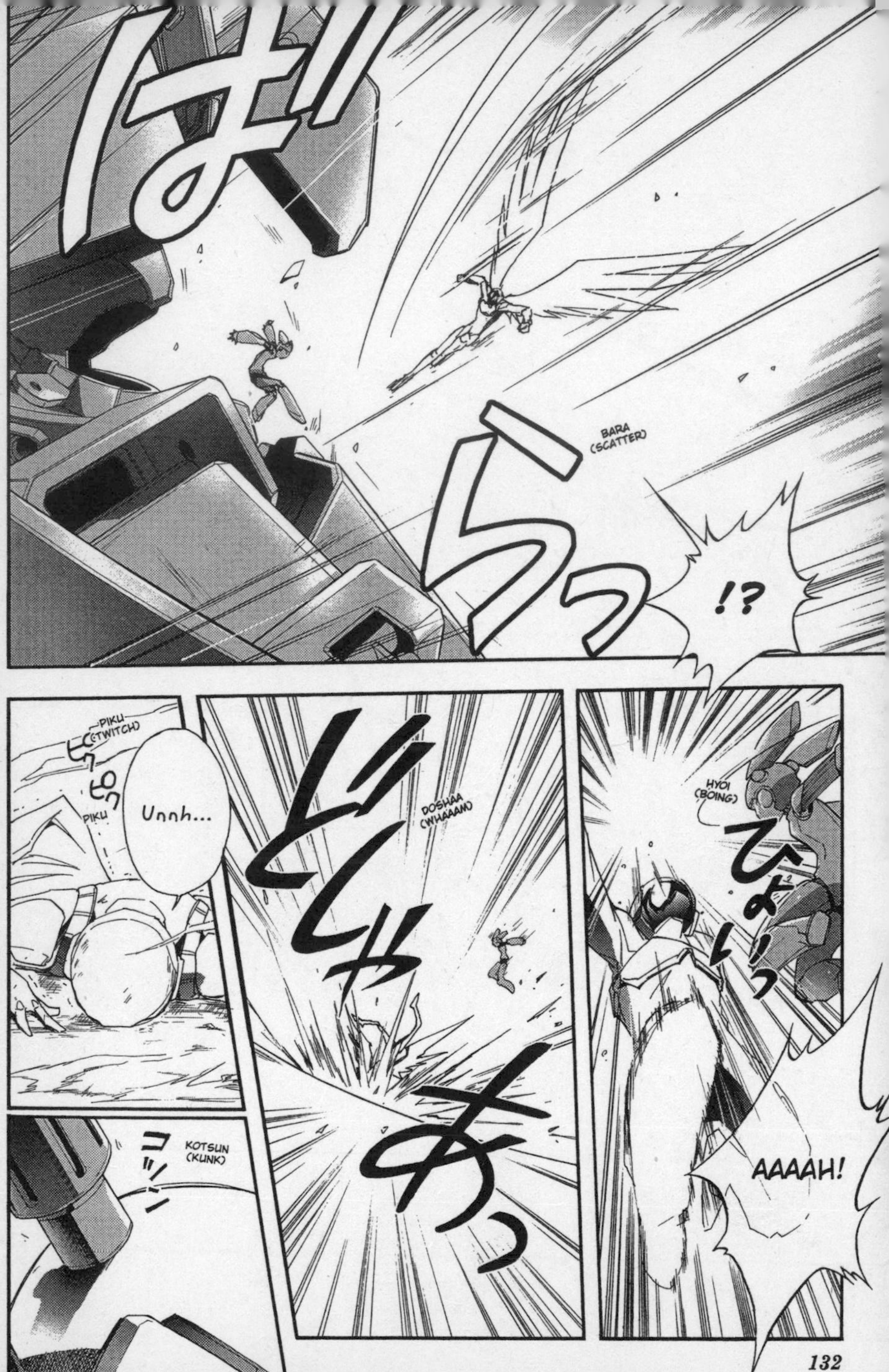
ばらっ
BARA (SCATTER)
!?
ひょいっ
HYOI (BOING)
AAAAH!
どしゃあっ
DOSHAA (WHAAAM)
ピク ピク
PIKU (TWITCH)
PIKU
Unnh...
コツン
KOTSUN (KUNK)

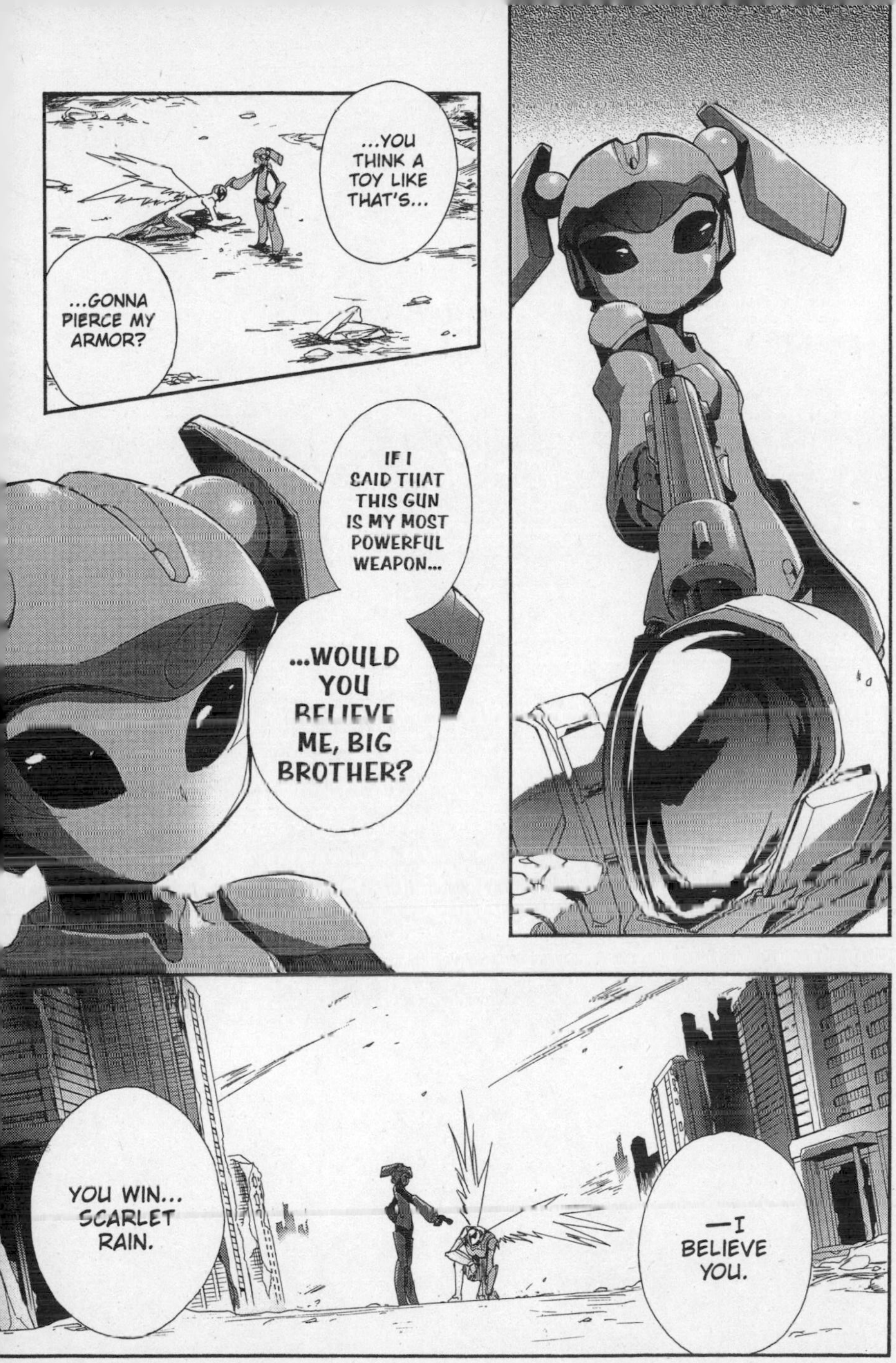
...YOU THINK A TOY LIKE THAT'S...
...GONNA PIERCE MY ARMOR?
IF I SAID THAT THIS GUN IS MY MOST POWERFUL WEAPON...
...WOULD YOU BELIEVE ME, BIG BROTHER?
—I BELIEVE YOU.
YOU WIN... SCARLET RAIN.

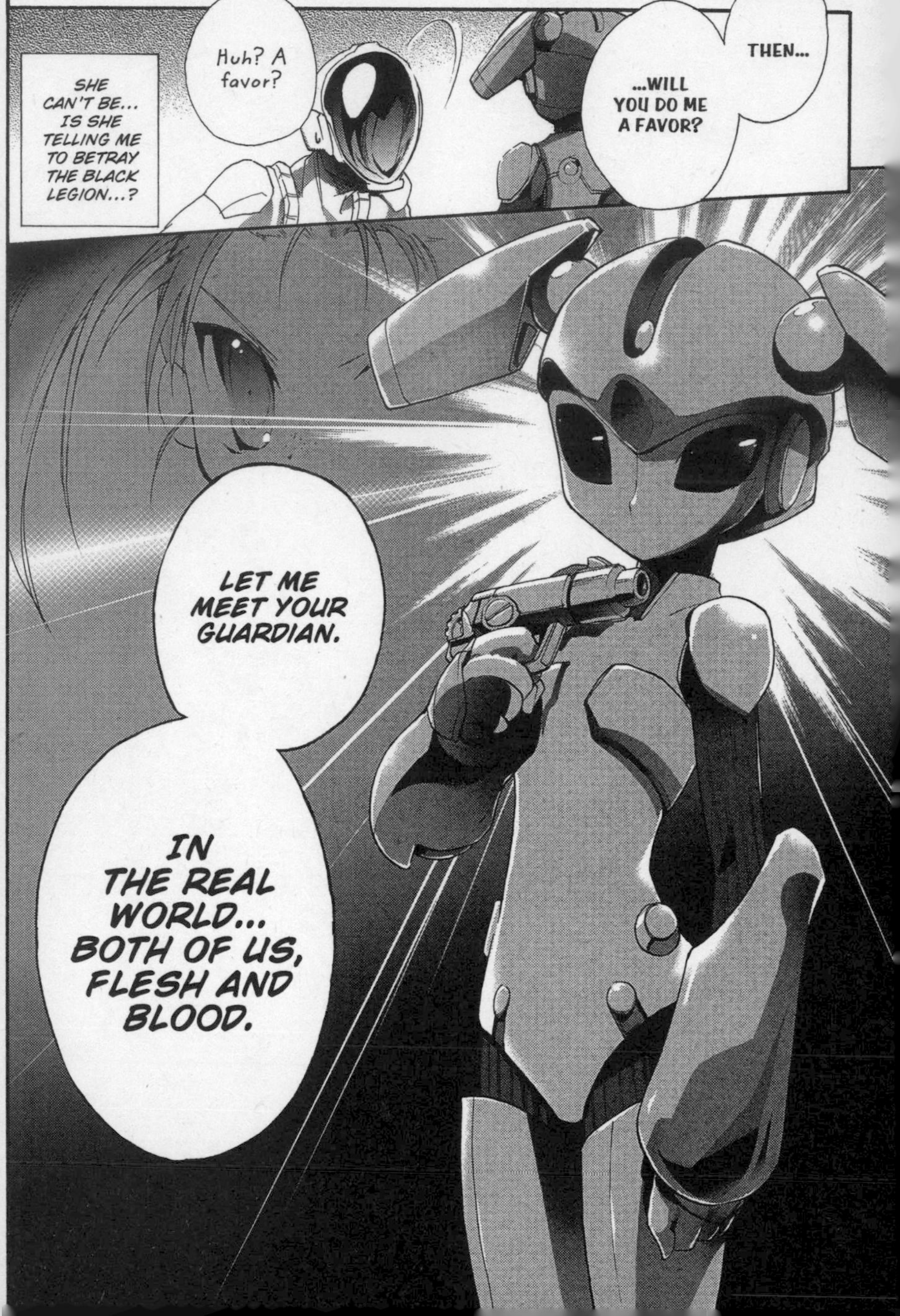
THEN...
...WILL YOU DO ME A FAVOR?
Huh? A favor?
SHE CAN'T BE... IS SHE TELLING ME TO BETRAY THE BLACK LEGION...?
LET ME MEET YOUR GUARDIAN.
IN THE REAL WORLD... BOTH OF US, FLESH AND BLOOD.

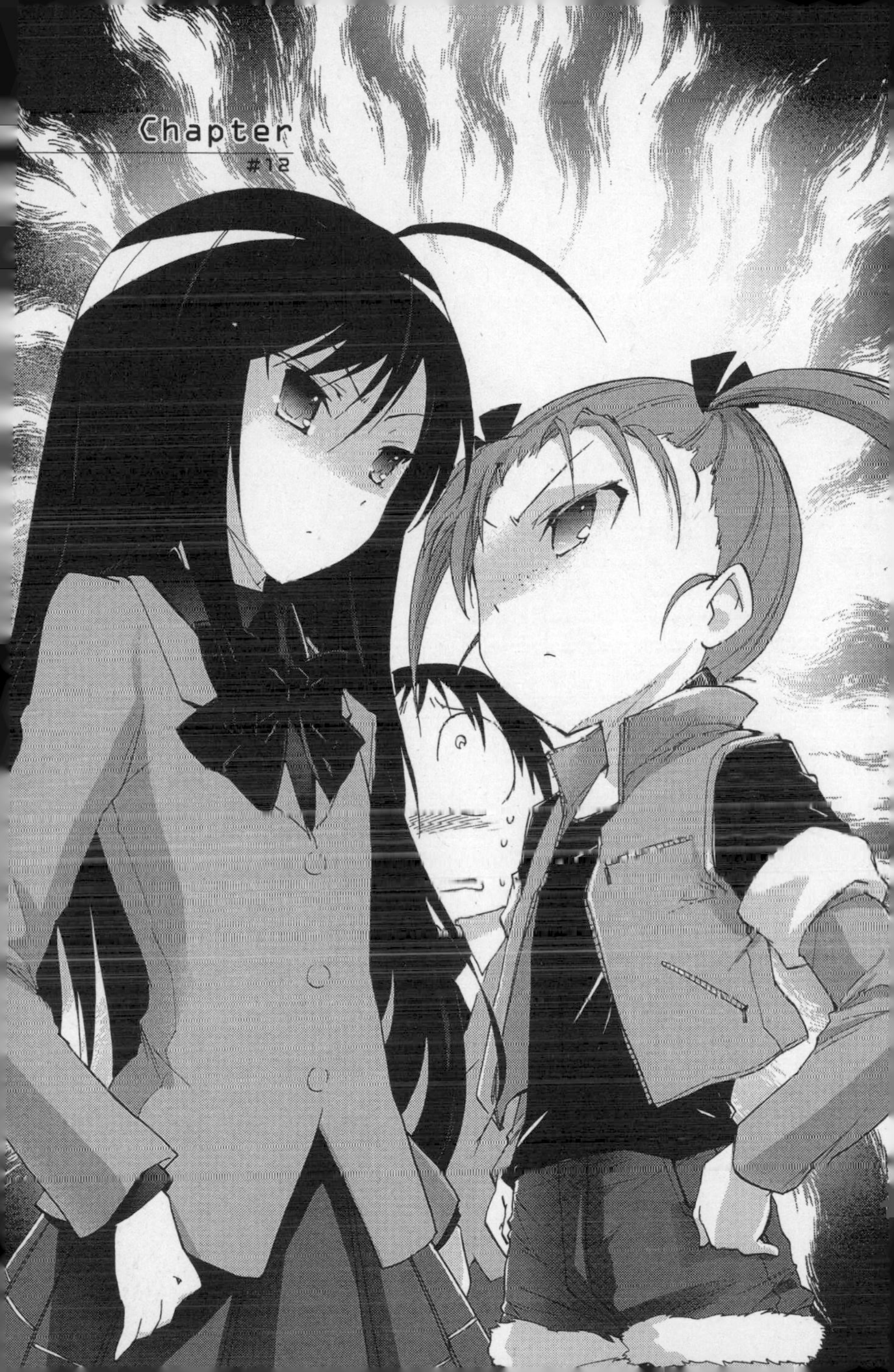
Chapter
#12

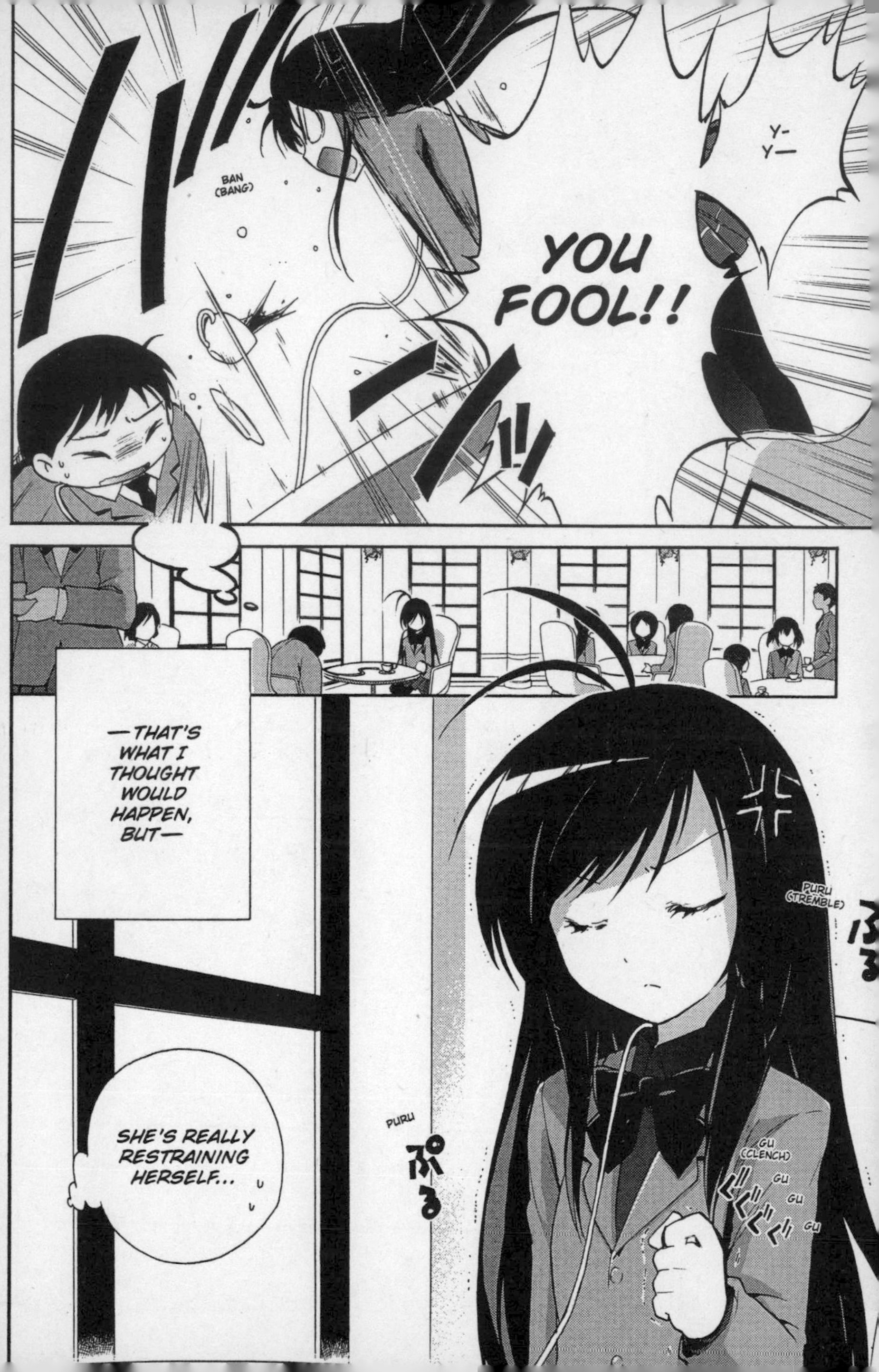
Y-
Y—
YOU FOOL!!
BAN (BANG)
PURU (TREMBLE)
ふる
GU (CLENCH)
ぐぐぐぐ
GU
GU
GU
PURU
ぷる
—THAT'S WHAT I THOUGHT WOULD HAPPEN, BUT—
SHE'S REALLY RESTRAINING HERSELF...

※SOCIAL ENGINEERING = A METHOD OF HACKING SECURITY WITHOUT USING A NETWORK THROUGH CONTACT WITH THE TARGET OFFLINE AND PHYSICAL MEANS.

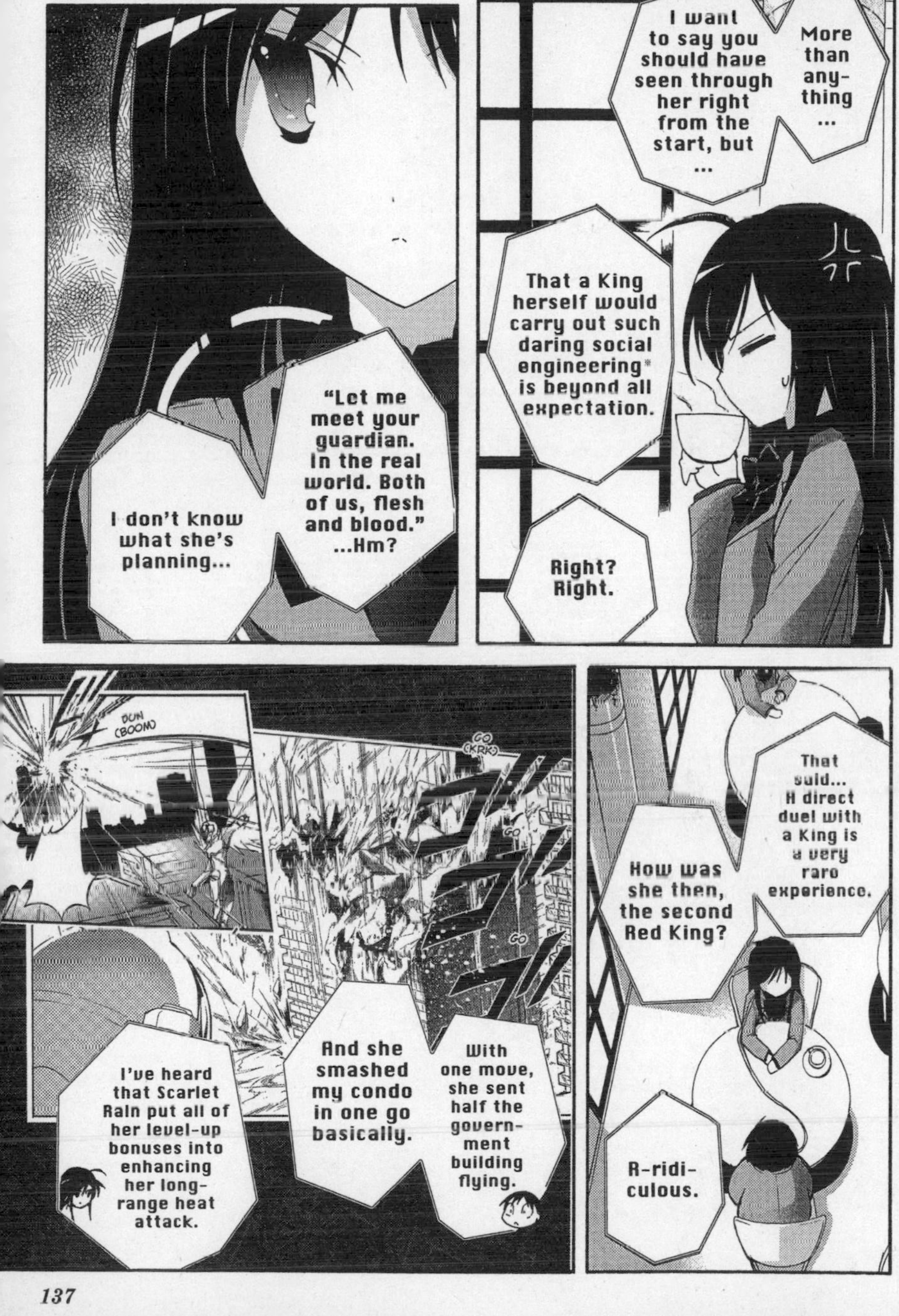

More than anything...
I want to say you should have seen through her right from the start, but...
That a King herself would carry out such daring social engineering* is beyond all expectation.
Right? Right.
"Let me meet your guardian. In the real world. Both of us, flesh and blood." ...Hm?
I don't know what she's planning...
That said... A direct duel with a King is a very rare experience.
How was she then, the second Red King?
R-ridiculous.
BUN (BOOM)
GO (KRK)
GO
GO
With one move, she sent half the government building flying.
And she smashed my condo in one go basically.
I've heard that Scarlet Rain put all of her level-up bonuses into enhancing her long-range heat attack.

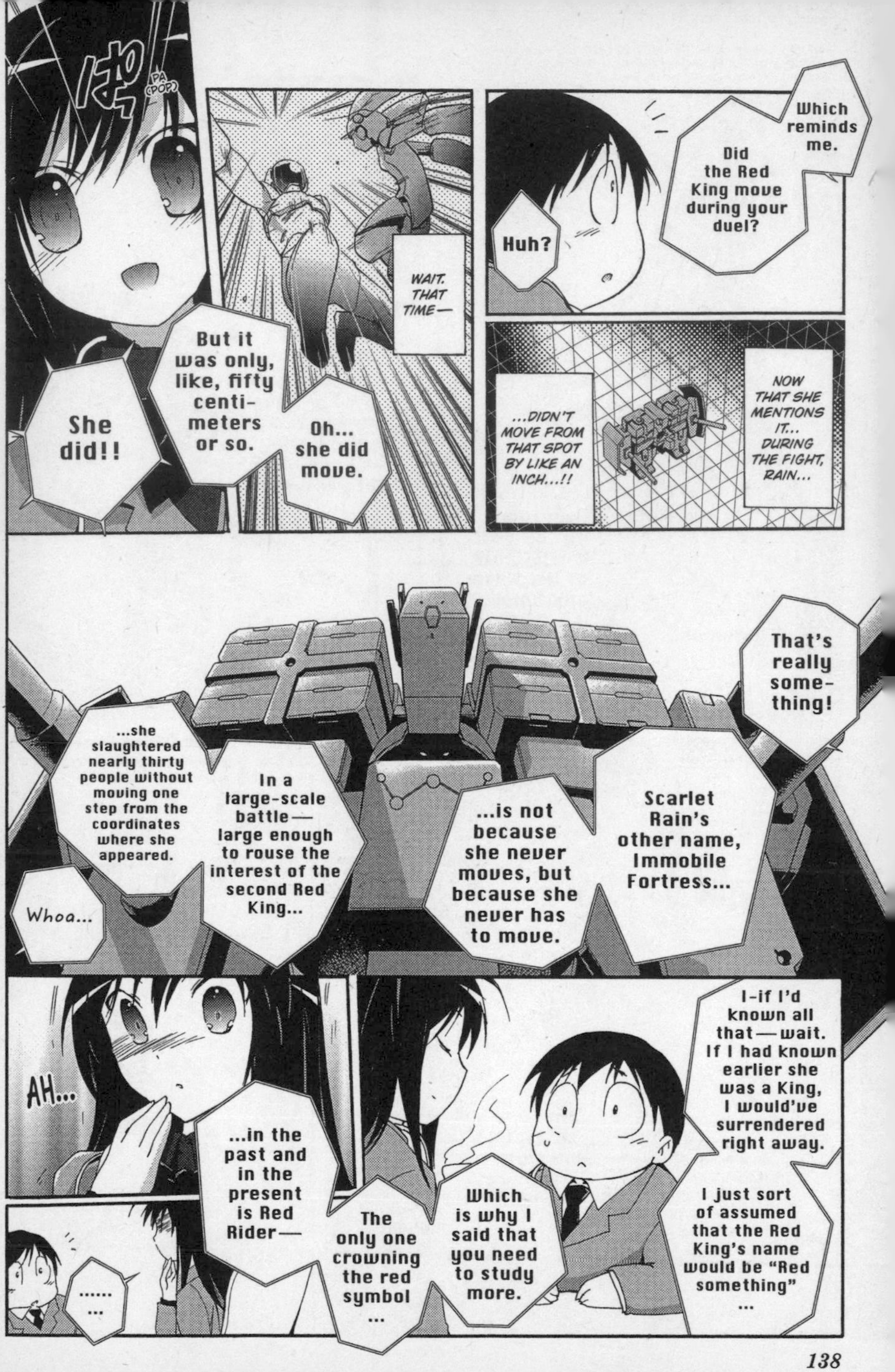
Which reminds me.
Did the Red King move during your duel?
Huh?
NOW THAT SHE MENTIONS IT... DURING THE FIGHT, RAIN...
...DIDN'T MOVE FROM THAT SPOT BY LIKE AN INCH...!!
WAIT. THAT TIME—
ぱっ PA (POP)
She did!!
Oh... she did move.
But it was only, like, fifty centi-meters or so.
That's really some-thing!
Scarlet Rain's other name, Immobile Fortress...
...is not because she never moves, but because she never has to move.
In a large-scale battle—large enough to rouse the interest of the second Red King...
...she slaughtered nearly thirty people without moving one step from the coordinates where she appeared.
Whoa...
I-if I'd known all that—wait. If I had known earlier she was a King, I would've surrendered right away.
I just sort of assumed that the Red King's name would be "Red something"...
Which is why I said that you need to study more.
The only one crowning the red symbol...
...in the past and in the present is Red Rider—
AH...
......
...

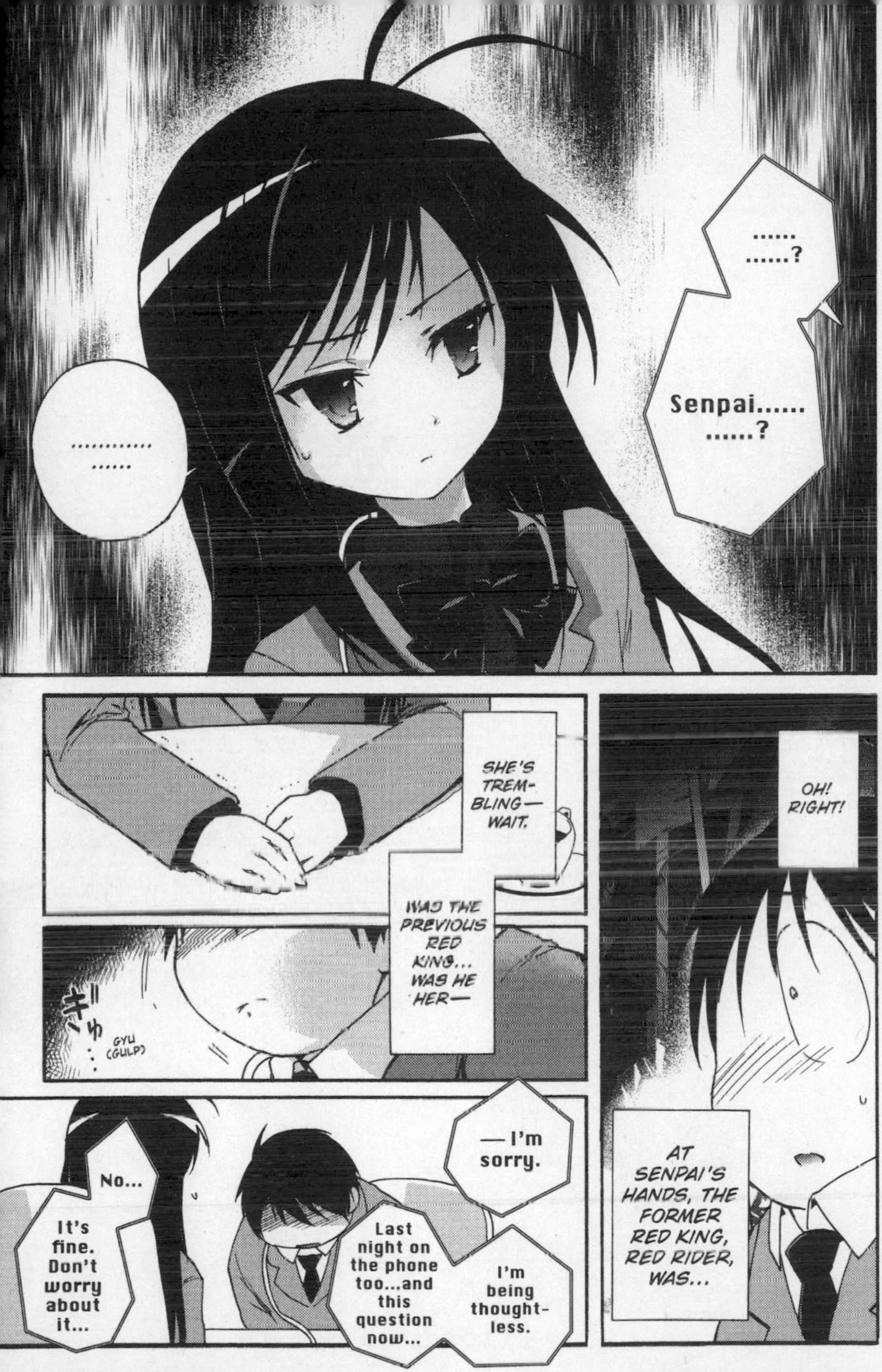
......
......?
Senpai......
......?
....
......
SHE'S TREMBLING—WAIT.
WAS THE PREVIOUS RED KING... WAS HE HER—
GYU (GULP)
OH! RIGHT!
AT SENPAI'S HANDS, THE FORMER RED KING, RED RIDER, WAS...
—I'm sorry.
Last night on the phone too...and this question now...
I'm being thoughtless.
No...
It's fine. Don't worry about it...

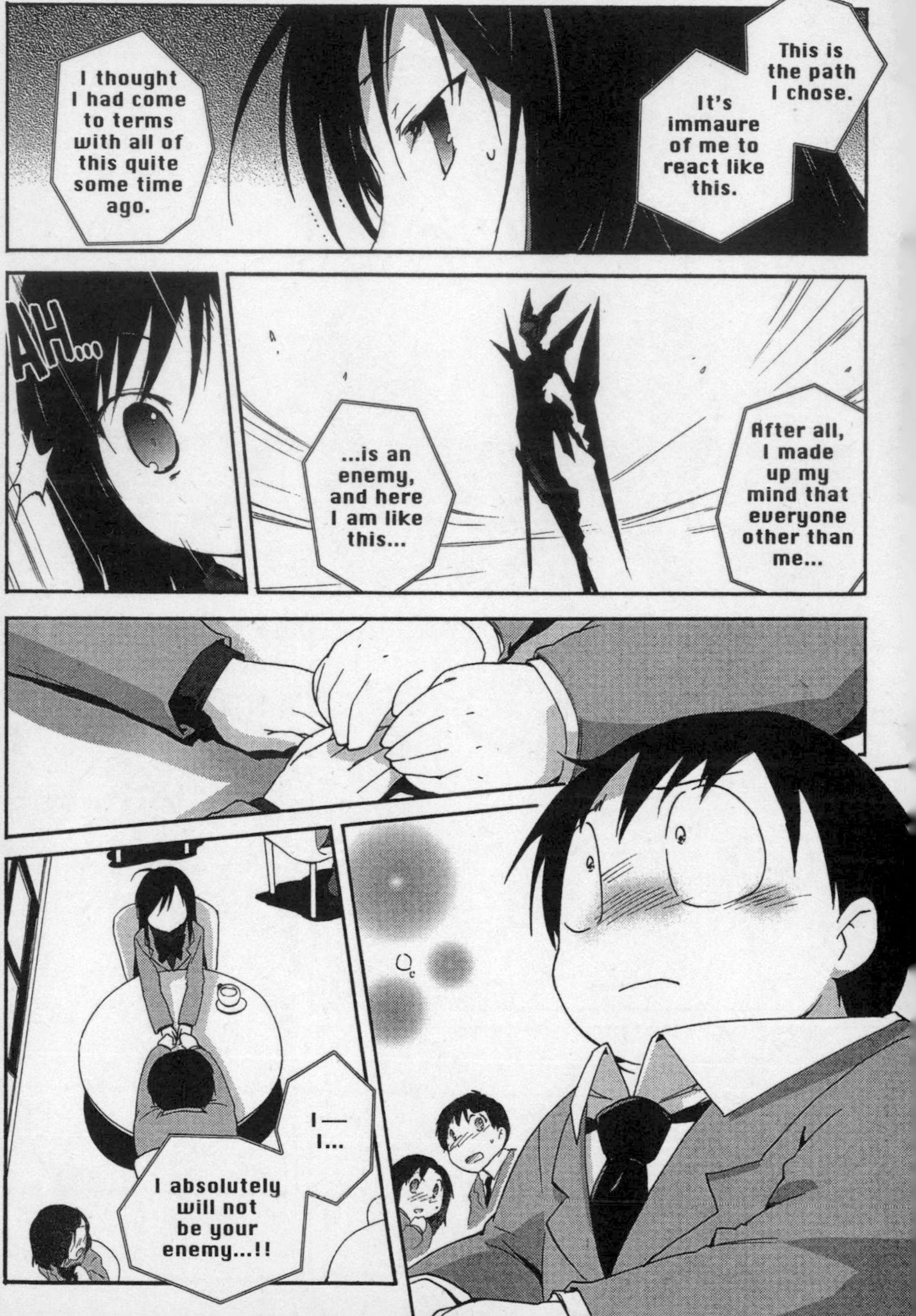
This is the path I chose.
It's immaure of me to react like this.
I thought I had come to terms with all of this quite some time ago.
After all, I made up my mind that everyone other than me...
...is an enemy, and here I am like this...
AH...
I— I...
I absolutely will not be your enemy...!!

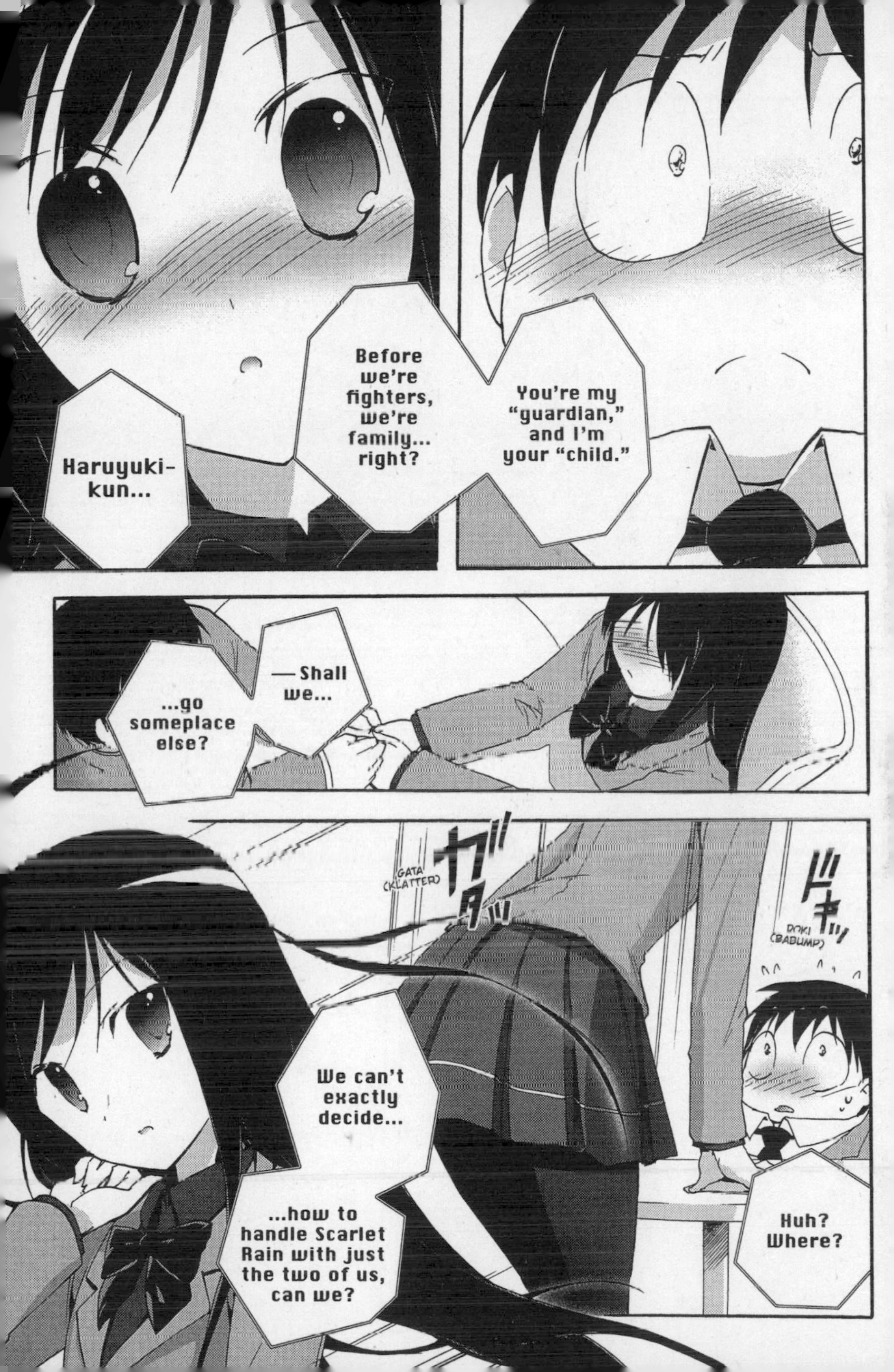
You're my "guardian," and I'm your "child."
Before we're fighters, we're family... right?
Haruyuki-kun...
—Shall we...
...go someplace else?
DOKI (BABUMP)
GATA (KLATTER)
Huh? Where?
We can't exactly decide...
...how to handle Scarlet Rain with just the two of us, can we?

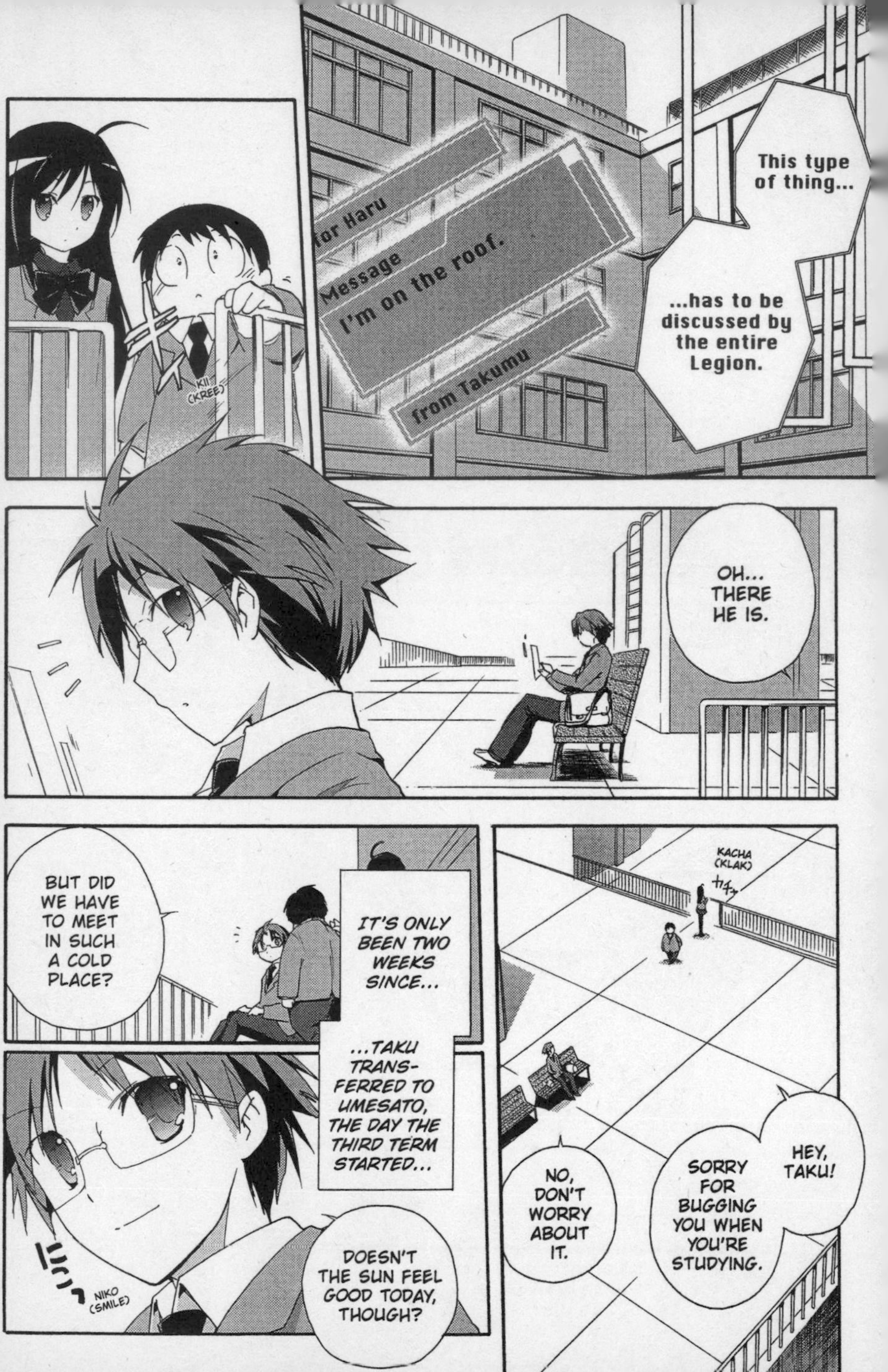
for Haru
Message
I'm on the roof.
from Takumu
This type of thing...
...has to be discussed by the entire Legion.
KII (KREE)
OH... THERE HE IS.
KACHA (KLAK)
HEY, TAKU!
SORRY FOR BUGGING YOU WHEN YOU'RE STUDYING.
NO, DON'T WORRY ABOUT IT.
IT'S ONLY BEEN TWO WEEKS SINCE...
BUT DID WE HAVE TO MEET IN SUCH A COLD PLACE?
...TAKU TRANSFERRED TO UMESATO, THE DAY THE THIRD TERM STARTED...
DOESN'T THE SUN FEEL GOOD TODAY, THOUGH?
NIKO (SMILE)

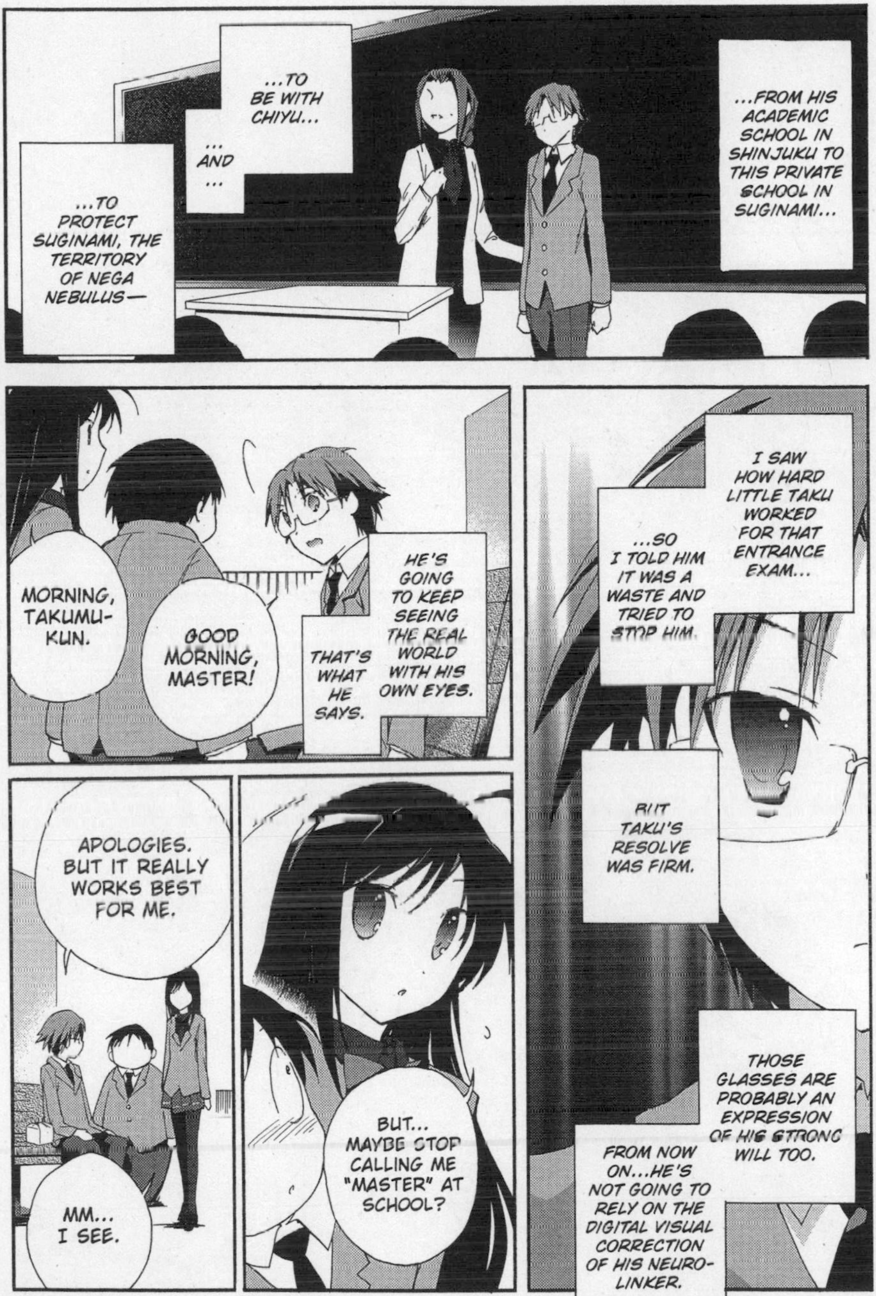
...FROM HIS ACADEMIC SCHOOL IN SHINJUKU TO THIS PRIVATE SCHOOL IN SUGINAMI...
...TO BE WITH CHIYU...
...AND...
...TO PROTECT SUGINAMI, THE TERRITORY OF NEGA NEBULUS—
I SAW HOW HARD LITTLE TAKU WORKED FOR THAT ENTRANCE EXAM...
...SO I TOLD HIM IT WAS A WASTE AND TRIED TO STOP HIM.
BUT TAKU'S RESOLVE WAS FIRM.
THOSE GLASSES ARE PROBABLY AN EXPRESSION OF HIS STRONG WILL TOO.
FROM NOW ON...HE'S NOT GOING TO RELY ON THE DIGITAL VISUAL CORRECTION OF HIS NEURO-LINKER.
HE'S GOING TO KEEP SEEING THE REAL WORLD WITH HIS OWN EYES.
THAT'S WHAT HE SAYS.
GOOD MORNING, MASTER!
MORNING, TAKUMU-KUN.
BUT... MAYBE STOP CALLING ME "MASTER" AT SCHOOL?
APOLOGIES. BUT IT REALLY WORKS BEST FOR ME.
MM... I SEE.

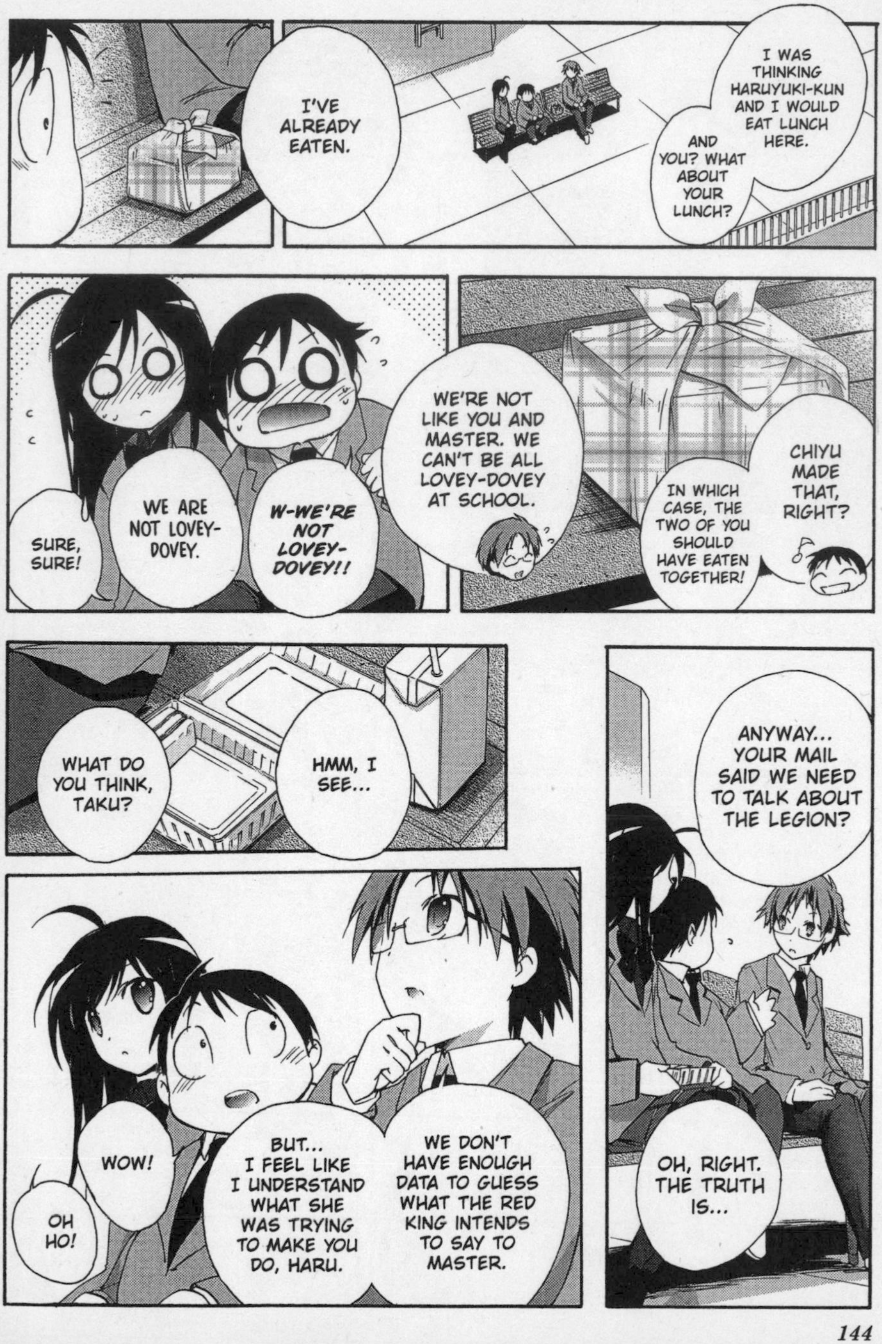
I WAS THINKING HARUYUKI-KUN AND I WOULD EAT LUNCH HERE.
AND YOU? WHAT ABOUT YOUR LUNCH?
I'VE ALREADY EATEN.
CHIYU MADE THAT, RIGHT?
IN WHICH CASE, THE TWO OF YOU SHOULD HAVE EATEN TOGETHER!
WE'RE NOT LIKE YOU AND MASTER. WE CAN'T BE ALL LOVEY-DOVEY AT SCHOOL.
W-WE'RE NOT LOVEY-DOVEY!!
WE ARE NOT LOVEY-DOVEY.
SURE, SURE!
ANYWAY... YOUR MAIL SAID WE NEED TO TALK ABOUT THE LEGION?
OH, RIGHT. THE TRUTH IS...
HMM, I SEE...
WHAT DO YOU THINK, TAKU?
WE DON'T HAVE ENOUGH DATA TO GUESS WHAT THE RED KING INTENDS TO SAY TO MASTER.
BUT... I FEEL LIKE I UNDERSTAND WHAT SHE WAS TRYING TO MAKE YOU DO, HARU.
WOW!
OH HO!

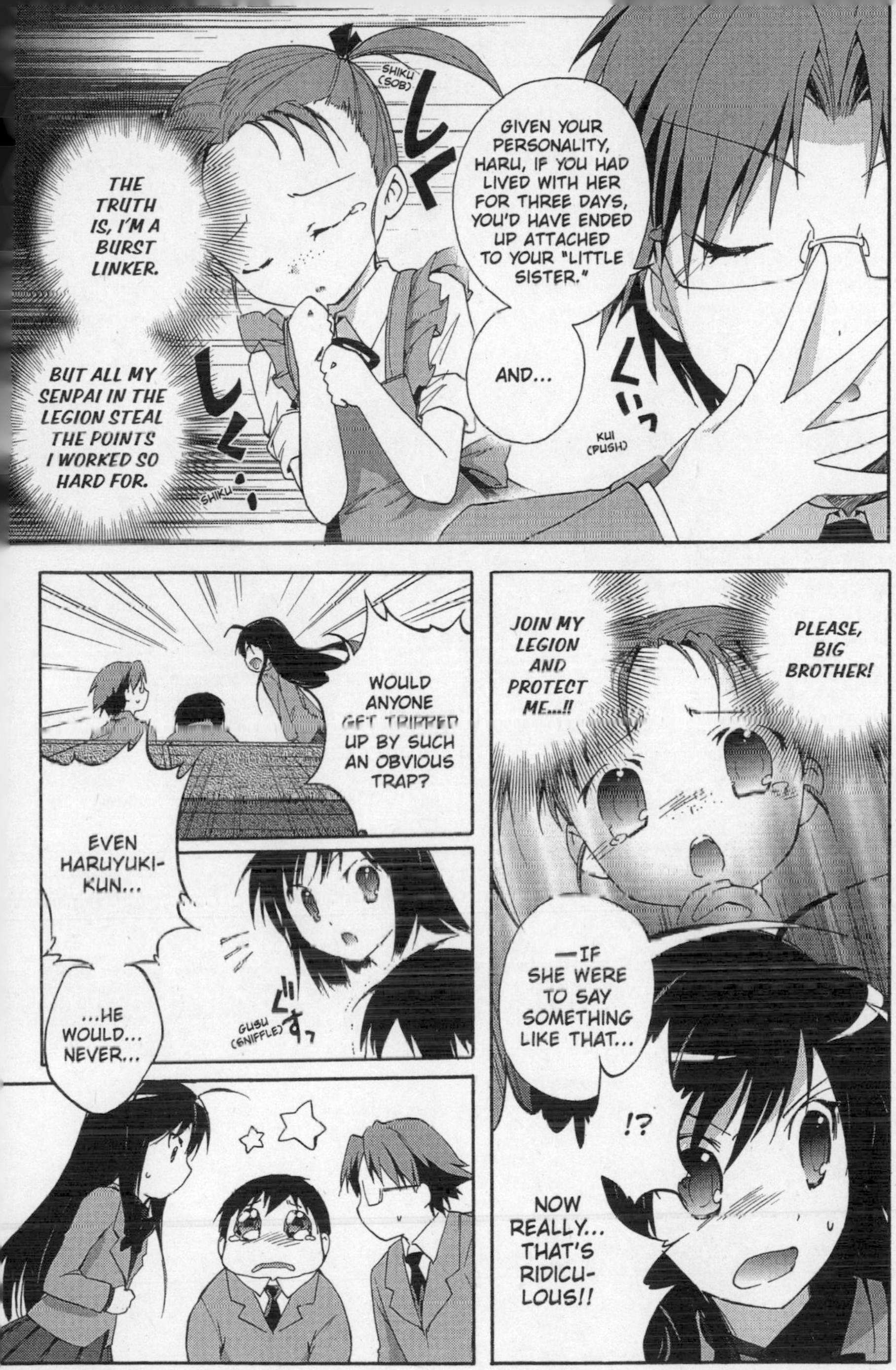

GIVEN YOUR PERSONALITY, HARU, IF YOU HAD LIVED WITH HER FOR THREE DAYS, YOU'D HAVE ENDED UP ATTACHED TO YOUR "LITTLE SISTER."
AND...
KUI (PUSH)
SHIKU (SOB)
THE TRUTH IS, I'M A BURST LINKER.
BUT ALL MY SENPAI IN THE LEGION STEAL THE POINTS I WORKED SO HARD FOR.
SHIKU
PLEASE, BIG BROTHER!
JOIN MY LEGION AND PROTECT ME...!!
—IF SHE WERE TO SAY SOMETHING LIKE THAT...
!?
NOW REALLY... THAT'S RIDICULOUS!!
WOULD ANYONE GET TRIPPED UP BY SUCH AN OBVIOUS TRAP?
EVEN HARUYUKI-KUN...
GUSU (SNIFFLE)
...HE WOULD... NEVER...

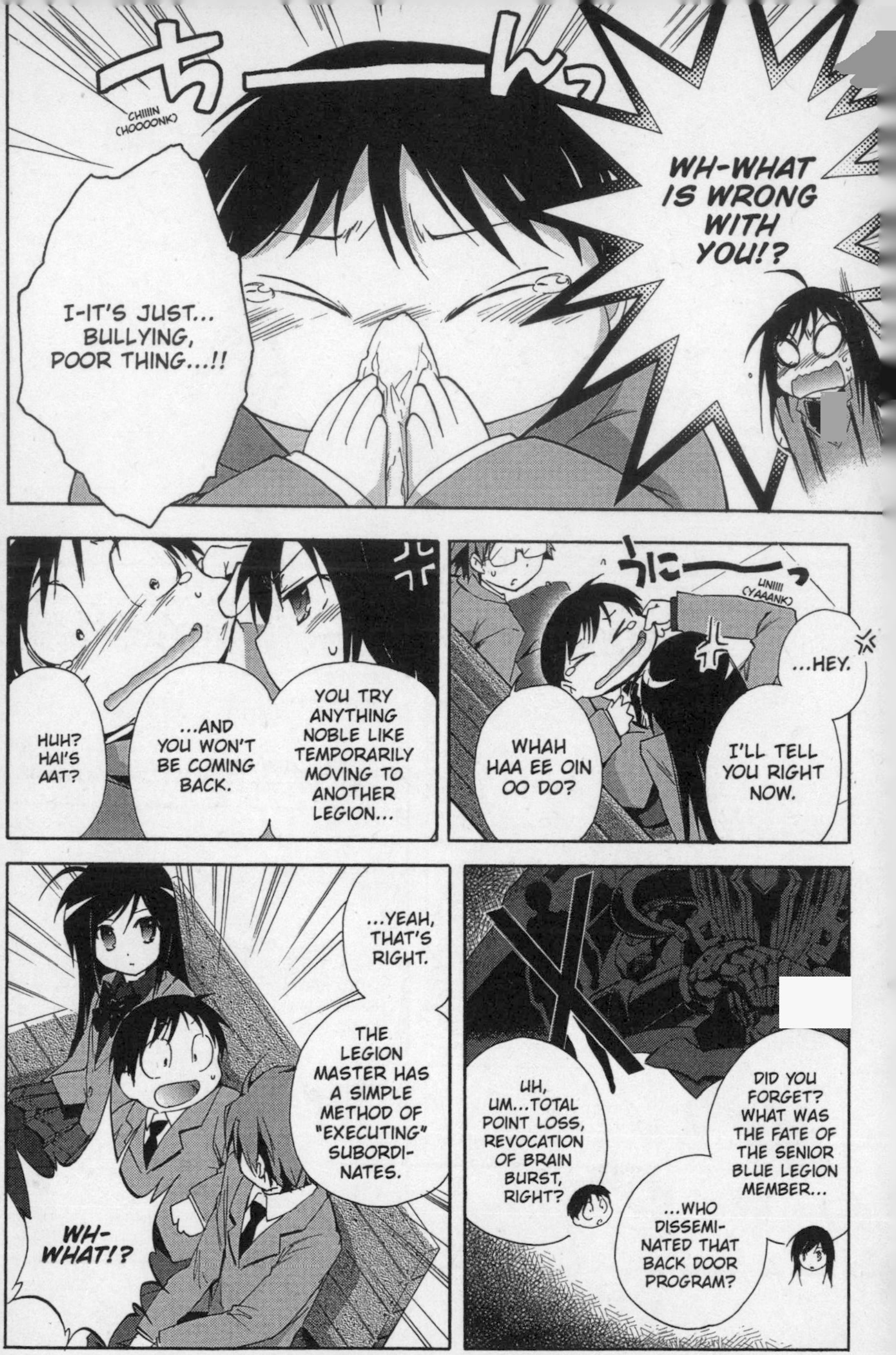

ちーんっ
CHIIIIN (HOOOONK)
I-IT'S JUST... BULLYING, POOR THING...!!
WH-WHAT IS WRONG WITH YOU!?
...HEY.
I'LL TELL YOU RIGHT NOW.
うにーーっ
UNIIII (YAAANK)
WHAH HAA EE OIN OO DO?
YOU TRY ANYTHING NOBLE LIKE TEMPORARILY MOVING TO ANOTHER LEGION...
...AND YOU WON'T BE COMING BACK.
HUH? HAI'S AAT?
DID YOU FORGET? WHAT WAS THE FATE OF THE SENIOR BLUE LEGION MEMBER...
...WHO DISSEMINATED THAT BACK DOOR PROGRAM?
UH, UM...TOTAL POINT LOSS, REVOCATION OF BRAIN BURST, RIGHT?
...YEAH, THAT'S RIGHT.
THE LEGION MASTER HAS A SIMPLE METHOD OF "EXECUTING" SUBORDINATES.
WH-WHAT!?

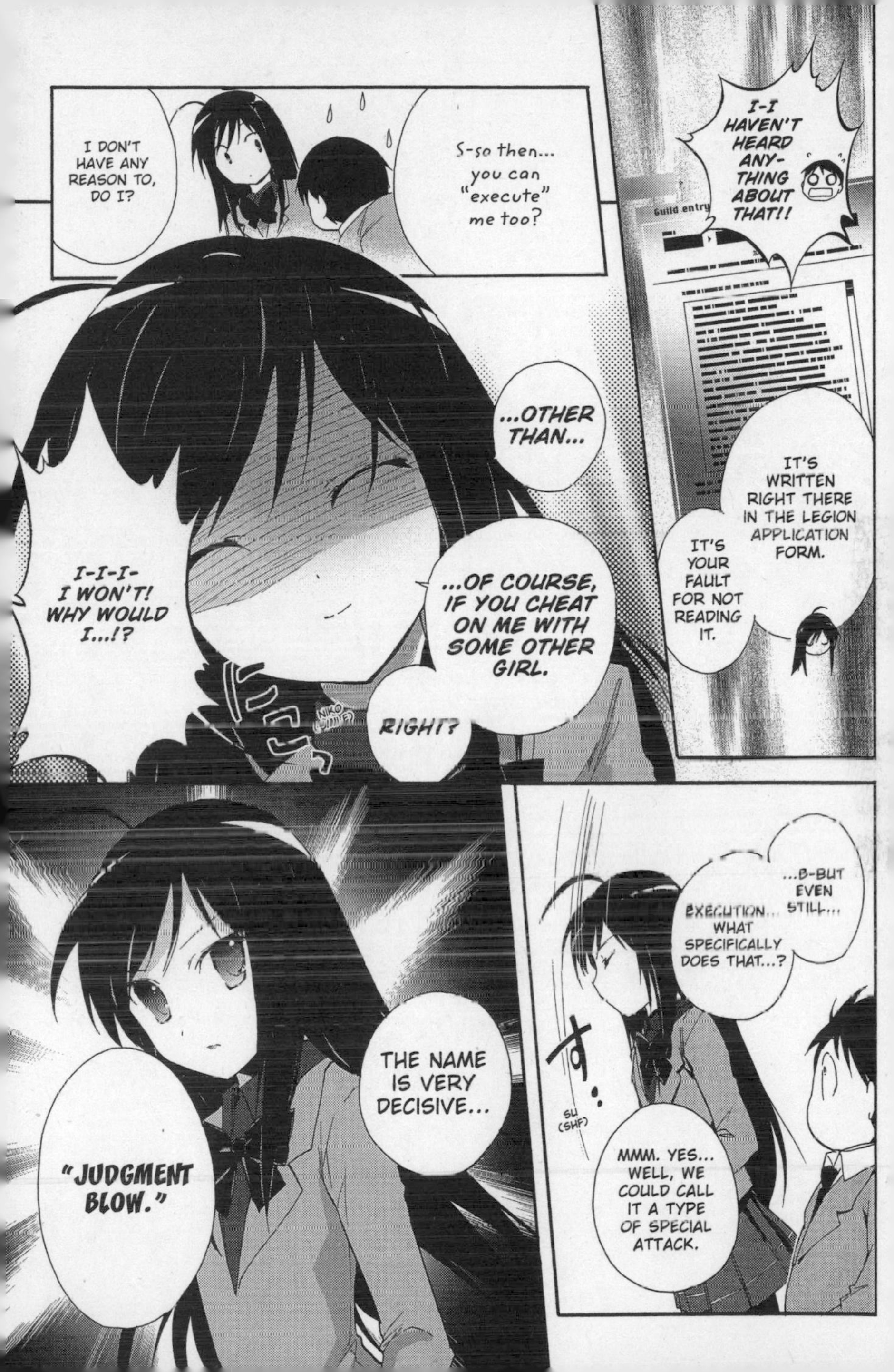
I-I HAVEN'T HEARD ANYTHING ABOUT THAT!!
Guild entry
IT'S WRITTEN RIGHT THERE IN THE LEGION APPLICATION FORM.
IT'S YOUR FAULT FOR NOT READING IT.
S-so then... you can "execute" me too?
I DON'T HAVE ANY REASON TO, DO I?
...OTHER THAN...
...OF COURSE, IF YOU CHEAT ON ME WITH SOME OTHER GIRL.
RIGHT?
I-I-I-I WON'T! WHY WOULD I...!?
...B-BUT EVEN STILL...
EXECUTION... WHAT SPECIFICALLY DOES THAT...?
SU (SHF)
MMM. YES... WELL, WE COULD CALL IT A TYPE OF SPECIAL ATTACK.
THE NAME IS VERY DECISIVE...
"JUDGMENT BLOW."

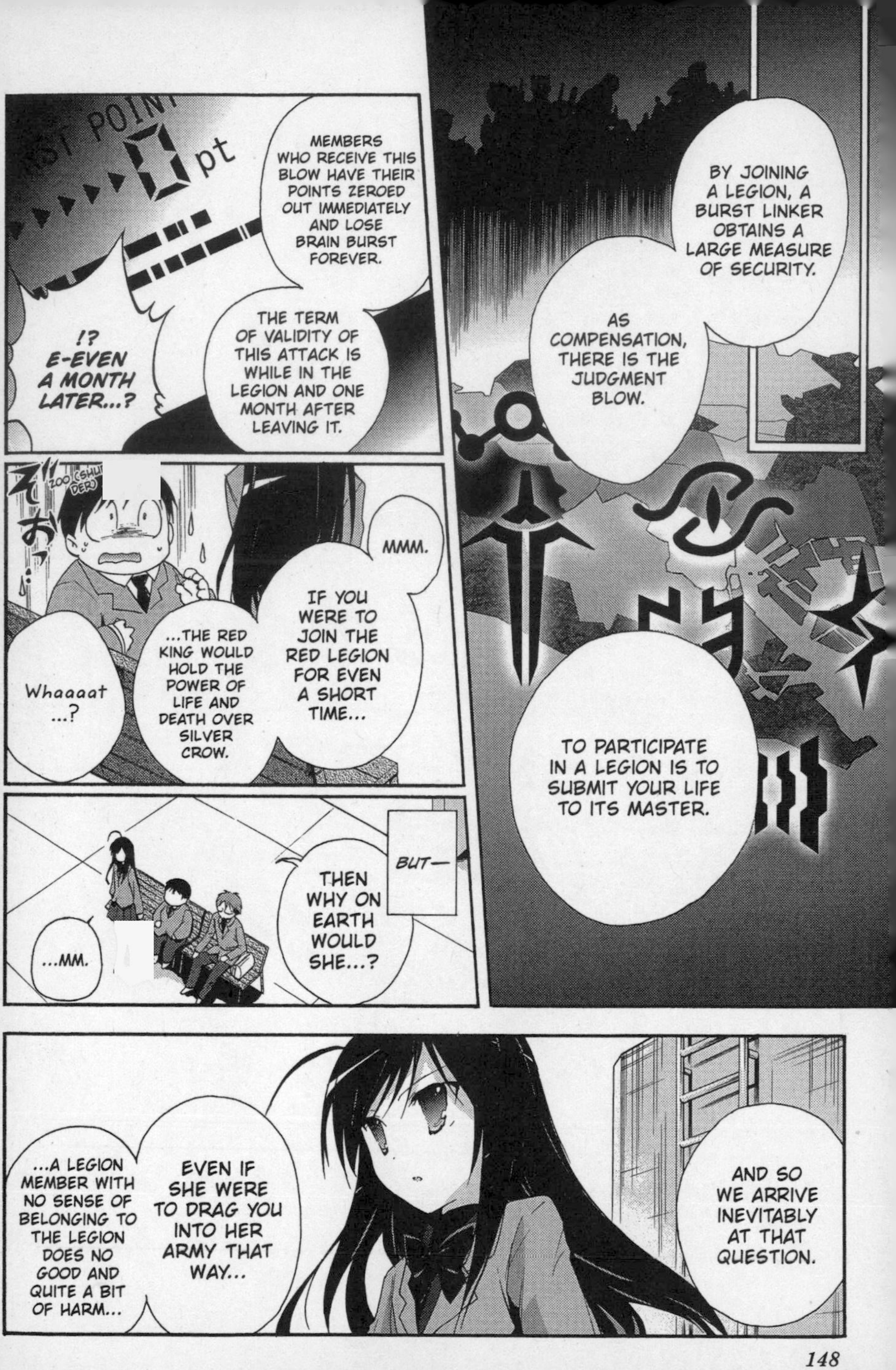
BY JOINING A LEGION, A BURST LINKER OBTAINS A LARGE MEASURE OF SECURITY.
AS COMPENSATION, THERE IS THE JUDGMENT BLOW.
TO PARTICIPATE IN A LEGION IS TO SUBMIT YOUR LIFE TO ITS MASTER.
MEMBERS WHO RECEIVE THIS BLOW HAVE THEIR POINTS ZEROED OUT IMMEDIATELY AND LOSE BRAIN BURST FOREVER.
THE TERM OF VALIDITY OF THIS ATTACK IS WHILE IN THE LEGION AND ONE MONTH AFTER LEAVING IT.
!? E-EVEN A MONTH LATER...?
ZOO (SHU DER)
MMM.
IF YOU WERE TO JOIN THE RED LEGION FOR EVEN A SHORT TIME...
...THE RED KING WOULD HOLD THE POWER OF LIFE AND DEATH OVER SILVER CROW.
Whaaaat ...?
BUT—
THEN WHY ON EARTH WOULD SHE...?
...MM.
AND SO WE ARRIVE INEVITABLY AT THAT QUESTION.
EVEN IF SHE WERE TO DRAG YOU INTO HER ARMY THAT WAY...
...A LEGION MEMBER WITH NO SENSE OF BELONGING TO THE LEGION DOES NO GOOD AND QUITE A BIT OF HARM...

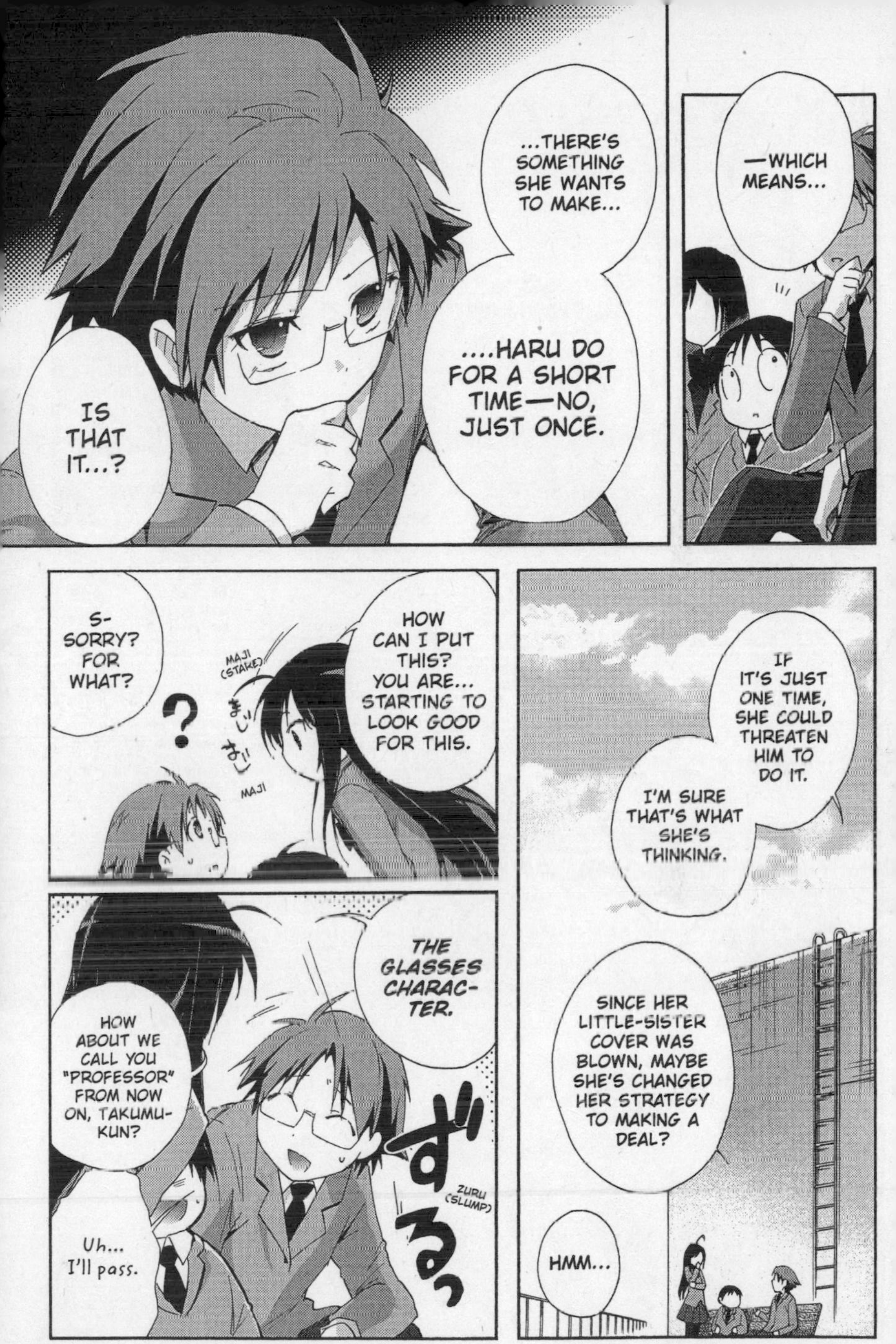
—WHICH MEANS...
...THERE'S SOMETHING SHE WANTS TO MAKE...
....HARU DO FOR A SHORT TIME—NO, JUST ONCE.
IS THAT IT...?
IF IT'S JUST ONE TIME, SHE COULD THREATEN HIM TO DO IT.
I'M SURE THAT'S WHAT SHE'S THINKING.
SINCE HER LITTLE-SISTER COVER WAS BLOWN, MAYBE SHE'S CHANGED HER STRATEGY TO MAKING A DEAL?
HMM...
HOW CAN I PUT THIS? YOU ARE... STARTING TO LOOK GOOD FOR THIS.
MAJI (STARE)
まじまじ
MAJI
?
S-SORRY? FOR WHAT?
THE GLASSES CHARACTER.
HOW ABOUT WE CALL YOU "PROFESSOR" FROM NOW ON, TAKUMU-KUN?
ZURU (SLUMP)
ずるっ
Uh... I'll pass.

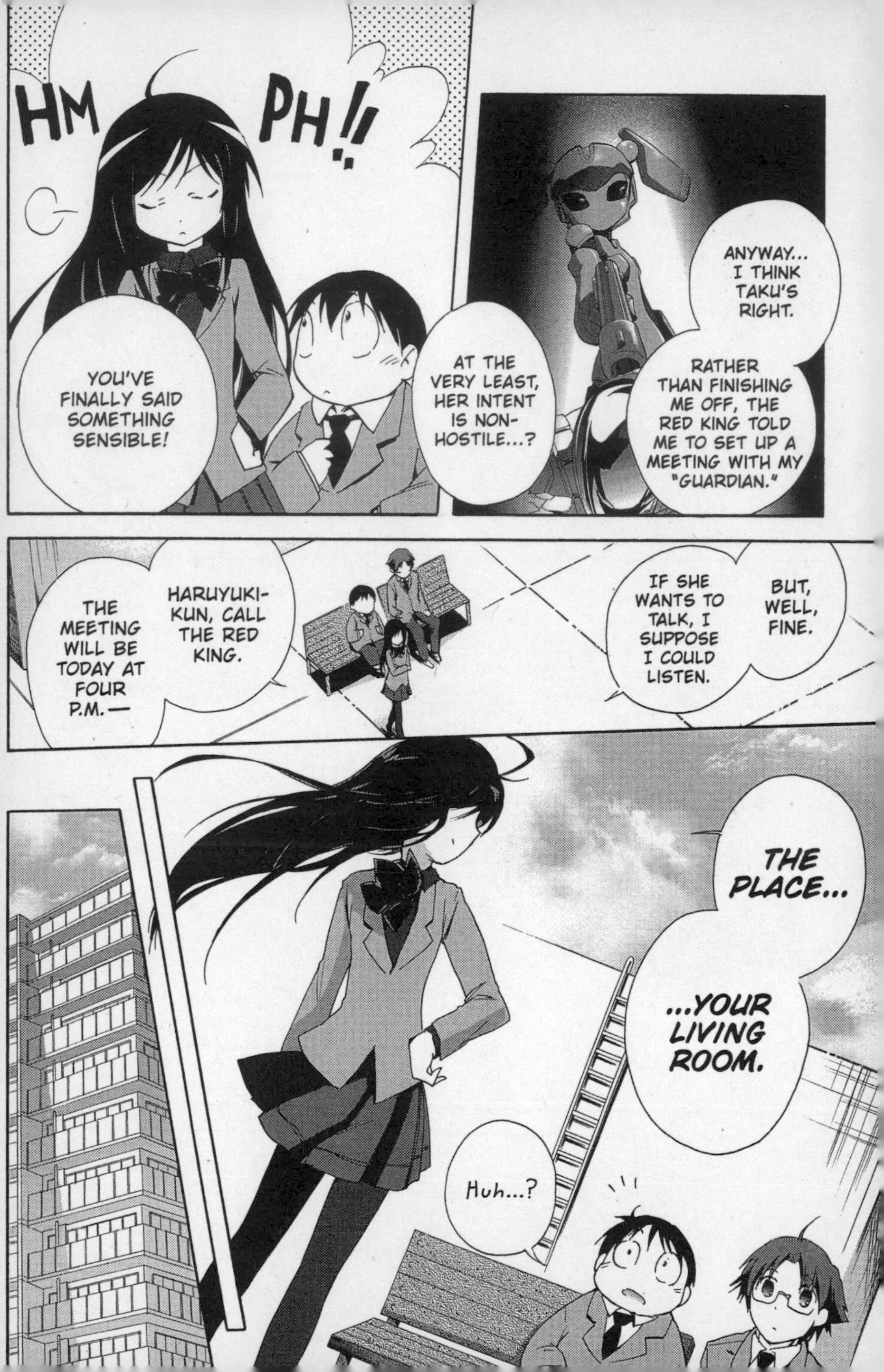
ANYWAY... I THINK TAKU'S RIGHT.
RATHER THAN FINISHING ME OFF, THE RED KING TOLD ME TO SET UP A MEETING WITH MY "GUARDIAN."
AT THE VERY LEAST, HER INTENT IS NON-HOSTILE...?
HMPH!!
YOU'VE FINALLY SAID SOMETHING SENSIBLE!
BUT, WELL, FINE.
IF SHE WANTS TO TALK, I SUPPOSE I COULD LISTEN.
HARUYUKI-KUN, CALL THE RED KING.
THE MEETING WILL BE TODAY AT FOUR P.M.—
THE PLACE...
...YOUR LIVING ROOM.
Huh...?

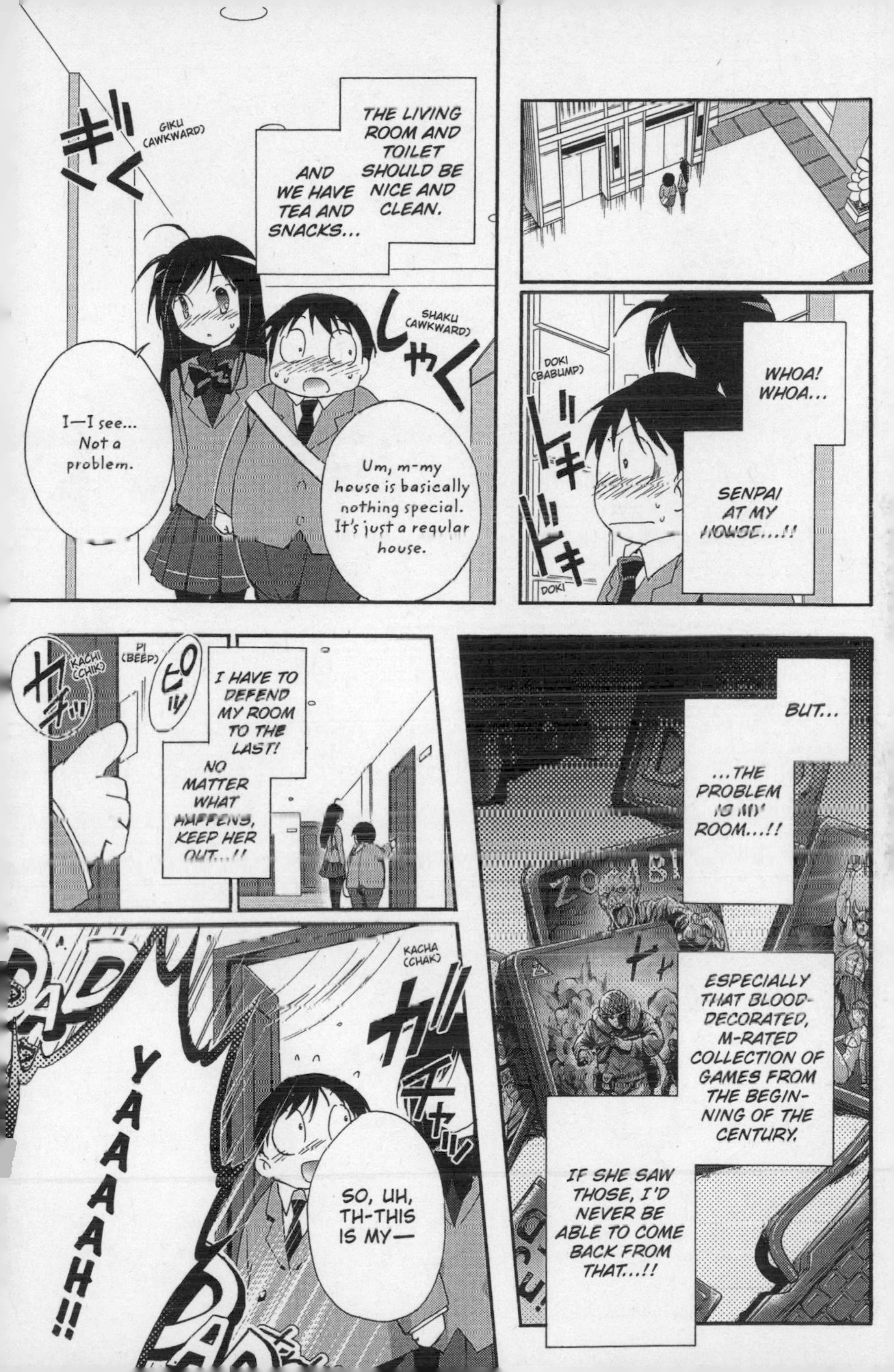

WHOA! WHOA...
SENPAI AT MY HOUSE...!!
DOKI (BABUMP)
DOKI
THE LIVING ROOM AND TOILET SHOULD BE NICE AND CLEAN.
AND WE HAVE TEA AND SNACKS...
SHAKU (AWKWARD)
Um, m-my house is basically nothing special. It's just a regular house.
GIKU (AWKWARD)
I—I see... Not a problem.
BUT...
...THE PROBLEM IS MY ROOM...!!
ESPECIALLY THAT BLOOD-DECORATED, M-RATED COLLECTION OF GAMES FROM THE BEGIN-NING OF THE CENTURY.
IF SHE SAW THOSE, I'D NEVER BE ABLE TO COME BACK FROM THAT...!!
I HAVE TO DEFEND MY ROOM TO THE LAST!
NO MATTER WHAT HAPPENS, KEEP HER OUT...!!
PI (BEEP)
KACHI (CHIK)
KACHA (CHAK)
SO, UH, TH-THIS IS MY—
YAAAAAH!!

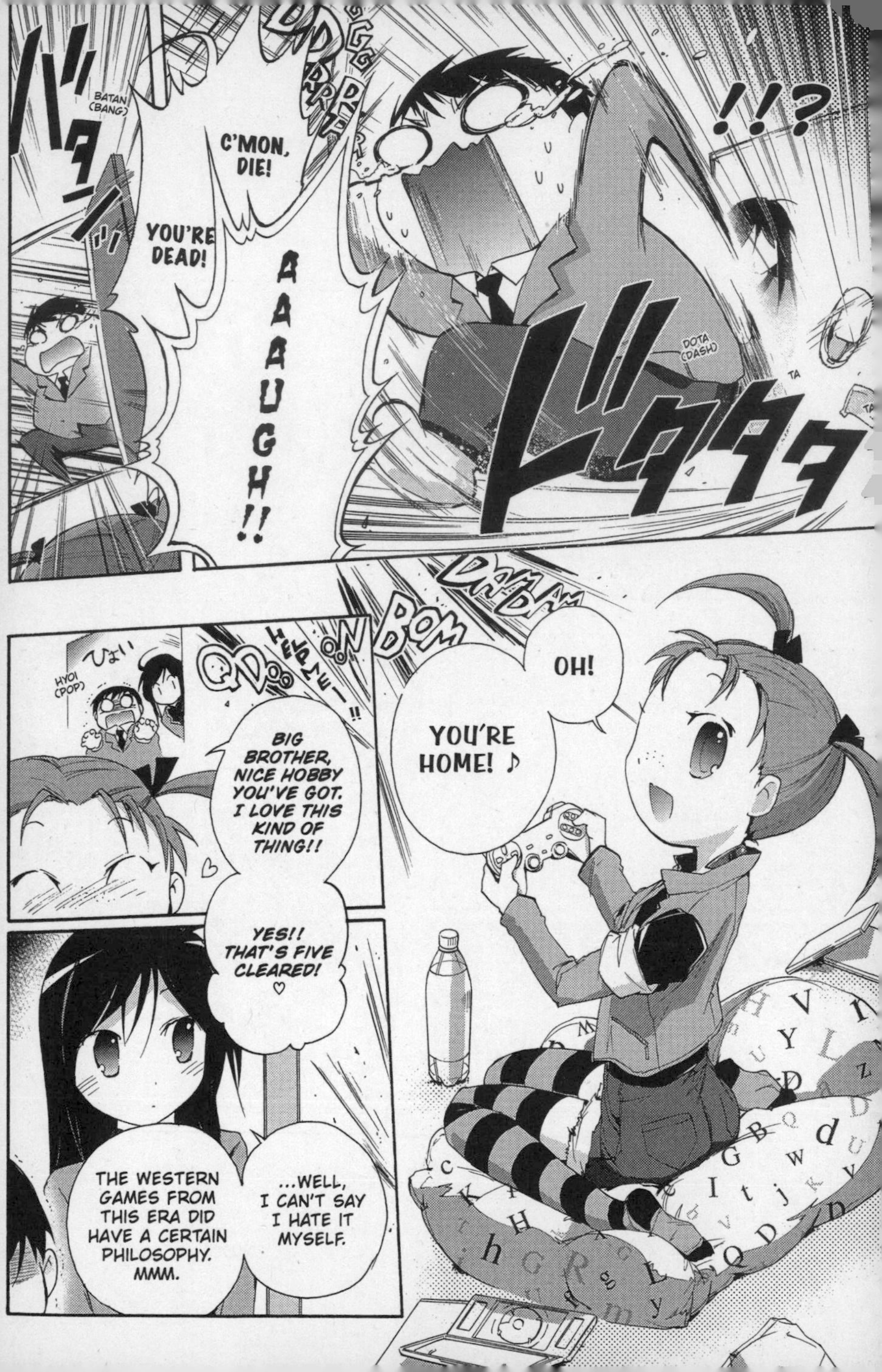
!!?
DOTA (DASH)
TA
TA
AAAUGH!!
C'MON, DIE!
YOU'RE DEAD!
BATAN (BANG)
OH!
YOU'RE HOME! ♪
HYOI (POP)
ひょい
HELP ME—!!
BIG BROTHER, NICE HOBBY YOU'VE GOT. I LOVE THIS KIND OF THING!!
YES!! THAT'S FIVE CLEARED! ♡
...WELL, I CAN'T SAY I HATE IT MYSELF.
THE WESTERN GAMES FROM THIS ERA DID HAVE A CERTAIN PHILOSOPHY. MMM.

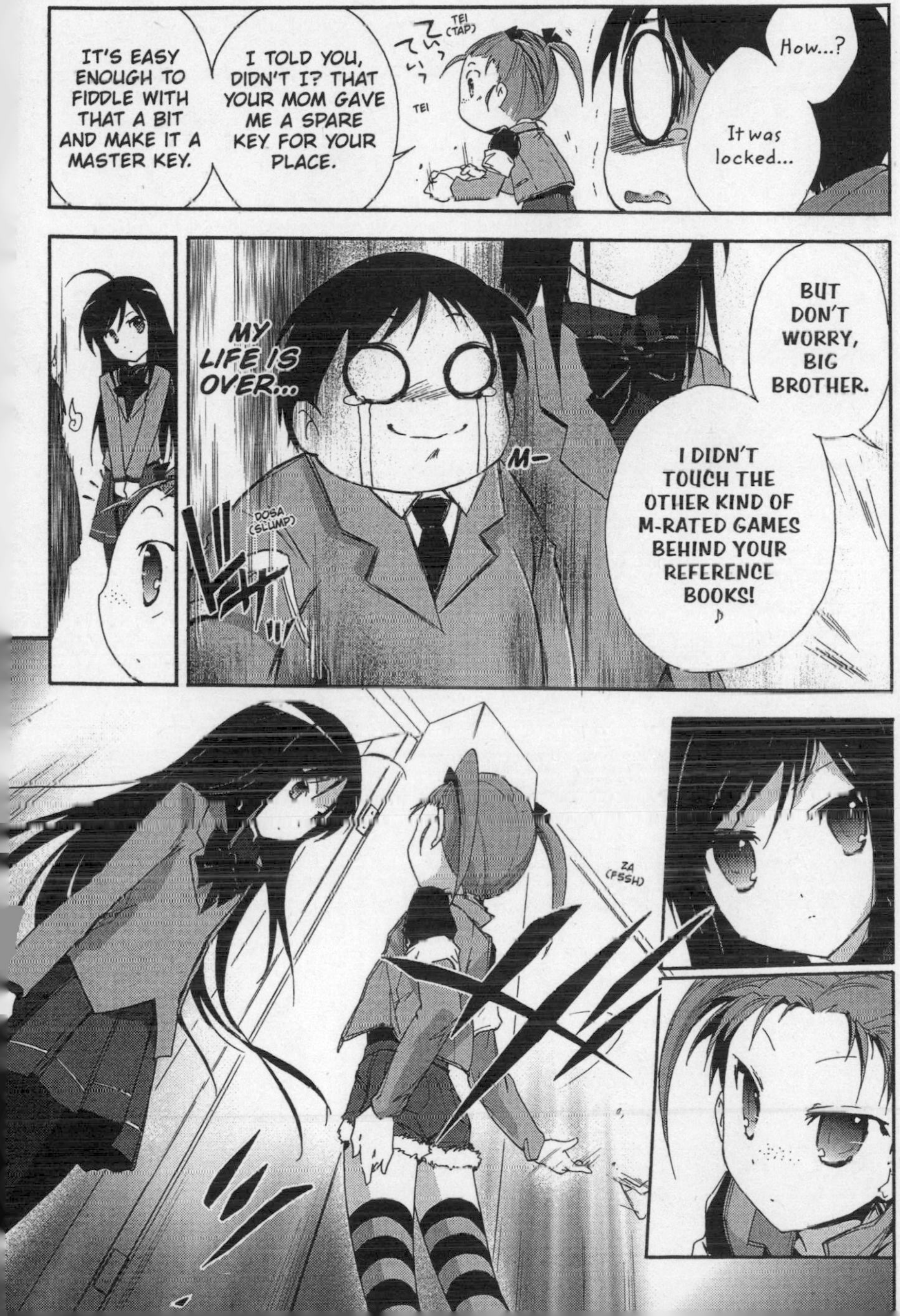
How...?
It was locked...
TEI (TAP)
TEI
I TOLD YOU, DIDN'T I? THAT YOUR MOM GAVE ME A SPARE KEY FOR YOUR PLACE.
IT'S EASY ENOUGH TO FIDDLE WITH THAT A BIT AND MAKE IT A MASTER KEY.
BUT DON'T WORRY, BIG BROTHER.
I DIDN'T TOUCH THE OTHER KIND OF M-RATED GAMES BEHIND YOUR REFERENCE BOOKS! ♪
M-
MY LIFE IS OVER...
DOSA (SLUMP)
ZA (FSSH)

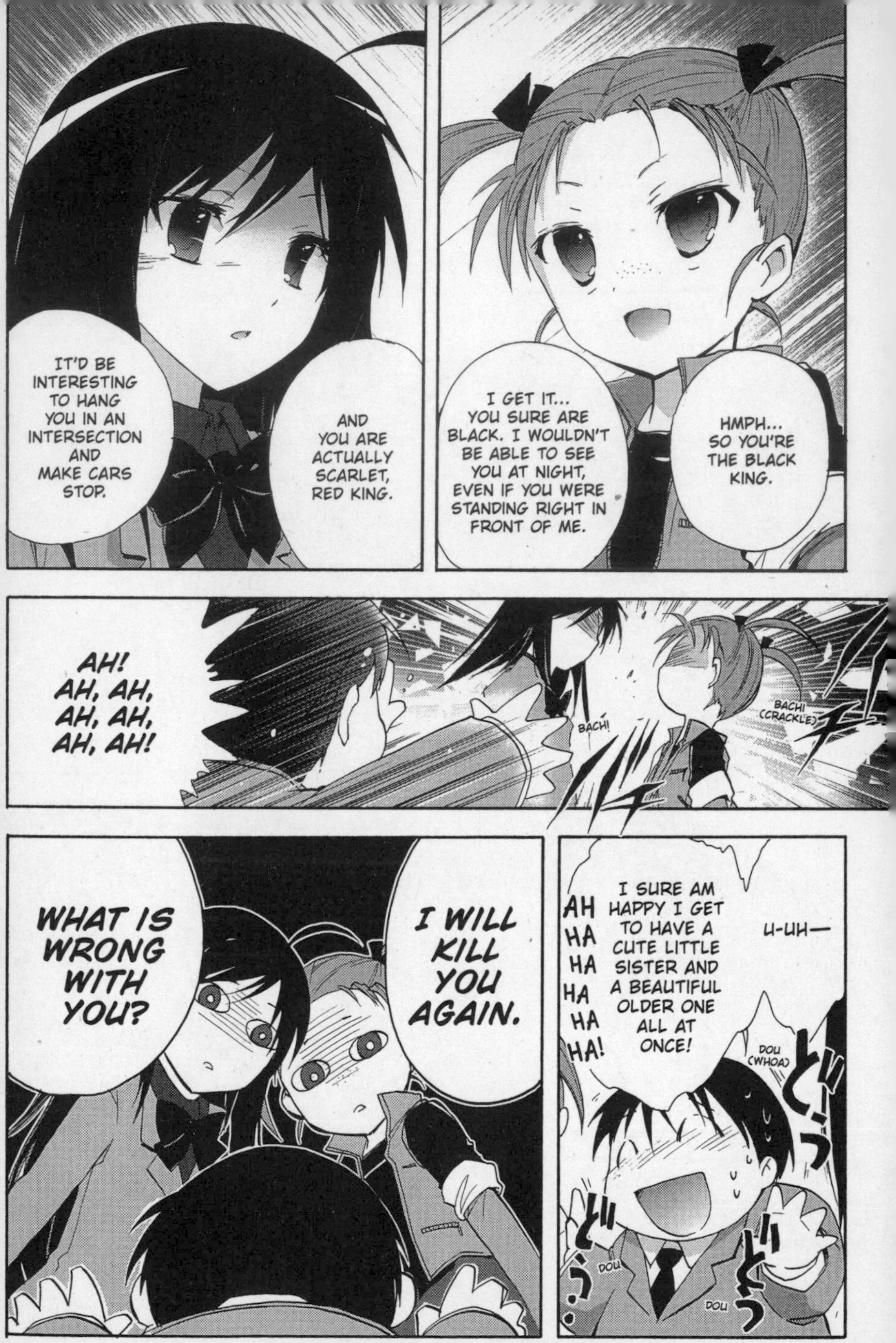
HMPH... SO YOU'RE THE BLACK KING.
I GET IT... YOU SURE ARE BLACK. I WOULDN'T BE ABLE TO SEE YOU AT NIGHT, EVEN IF YOU WERE STANDING RIGHT IN FRONT OF ME.
AND YOU ARE ACTUALLY SCARLET, RED KING.
IT'D BE INTERESTING TO HANG YOU IN AN INTERSECTION AND MAKE CARS STOP.
BACHI (CRACKLE)
BACHI!
AH! AH, AH, AH, AH, AH, AH!
U-UH—
I SURE AM HAPPY I GET TO HAVE A CUTE LITTLE SISTER AND A BEAUTIFUL OLDER ONE ALL AT ONCE!
AH HA HA HA HA HA!
DOU (WHOA)
DOU
DOU
I WILL KILL YOU AGAIN.
WHAT IS WRONG WITH YOU?

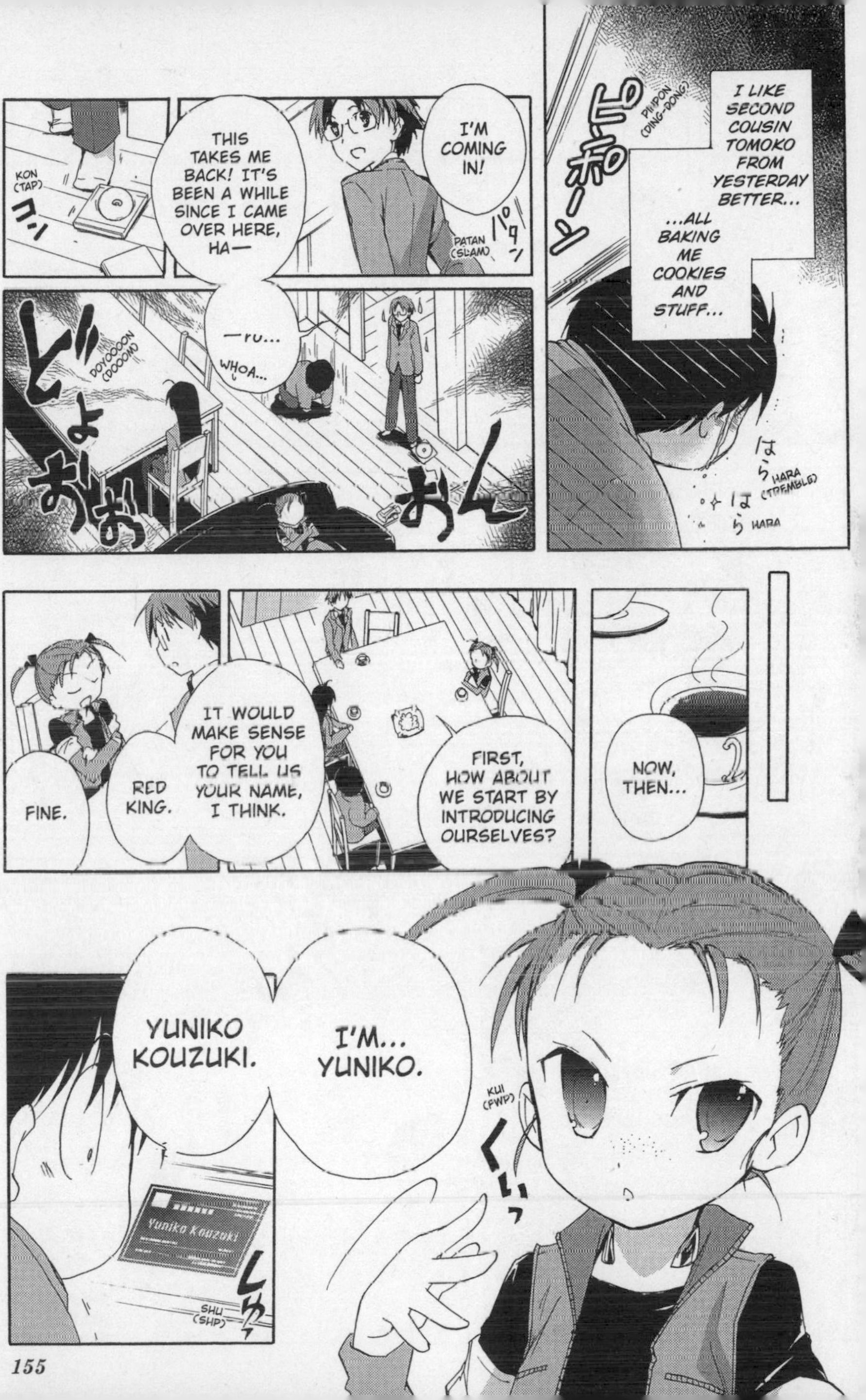
PIIPON (DING-DONG)
ピンポーン
I LIKE SECOND COUSIN TOMOKO FROM YESTERDAY BETTER...
...ALL BAKING ME COOKIES AND STUFF...
はら HARA (TREMBLE)
はら HARA
I'M COMING IN!
PATAN (SLAM)
パタン
THIS TAKES ME BACK! IT'S BEEN A WHILE SINCE I CAME OVER HERE, HA—
KON (TAP)
コン
—YU...
WHOA...
DOYOOOON (DOOOM)
どよおおん
NOW, THEN...
FIRST, HOW ABOUT WE START BY INTRODUCING OURSELVES?
IT WOULD MAKE SENSE FOR YOU TO TELL US YOUR NAME, I THINK.
RED KING.
FINE.
I'M... YUNIKO.
KUI (FWP)
くいっ
YUNIKO KOUZUKI.
Yuniko Kouzuki
SHU (SHP)
しゅっ

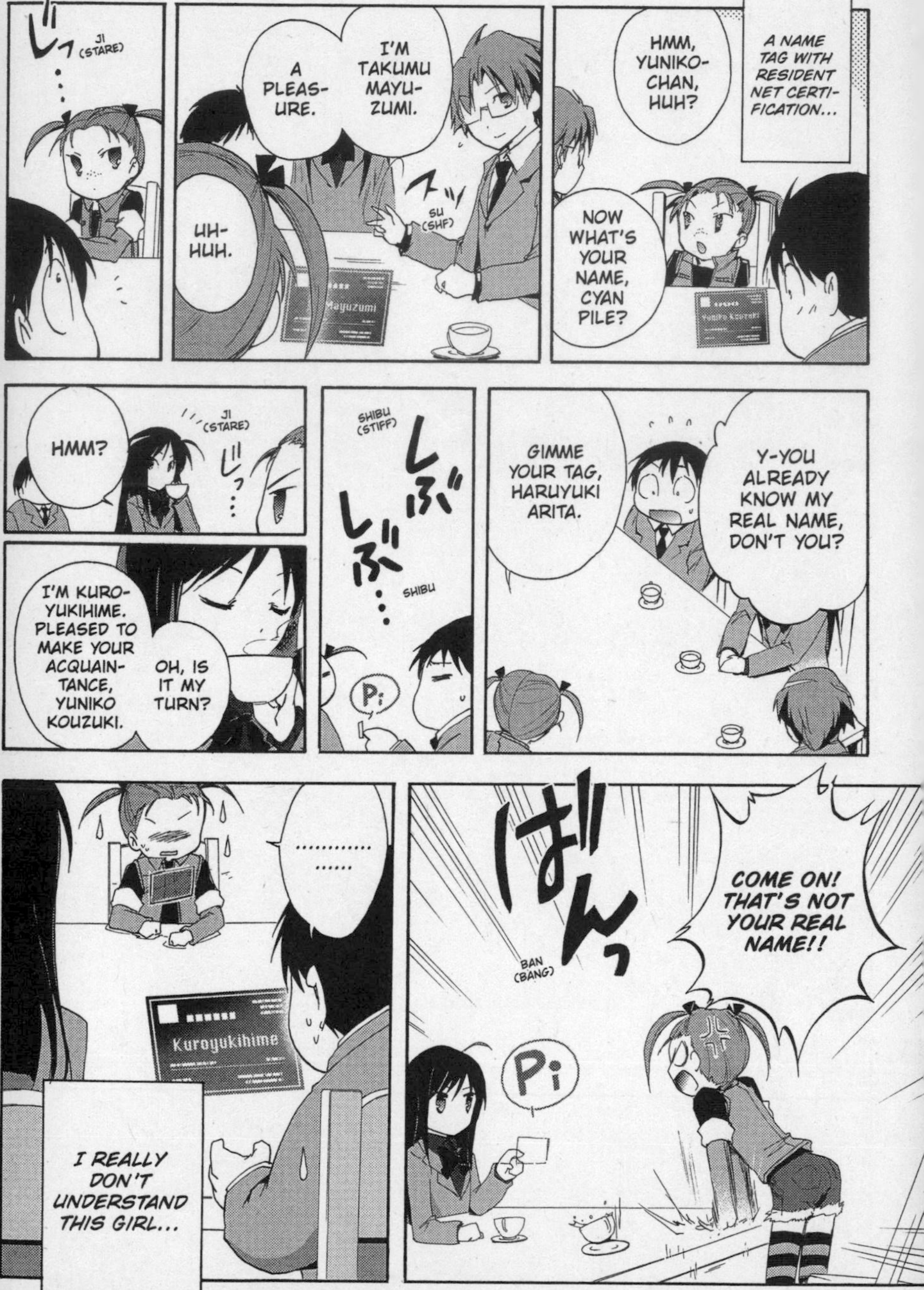
A NAME TAG WITH RESIDENT NET CERTIFICATION...
HMM, YUNIKO-CHAN, HUH?
NOW WHAT'S YOUR NAME, CYAN PILE?
I'M TAKUMU MAYUZUMI.
A PLEASURE.
SU (SHF)
Mayuzumi
UH-HUH.
JI (STARE)
...
Y-YOU ALREADY KNOW MY REAL NAME, DON'T YOU?
GIMME YOUR TAG, HARUYUKI ARITA.
SHIBU (STIFF)
SHIBU
Pi
HMM?
JI (STARE)
OH, IS IT MY TURN?
I'M KURO-YUKIHIME. PLEASED TO MAKE YOUR ACQUAINTANCE, YUNIKO KOUZUKI.
BAN (BANG)
COME ON! THAT'S NOT YOUR REAL NAME!!
Pi
....
Kuroyukihime
I REALLY DON'T UNDERSTAND THIS GIRL...

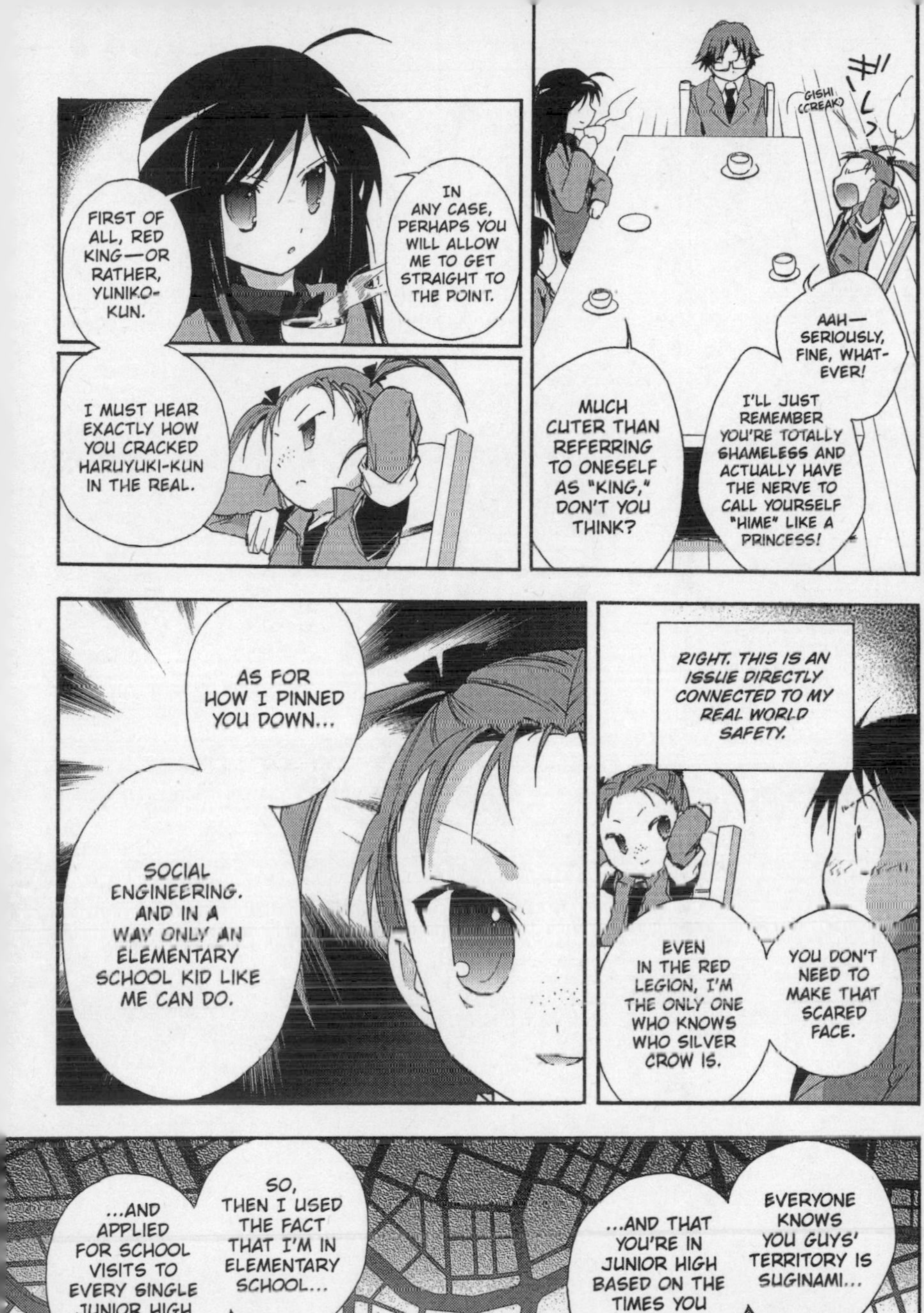
GISHI (CREAK)
AAH—SERIOUSLY, FINE, WHATEVER!
I'LL JUST REMEMBER YOU'RE TOTALLY SHAMELESS AND ACTUALLY HAVE THE NERVE TO CALL YOURSELF "HIME" LIKE A PRINCESS!
MUCH CUTER THAN REFERRING TO ONESELF AS "KING," DON'T YOU THINK?
IN ANY CASE, PERHAPS YOU WILL ALLOW ME TO GET STRAIGHT TO THE POINT.
FIRST OF ALL, RED KING—OR RATHER, YUNIKO-KUN.
I MUST HEAR EXACTLY HOW YOU CRACKED HARUYUKI-KUN IN THE REAL.
RIGHT. THIS IS AN ISSUE DIRECTLY CONNECTED TO MY REAL WORLD SAFETY.
YOU DON'T NEED TO MAKE THAT SCARED FACE.
EVEN IN THE RED LEGION, I'M THE ONLY ONE WHO KNOWS WHO SILVER CROW IS.
AS FOR HOW I PINNED YOU DOWN...
SOCIAL ENGINEERING. AND IN A WAY ONLY AN ELEMENTARY SCHOOL KID LIKE ME CAN DO.
EVERYONE KNOWS YOU GUYS' TERRITORY IS SUGINAMI...
...AND THAT YOU'RE IN JUNIOR HIGH BASED ON THE TIMES YOU SHOWED UP.
SO, THEN I USED THE FACT THAT I'M IN ELEMENTARY SCHOOL...
...AND APPLIED FOR SCHOOL VISITS TO EVERY SINGLE JUNIOR HIGH IN SUGINAMI WARD.

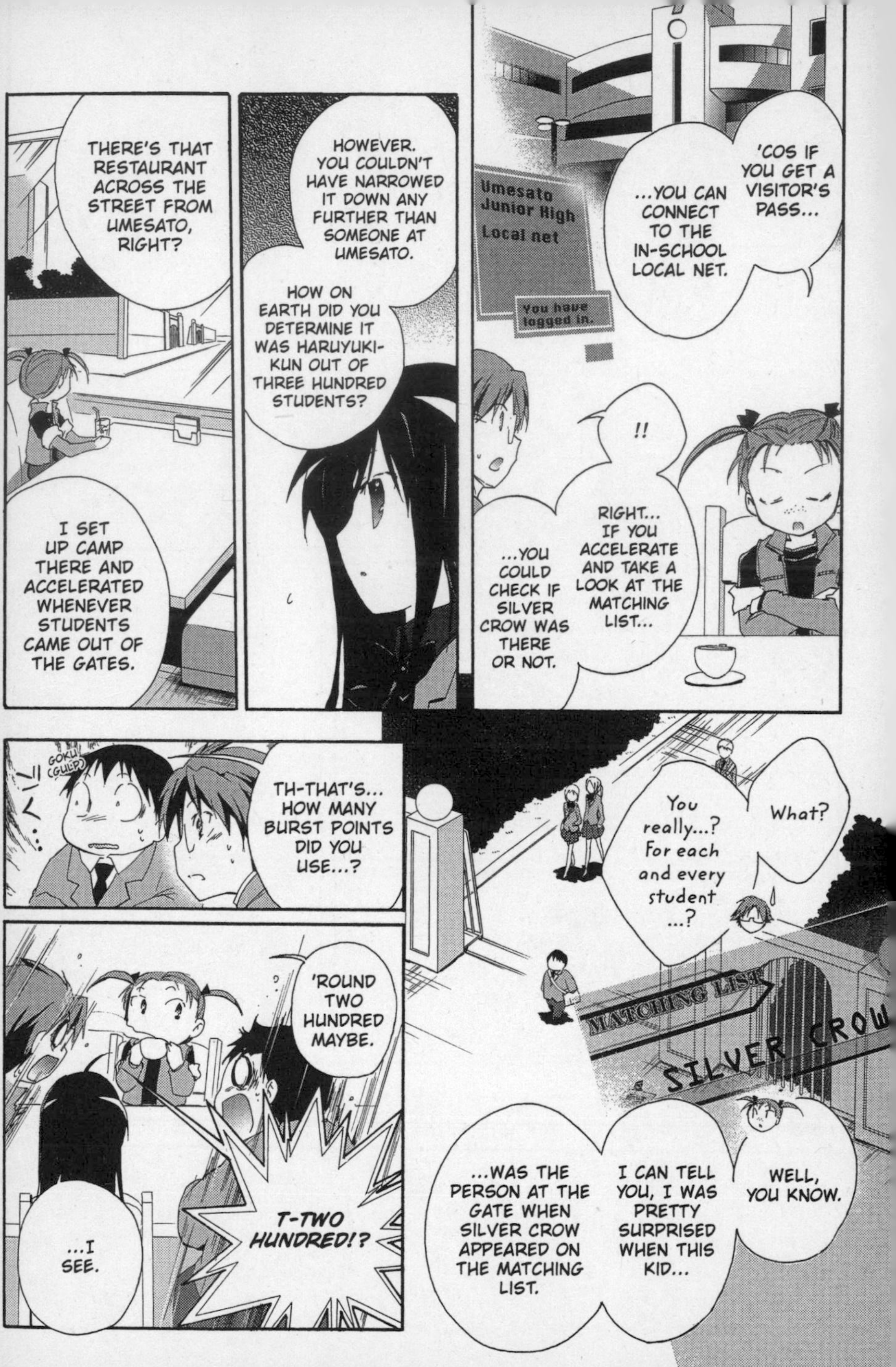
'COS IF YOU GET A VISITOR'S PASS...
...YOU CAN CONNECT TO THE IN-SCHOOL LOCAL NET.
Umesato Junior High Local net
You have logged in.
!!
RIGHT... IF YOU ACCELERATE AND TAKE A LOOK AT THE MATCHING LIST...
...YOU COULD CHECK IF SILVER CROW WAS THERE OR NOT.
HOWEVER. YOU COULDN'T HAVE NARROWED IT DOWN ANY FURTHER THAN SOMEONE AT UMESATO.
HOW ON EARTH DID YOU DETERMINE IT WAS HARUYUKI-KUN OUT OF THREE HUNDRED STUDENTS?
THERE'S THAT RESTAURANT ACROSS THE STREET FROM UMESATO, RIGHT?
I SET UP CAMP THERE AND ACCELERATED WHENEVER STUDENTS CAME OUT OF THE GATES.
What?
You really...? For each and every student ...?
MATCHING LIST
SILVER CROW
WELL, YOU KNOW.
I CAN TELL YOU, I WAS PRETTY SURPRISED WHEN THIS KID...
...WAS THE PERSON AT THE GATE WHEN SILVER CROW APPEARED ON THE MATCHING LIST.
GOKU (GULP)
TH-THAT'S... HOW MANY BURST POINTS DID YOU USE...?
'ROUND TWO HUNDRED MAYBE.
T-TWO HUNDRED!?
...I SEE.

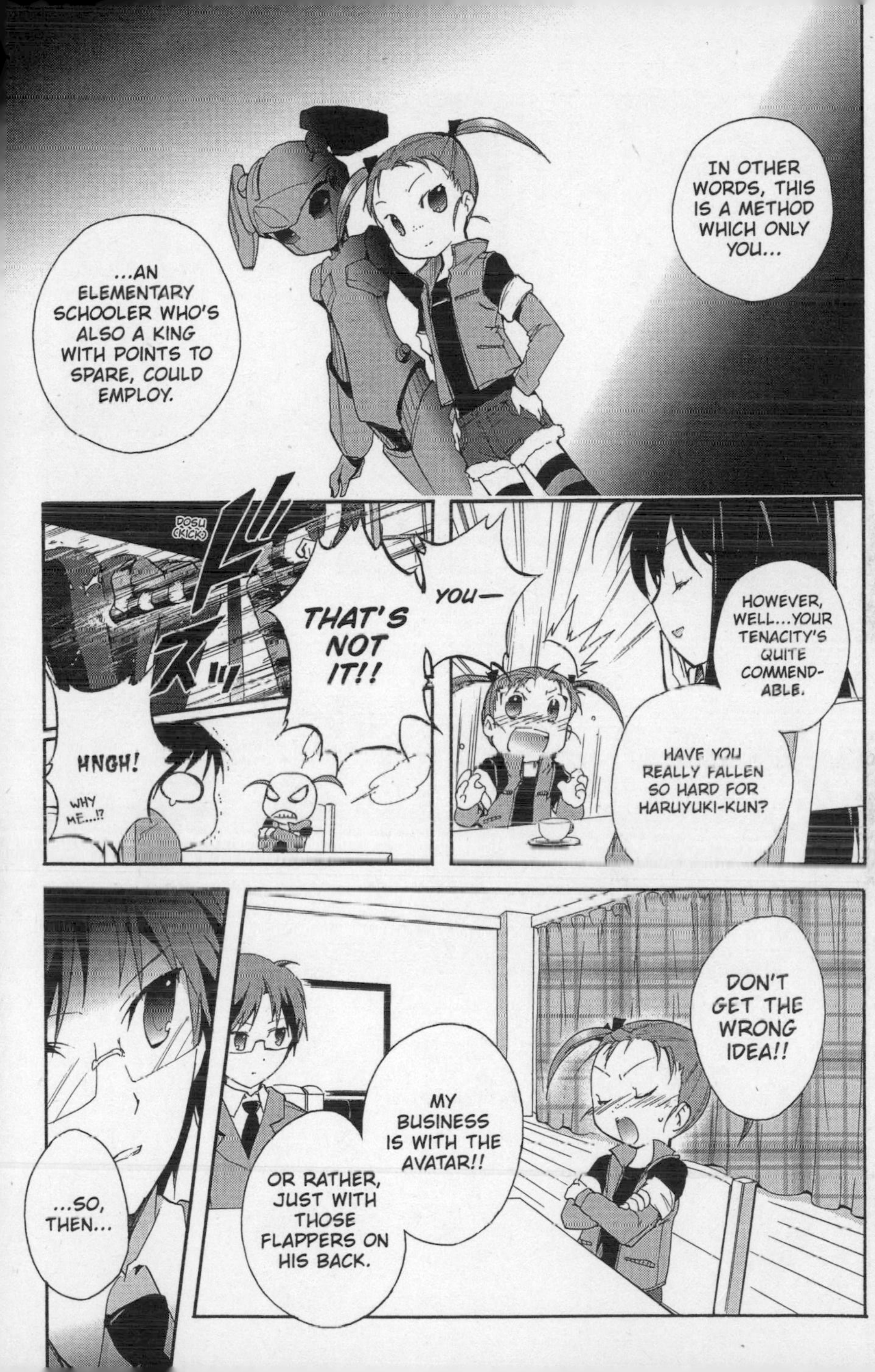
IN OTHER WORDS, THIS IS A METHOD WHICH ONLY YOU...
...AN ELEMENTARY SCHOOLER WHO'S ALSO A KING WITH POINTS TO SPARE, COULD EMPLOY.
HOWEVER, WELL...YOUR TENACITY'S QUITE COMMENDABLE.
HAVE YOU REALLY FALLEN SO HARD FOR HARUYUKI-KUN?
YOU—
THAT'S NOT IT!!
DOSU (KICK)
HNGH!
WHY ME...!?
DON'T GET THE WRONG IDEA!!
MY BUSINESS IS WITH THE AVATAR!!
OR RATHER, JUST WITH THOSE FLAPPERS ON HIS BACK.
...SO, THEN...

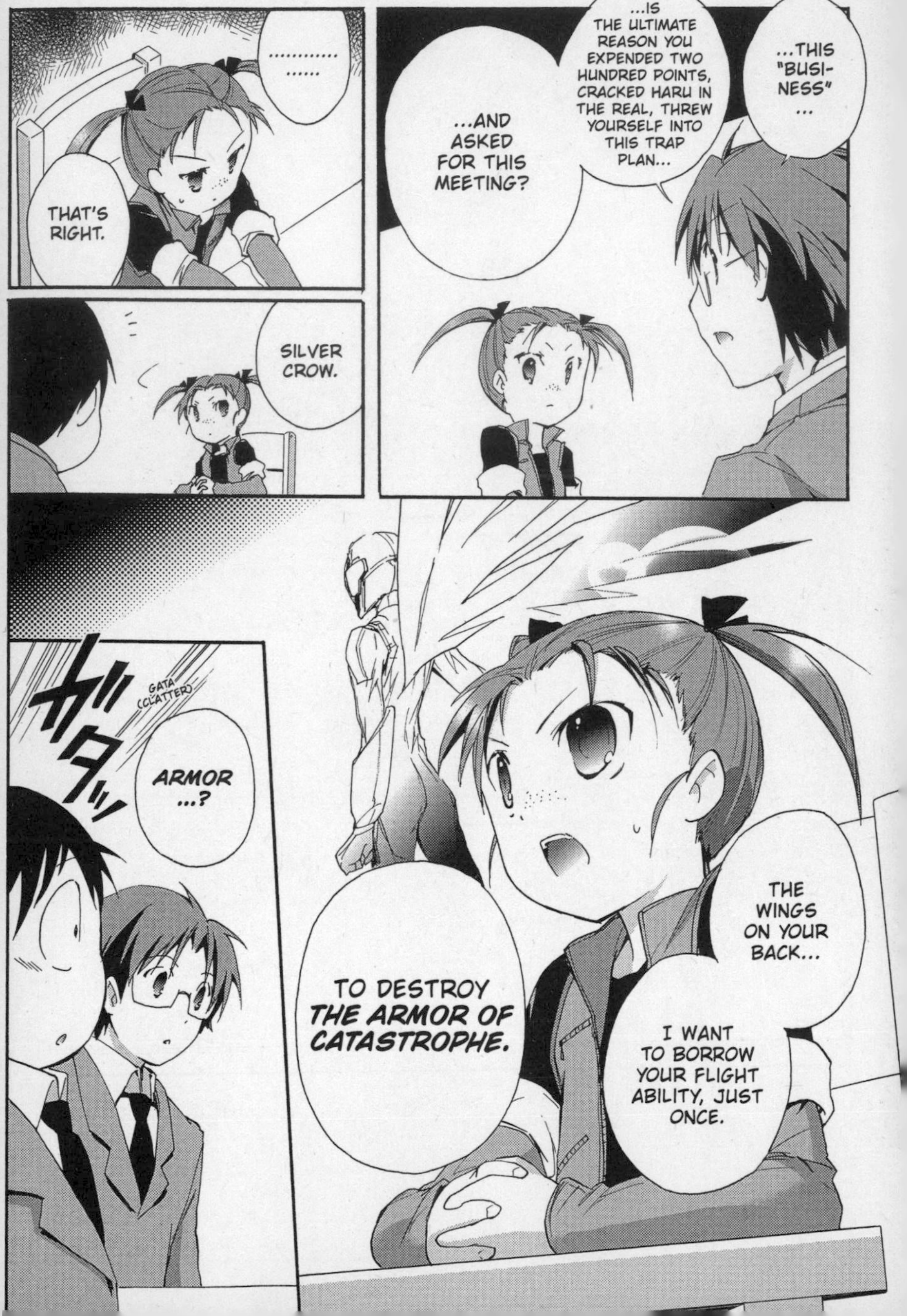
...THIS "BUSINESS" ...
...IS THE ULTIMATE REASON YOU EXPENDED TWO HUNDRED POINTS, CRACKED HARU IN THE REAL, THREW YOURSELF INTO THIS TRAP PLAN...
...AND ASKED FOR THIS MEETING?
....
THAT'S RIGHT.
SILVER CROW.
THE WINGS ON YOUR BACK...
I WANT TO BORROW YOUR FLIGHT ABILITY, JUST ONCE.
TO DESTROY *THE ARMOR OF CATASTROPHE.*
GATA (CLATTER)
ARMOR ...?

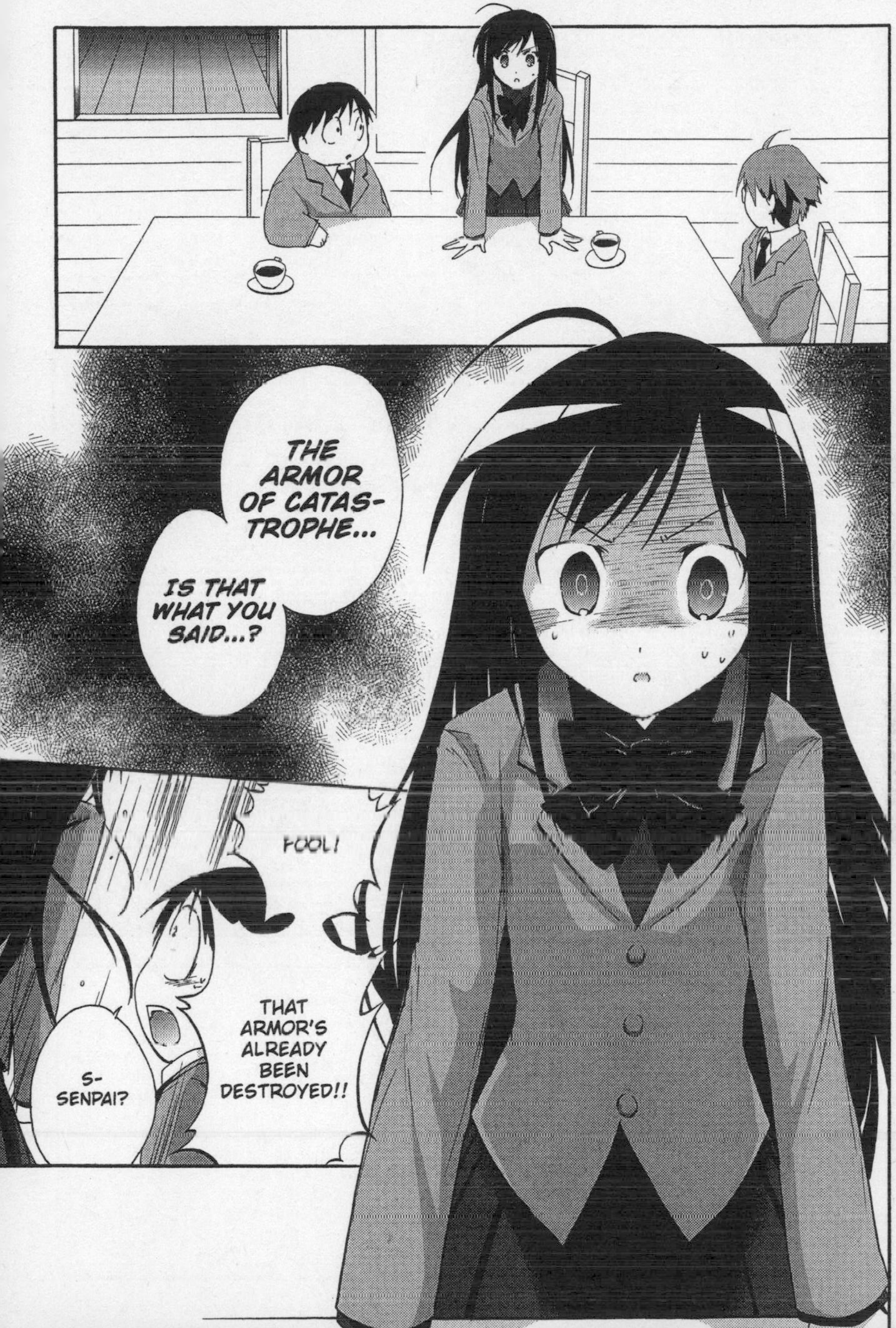
THE ARMOR OF CATAS-TROPHE...
IS THAT WHAT YOU SAID...?
FOOL!
THAT ARMOR'S ALREADY BEEN DESTROYED!!
S-SENPAI?

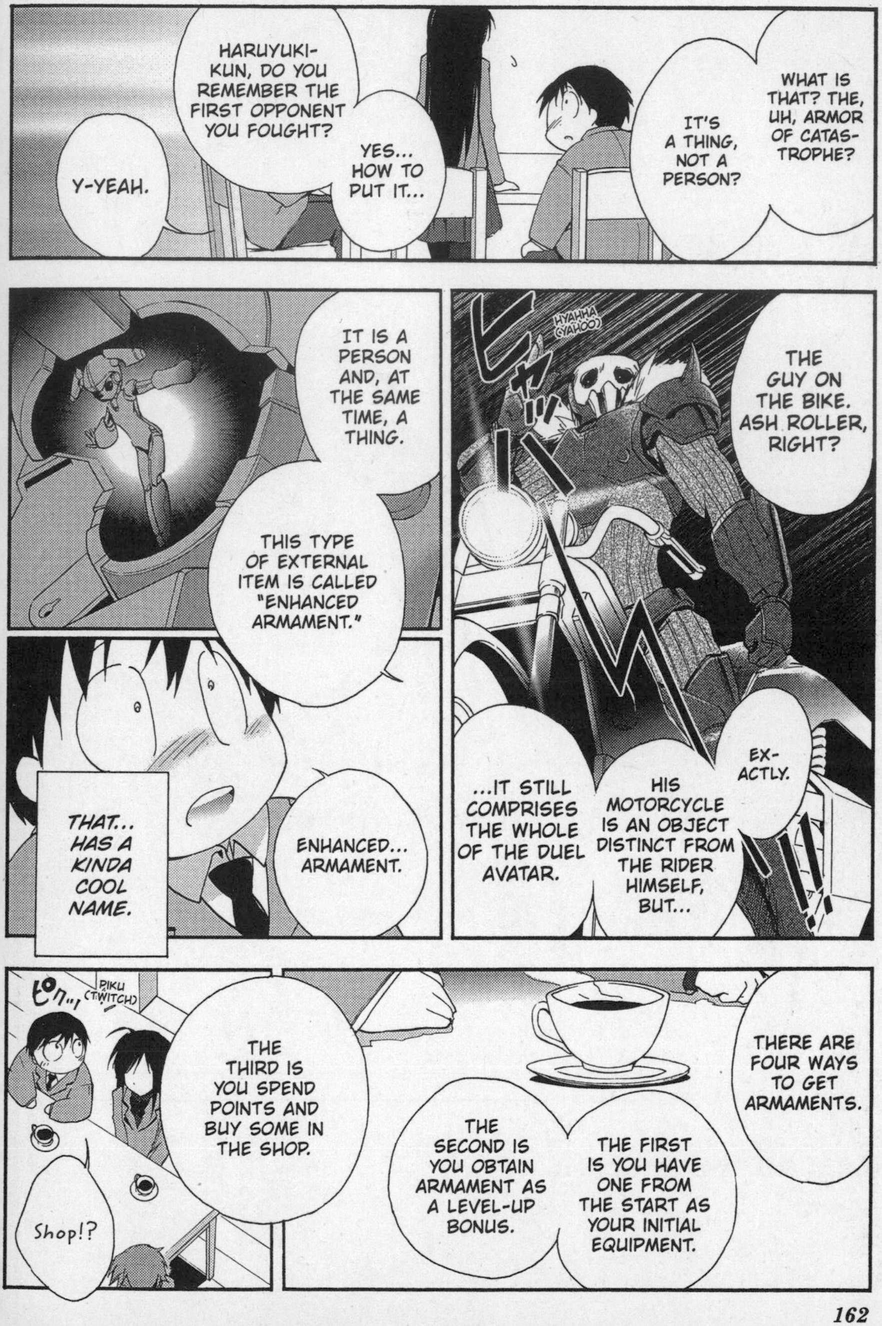
WHAT IS THAT? THE, UH, ARMOR OF CATASTROPHE?
IT'S A THING, NOT A PERSON?
HARUYUKI-KUN, DO YOU REMEMBER THE FIRST OPPONENT YOU FOUGHT?
YES... HOW TO PUT IT...
Y-YEAH.
HYAHHA (YAHOO)
THE GUY ON THE BIKE. ASH ROLLER, RIGHT?
EX-ACTLY.
HIS MOTORCYCLE IS AN OBJECT DISTINCT FROM THE RIDER HIMSELF, BUT...
...IT STILL COMPRISES THE WHOLE OF THE DUEL AVATAR.
IT IS A PERSON AND, AT THE SAME TIME, A THING.
THIS TYPE OF EXTERNAL ITEM IS CALLED "ENHANCED ARMAMENT."
ENHANCED... ARMAMENT.
THAT... HAS A KINDA COOL NAME.
THERE ARE FOUR WAYS TO GET ARMAMENTS.
THE FIRST IS YOU HAVE ONE FROM THE START AS YOUR INITIAL EQUIPMENT.
THE SECOND IS YOU OBTAIN ARMAMENT AS A LEVEL-UP BONUS.
THE THIRD IS YOU SPEND POINTS AND BUY SOME IN THE SHOP.
PIKU (TWITCH)
Shop!?

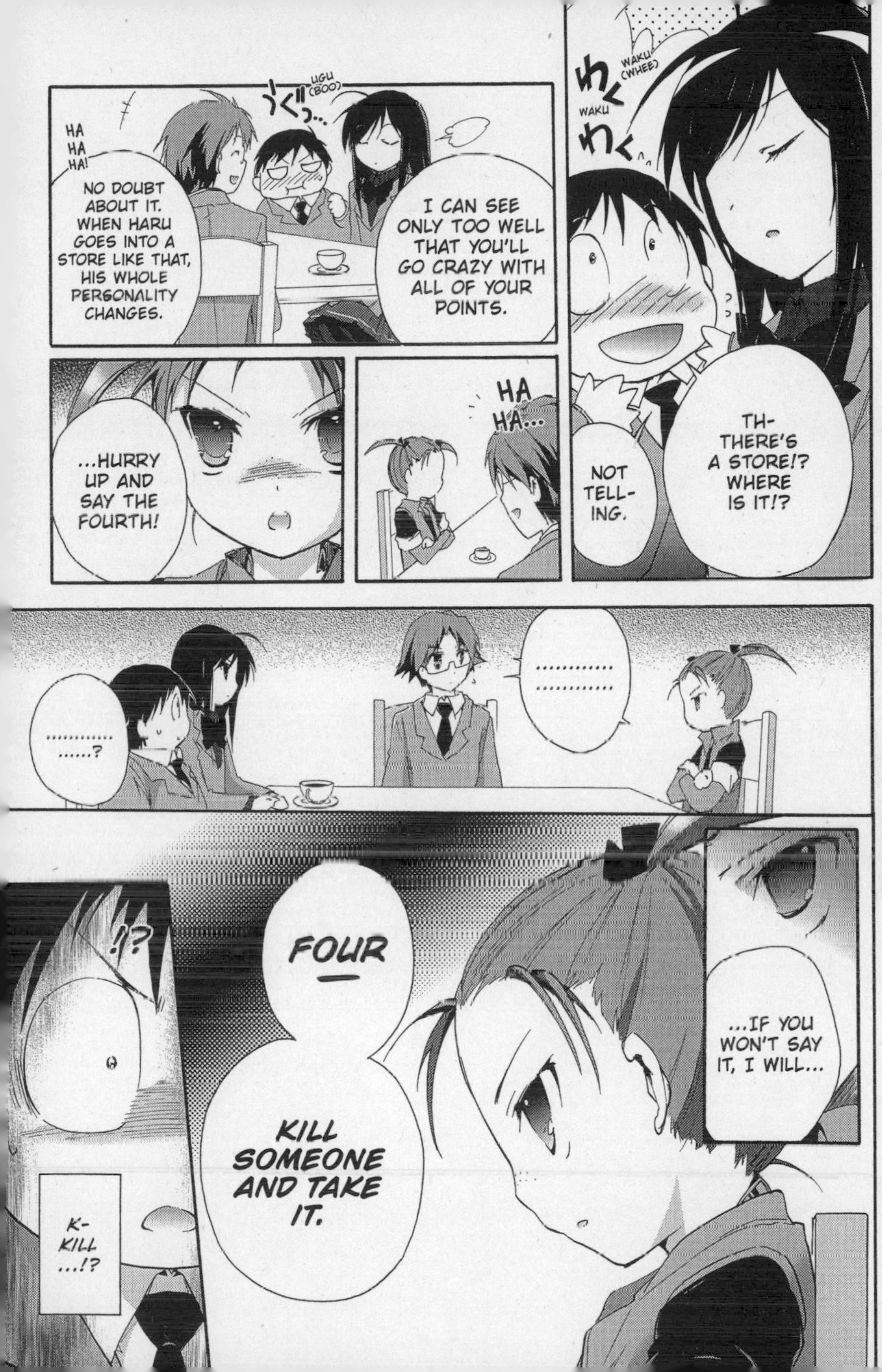
わくわく
WAKU (WHEE) WAKU
TH-THERE'S A STORE!? WHERE IS IT!?
NOT TELLING.
I CAN SEE ONLY TOO WELL THAT YOU'LL GO CRAZY WITH ALL OF YOUR POINTS.
うぐっ…
UGU (BOO)
HA HA HA!
NO DOUBT ABOUT IT. WHEN HARU GOES INTO A STORE LIKE THAT, HIS WHOLE PERSONALITY CHANGES.
HA HA...
...HURRY UP AND SAY THE FOURTH!
....
..................?
...IF YOU WON'T SAY IT, I WILL...
FOUR —
KILL SOMEONE AND TAKE IT.
!?
K-KILL ...!?

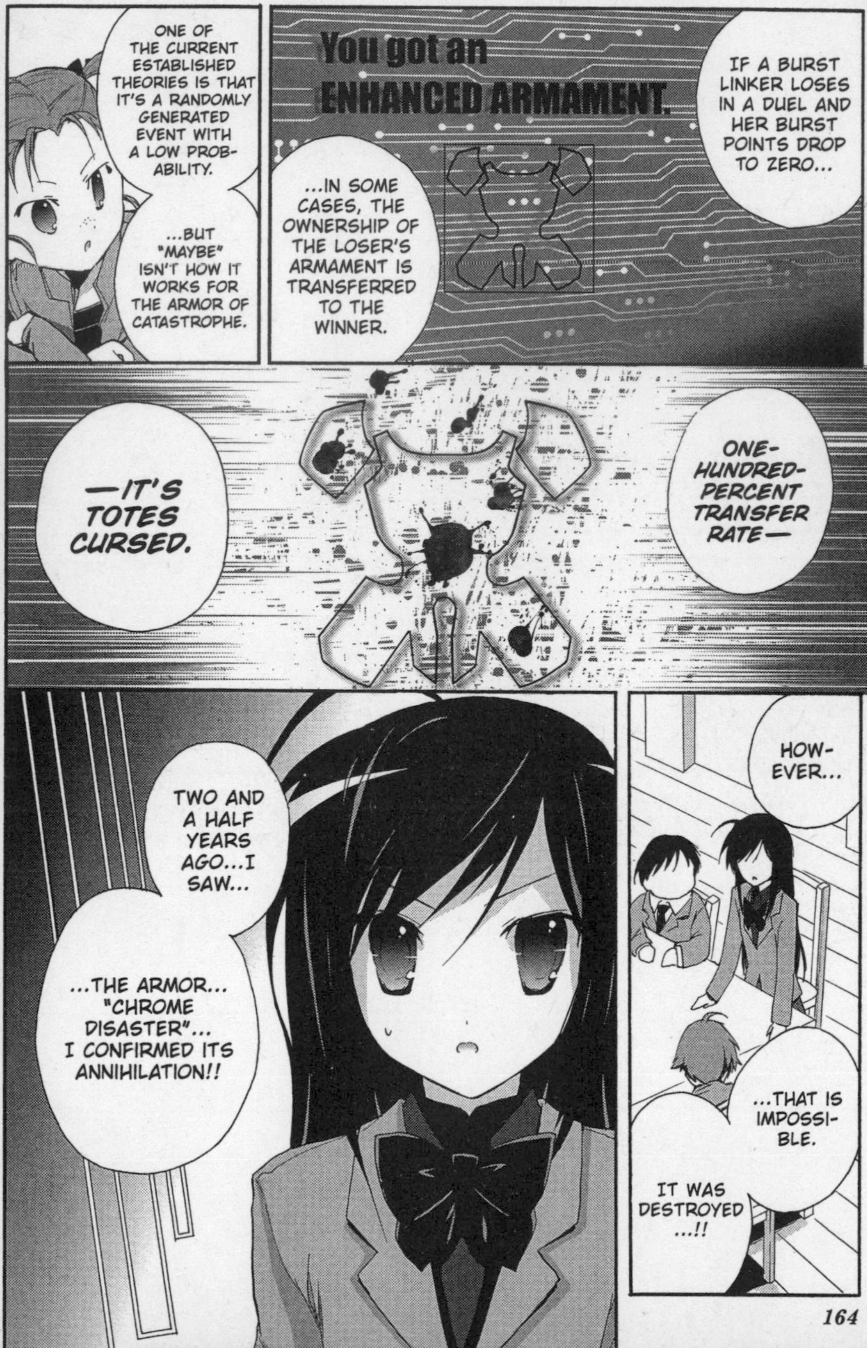

IF A BURST LINKER LOSES IN A DUEL AND HER BURST POINTS DROP TO ZERO...
You got an ENHANCED ARMAMENT.
...IN SOME CASES, THE OWNERSHIP OF THE LOSER'S ARMAMENT IS TRANSFERRED TO THE WINNER.
ONE OF THE CURRENT ESTABLISHED THEORIES IS THAT IT'S A RANDOMLY GENERATED EVENT WITH A LOW PROBABILITY.
...BUT "MAYBE" ISN'T HOW IT WORKS FOR THE ARMOR OF CATASTROPHE.
ONE-HUNDRED-PERCENT TRANSFER RATE—
—IT'S TOTES CURSED.
HOWEVER...
...THAT IS IMPOSSIBLE.
IT WAS DESTROYED ...!!
TWO AND A HALF YEARS AGO...I SAW...
...THE ARMOR... "CHROME DISASTER"... I CONFIRMED ITS ANNIHILATION!!

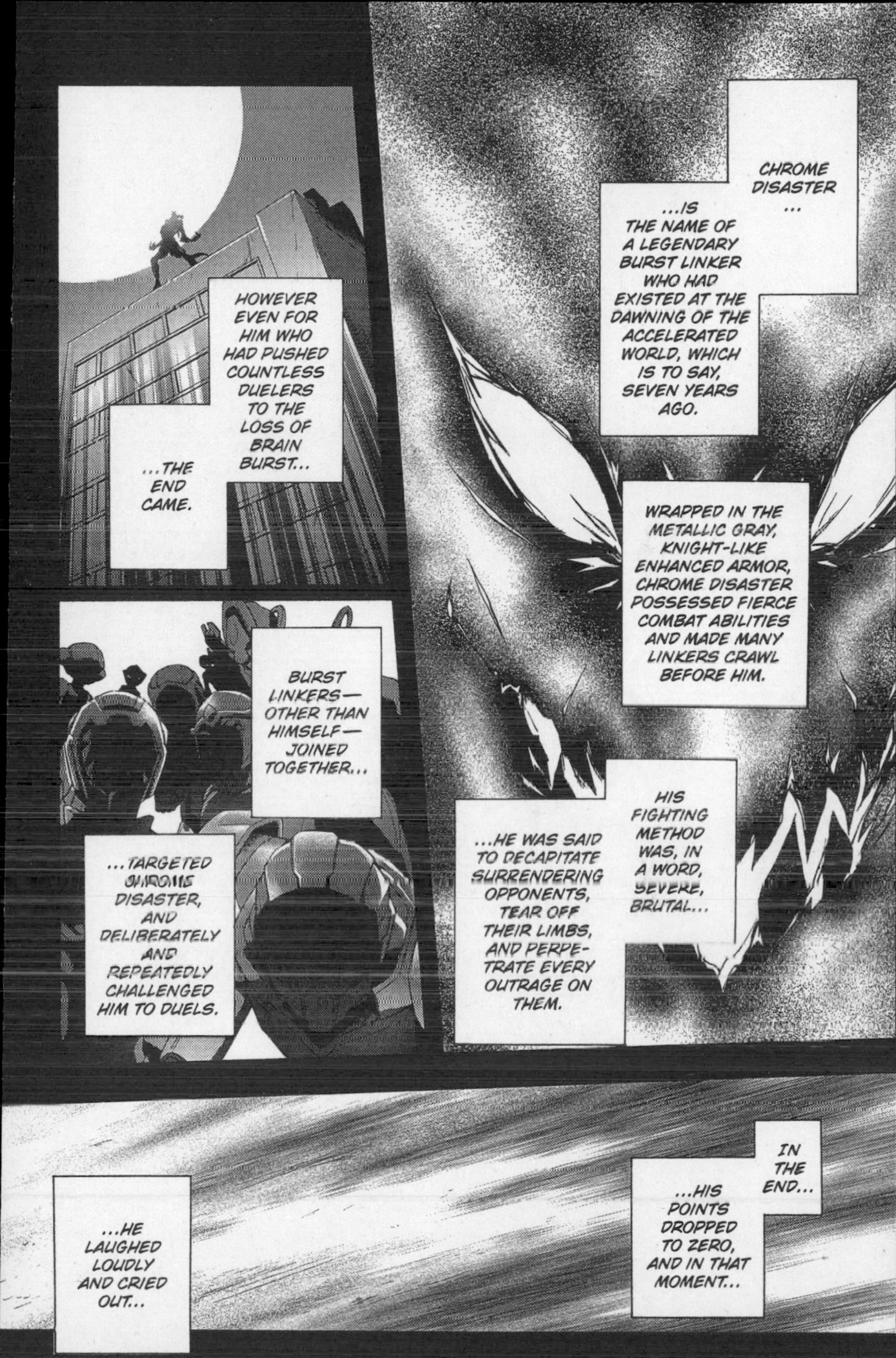
CHROME DISASTER...
...IS THE NAME OF A LEGENDARY BURST LINKER WHO HAD EXISTED AT THE DAWNING OF THE ACCELERATED WORLD, WHICH IS TO SAY, SEVEN YEARS AGO.
WRAPPED IN THE METALLIC GRAY, KNIGHT-LIKE ENHANCED ARMOR, CHROME DISASTER POSSESSED FIERCE COMBAT ABILITIES AND MADE MANY LINKERS CRAWL BEFORE HIM.
HIS FIGHTING METHOD WAS, IN A WORD, SEVERE, BRUTAL...
...HE WAS SAID TO DECAPITATE SURRENDERING OPPONENTS, TEAR OFF THEIR LIMBS, AND PERPETRATE EVERY OUTRAGE ON THEM.
HOWEVER EVEN FOR HIM WHO HAD PUSHED COUNTLESS DUELERS TO THE LOSS OF BRAIN BURST...
...THE END CAME.
BURST LINKERS—OTHER THAN HIMSELF—JOINED TOGETHER...
...TARGETED CHROME DISASTER, AND DELIBERATELY AND REPEATEDLY CHALLENGED HIM TO DUELS.
IN THE END...
...HIS POINTS DROPPED TO ZERO, AND IN THAT MOMENT...
...HE LAUGHED LOUDLY AND CRIED OUT...

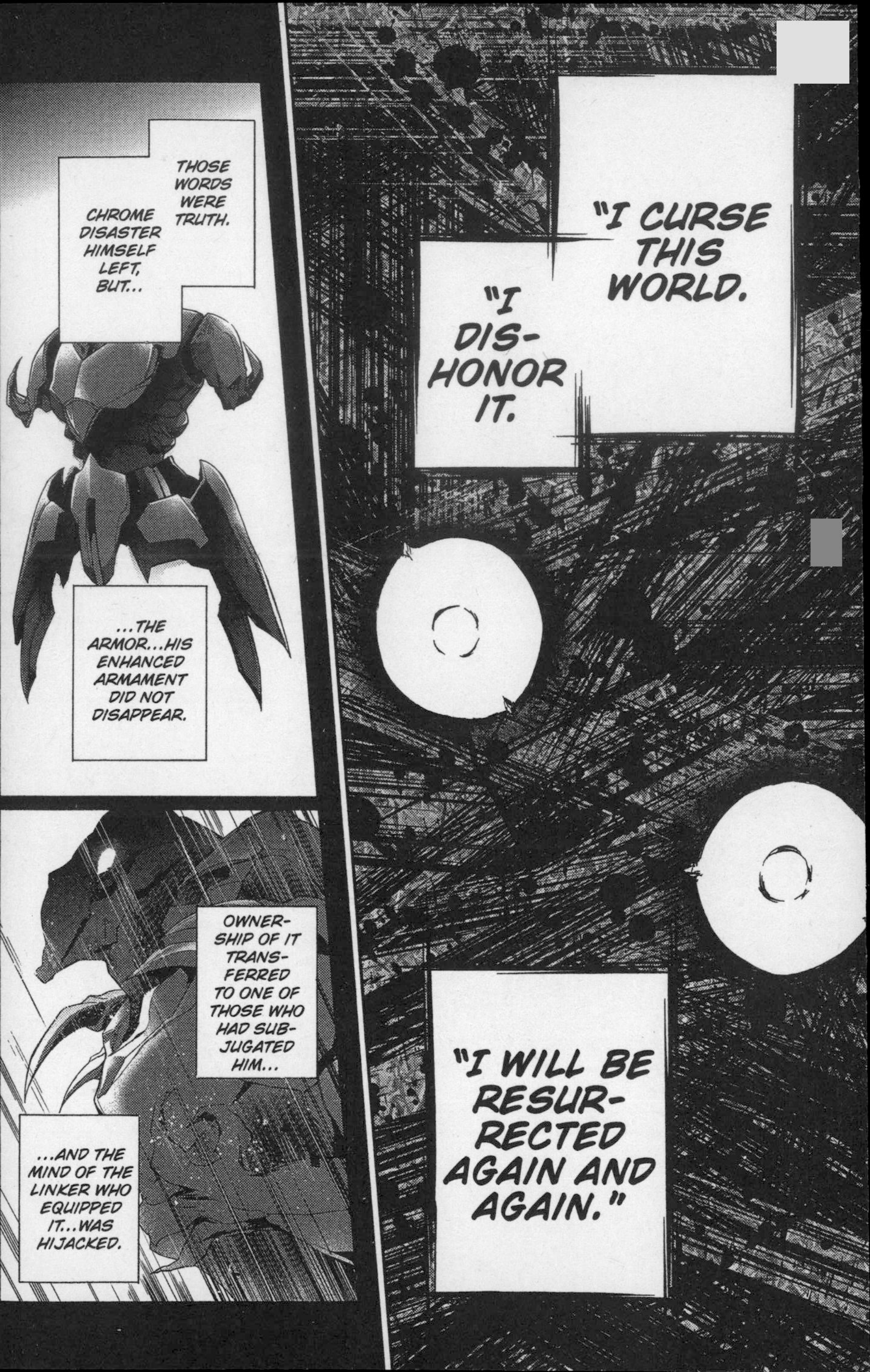
"I CURSE THIS WORLD.
"I DIS-HONOR IT.
"I WILL BE RESUR-RECTED AGAIN AND AGAIN."
THOSE WORDS WERE TRUTH.
CHROME DISASTER HIMSELF LEFT, BUT...
...THE ARMOR...HIS ENHANCED ARMAMENT DID NOT DISAPPEAR.
OWNER-SHIP OF IT TRANS-FERRED TO ONE OF THOSE WHO HAD SUB-JUGATED HIM...
...AND THE MIND OF THE LINKER WHO EQUIPPED IT...WAS HIJACKED.

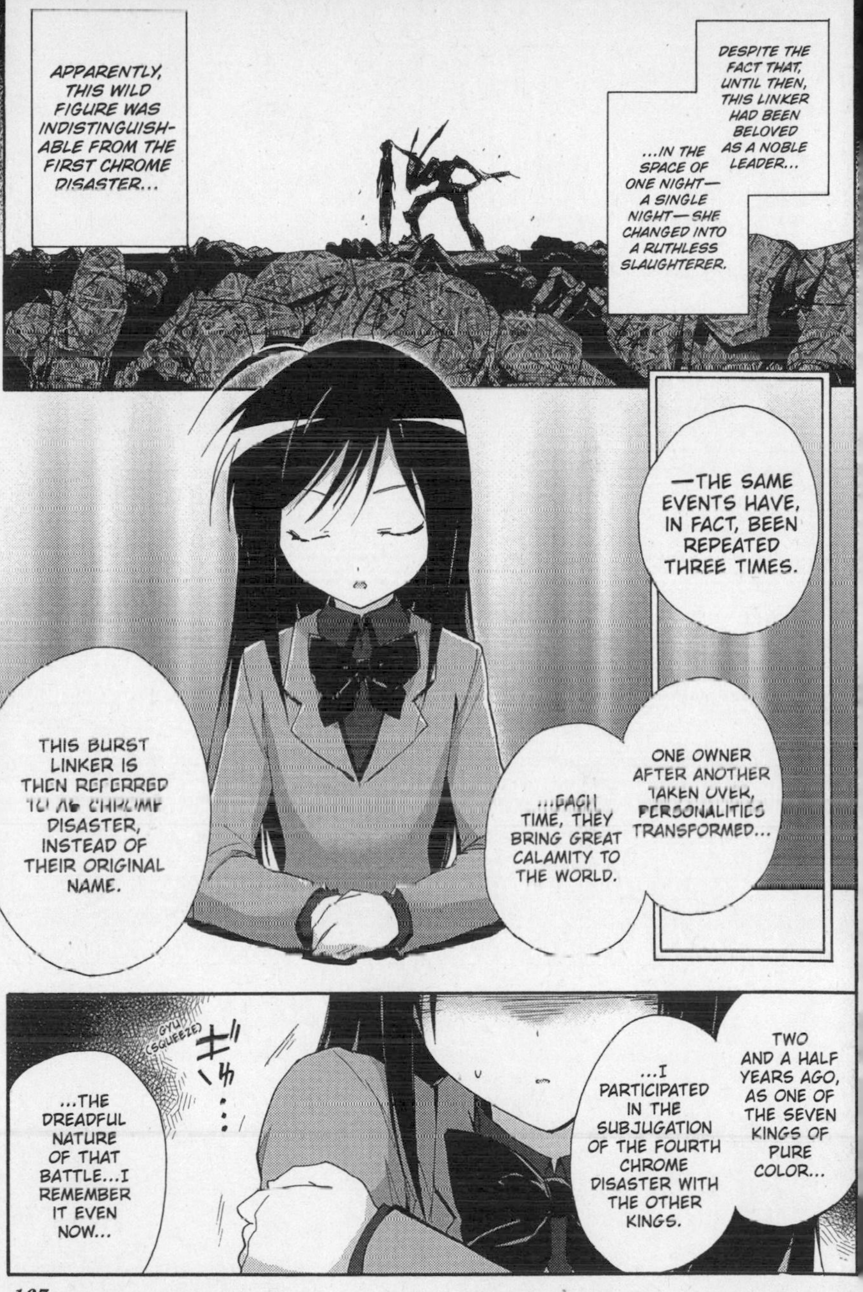
DESPITE THE FACT THAT, UNTIL THEN, THIS LINKER HAD BEEN BELOVED AS A NOBLE LEADER...
...IN THE SPACE OF ONE NIGHT—A SINGLE NIGHT—SHE CHANGED INTO A RUTHLESS SLAUGHTERER.
APPARENTLY, THIS WILD FIGURE WAS INDISTINGUISHABLE FROM THE FIRST CHROME DISASTER...
—THE SAME EVENTS HAVE, IN FACT, BEEN REPEATED THREE TIMES.
ONE OWNER AFTER ANOTHER TAKEN OVER, PERSONALITIES TRANSFORMED...
...EACH TIME, THEY BRING GREAT CALAMITY TO THE WORLD.
THIS BURST LINKER IS THEN REFERRED TO AS CHROME DISASTER, INSTEAD OF THEIR ORIGINAL NAME.
TWO AND A HALF YEARS AGO, AS ONE OF THE SEVEN KINGS OF PURE COLOR...
...I PARTICIPATED IN THE SUBJUGATION OF THE FOURTH CHROME DISASTER WITH THE OTHER KINGS.
GYU (SQUEEZE)
...THE DREADFUL NATURE OF THAT BATTLE...I REMEMBER IT EVEN NOW...

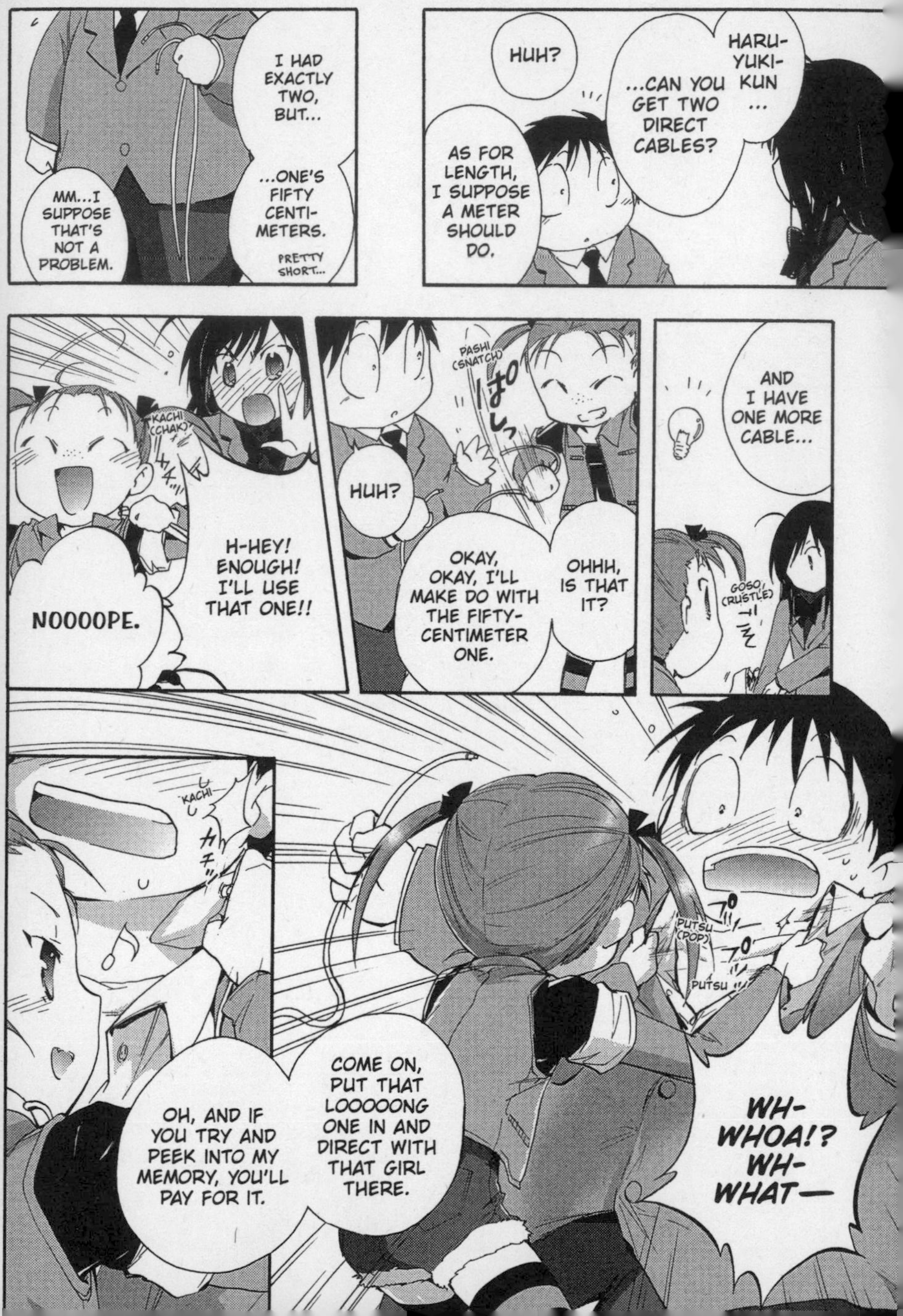
HARU-YUKI-KUN ...
...CAN YOU GET TWO DIRECT CABLES?
HUH?
AS FOR LENGTH, I SUPPOSE A METER SHOULD DO.
I HAD EXACTLY TWO, BUT...
...ONE'S FIFTY CENTI-METERS.
PRETTY SHORT...
MM...I SUPPOSE THAT'S NOT A PROBLEM.
AND I HAVE ONE MORE CABLE...
GOSO (RUSTLE)
PASHI (SNATCH)
OHHH, IS THAT IT?
OKAY, OKAY, I'LL MAKE DO WITH THE FIFTY-CENTIMETER ONE.
HUH?
KACHI (CHAK)
H-HEY! ENOUGH! I'LL USE THAT ONE!!
NOOOOPE.
WH-WHOA!? WH-WHAT—
PUTSU (POP)
PUTSU
COME ON, PUT THAT LOOOOONG ONE IN AND DIRECT WITH THAT GIRL THERE.
KACHI
OH, AND IF YOU TRY AND PEEK INTO MY MEMORY, YOU'LL PAY FOR IT.

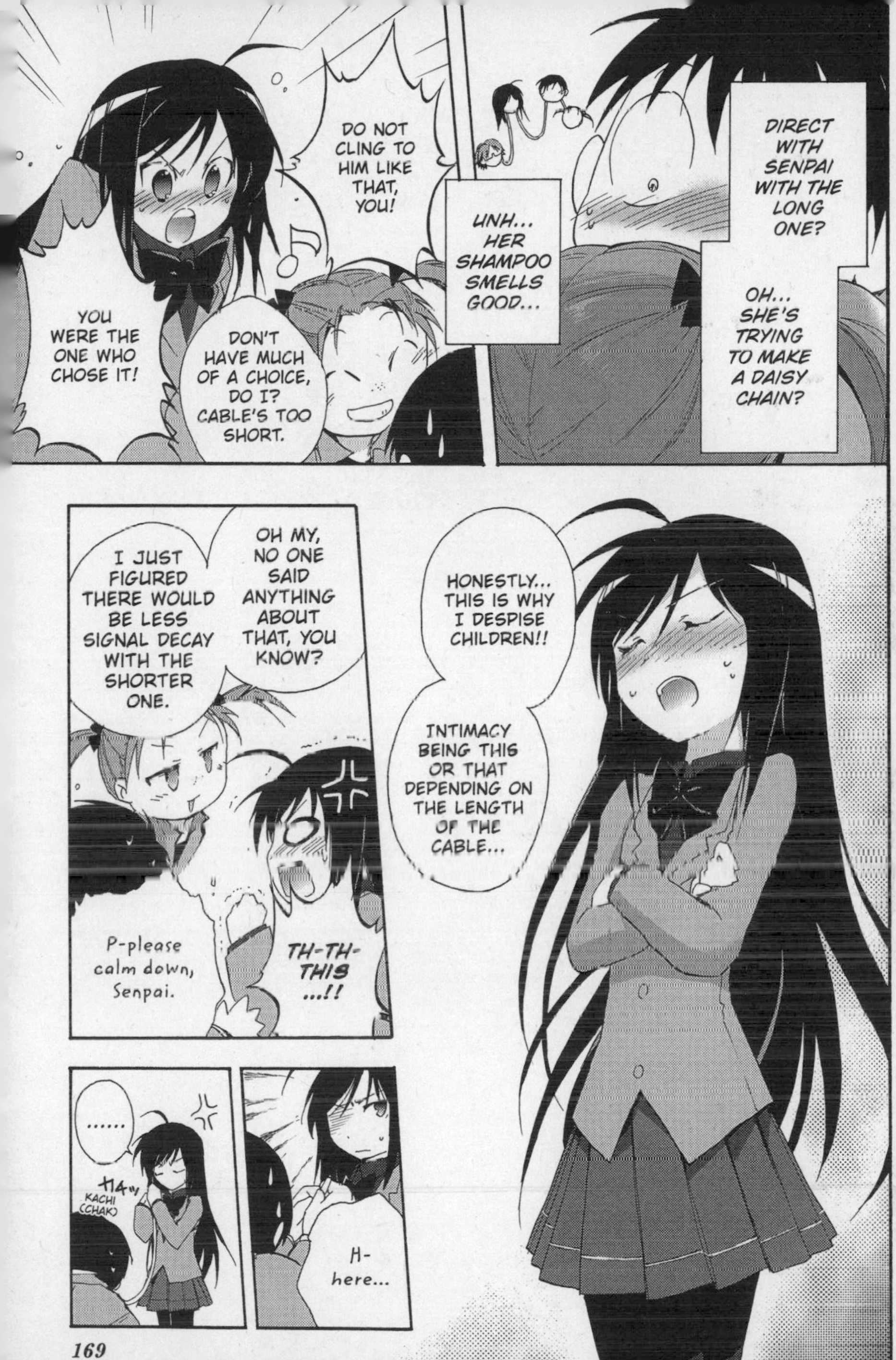
DIRECT WITH SENPAI WITH THE LONG ONE?
OH... SHE'S TRYING TO MAKE A DAISY CHAIN?
UNH... HER SHAMPOO SMELLS GOOD...
DO NOT CLING TO HIM LIKE THAT, YOU!
DON'T HAVE MUCH OF A CHOICE, DO I? CABLE'S TOO SHORT.
YOU WERE THE ONE WHO CHOSE IT!
HONESTLY... THIS IS WHY I DESPISE CHILDREN!!
INTIMACY BEING THIS OR THAT DEPENDING ON THE LENGTH OF THE CABLE...
OH MY, NO ONE SAID ANYTHING ABOUT THAT, YOU KNOW?
I JUST FIGURED THERE WOULD BE LESS SIGNAL DECAY WITH THE SHORTER ONE.
TH-TH-THIS ...!!
P-please calm down, Senpai.
H-here...
......
KACHI (CHAK)

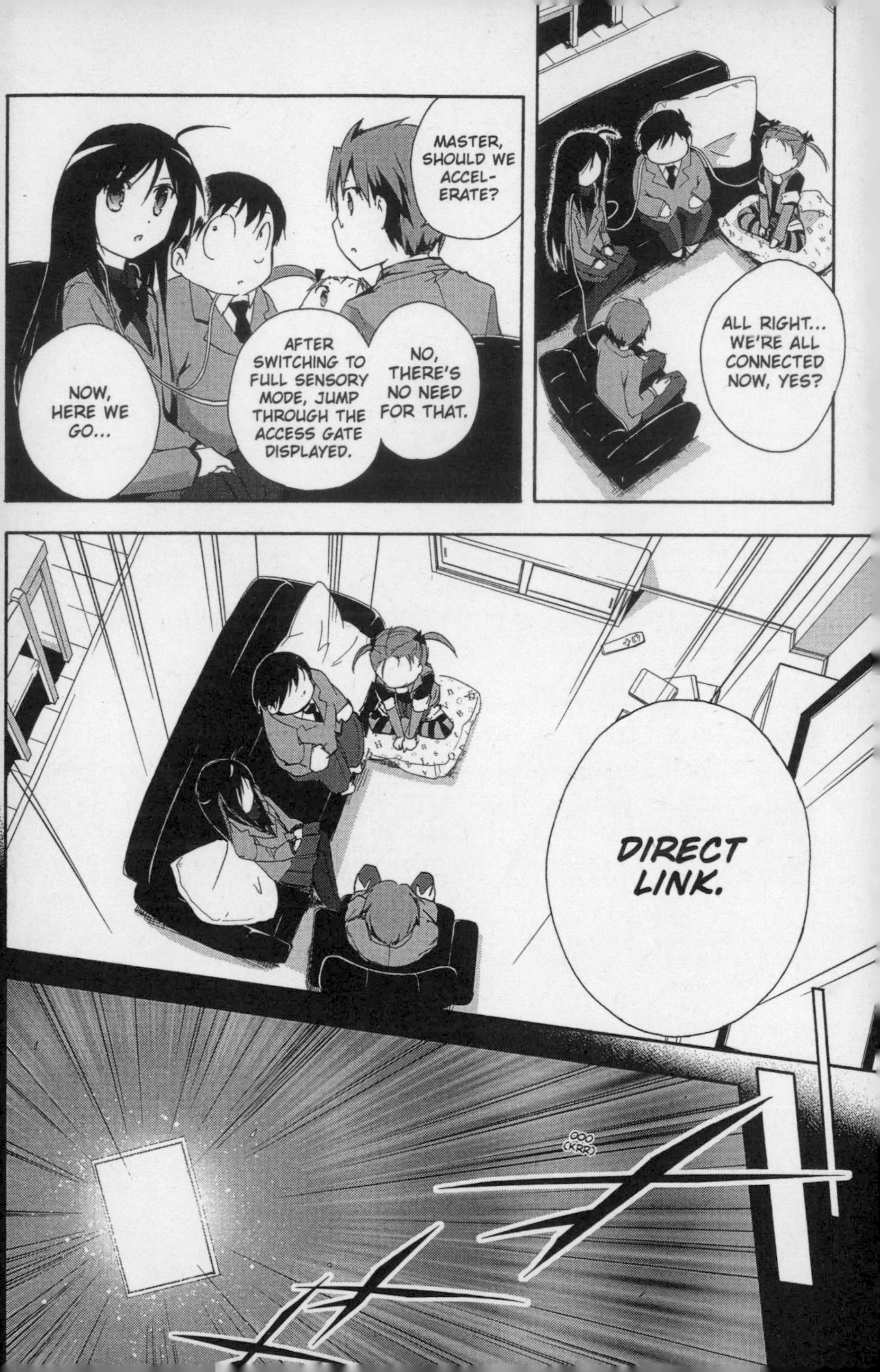
ALL RIGHT... WE'RE ALL CONNECTED NOW, YES?
MASTER, SHOULD WE ACCEL-ERATE?
NO, THERE'S NO NEED FOR THAT.
AFTER SWITCHING TO FULL SENSORY MODE, JUMP THROUGH THE ACCESS GATE DISPLAYED.
NOW, HERE WE GO...
DIRECT LINK.
(KRR)

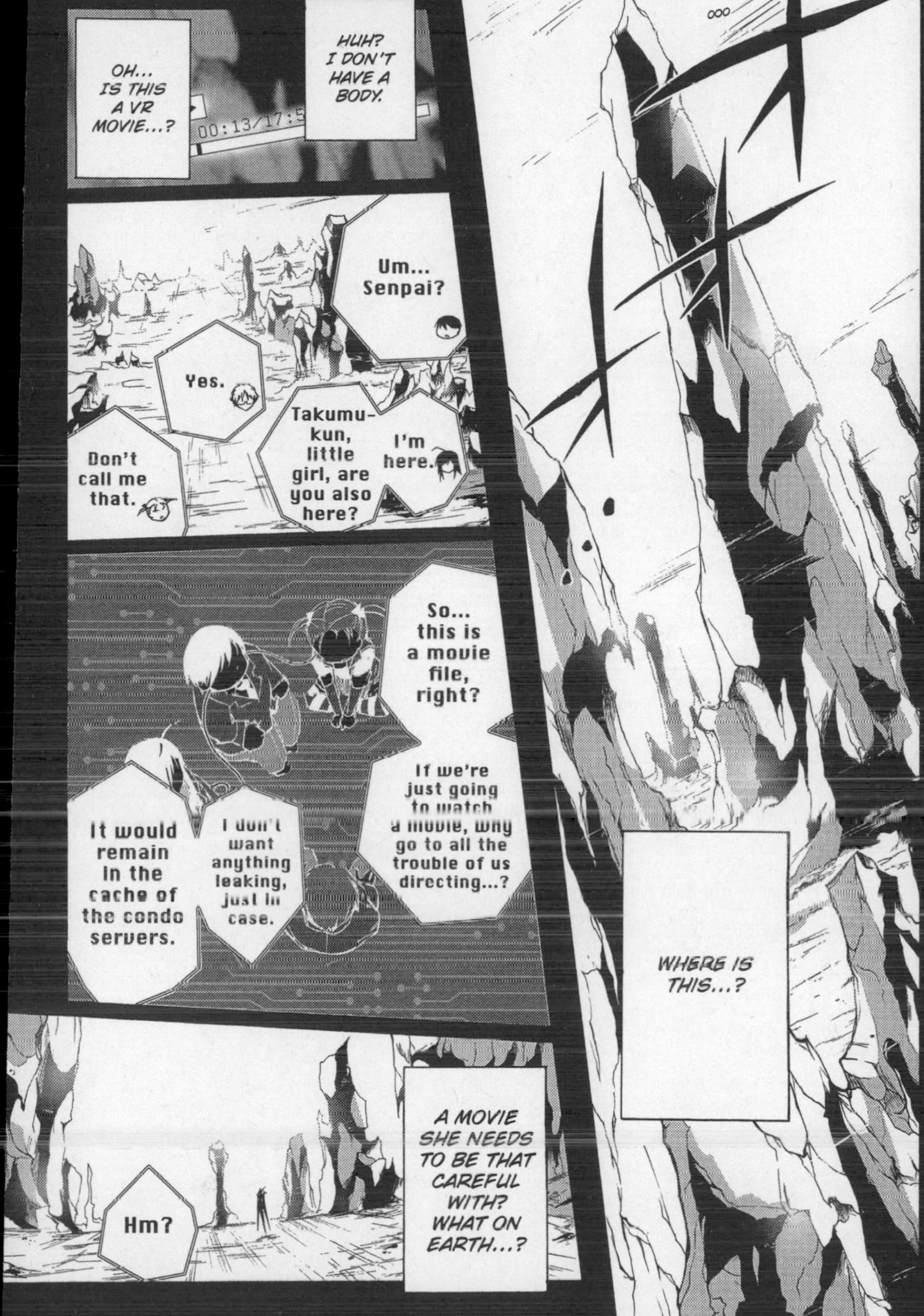
ooo
WHERE IS THIS...?
HUH? I DON'T HAVE A BODY.
OH... IS THIS A VR MOVIE...?
00:13/17:5
Um... Senpai?
I'm here.
Takumu-kun, little girl, are you also here?
Yes.
Don't call me that.
So... this is a movie file, right?
If we're just going to watch a movie, why go to all the trouble of us directing...?
I don't want anything leaking, just in case.
It would remain in the cache of the condo servers.
A MOVIE SHE NEEDS TO BE THAT CAREFUL WITH? WHAT ON EARTH...?
Hm?

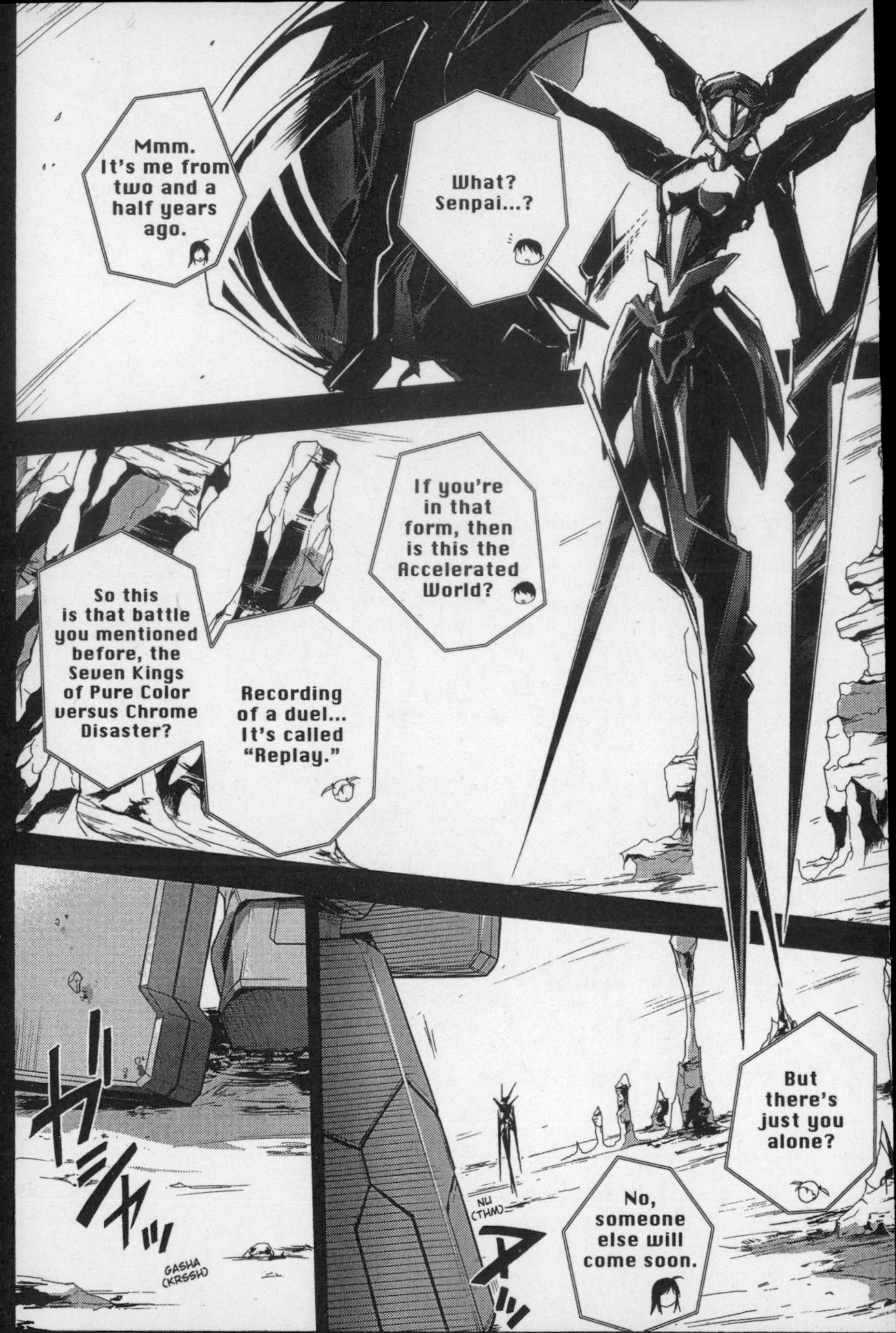
What? Senpai...?
Mmm. It's me from two and a half years ago.
If you're in that form, then is this the Accelerated World?
Recording of a duel... It's called "Replay."
So this is that battle you mentioned before, the Seven Kings of Pure Color versus Chrome Disaster?
But there's just you alone?
No, someone else will come soon.
NU (THM)
GASHA (KRSSH)

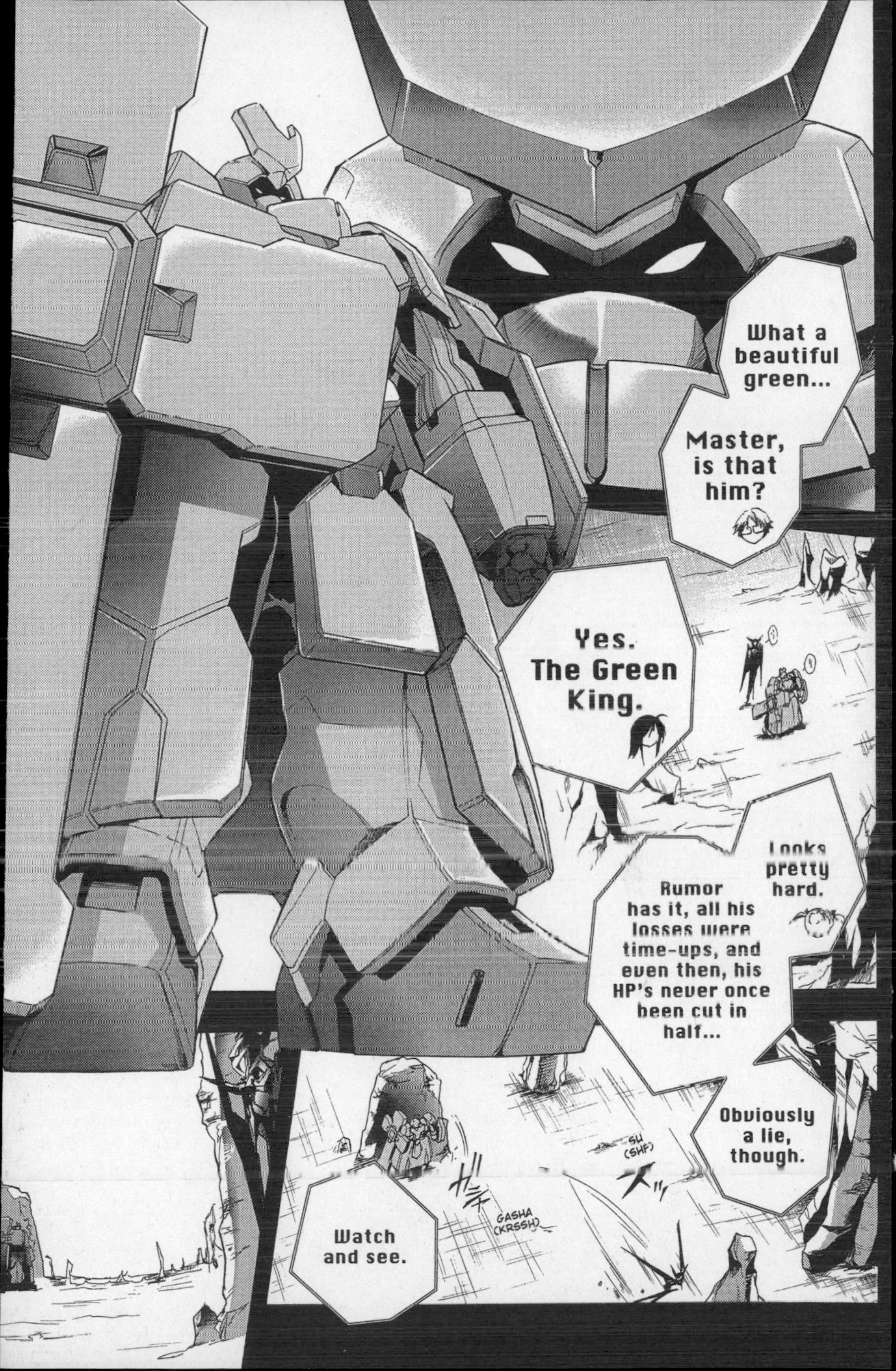
What a beautiful green...
Master, is that him?
Yes. The Green King.
Looks pretty hard.
Rumor has it, all his losses were time-ups, and even then, his HP's never once been cut in half...
Obviously a lie, though.
SU (SHF)
GASHA (KRSSH)
Watch and see.

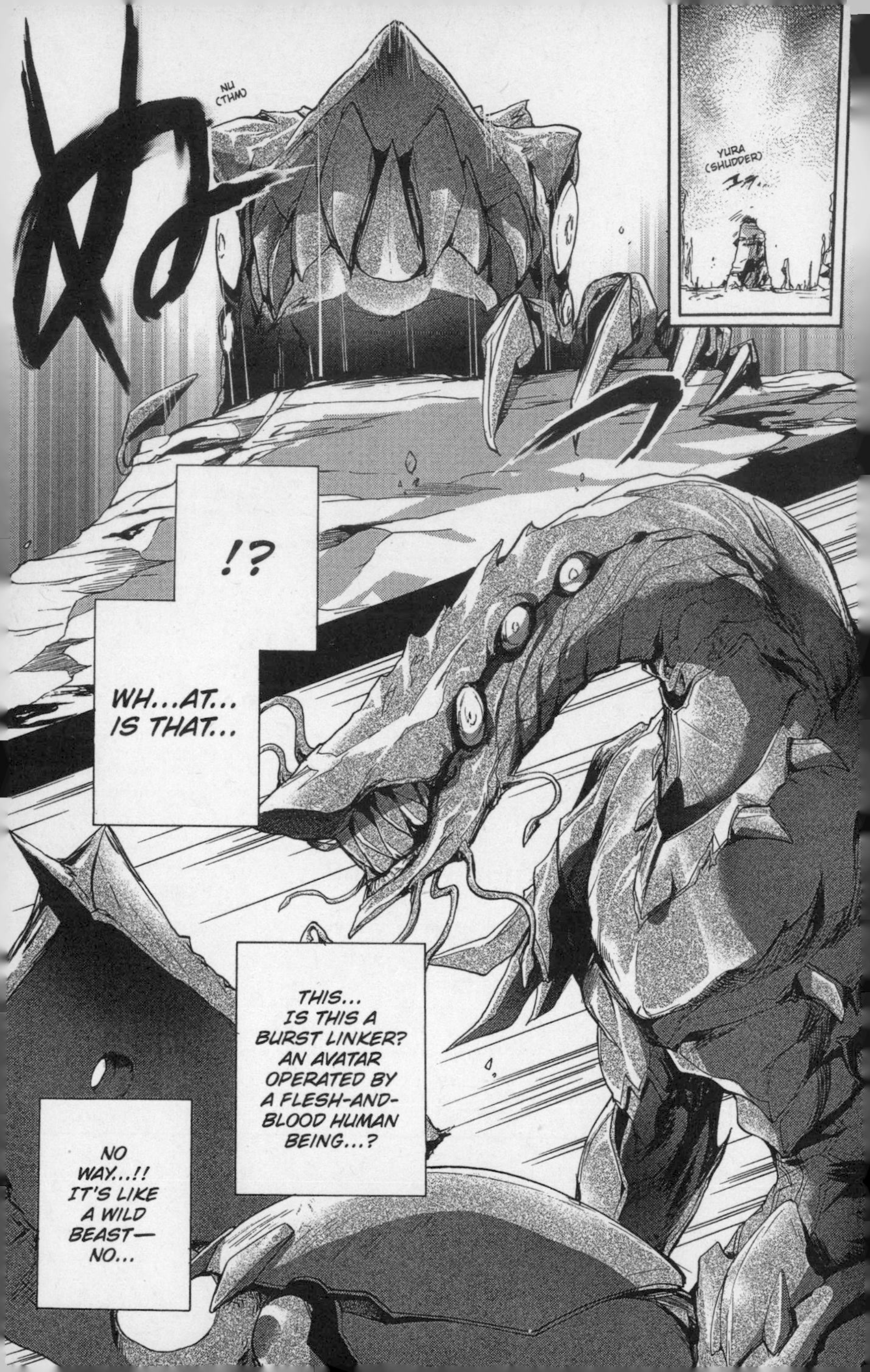
YURA (SHUDDER)
NU (THM)
!?
WH...AT... IS THAT...
THIS... IS THIS A BURST LINKER? AN AVATAR OPERATED BY A FLESH-AND-BLOOD HUMAN BEING...?
NO WAY...!! IT'S LIKE A WILD BEAST— NO...

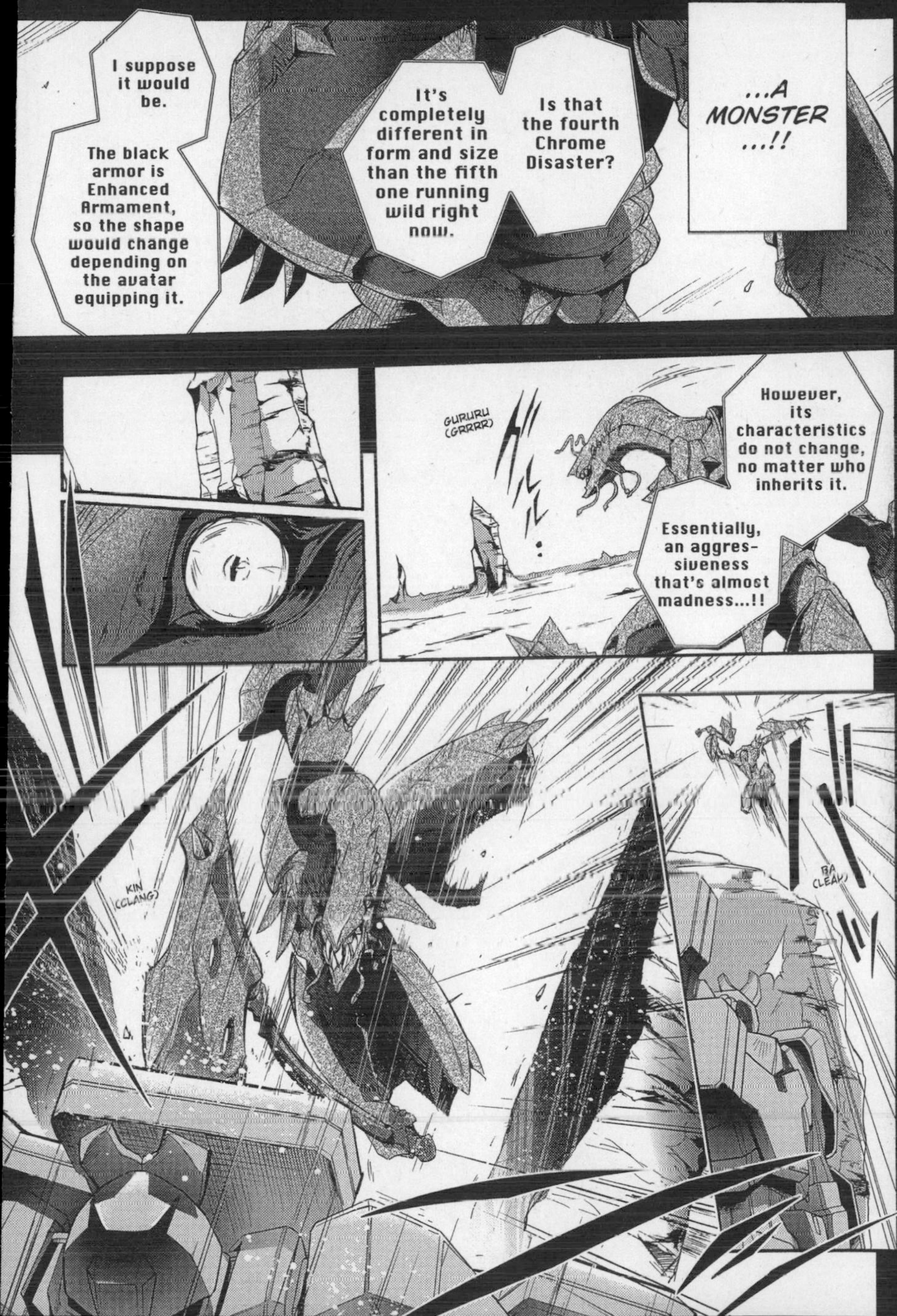
...A MONSTER ...!!
Is that the fourth Chrome Disaster?
It's completely different in form and size than the fifth one running wild right now.
I suppose it would be.
The black armor is Enhanced Armament, so the shape would change depending on the avatar equipping it.
GURURU (GRRRR)
However, its characteristics do not change, no matter who inherits it.
Essentially, an aggres-siveness that's almost madness...!!
BA
KIN (CLANG)

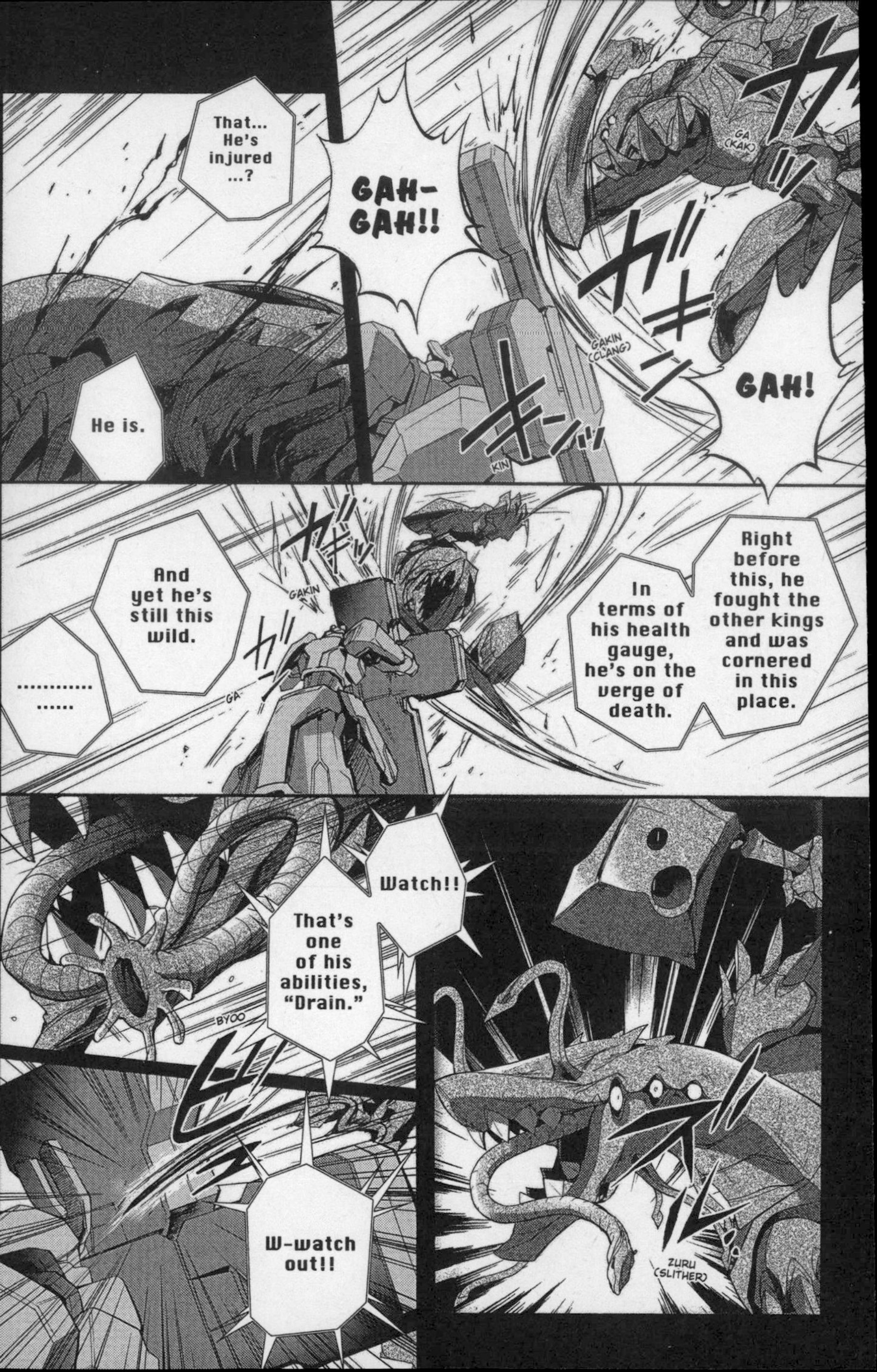
GA (KAK)
GAH-GAH!!
GAKIN (CLANG)
GAH!
KIN
That... He's injured ...?
He is.
Right before this, he fought the other kings and was cornered in this place.
In terms of his health gauge, he's on the verge of death.
GAKIN
GA
And yet he's still this wild.
....
ZURU (SLITHER)
Watch!!
That's one of his abilities, "Drain."
BYOO
W-watch out!!

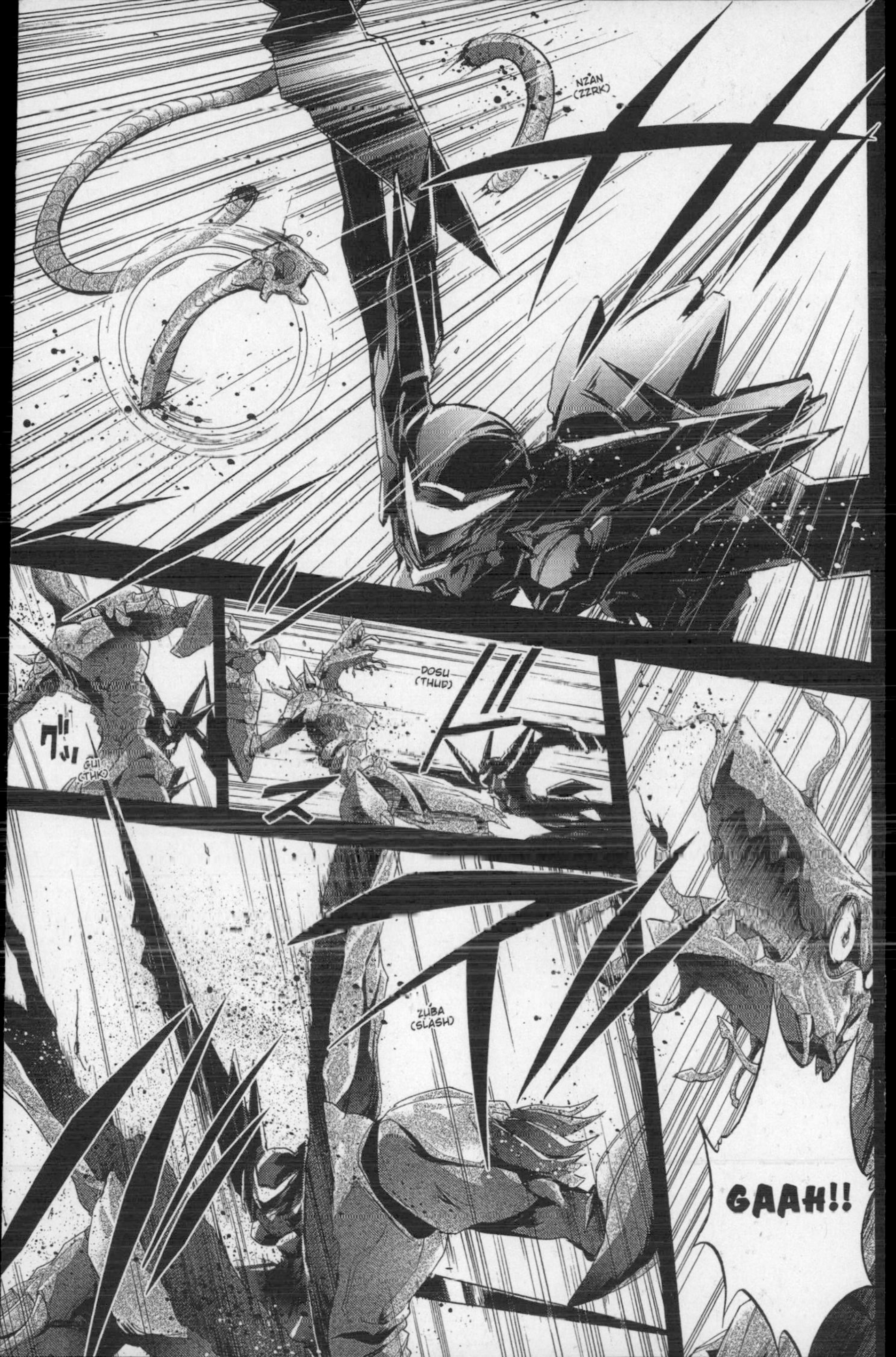
NZAN
(ZZRK)
DOSU
(THUD)
GUI
(THK)
ZUBA
(SLASH)
GAAH!!

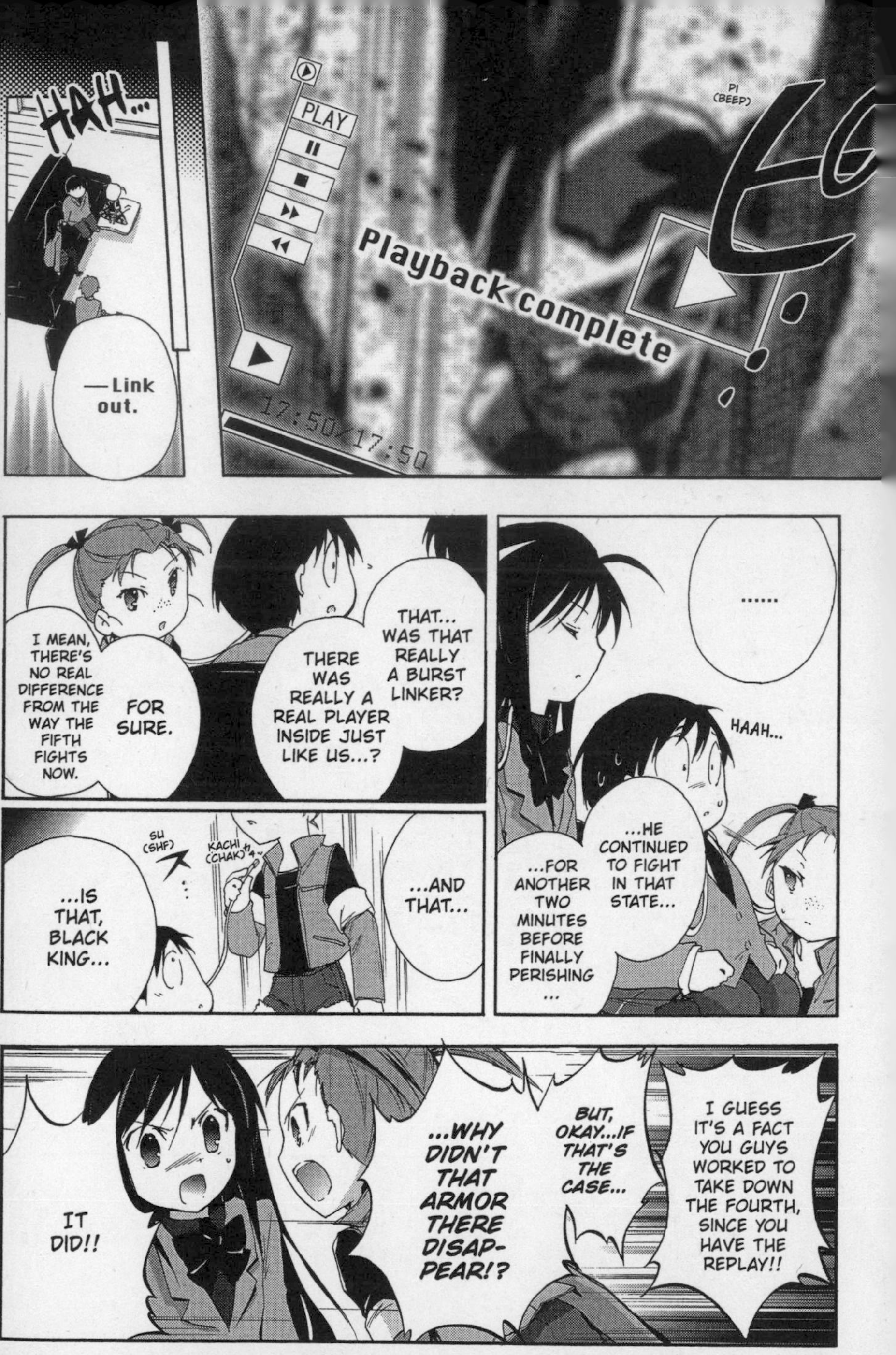
PI
(BEEP)
PLAY
Playback complete
17:50/17:50
HAH...
—Link out.
......
HAAH...
...HE CONTINUED TO FIGHT IN THAT STATE...
...FOR ANOTHER TWO MINUTES BEFORE FINALLY PERISHING ...
THAT... WAS THAT REALLY A BURST LINKER?
THERE WAS REALLY A REAL PLAYER INSIDE JUST LIKE US...?
FOR SURE.
I MEAN, THERE'S NO REAL DIFFERENCE FROM THE WAY THE FIFTH FIGHTS NOW.
...AND THAT...
KACHI
(CHAK)
SU
(SHF)
...IS THAT, BLACK KING...
I GUESS IT'S A FACT YOU GUYS WORKED TO TAKE DOWN THE FOURTH, SINCE YOU HAVE THE REPLAY!!
BUT, OKAY...IF THAT'S THE CASE...
...WHY DIDN'T THAT ARMOR THERE DISAPPEAR!?
IT DID!!

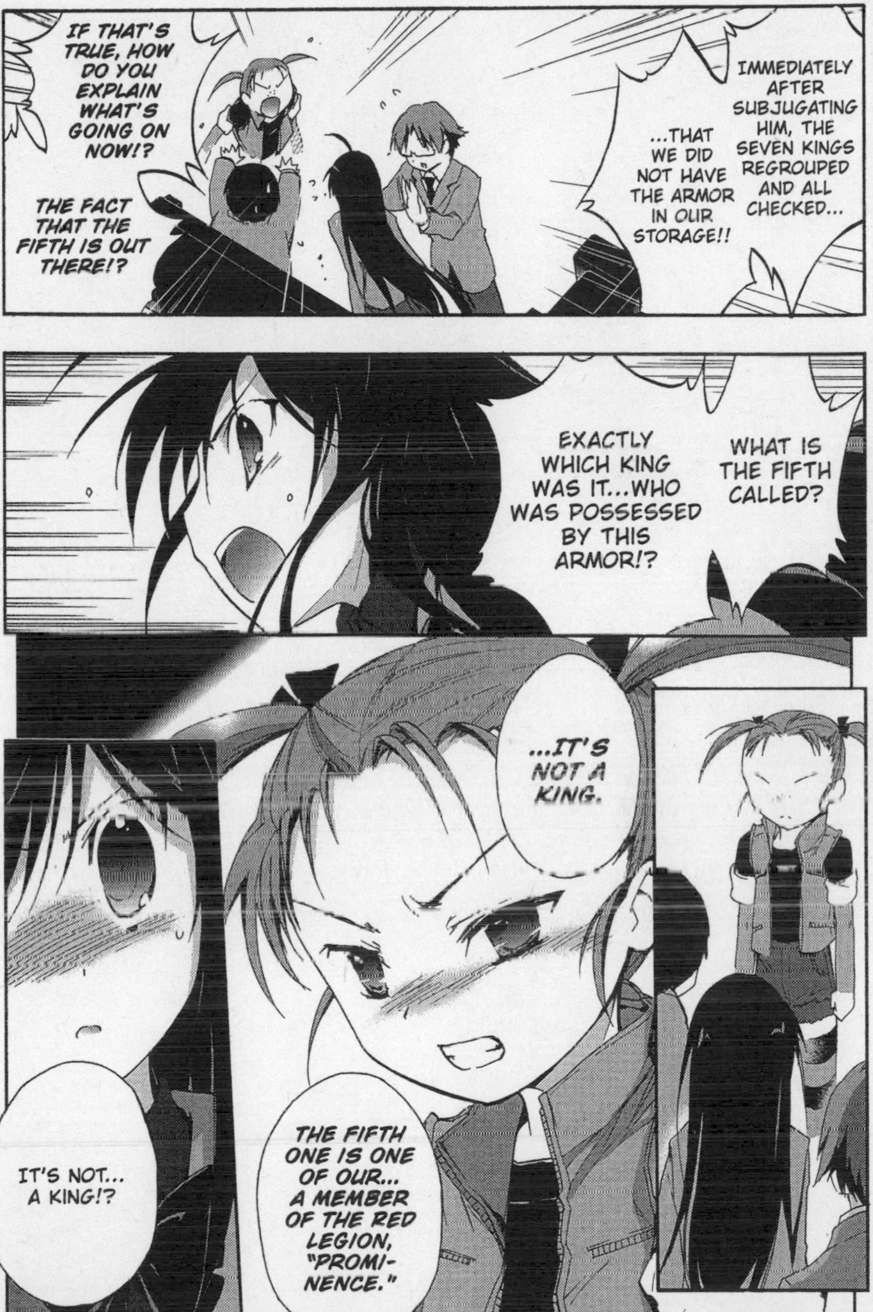
IMMEDIATELY AFTER SUBJUGATING HIM, THE SEVEN KINGS REGROUPED AND ALL CHECKED...
...THAT WE DID NOT HAVE THE ARMOR IN OUR STORAGE!!
IF THAT'S TRUE, HOW DO YOU EXPLAIN WHAT'S GOING ON NOW!?
THE FACT THAT THE FIFTH IS OUT THERE!?
WHAT IS THE FIFTH CALLED?
EXACTLY WHICH KING WAS IT...WHO WAS POSSESSED BY THIS ARMOR!?
...IT'S NOT A KING.
THE FIFTH ONE IS ONE OF OUR... A MEMBER OF THE RED LEGION, "PROMINENCE."
IT'S NOT... A KING!?

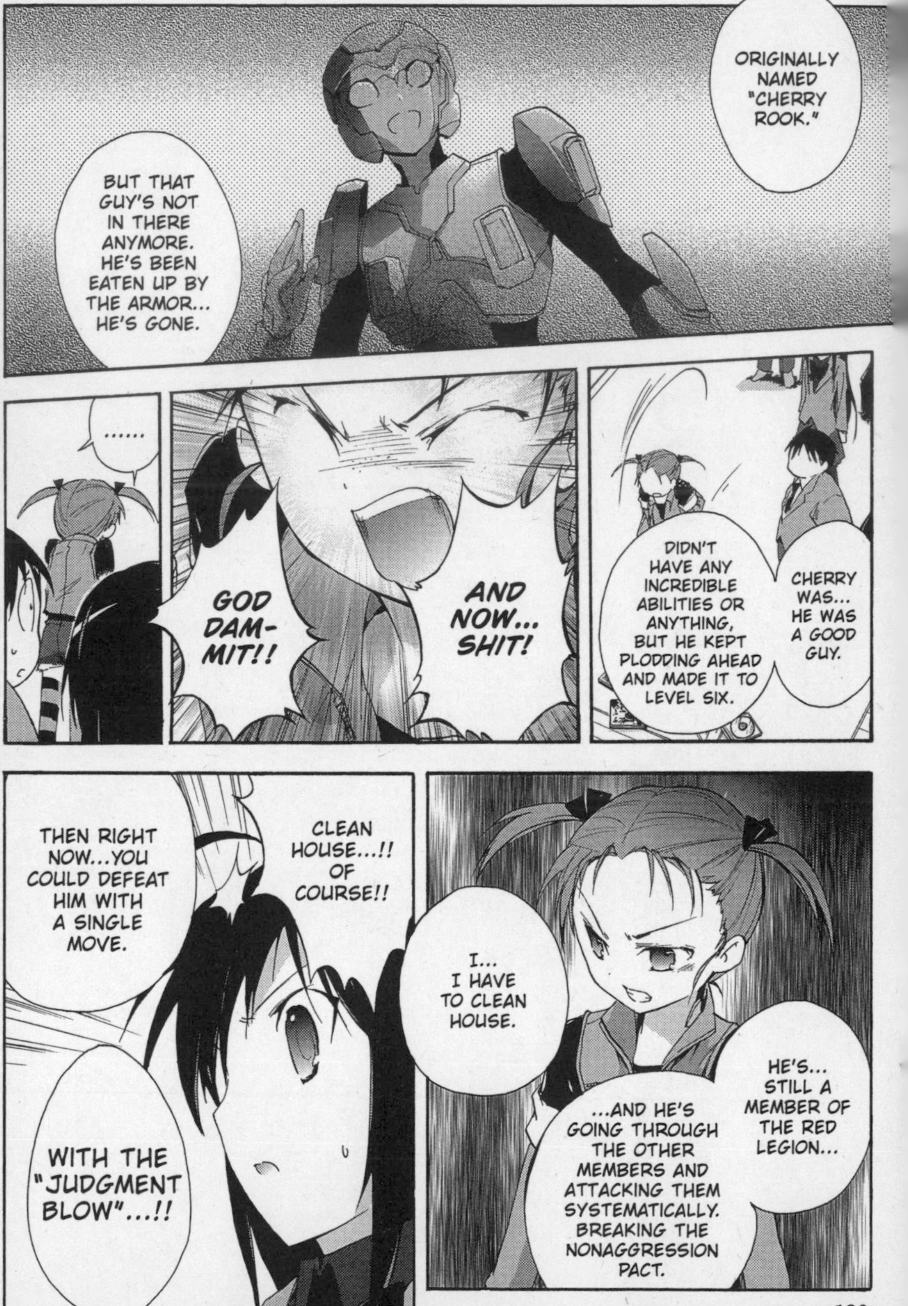
ORIGINALLY NAMED "CHERRY ROOK."
BUT THAT GUY'S NOT IN THERE ANYMORE. HE'S BEEN EATEN UP BY THE ARMOR... HE'S GONE.
CHERRY WAS... HE WAS A GOOD GUY.
DIDN'T HAVE ANY INCREDIBLE ABILITIES OR ANYTHING, BUT HE KEPT PLODDING AHEAD AND MADE IT TO LEVEL SIX.
AND NOW... SHIT!
GOD DAM-MIT!!
......
HE'S... STILL A MEMBER OF THE RED LEGION...
...AND HE'S GOING THROUGH THE OTHER MEMBERS AND ATTACKING THEM SYSTEMATICALLY. BREAKING THE NONAGGRESSION PACT.
I... I HAVE TO CLEAN HOUSE.
CLEAN HOUSE...!! OF COURSE!!
THEN RIGHT NOW...YOU COULD DEFEAT HIM WITH A SINGLE MOVE.
WITH THE "JUDGMENT BLOW"...!!

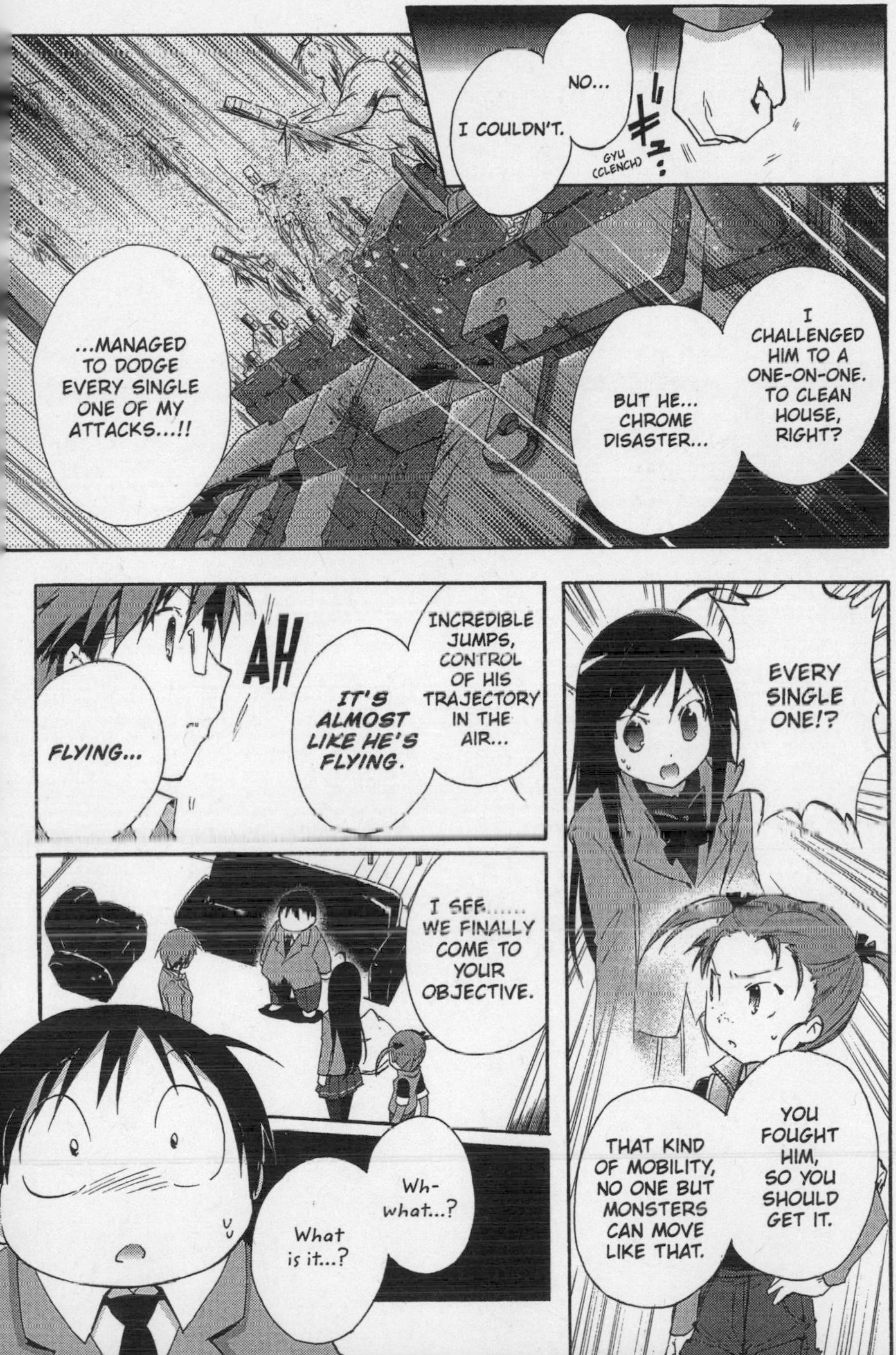
NO...
I COULDN'T.
GYU (CLENCH)
I CHALLENGED HIM TO A ONE-ON-ONE. TO CLEAN HOUSE, RIGHT?
BUT HE... CHROME DISASTER...
...MANAGED TO DODGE EVERY SINGLE ONE OF MY ATTACKS...!!
EVERY SINGLE ONE!?
YOU FOUGHT HIM, SO YOU SHOULD GET IT.
THAT KIND OF MOBILITY, NO ONE BUT MONSTERS CAN MOVE LIKE THAT.
INCREDIBLE JUMPS, CONTROL OF HIS TRAJECTORY IN THE AIR...
IT'S ALMOST LIKE HE'S FLYING.
AH
FLYING...
I SEE...... WE FINALLY COME TO YOUR OBJECTIVE.
Wh- what...?
What is it...?

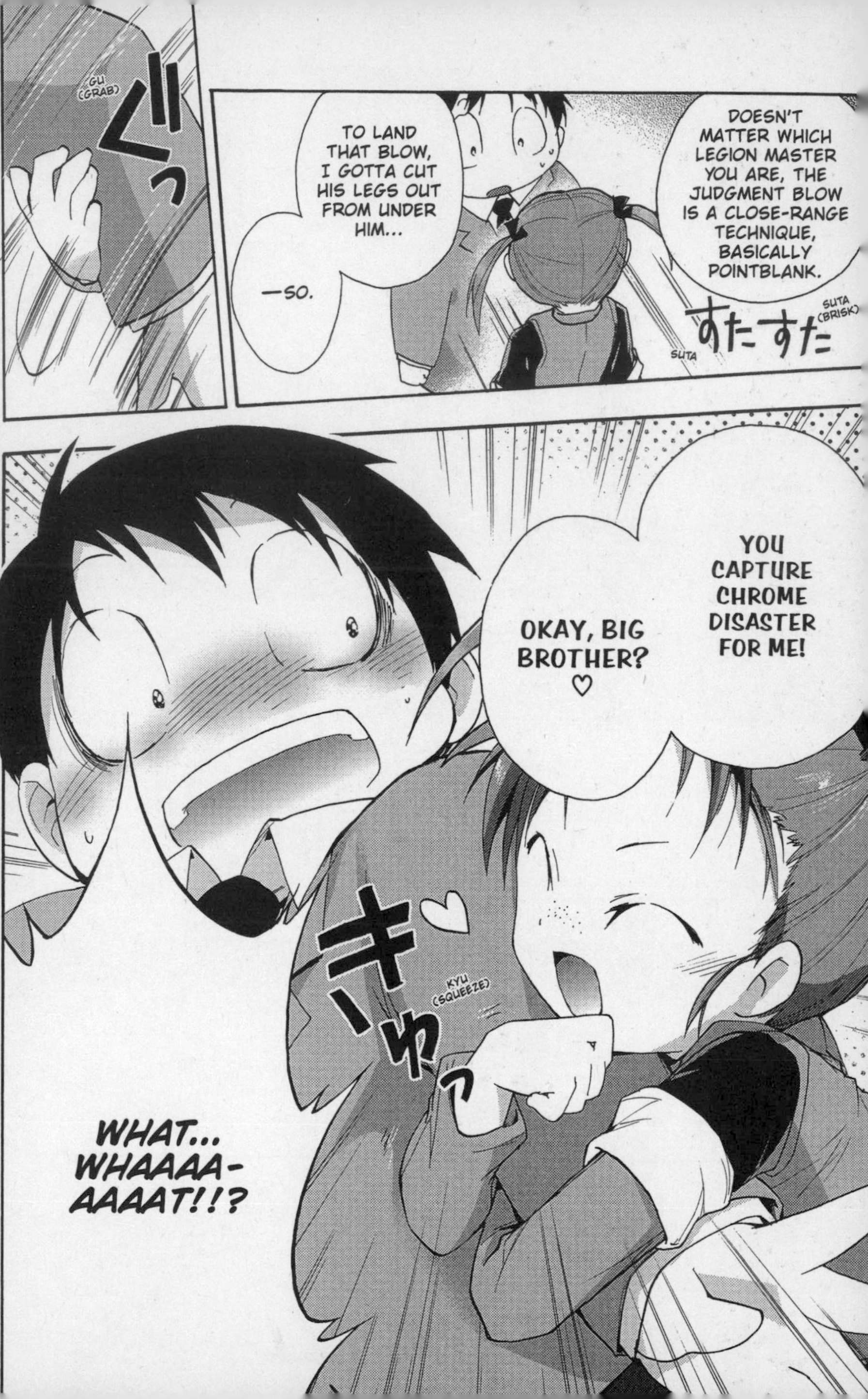
DOESN'T MATTER WHICH LEGION MASTER YOU ARE, THE JUDGMENT BLOW IS A CLOSE-RANGE TECHNIQUE, BASICALLY POINTBLANK.
すたすた
SUTA SUTA (BRISK)
TO LAND THAT BLOW, I GOTTA CUT HIS LEGS OUT FROM UNDER HIM...
—SO.
ぐっ
GU (GRAB)
YOU CAPTURE CHROME DISASTER FOR ME!
OKAY, BIG BROTHER? ♡
きゅっ
KYU (SQUEEZE)
WHAT... WHAAAAA-AAAAT!!?

►►►ACCEL·WORLD

THE NEXT PAGES ARE A LITTLE ANNOUNCEMENT MANGA I DID BETWEEN VOLUMES TWO AND THREE.

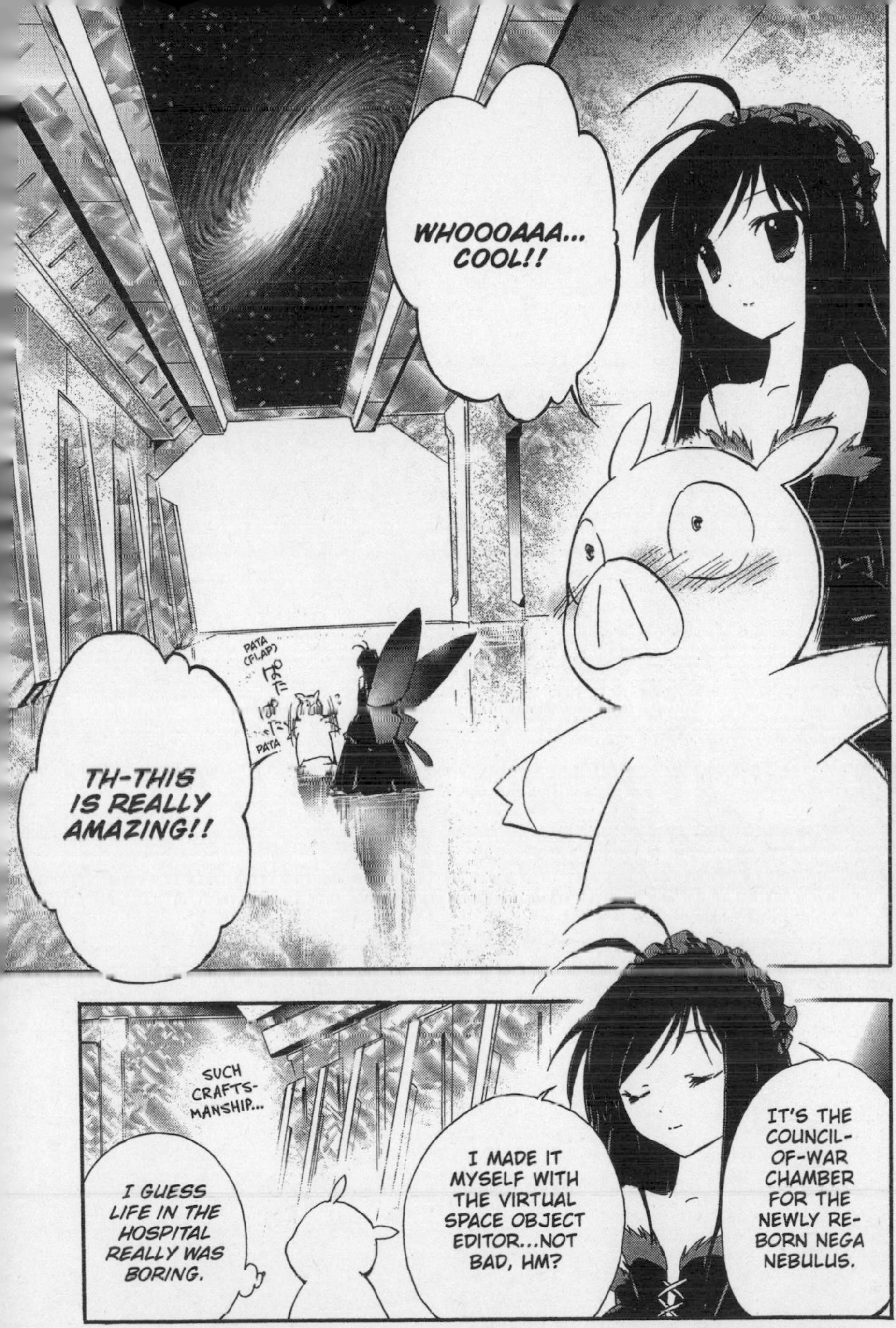
WHOOOAAA... COOL!!
PATA (FLAP)
ぱた ぱた
PATA
TH-THIS IS REALLY AMAZING!!
IT'S THE COUNCIL-OF-WAR CHAMBER FOR THE NEWLY RE-BORN NEGA NEBULUS.
I MADE IT MYSELF WITH THE VIRTUAL SPACE OBJECT EDITOR...NOT BAD, HM?
SUCH CRAFTS-MANSHIP...
I GUESS LIFE IN THE HOSPITAL REALLY WAS BORING.

※THIS COMIC IS A SPECIAL EPISODE TO ANNOUNCE VOLUMES ONE AND TWO AND DRAWN BETWEEN THE SERIALIZED CHAPTERS EIGHT (COLLECTED IN VOLUME TWO) AND NINE (COLLECTED IN THIS VOLUME).

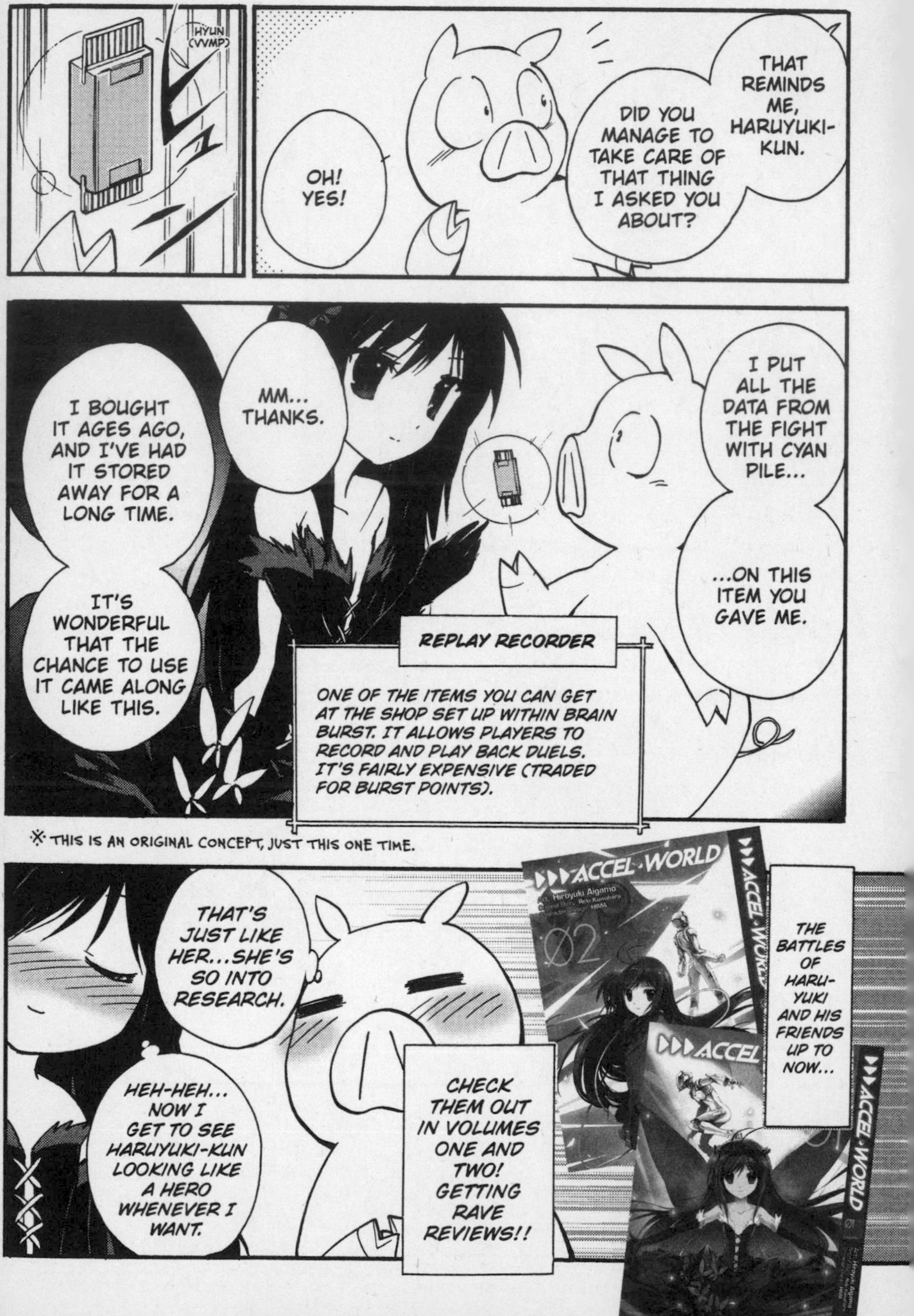
THAT REMINDS ME, HARUYUKI-KUN.
DID YOU MANAGE TO TAKE CARE OF THAT THING I ASKED YOU ABOUT?
OH! YES!
HYUN (VVMP)
I PUT ALL THE DATA FROM THE FIGHT WITH CYAN PILE...
...ON THIS ITEM YOU GAVE ME.
MM... THANKS.
I BOUGHT IT AGES AGO, AND I'VE HAD IT STORED AWAY FOR A LONG TIME.
IT'S WONDERFUL THAT THE CHANCE TO USE IT CAME ALONG LIKE THIS.
REPLAY RECORDER
ONE OF THE ITEMS YOU CAN GET AT THE SHOP SET UP WITHIN BRAIN BURST. IT ALLOWS PLAYERS TO RECORD AND PLAY BACK DUELS. IT'S FAIRLY EXPENSIVE (TRADED FOR BURST POINTS).
※ THIS IS AN ORIGINAL CONCEPT, JUST THIS ONE TIME.
THE BATTLES OF HARUYUKI AND HIS FRIENDS UP TO NOW...
ACCEL·WORLD
Art: Hiroyuki Aigamo
02
ACCEL
ACCEL·WORLD
CHECK THEM OUT IN VOLUMES ONE AND TWO! GETTING RAVE REVIEWS!!
THAT'S JUST LIKE HER...SHE'S SO INTO RESEARCH.
HEH-HEH... NOW I GET TO SEE HARUYUKI-KUN LOOKING LIKE A HERO WHENEVER I WANT.

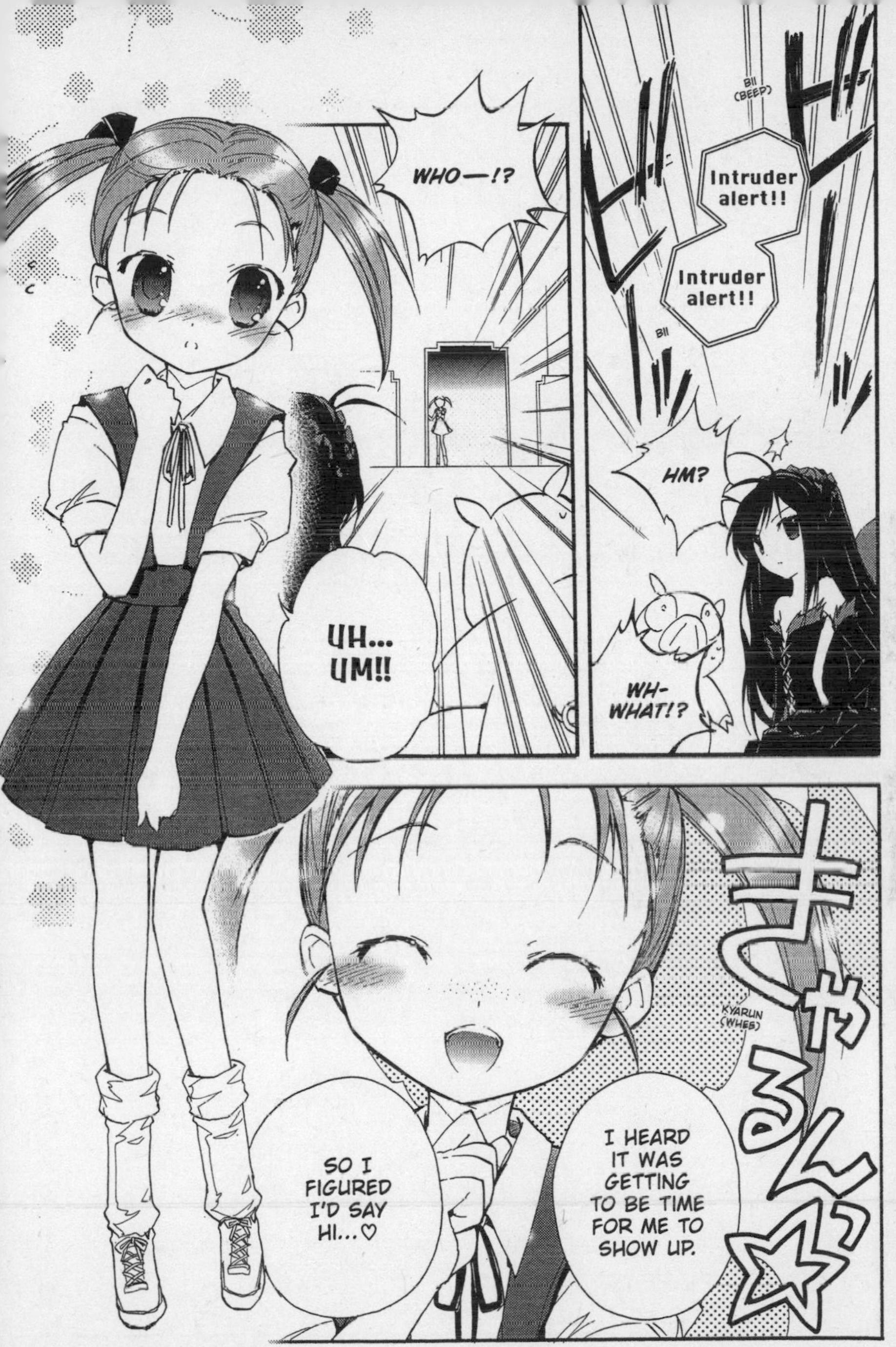
BII (BEEP)
Intruder alert!!
Intruder alert!!
BII
HM?
WH-WHAT!?
WHO—!?
UH... UM!!
KYARUN (WHEE)
I HEARD IT WAS GETTING TO BE TIME FOR ME TO SHOW UP.
SO I FIGURED I'D SAY HI...♡

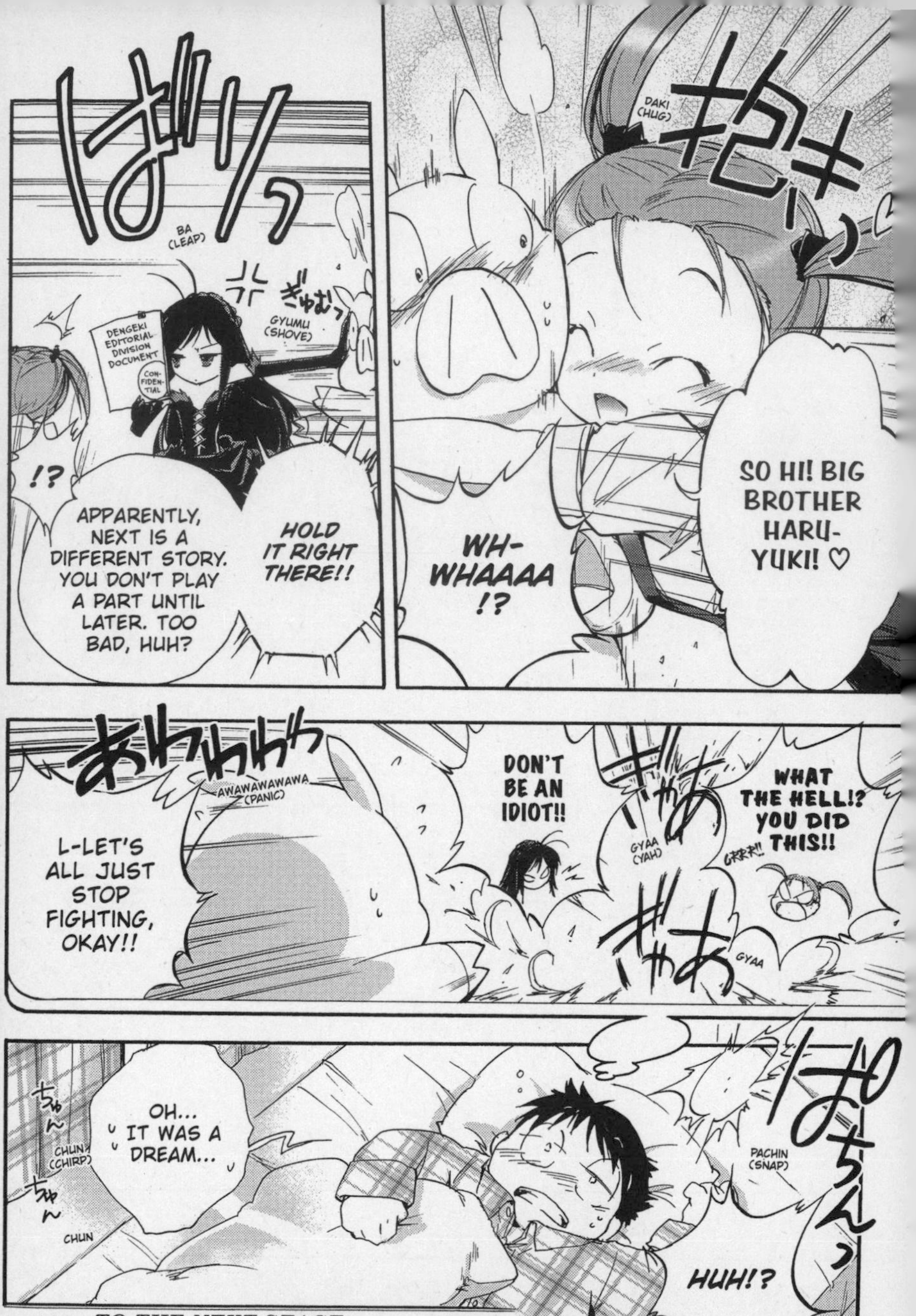
DAKI (HUG)
SO HI! BIG BROTHER HARU-YUKI! ♡
WH-WHAAAA!?
BA (LEAP)
GYUMU (SHOVE)
DENGEKI EDITORIAL DIVISION DOCUMENT
CON-FIDEN-TIAL
!?
HOLD IT RIGHT THERE!!
APPARENTLY, NEXT IS A DIFFERENT STORY. YOU DON'T PLAY A PART UNTIL LATER. TOO BAD, HUH?
WHAT THE HELL!? YOU DID THIS!!
GYAA (YAH)
GYAA
DON'T BE AN IDIOT!!
AWAWAWAWAWA (PANIC)
L-LET'S ALL JUST STOP FIGHTING, OKAY!!
PACHIN (SNAP)
HUH!?
OH... IT WAS A DREAM...
CHUN (CHIRP)
CHUN
◂◂◂ TO THE NEXT STAGE

To Be Continued in the Next Stage...!!

DUEL AVATAR DESIGN ASSISTANCE: YOSUKE KABASHIMA, NORIYUKI JINGU, TAKUMI SAKURA, HIROYUKI TAIGA, AND MASAHIRO YAMANE

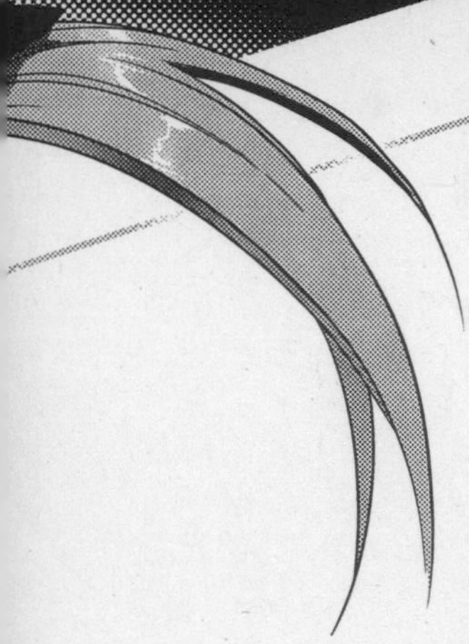

◎AFTERWORD◎

Thank you so much for picking up Volume Three of the manga version of *Accel World*!

The anime started in April, and the acceleration and heat is so much, it gives you goose bumps, right? I totally want to throw myself into this and keep drawing the rest. I hope you'll keep cheering me on!

合鴨ひろゆき拝.

Hiroyuki Aigamo

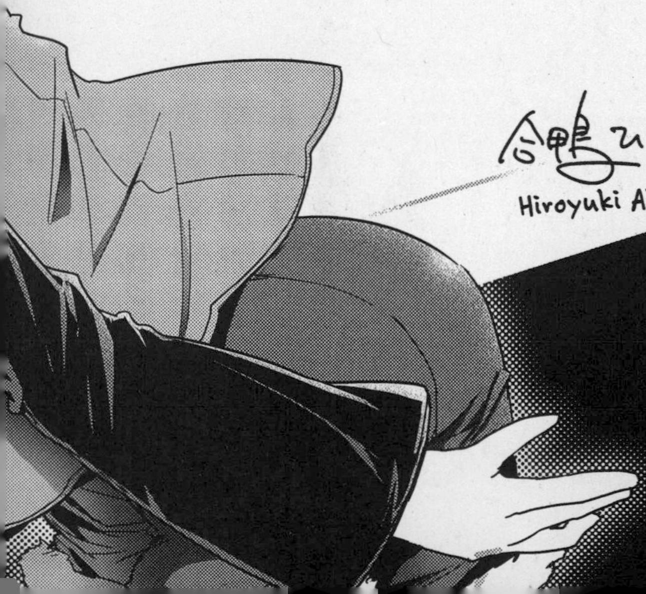

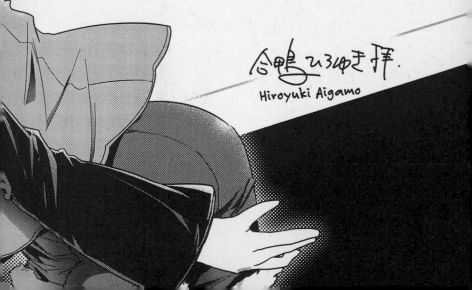

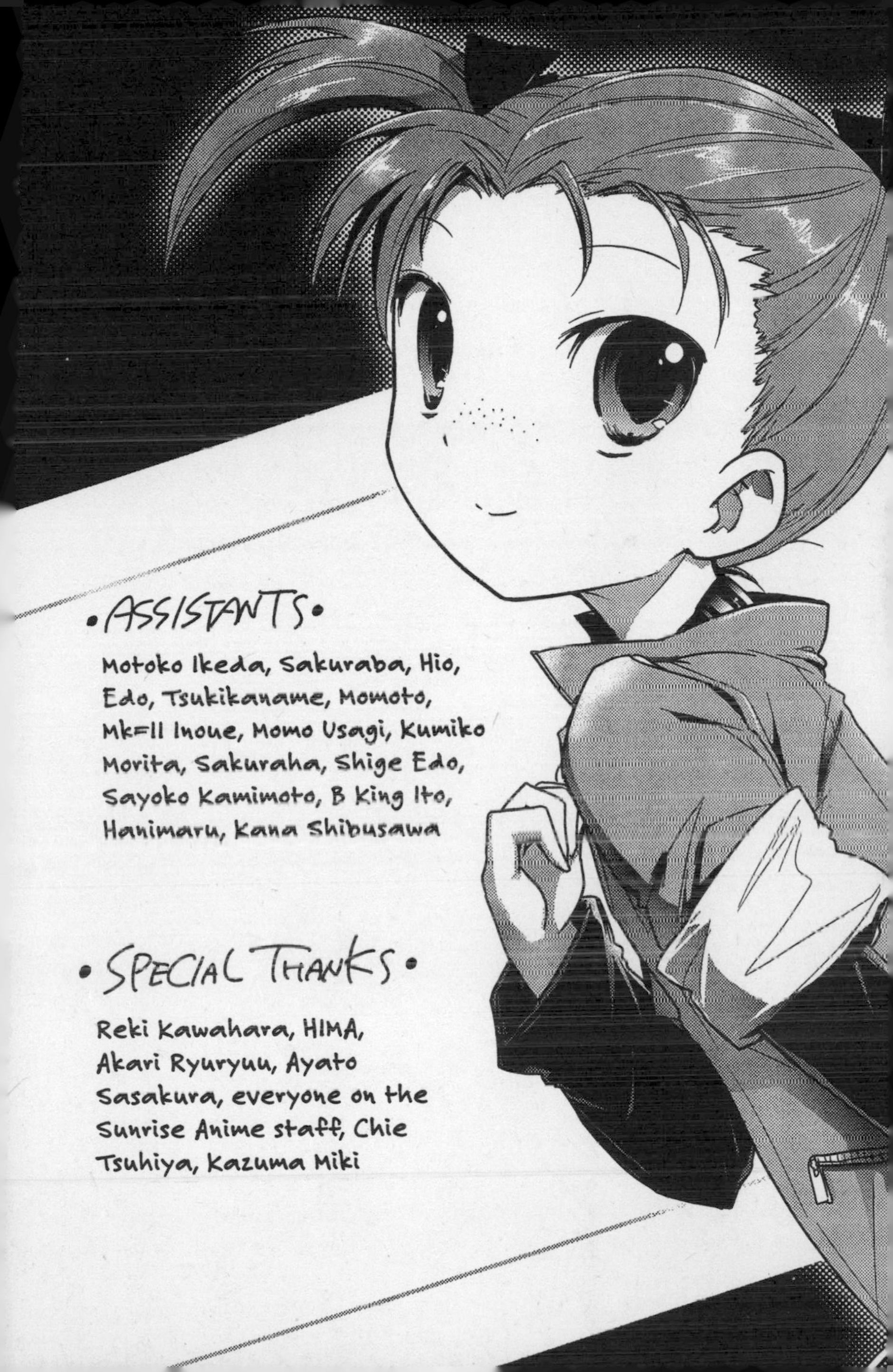

• ASSISTANTS •

Motoko Ikeda, Sakuraba, Hio, Edo, Tsukikaname, Momoto, Mk=II Inoue, Momo Usagi, Kumiko Morita, Sakuraha, Shige Edo, Sayoko Kamimoto, B King Ito, Hanimaru, Kana Shibusawa

• SPECIAL THANKS •

Reki Kawahara, HIMA, Akari Ryuryuu, Ayato Sasakura, everyone on the Sunrise Anime staff, Chie Tsuhiya, Kazuma Miki

CONGRATULATIONS ON THE PUBLICATION OF VOLUME THREE!

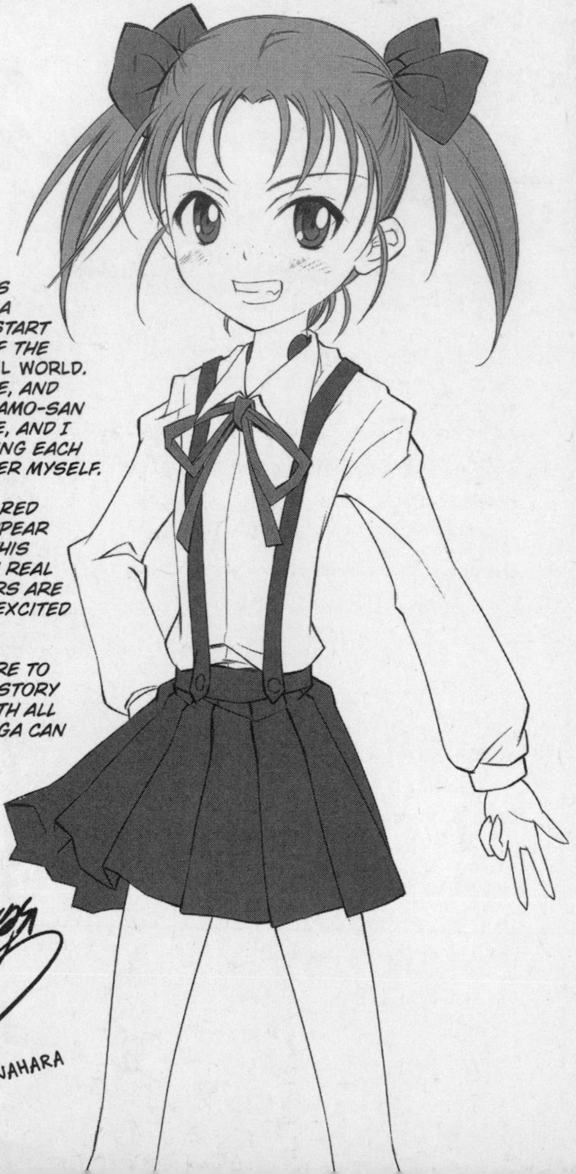

IT SEEMS SOON, BUT IT'S ALREADY BEEN TWO AND A HALF YEARS SINCE THE START OF THE SERIALIZATION OF THE MANGA VERSION OF ACCEL WORLD. THE HARU, KUROYUKIHIME, AND THEIR FRIENDS THAT AIGAMO-SAN DRAWS ARE REALLY ALIVE, AND I LOOK FORWARD TO READING EACH INSTALLMENT AS A READER MYSELF.

AQUA CURRENT AND THE RED KING NIKO, WHO BOTH APPEAR FOR THE FIRST TIME IN THIS VOLUME, ARE SO CUTE IN REAL LIFE, WHILE THEIR AVATARS ARE SO COOL; I GOT PRETTY EXCITED WHILE I WAS READING.

THERE'S STILL A LOT MORE TO GET TO IN THE ORIGINAL STORY (LOL), SO I'M HOPING WITH ALL MY HEART THAT THE MANGA CAN ALSO GO ON FOREVER.
THANK YOU SO MUCH ONCE AGAIN!

REKI KAWAHARA

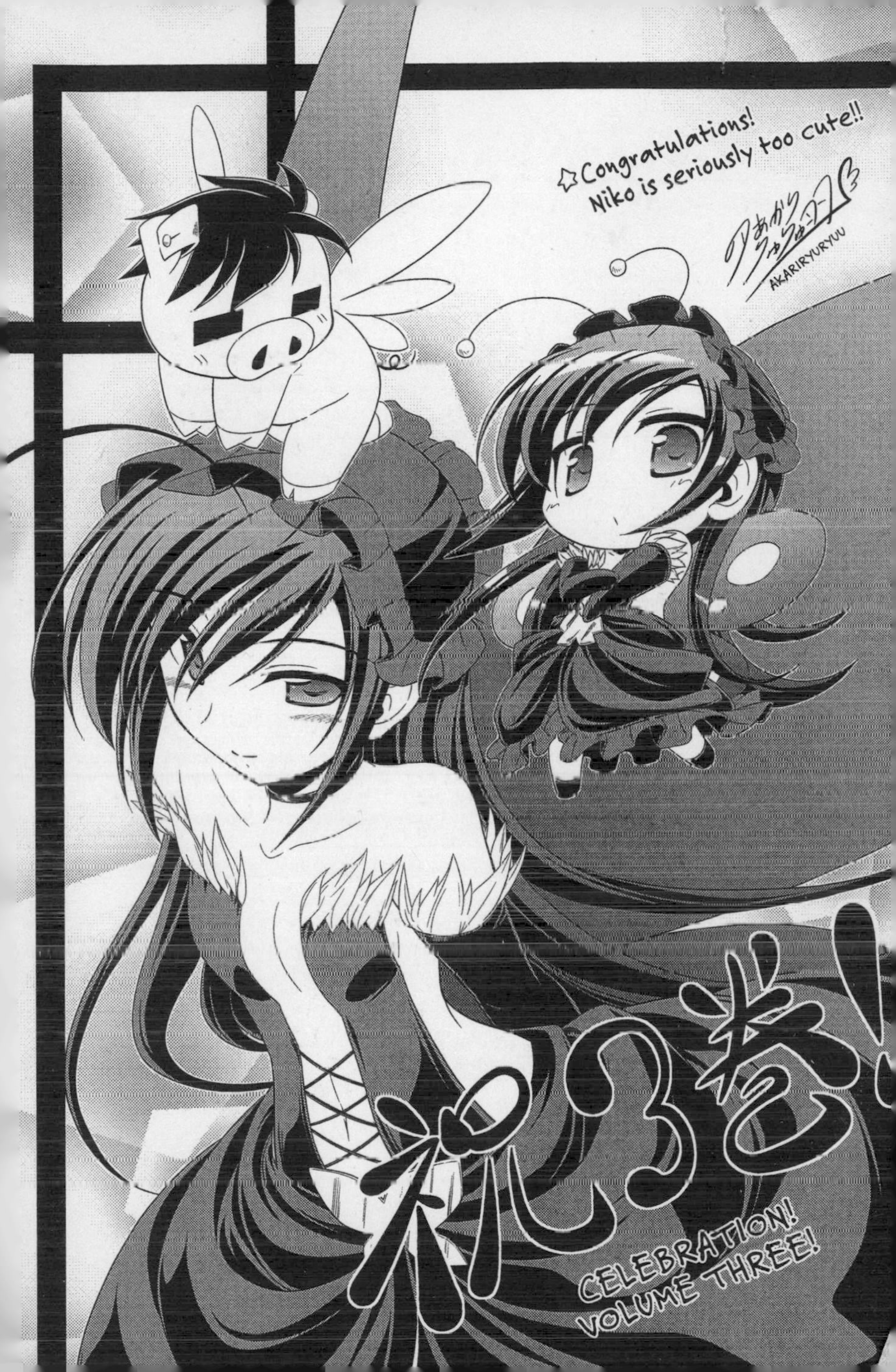
☆Congratulations!
Niko is seriously too cute!!
あかりりゅりゅう
AKARIRYURYUU
祝3巻!
CELEBRATION!
VOLUME THREE!

ACCEL WORLD 3

ART: HIROYUKI AIGAMO
ORIGINAL STORY: REKI KAWAHARA
CHARACTER DESIGN: HIMA

Translation: Jocelyne Allen
Lettering: Brndn Blakeslee and Lys Blakeslee

ACCEL WORLD
© REKI KAWAHARA / HIROYUKI AIGAMO 2012
All rights reserved.
Edited by ASCII MEDIA WORKS
First published in Japan in 2012 by KADOKAWA CORPORATION, Tokyo.
English translation rights arranged with KADOKAWA CORPORATION, Tokyo, through Tuttle-Mori Agency, Inc., Tokyo.

Translation © 2015 by Hachette Book Group, Inc.

Yen Press
Hachette Book Group
1290 Avenue of the Americas
New York, NY 10104

www.HachetteBookGroup.com
www.YenPress.com

Yen Press is an imprint of Hachette Book Group, Inc. The Yen Press name and logo are trademarks of Hachette Book Group, Inc.

The publisher is not responsible for websites (or their content) that are not owned by the publisher.

First Yen Press Edition: March 2015

ISBN: 978-0-316-29635-9

10 9 8 7 6 5 4 3 2 1

BVG

Printed in the United States of America